FEARFUL MAJESTY

ALSO BY BENSON BOBRICK

Labyrinths of Iron

FEARFUL MAJESTY

The Life and Reign of Ivan the Terrible

BENSON BOBRICK

PARAGON HOUSE   NEW YORK

TO DANIELLE

First paperback edition, 1989

Published in the United States by

Paragon House Publishers
90 Fifth Avenue
New York, NY 10011

Copyright © 1987 by Benson Bobrick

All rights reserved. No part of this book may be reproduced, in any
form, without written permission
from the publishers, unless by a reviewer who wishes to quote brief
passages.

Material reprinted from *The Musrovia of Antonio Passevino, S.J.*, translated by
Hugh F. Graham by permission of the University of Pittsburgh Press, © 1977
by University Center for International Studies, University of Pittsburgh.

Excerpts from *Prince A.M. Kurbsky: History of Ivan IV*, translated by J.L.I.
Fennell. Reprinted by permission of the Cambridge University Press, © 1965.

The Correspondence Between Prince A.M. Kurbsky and Tsar Ivan IV, translated by
J.L.I. Fennell. Reprinted by permission of the Cambridge University Press, ©
1955.

Excerpts from *Tsar Ivan IV's Reply to Jan Rokyta*, translated by V.A. Tumins.
Reprinted by permission of Mouton de Gruyter Publishers, © 1971.

Reprinted by arrangement with G.P. Putnam's Sons

Library of Congress Cataloging-in-Publication Data

Bobrick, Benson, 1947–
Fearful majesty : the life and reign of Ivan the Terrible / Benson
Bobrick. — 1st pbk. ed.
p.   cm.
Reprint. Originally published: New York : Putnam, c1987.
Bibliography: p.
Includes index.
ISBN 1-55778-226-1
1. Ivan IV, Czar of Russia, 1530–1584.   2. Soviet
Union—Kings and rulers—Biography.   3. Soviet Union—History—
Ivan IV, 1533–1584.
I. Title.
[DK106.B63   1990]
947'.043'0924—dc19
[B]   88-26778
CIP

Printed and bound in Canada.

Acknowledgments

This book has been long in the making, and I am grateful to all who helped along the way. At one time or another I received needed information or advice from my brother Peter Bobrick (on whom I could always rely for expert translations from the German); from Diana Ajjan, Hugh F. Graham, John W. Hawkins, Joe Kanon, Tim Meyer, Christine Schillig, Cecilia de Querol, Fred Sawyer, Peter von Wahlde, and Victoria Zubkina; from Victoria Edwards at Sovfoto; and from various members on staff at the New York Public Library, Butler Library at Columbia University, the Library of Congress, and the Library of the British Museum. I should also like to acknowledge here, too, those numerous yet exemplary scholars and historians whose bookish company I was privileged to keep in the quiet of my study every day. If my own book has anything new or useful to offer, it is surely because I was able to take my "prospect round" from atop the shoulders of their work. My extensive Bibliography represents an earnest attempt at a full and democratic roll-call of my debt.

Finally, I am especially grateful to my editor, Lee Ann Chearneyi, who gave me leave to write as I wished, but not license to be redundant or pointlessly obscure; to Marguerite Woerner for crucial technical assistance; and above all to my wife, Danielle, whose intercessory support helped prevent the sometimes tyrannical exactions of my task from inscribing my name (in a manner of speaking) as a posthumous addition to Ivan's dread Synodical.

Contents

Part One: MUSCOVY

Part Two: EMPIRE

Rulers of Russia (to 1598)

(Ancestors of IVAN IV are capitalized)

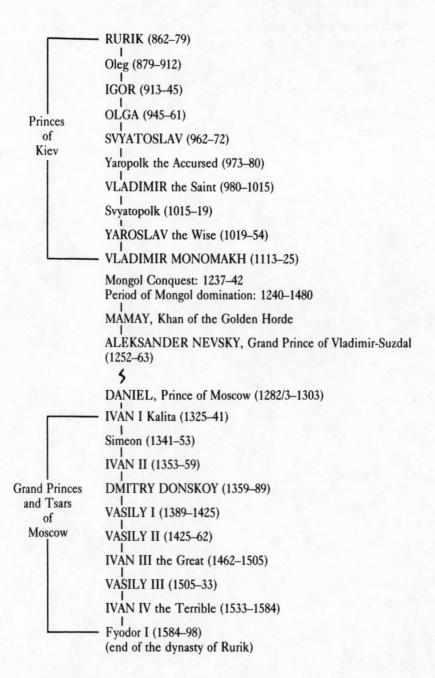

Princes of Kiev

RURIK (862–79)

Oleg (879–912)

IGOR (913–45)

OLGA (945–61)

SVYATOSLAV (962–72)

Yaropolk the Accursed (973–80)

VLADIMIR the Saint (980–1015)

Svyatopolk (1015–19)

YAROSLAV the Wise (1019–54)

VLADIMIR MONOMAKH (1113–25)

Mongol Conquest: 1237–42
Period of Mongol domination: 1240–1480

MAMAY, Khan of the Golden Horde

ALEKSANDER NEVSKY, Grand Prince of Vladimir-Suzdal (1252–63)

DANIEL, Prince of Moscow (1282/3–1303)

Grand Princes and Tsars of Moscow

IVAN I Kalita (1325–41)

Simeon (1341–53)

IVAN II (1353–59)

DMITRY DONSKOY (1359–89)

VASILY I (1389–1425)

VASILY II (1425–62)

IVAN III the Great (1462–1505)

VASILY III (1505–33)

IVAN IV the Terrible (1533–1584)

Fyodor I (1584–98)
(end of the dynasty of Rurik)

GENEALOGY OF IVAN IV, "the Terrible"

Chart One

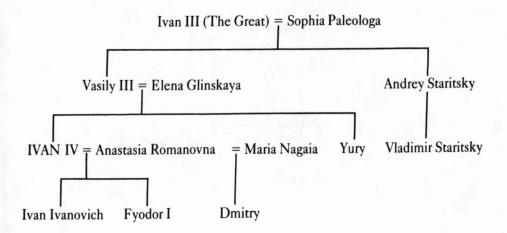

Ivan III (The Great) = Sophia Paleologa

Vasily III = Elena Glinskaya   Andrey Staritsky

IVAN IV = Anastasia Romanovna   = Maria Nagaia   Yury   Vladimir Staritsky

Ivan Ivanovich   Fyodor I   Dmitry

GENEALOGY OF IVAN IV, "the Terrible"

Chart Two

(Byzantine Dynasty of the Paleologi)
1261–1453

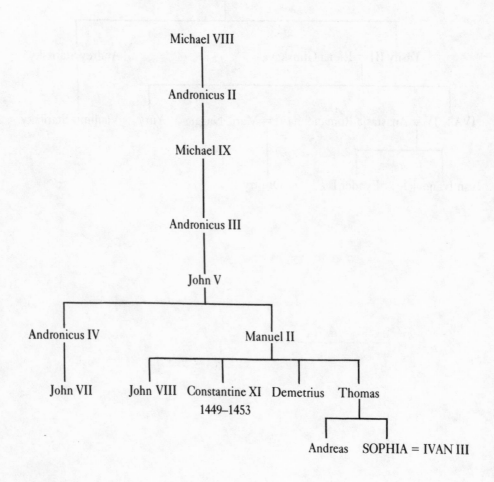

Michael VIII

Andronicus II

Michael IX

Andronicus III

John V

Andronicus IV   Manuel II

John VII   John VIII   Constantine XI   Demetrius   Thomas
                         1449–1453

Andreas   SOPHIA = IVAN III

GENEALOGY OF IVAN IV, "the Terrible"

Chart Three

(The Glinskys)

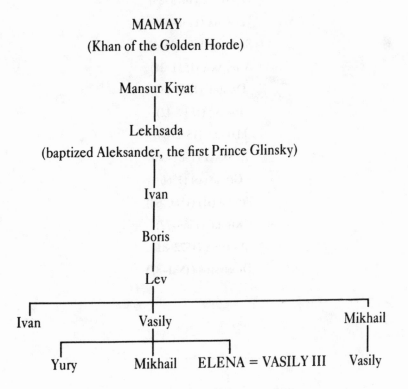

MAMAY
(Khan of the Golden Horde)

Mansur Kiyat

Lekhsada
(baptized Aleksander, the first Prince Glinsky)

Ivan

Boris

Lev

Ivan   Vasily   Mikhail

Yury   Mikhail   ELENA = VASILY III   Vasily

Metropolitans of Moscow

IONA (1448–61)

FEODOSY (1461–64)

PHILIP (I) (1464–73)

GERONTY (1473–89)

ZOSIMA (1490–94)

SIMEON (1495–1511)

VARLAAM (1511–21)

DANIEL (1522–39)

JOASAF (1539–42)

MAKARY (1542–63)

AFANASY (1564–66)

GHERMAN (1566)

PHILIP (II) (1566–68)

KIRILL (1568–72)

ANTONY (1572–81)

DIONYSIUS (1581–87)

Preface

In 1492, the year Columbus "discovered America," most Russians expected the world to end. Like the Byzantines, they dated their calendar from the Creation, believed the world had been created in 5508 B.C., and that it would endure for 7000 years—a calculation based on the idea of the Cosmic Week, as extrapolated from the week of Creation: for to God a thousand years are as one day. As 1492 approached, the apocalyptic signs were unmistakable, as long-standing prophecies appeared to be fulfilled. The greatest of these by far was the fall, after the reign and splendor of over a thousand years, of Constantinople to the Turks—"the Ishmaelites"—an event that marked the end of the Byzantine Empire and seemed to warrant comparison with the destruction of Jerusalem by the Romans and Christ's death upon the Cross. Such was the general foreboding, that the Russian Church actually failed to calculate the date of Easter for the following year.

The world survived, of course; the Last or "Terrible" Judgment (as the Eastern Orthodox called it) was delayed, and when a new Easter calendar was compiled for the eighth millennium by the Metropolitan of Moscow (the primate of the Russian Church), the grand prince was described in the prologue as "the new Emperor Constantine"—and Moscow as "the New City of Constantine"—thereby laying claim to the religious and political inheritance of Byzantium. In 1547, Ivan IV ("the Terrible") officially ratified this claim by assuming the title of Tsar. At the same time, he married Anastasia Romanovna, a member of the family later known as Romanov, destined to supplant the House of Rurik as the ruling dynasty of the realm. His coronation was thus the seminal setting for the course Russian history would follow from that day forward until 1917.

Ivan's reign, though chronologically remote, has relevance for anyone caring to understand the people of Russia and the place of their nation in the world. Indeed, despite the Revolution of 1917, some part of the Russian soul will always remain Muscovite, and to a degree most readers might find surprising the Soviet state elaborated under Stalin represented less a repudiation of the world of the tsars than a kind of recrudescence of the Muscovy Ivan ruled. Traces of old Muscovy continue to this day, and are broadly reflected in everything from popular customs to government organization and foreign relations. It is in Ivan's time, for example, that Russia's great confrontation with the West begins, and ideas formed then seem almost to have been cast and set in a mold. "Evil Empire" speeches belong to a long tradition, and one urgent admonition delivered in 1569 by the king of Poland (describing Russia as "an enemy to all liberty under the heavens") stands as the progenitor of all such diatribes.

Ivan was cruel—and "terrible"—and great. His considerable reign saw the conquest of the Tartar strongholds of Kazan and Astrakhan, and (despite a disastrous drive to the Baltic) the consolidation of Russia as a nation from the Caspian to the White Sea. His ongoing duel with the princely aristocracy, or boyars, laid the foundations for an autocracy supported by a nonhereditary serving class, while his permanent initiatives in opening up diplomatic ties to Europe bound Russia ever after to the West. No ruler of the age had more staying power. Eight popes would succeed each other to the Holy See, four monarchs each to the thrones of France, Poland, Portugal, Germany, and England, three to the throne of Sweden, and three Turkish sultans to the Sublime Porte before Ivan met his own demise. Within Muscovy itself, his judicial and other reforms for a time made him an exceptionally popular ruler, and though his *Oprichnina*—or "government apart"—would eventually develop into a terror machine, its inception brought lowborn gentry into the councils of government and arguably at first had the welfare of the country at heart. In certain respects, at least, he may not have been unworthy of the adoration bestowed on him by Peter the Great, or of his twentieth-century reincarnation as the ambiguous national hero of Sergey Eisenstein's film.

Yet however great his achievements, they were matched by his despotism and atrocities; and despite his colossal stature, historians disagree about him on almost every level and on many important details. He has remained the most controversial of tsars, and part of his fascination for a student of history lies in the changing fortunes of his fame.

A decisive verdict is made difficult by serious gaps in the factual evidence on which a biography can be based. This is true with regard to Ivan in particular, and to his period in general—one of the most abstruse in Russian history. The situation so dismayed the great historian S. F. Platonov in 1923 that he doubted a biography of Ivan could be written, though he wrote one himself nevertheless.

The obstacles today are less daunting than they were. In the past half-century research in the field has claimed the talents of a number of remarkable scholars, east and west, whose insights and discoveries have been considerable. By and large, however, this new archive of material has remained the preserve of specialists, and is scattered far and wide through learned journals seldom read beyond the halls of academe. This book is substantially an attempt to gather much of the best of it under a single roof.

Beyond that, I have tried to place Ivan more clearly in his contemporary context, to fill in the historical background and often neglected landscape of ideas, and to evoke Muscovy itself as vividly as possible—for even among popular historians it can no longer suffice to say merely that Russia was "barbarous" and "medieval" before Peter the Great. However, though I have occasionally tried to carry my own lamp into the recesses of the story, I cannot claim to have resolved the fundamental contradictions that must baffle any biographer of Ivan IV. On the contrary, I learned to live with them—even as his contemporaries did. One contemporary miniature remains for me inimitably succinct: "He was a goodlie man of person and presence, waell favored, high forehead, shrill voice; a right Sithian; full of readie wisdom; cruel, bloudye, merciles."

A Note on Names and Dates

No two books on Russian history agree completely on the spelling of names. In this book anglicized (if not always English) forms have been used, for ease of recognition and pronunciation. The soft sign, usually rendered by an apostrophe (as in Sil'vester), has been dropped.

All dates are according to the Julian or Old Style calendar in use in Western Europe until 1582. Sixteenth-century Russians celebrated their New Year on September 1 and based their calendar on the date of the creation of the world, which they placed in 5508 B.C.

"[Mercy] becomes
The throned monarch better than his crown;
His sceptre shows the force of temporal power,
The attribute to awe and majesty,
Wherein doth sit the dread and fear of kings;
But mercy is above this sceptred sway."

—SHAKESPEARE,
The Merchant of Venice,
Act 4, Scene 1, ll. 188–193.

"If all the pictures and patterns of a merciless prince were lost in the world, they might all again be painted to the life out of the story of this King. For, how many servants did he advance in haste and with what change of his fancy ruined again, no man knowing for what offense? To how many others, of more desert, gave he abundant flowers from whence to gather honey, and in the end of harvest burnt them in the hive? How many wives did he cut off, and cast off, as his fancy and affection changed? How many princes of the blood (whereof some of them for age could hardly crawl toward the block), with a world of others of degrees did he execute?"

—SIR WALTER RALEGH,
History of the World, on Henry VIII

MUSCOVY

part one

MUSCOVY

1.

The Death of Vasily III

In 1533, Vasily III, grand prince of Muscovy and the father of Ivan IV ("the Terrible"), Russia's first tsar, was in his fifty-fourth year (and the twenty-eighth of his reign) when his life was cut short. No one was more surprised at this development than Vasily himself. Though he had reached a comparatively venerable age, throughout his careworn years as sovereign he had never felt so rambunctious. Seven years before, he had cast off a barren, gloomy, and hypochondriacal wife for a Lithuanian princess half his age whose beauty and animal vitality absolutely infatuated him. He had defied the whole Eastern Orthodox Church to have her, and she had since borne him two sons, securing the succession after a quarter century of doubt. His might unchallenged and supreme, still in love, lusty and optimistic, as he set out in September for a holiday of hunting and feasting at Volokolamsk northwest of Moscow, he cannot have been much alarmed when a crimson sore containing a tiny pimple appeared on his lower left thigh.

Vasily belonged to the House of Rurik, an august dynasty of semilegendary origin which had monopolized the throne of Russia from her birth as a nation in the ninth century A.D. No noble house in European history, in fact, was ever to rule so long. Only the Hapsburgs of Austria could claim a comparable longevity, while relatively speaking the long train of Romanovs would make up a modest span.

Yet few nations had endured a more turbulent medieval past.

According to the Russian *Primary Chronicle*, in the year 862 clan elders of various warring Slavic tribes, exasperated at their inability to bring peace to the Russian plain, had summoned Viking chieftains from overseas "to come and rule over us and create order in the land." A certain Rurik came, with his brothers Sineus and Truvor, in answer to their call.

Rurik has been identified as Roric the Dane or Roric of Jutland, known in western annals as *fel Christianitatis* or "the gall of Christendom." Before departing for Russia, he had raided settlements along the banks of the river Elbe, ravaged part of northern France, and with an armada of 350 boats had sacked the coast of England. The military confraternity of Norsemen to which he belonged was called the Varangians (from "vaeringr"— "associate under oath"), mercenary merchant-warriors who also by way of the Western Dvina, Dnieper, and Volga Rivers, explored routes all the way to the Black and Caspian seas. Some entered the service of the Byzantine emperor in Constantinople, where they served as shock troops or imperial guards. Rurik remained on Slav territory and (invited or not) established himself at Novgorod.

Like the Normans in England, the Varangians soon merged with the native population. No one really knows, for example, whether the word "Russe" is Slavic or Norse.

Rurik was succeeded by Oleg, who transferred his rule to Kiev on the Dnieper, the road to Byzantium; Oleg by Igor, Rurik's son; and Igor by Olga, who acted as regent until her grandson, Sviatoslav, came to power in 962. Meanwhile, a century of steady expansion had transformed the "Russe" conglomeration of tribes into a regional power. Commercial competition with Constantinople made conflict inevitable, and though the Byzantines on the whole prevailed, advantageous new trade agreements were wrung from the imperial city with each armistice.

Sviatoslav, a pagan, was a noble if savage warrior-prince. His illegitimate son and successor was a saint, Vladimir I, who converted to Christianity in 988 and compelled his subjects to follow his example, thus bringing Russia within the orbit of Greek Orthodox Christianity. The local pagan temples and idols were overthrown, and the people of Kiev baptized *en masse* in the waters of the Dnieper, much as the Saxons had been "evangelized" by Charlemagne. Politically, Vladimir consolidated his realm from the Baltic to the Ukraine.

Upon his death civil war ensued between his sons. One of them, Svyatopolk, assassinated his brothers Boris and Gleb in a grab for absolute power. He became the most famous villain in Russian history—Svyatopolk the Accursed. Boris and Gleb, who went to their deaths like martyrs, were canonized. Svyatopolk in turn was toppled by another brother, Yaroslav, known to history as Yaroslav the Wise, a statesman, scholar, and patron of the arts who promoted Christian culture in Kiev with libraries and schools. He beautified the capital with a palace and its own Cathedral, and drafted the *Russkaya Pravda*, the first Russian Law Code.

Yaroslav married the daughter of the Byzantine emperor Constantine IX

Monomachos. Their offspring was another remarkable man, Vladimir II Monomakh, who ruled from 1113 to 1125 and proved an energetic statesman, a skillful military leader, and a gifted writer. Meanwhile, the government of Kiev had evolved into a kind of limited monarchy, with a grand prince, an independent nobility, and *veches* or town assemblies with real influence on state and local affairs.

In international relations, through dynastic union (the centerpiece of medieval diplomacy) and other ties, Russia fully belonged to the "extended family" of European nations. At one time or another, its rulers contracted matrimonial alliances with Hungary, Bohemia, Poland, Germany, Norway, Sweden, and France. Vladimir II himself married the daughter of King Harold of England; the missal on which French kings for centuries swore their coronation oaths belonged originally to the daughter of Yaroslav the Wise who had married King Louis I.

Russia's political maturation was accompanied by a flourishing and diversified economy, with agriculture, trade, and industry. But forces presaging disunity and chaos were churning about the borders of the land. The shores of the Black Sea and the Don and Volga river basins to the east were the domain of roving tribesmen of Turkic and Mongol origin. A war without end developed against these nomads of the steppes—the Khazars, the Pechenegs, and the Polovtsy—who repeatedly advanced in human-wave assaults against the fledgling civilization. Gradually, the suburbs of the capital were turned into a wasteland. The nomads occupied the mouth of the Dnieper, severed Russian trade with Constantinople, and drove the population west into Galicia and Volynia, and northeast toward Suzdal on the upper Volga. Kiev's mercantile economy (the most advanced in Europe) was destroyed and replaced by an agricultural society to the north. This retrograde development in Russian economic history was paralleled by political dissolution.

"The grass bends in sorrow," wrote the poet of *The Lay of the Host of Igor*, the greatest of early Russian epics, "and the tree is bowed down to earth by woe. . . . Victory over the infidels is gone, for now brother said to brother: 'This is mine, and that is mine also,' and the princes began to say of little things, 'Lo! this is a great matter,' and to forge discord against themselves. And on all sides the infidels were victorious."

A grim struggle for power ensued among various members of the ruling family, who in administering their scattered appanage domains had divergent regional goals. The absence of the concept of primogeniture contributed to the disarray, through a continuing subdivision of property among princely offspring. Among the rival principalities, Vladimir-Suzdal in the north emerged as the most powerful, and in 1169 its capital became the seat of the grand prince.

Après cela, le déluge. In 1223, the Mongol cavalry of Genghis Khan charged across the Caucasus and conquered the entire region between the Don and Volga rivers. His grandson, Batu, pushing farther west, captured Vladimir, Pereslavl, and Chernigov in 1238 and Kiev in 1240. The carnage was dreadful. A papal legate who crossed southern Russia in 1245 wrote: "We found lying in the field countless skulls and bones. Kiev, which had been extremely large and prosperous, has been reduced to nothing." Though Novgorod was spared destruction, its valiant duke Aleksander Nevsky, who had recently defeated two invasions from the West—the Swedes on the banks of the Neva River in 1240, and the Teutonic Knights on the ice of Lake Peipus in 1242—chose to submit rather than subject his people to inevitable massacre. Batu established his headquarters at Sarai on the lower Volga, and the Golden Horde, as it was called, became the Eastern European branch of the Great Horde of the Mongol Empire.

Mongol (or Tartar[1]) domination of Russia was destined to last two and a half centuries.

But "though an empire can be won on horseback, it cannot be ruled from the saddle," and the Mongols (whom Pushkin called "Arabs without Aristotle or Algebra") needed proxies to administer their conquered domains. In Russia they enlisted—and handsomely rewarded—compliant princes willing to enforce their cruel and benighted rule.

Such was the background for the rise of Moscow.

The city of Moscow had begun as a tiny hamlet on a bend of the Moscow River. To this day no one knows where the name comes from, though to the Muscovite of the sixteenth century (for whom Biblical and Russian history were intertwined) it was somehow connected to "our forefather Mosokh, son of Japheth, grandson of Noah." Archaeological excavations reveal that some sort of settlement existed on the site as early as Neolithic times, but Moscow itself is not mentioned in the chronicles until 1147, when it enters recorded history as a frontier habitation between Suzdal and Ryazan. In 1156, the Suzdal prince, Yury Dolgoruky, seduced a local princess who, though married, passionately returned his attentions because "he did everything according to her desire." When her husband protested, Yury killed him and confiscated his estate. In the following year he surrounded the property with a wooden palisade.

Thus began the Kremlin, situated on a bluff above the Moscow River, as a modest triangular fort. Before long it became the "kreml" or central citadel of a town, and the town, like the fortress, grew. Located near the headwaters of four major rivers (the Oka, the Volga, the Dnieper, and the Don), with their numerous tributaries linked variously to each other and to lesser rivers and streams, Moscow lay at the crossroads of that remarkable network of water highways which bind European Russia together as though by deliberate plan.

In the vicinity of Moscow there were few elevations to impede the town's expansion except for the high southwestern bank of the Moscow River, known as the Sparrow Hills. By the fourteenth century it had become the capital of a dynamic principality, and under Ivan I ("Moneybags") Kalita, a thrifty and industrious prince, achieved preeminence in the northeast. Because Moscow princes were exceptionally willing to act as Mongol surrogates—collecting taxes, helping to suppress revolts, and even betraying rivals to the foe—they were repeatedly invested by their overlords with the title of "grand prince," even though they belonged to a junior branch of the House of Rurik. After the metropolitan or chief hierarch of the Church transferred his see to Moscow in 1325, which enormously enhanced the city's prestige, the ecclesiastical establishment pursued a similar policy, obliging the Russian congregation to pray for the khan in church in return for substantial tax immunities and other privileges. Finally, the principle of primogeniture, established for the House of Moscow by Dmitry Donskoy, prince from 1359 to 1389, greatly assisted in the increase of its power.

This shrewd maneuvering paid off, as Moscow eventually achieved sufficient strength to turn on its benefactors and emerge as the national champions against Mongol tyranny. On September 8, 1380, "in a clean field beyond the Don, on the birthday of the Mother of God," Donskoy met and defeated Khan Mamay of the Golden Horde in the Battle of Kulikovo Field. Though in the following year the Tartars would avenge their humiliation, Donskoy had destroyed the myth of Mongol invincibility. The Russian declaration of independence had been signed in blood.

Renovations of the Kremlin reflected the growth in Moscow's might. Under Ivan Kalita the original palisade had been reinforced by earthen ramparts; in 1367, Donskoy doubled the area of enclosure and replaced the old fortifications with a white-stone wall. From this time onward Moscow began its subjugation of neighboring principalities, in a progressive effort to make itself the capital of a great northern Russian state.

Meanwhile the old Russia of Kiev had long since disappeared. The Poles had conquered Galicia, and one by one the Lithuanians (driven southward by a war of extermination waged against them by the Teutonic Knights) succeeded in subjugating the principalities of Volynia, Polotsk, Smolensk,

Kiev, and Chernigov. When Poland and Lithuania were joined by dynastic union in 1386 all this territory (sometimes called Western Russia) appeared to pass forever into alien hands.

Concurrently, the Mongol Empire had begun to break up, with the Golden Horde resolving into lesser succession states founded as khanates: in the Crimea (1430), Kazan (1436) and Astrakhan (1466). In 1452 Moscow established a small Tartar khanate of its own called Kasimov, centered on the Oka River town of Gorodets, as a haven for Tartar renegades, which later proved a reliable source of auxiliary troops for the army and of officials to staff pro-Muscovite Tartar regimes.

The way had also been prepared for the establishment of a true national church, following the "apostasy" of the Greeks in courting union with Rome at Florence in 1439, and the subsequent fall of Constantinople to the Turks in 1453.

All these developments set the stage for the triumphant reign of Ivan III "the Great," who ascended the Moscow throne in 1462. A tall, slightly hunchbacked, patient but determined monarch, he made it his task by cunning, force, and persuasion to annex numerous surrounding principalities to his expanding state—including Yaroslavl in 1463, Perm in 1472, Rostov in 1474, Novgorod (a democratic republic) and its vast northern possessions by 1478, Tver and Vyatka in 1485, and Vyazma and Chernigov by 1498. In 1500, one of his brothers bequeathed him half of Ryazan. Meanwhile he had married Sophia Paleologa, the niece of the last Byzantine emperor, began to adopt Byzantine court ceremonial, titles, and heraldry, including the Byzantine two-headed eagle as his insignia of sovereignty, and in 1480, in a great, bloodless victory that marked the end of the Tartar yoke, faced down the remnant of the Golden Horde at the Ugra River. Soon thereafter he assumed the title of *samoderzhets*, the Slavic equivalent of the Byzantine *autokrator*, or autocrat, and in the manner of the Byzantine emperors of old affirmed that he had received his investiture from God.

The changing status of the Muscovite grand prince encouraged cautious but persistent efforts by the Kremlin to re-enter the international political community. Envoys were dispatched to Denmark, Vienna, Hungary, Venice, and Constantinople, while diplomats arrived from abroad to discuss everything from a crusade against the Turks to the procurement of falcons for the German imperial court. Less peaceably, Moscow's expansion—by incorporating territory that had once insulated her from foreign powers—brought her face to face with Swedish Finland, German Livonia, and Lithuania along a long and irregular western frontier. In the south and east she also now faced the Tartar khanates of Crimea and Kazan. Every one of these states was fundamentally hostile to her growth.

They had much to fear. In 1493, Ivan III claimed as his patrimony all lands held by Lithuania that had once formed part of the Russia of Kiev, and in 1500 scored considerable gains near Polotsk, Smolensk, and Chernigov-Seversk.

His son Vasily III, crowned in 1505, not only completed his father's northern objectives by annexing the principality of Pskov in 1510 (the last stronghold of democratic traditions in Russia) and the remainder of Ryazan in 1517, but in 1514, after three bloody campaigns, detached Smolensk from Lithuania despite a grave defeat on the Orsha River in which tens of thousands died.

Thus, by 1533, all Russians were called Muscovites, and Russia Muscovy, because Moscow had the power.

That power was stern, as perhaps it had to be, to overthrow the Tartar yoke; but it also brought a new oppression. On the one hand Vasily reigned at a time when throughout Europe old aristocratic and feudal societies were completing their transformation into centralized monarchical states. Muscovy, the most Western of Asiatic, most Eastern of European states, decidedly belonged to this overall pattern of development. But the style of Muscovite governance (Byzantine kingship cast in a Mongol mold), as well as the economic and social configuration of its expanding kingdom, differed markedly from its Western counterparts. Muscovy remained an agricultural society fundamentally supported by the toil of its peasantry, with a merchant class but no social equivalent to the independent merchant guilds of the more industrialized West. There was a gentry, but its hallmark as a rising middle class was not entrepreneurship but state service. State service in fact was what Muscovy was all about. The grand prince enjoyed an authority over his individual subjects that was tyrannical, with some institutional but no real constitutional restraints. The Russian people were encouraged to regard their sovereign as omniscient, omnipresent, and semidivine; they called him God's key-bearer or chamberlain, and believed him to be God's agent on earth. In the words of Sigismund von Herberstein, twice German ambassador to Russia during the reign of Vasily III:

> In the power which he exercises over his subjects he easily outstrips the rulers of the whole world. He makes use of his authority in spiritual as well as temporal affairs; he freely and of his own will decides concerning the lives and property of everybody; of the councilors whom he has, none is of such authority that he dares to disagree or in any way to resist. They say publicly that the will of the prince is the will of God. ''

Under Vasily, all subjects, lowborn or high, began to refer to themselves as "slaves" when addressing the grand prince. The conception of the sover-

grandpuire who suppose ruler and precator of God

eign as "the living law," and of his sovereignty as the earthly reflection of divine wisdom and power, was thoroughly Byzantine, as was his duty as viceregent of God to act as Defender of the Faith—"the orthodox and pious ruler in spiritual union with his flock." But the Mongol Khan, the other great exemplar to which the Muscovites looked for their understanding of imperial rule, had stood for arbitrary despotism, a ruler separated from his subjects and responsible to none. These two forms of absolutism were entwined—or twisted—together so that the Muscovite sovereign emerged as a kind of khan in Byzantine garb.

Vasily could not divorce so he put his wife in a convent

Vasily was prepared to go to any lengths to see that his line did not demise, and his uncanonical divorce (like that of England's Henry VIII) was arguably the crucial event of his reign. Though his first wife, Solomonia Saburova, had been selected according to royal custom from a bride-show of 1500 virgins summoned to the capital, Vasily had chosen badly, and after twenty years of childless and disagreeable wedlock—yet barred from divorce because lack of issue was not recognized as adequate grounds—began to despair. According to the chroniclers, he bitterly apostrophized birds' nests, flourishing gardens, rivers rich in fish, and other examples of fecund nature from which he felt estranged, even as Solomonia, quite as dismayed, resorted to exorcists and witches "to make the Grand Prince love her and enable her to conceive." One advised her to moisten her white garments with water; another, to rub herself all over with honey and oil. Such measures failed to arouse him, however, and in the fall of 1525 he reportedly met with his boyars, wept, and said: "Who will rule the Russian land when I am gone? My brothers? They cannot even manage their own appanage estates." The boyars replied: "Sovereign, when a fig tree is barren it is cut down and removed from the vineyard." This was just what he wanted to hear, and on November 28, over the objections of the Eastern patriarchs and many holy monks on Mt. Athos to whom he appealed—but with the approval of his own submissive Metropolitan, Daniel—Vasily obtained an annulment and thrust Solomonia into a convent in the principality of Suzdal.

As with Henry VIII, dynastic considerations took precedence over imperatives of faith, but in order to retroactively sanctify the act later official court chronicles made Solomonia insist upon her tonsure over Vasily's objections: "Knowing that she was barren," we read, "like Sarah of old, the Grand Princess entreated the Grand Prince to allow her to enter the cloister. He said: 'How can I sunder my marriage and take another? I am a pious sovereign who fulfills God's commandments and the prescribed law.' But she tearfully and earnestly entreated, and finally begged the Metropolitan to intercede. He did, and the Grand Prince obeyed him." In fact, when Daniel came to the convent to cut off her hair, he found her weeping and sobbing, and when he tried to place the cowl on her head, she fought him off, hurled it to the ground and stamped on it. One of Vasily's councilors sternly upbraided her and struck her with his staff: " 'How dare you oppose our Lord's will or delay to execute his behests?' But she declared before everyone that she was forced to take the veil against her will, and called on God to avenge the monstrous wrong that had been done to her."

Subsequently, Solomonia declared that she was pregnant. Alarmed, Vasily sent a commission to the convent to ascertain if it were true. It wasn't, and he was probably relieved; for dynastic considerations aside, he had lately fallen in love with a Lithuanian exile and princess of royal Mongolian descent, Elena Glinskaya, whom he hastened to marry on January 21, 1526. The wedding took place in the Kremlin Cathedral of the Assumption, and after the metropolitan recited their vows, Vasily drank a glass of wine at a draught, let the glass fall to the ground and crushed it under his heel. The fragments were carefully collected and cast into the Moscow River. After the ceremony, choristers chanted long life to the newlyweds, the grand prince made a quick round of the local monasteries and churches, presided at the palace over a great feast of roast chicken, and was afterward escorted with his bride to their nuptial suite. There, thirty sheaves of rye were spread under the bed, candles stuck into tubs of wheat by the headboard, and the royal pair sprinkled with hops to assure their fertility. All night long outside their chamber the master of the horse patrolled with his sword drawn.

At the time of their wedding, Vasily was forty-seven, Elena twenty-three. Not long afterward, the grand prince began to dandify his dress, and in an unprecedented affront to Orthodox tradition, shaved off his beard to please her.

It was a very Western thing to do, and called attention to the fact that Elena, although raised in Moscow, had grown up in the household of her uncle, Mikhail Glinsky, a man of broad European education who had made a name for himself as a soldier, statesman, linguist, apothecary, and wit. As a condottiere or "knight errant," he had served in the army of Albrecht, duke of Saxony and under the Holy Roman Emperor Maximilian I. Returning to Lithuania, where his property and lineage made him a great lord of the land, he had been prized as a warrior and councilor of state. However, in 1506 he revolted against the crown in a bid to carve out a Lithuanian duchy for himself. Sigismund I of Poland "rode straight from his coronation in Cracow to drive him into exile," and Glinsky, unable to oppose the king's men, crossed with his family into Muscovy.

Vasily, who had connived at his rebellion, welcomed him with open arms—yet not with a complete embrace: in 1514, after the Muscovites took Smolensk, he failed to make him governor; and to ensure that Glinsky would not re-defect, imprisoned him in a Kremlin tower.

Glinsky had majesty in him, however, and after Elena's marriage prompted his release, his conspicuous abilities soon enabled him to emerge as one of Vasily's righthand men. He was appointed to the Boyar Duma, the chief administrative and legislative body of the realm, where he ranked third, and Vasily counted on his valor to safeguard his children's possession of the throne. The grand prince's brother, Yury, was especially to be feared. From the earliest days of Vasily's accession he had worn a lean and hungry look, and had all but openly rejoiced in Solomonia's sterility. When Elena then failed to produce an heir after three and a half years, there was probably no one more delighted in the kingdom—and none more chagrined when at six o'clock in the evening on August 25, 1530, she at last gave birth to a boy. The child's advent seemed a miracle.

At Trinity Monastery he was baptized "Ivan" on the tomb containing the relics of St. Sergius, whose powerful spiritual protection was invoked; and a year later on his name day, "The Feast of the Beheading of St. John the Baptist" (August 29, in the Orthodox calendar), Vasily fulfilled a vow he had made in accordance with ancient Russian custom and helped erect and consecrate in a single day a simple church of thanksgiving.

In 1532, a second son, Yury, was born—a deaf-mute, whose incapacities inevitably caused his parents to dote more assiduously on Ivan as the hope of the realm.

Many omens, prophecies, and dreams (most concocted later) embellish the story of Ivan's birth. But perhaps one or two are true. On the eve of his delivery, Elena reputedly dreamed that she was approached by a monk who "threw" an infant boy at her, and on the day of his birth, it is said, "the whole country was filled with the noise of thunder, and with awful flashes of lightning," presaging the "thunderous shocks" of his reign. It was reported, too, that a monk named Galaktion had predicted Vasily would have a son who would one day conquer Kazan; and indeed, far away in Kazan itself, the wife of the khan, upon learning of the child's birth, reputedly had a premonition and declared to the Muscovite envoy: "A Tsar is born among you: two teeth has he. With one he will devour us; but with the other—you." This agreed unpleasantly with a curse the patriarch of Jerusalem was said to have laid upon Vasily when he went through with his divorce: "If you do this evil thing, you shall have an evil son. Your nation shall become prey to terrors and tears. Rivers of blood will flow, the heads of the mighty will fall. Your cities will be devoured by flames."

The court, however, was astir with more mundane if salacious gossip, for it was rumored that Elena, slow to conceive, had taken a lover to save herself from Solomonia's fate. Therefore (it was said), "the child had two fathers, like Svyatopolk the Accursed."

For all that, his parents greeted his advent with unadulterated joy.

Yet Ivan was an ambiguous child, even as his genealogy brought together the clashing forces of medieval Russian history. In addition to the Byzantine strain contributed by his Greek grandmother, he was through his father a direct descendant of Dmitry Donskoy, who had defeated the Tartars on Kulikovo Field, but through his mother of Donskoy's antagonist, Khan Mamay of the Golden Horde.[2]

Ivan's two teeth[3] must have poked through slowly (he had incredibly late dentition, not complete before his fiftieth year!), and his infant lack of appetite was a matter of concern. In the summer of 1533, a carbuncle appeared on the nape of his neck. Elena wrote to Vasily, away at the time, who responded immediately with a flurry of questions: "Is it serious? What causes it? Is it hereditary? Can you tell me? Consult with other mothers you know; ask them to ask their friends. Tell me at once what you learn." Elena replied that the carbuncle was healing, but that she was suffering from various aches and pains. Vasily replied: "Are you better? Is there a mark on Ivan's neck? Tell me nothing but the truth."

Ivan recovered without complications; Elena's aches and pains disappeared. But late that September the inconspicuous pimple that had appeared on Vasily's thigh ripened into a boil. By the beginning of October, when he reached Volokolamsk, he was unsteady on his feet. Though he took the field with his dogs, he complained constantly of pain and returned to his lodge after an hour. Glinsky was sent for, and Vasily's two Western physicians, Theophilus (about whom little is known) and Nicholas Bulev, or "Nicholas the German," from Lübeck, a mystic mathematician, court astrologer, and herbalist. Though a Catholic (and therefore an apostate in the eyes of the Orthodox Church), Bulev's long service to Vasily had been exemplary, and the grand prince did not hesitate to put his life in his hands.

The three men consulted together and applied a poultice of meal, honey, and boiled onion to the sore to make it suppurate. Next an ointment was tried and "a great deal of pus oozed out." The pain increased, and his breath grew short. They administered a purgative of seeds, which left him exhausted. Divining that his days were numbered, Vasily secretly sent to the Kremlin for a copy of his father's will. He now redrafted his own and though he could barely sit up, made an effort to deliberate with his advisers about a Regency Council to rule during Ivan's minority. Meanwhile, the boil had developed into a huge abscess and "the pus filled a basin." Vasily had begun to fail when part of the core, "more than an inch and a half in diameter," came out. The swelling subsided, and in gratitude for his reprieve he suddenly announced his desire to become a monk. (As symbolized by a change in name, tonsuring was considered a real sacrament which even on one's deathbed bestowed pardon for the sins of the foregoing life. Not surprisingly, many a grand prince had taken advantage of it.)

Plans were made to return to the capital. Borne aloft on a horse-drawn litter, Vasily was turned repeatedly from side to side to ease his discomfort, but as they approached the village of Vorobevo south of Moscow on November 21, he suffered a relapse. A bridge was thrown across the Moscow River opposite the Novodevichy Monastery, but when the horses clattered onto the span a beam snapped and the traces were cut just in the nick of time. A few days later, he was ferried across below Dorogomilov.

Propped up in bed in the Kremlin Palace, Vasily gathered his principal advisers around him and began "a ceaseless round of conferences on the disposition of the realm." In addition to Glinsky and his youngest brother, Andrey Staritsky, the key boyars summoned to his bedside were Mikhail Zakharin, Prince Mikhail Vorontsov, Princes Vasily and Ivan Shuisky and Mikhail Tuchkov—the Regency Council of seven he designated to rule. Also consulted were the treasurer Peter Golovin and Ivan Shigona, his trusted courtier from Tver, while his confidential secretaries, Menshoy Putiatin and Fyodor Mishurin, drafted the final version of his testament.

Notably absent from this inner circle was Prince Yury, who had hovered about like a vulture since learning of Vasily's decline. The grand prince had gone to extraordinary lengths to keep the true situation from him. Now the die was cast. To prepare the stage for his departure, Vasily made a series of deathbed speeches to his brothers, the metropolitan, and the boyars. He demanded that they swear fidelity to his son Ivan, "stand together to keep order," and remain united against Mohammedans and Catholics. Looking straight at the boyars he said:

> You know that our power descends directly from Grand Prince Vladimir of Kiev. We are your natural rulers and you have always been our boyars. I commend Mikhail Lvovich Glinsky to you. Although he was an adult when

he came to us, you must not call him a sojourner, but regard him as though he were born here among us, because he is my close aide. Prince Glinsky, you must be ready to shed your blood to protect my wife and sons.

Gangrene set in, and the putrefying sore gave off an intolerable stench. Zakharin offered to pour vodka on it. Vasily rolled his eyes helplessly toward Bulev, who said: "I would cut myself to pieces to help you, but I am afraid only God can help you now."

Blood poisoning consumed him. Vasily "dozed and dreamed. He awoke and murmured: 'It is the Lord's will.' "

On the following day, December 3, he rallied, and discussed with Shigona, Zakharin, and Glinsky "what Elena would do and how the boyars should treat her." Toward evening he asked for some crushed almonds, but could do no more than raise them to his lips. Elena and little Ivan were brought to him for his blessing, accompanied by Agrafena, Ivan's nurse. Vasily commanded Agrafena never to let Ivan out of her sight. Elena became hysterical. "In whose hands have you left me?" she asked. "To whom do you remand our children?" Vasily replied: "I have designated Ivan as grand prince, and made arrangements for little Yury; and also for you according to custom," meaning he had bequeathed her a widow's appanage estate. He had more he wished to say to her, but she wailed so loudly that he was unable to make himself understood and she had to be taken from the room.

Night drew on. The miracle-working Icon of the Virgin of Vladimir was fetched. Someone asked Vasily's confessor if he had ever been present when the soul left the body. Not often, he said. A deacon began to sing the canon in honor of St. Catherine the Martyr. Vasily awoke, beholding a vision: "Catherine, mighty Christian martyr, thy will be done. Mistress, it is time!" He grasped her icon and kissed it, and kissed her relics, which were also placed in his hands.[4] Then he embraced the boyar, Mikhail Vorontsov, and forgave him some past offense.

"Tonsure me now!" he commanded, when suddenly a dispute arose: not everyone wanted him to become a monk. Some said: "Vladimir of Kiev was not tonsured before he died. But surely he went to the rest he deserved. And so too have other grand princes found righteous peace."

"Metropolitan," exclaimed Vasily, "am I to be left lying here?" He grasped his coverings and kissed them and stared at an icon of the Virgin above his head. Metropolitan Daniel sent for the robe and cowl and with the help of Abbot Joasaf of Trinity Monastery fastened a collar around his neck. As the procedure was hastily completed, Vasily's spirit, according to an eyewitness, left his body "in the form of a fine cloud." "And instead of a stench from the sore," claimed a posthumous panegyric, "the room was filled with perfume."

Thus did Grand Prince Vasily III, by the grace of God Lord of all Russia, of Vladimir, Moscow, Novgorod, Pskov, Smolensk, Tver, Yugorsk, Perm, Vyatka, Bulgaria,[5] Nizhny-Novgorod, Chernigov, Ryazan, Volokolamsk, Rzhev, Belaia, Rostov, Yaroslavl, Beloozero, Udorsk, Obdorsk, Kandinsk, and other places (for so his title read) pass at midnight, Wednesday, December 3, 1533, as the monk Varlaam, from this world.

Wrapped in a black taffeta cloth, his body was laid in a white-stone sarcophagus and carried the following morning, with all the city's church bells tolling, into Red Square. The three-and-one-half-year-old Ivan was crowned in the Cathedral of the Assumption and officials were dispatched throughout the country to administer the oath of allegiance to the entire population.

But the dominions enumerated in the grand prince's title were rather too much for an infant's shoulders to bear; and of course the regents thought so too, and soon ignored him and went about their affairs.

2.

The Realm of Muscovy

Though the kingdom Ivan inherited was not yet the transcontinental empire it was destined to become, it already occupied much of the great Central European plain that sweeps from the foot of the Carpathian Mountains to the Urals. In sheer land mass at least, if not in industrial concentration and might, it was one of the largest nations on earth, roughly equivalent in size to France, Spain, the British Isles, and Italy combined. It extended from the Pechora River in the north to the mouth of the Neva and Lake Ilmen in the west, from the upper Volga in the east, southwest to the Dnieper, to 200 miles south of Ryazan on the Don. Much of this territory, however, was sparsely inhabited wilderness, and most of Russia's ten to twelve million inhabitants were peasants who lived and worked in a condition of semienserfment on large aristocratic or monastic estates or in tiny villages and hamlets scattered over the land. Less than 10 percent of the population lived in cities or towns, of which there were about 150 in the year of Ivan's birth. The most prominent of these were Novgorod, Moscow, Pskov, and Smolensk, with populations ranging from up to 50,000.

Though Muscovy had an excellent pony express, there were no inns across its vast hinterland to accommodate the traveler, who had to provide food and shelter for himself. At the very least he carried some ground millet in a bag, a few pounds of salt pork, a hatchet, a tinderbox, a bottle of water, and a kettle. A long journey was easiest in winter, when on hard, smooth snow a horse-drawn sled could cover 400 miles in three days. A great noble would do this in style, in a great sled carpeted with a white bearskin or a thick Persian rug.

Though practically landlocked, with a small, unindented northern coast-line icebound much of the year, Muscovy's internal commerce and communi-cation was facilitated by a providential network of river highways, "that emptying themselves one into another, runne all into the Sea." The Volga (the greatest river in Europe) was said to empty into the Caspian Sea through seventy-two mouths.

Providence was more obscure with regard to climate, which was marked by fierce extremes: a blistering summer, and a long polar winter, a brief and tumultuous autumn and a still briefer spring. The average latitude of sixteenth-century Muscovy was coincident with that of Alaska. As far south as the Ukraine, the ground was covered by snow a quarter of the year, and northward toward the Arctic frozen eight months out of twelve. When the January cold came on, and the blizzards rolled up in a whirlwind from the Arctic gales, the very sap of the wood burning in the fire was seen to freeze at the brand's end. Even about Moscow the earth split into clefts, yet remained so hard that the dead were stacked stiff and uncorrupted in their coffins to await interment till spring.

"The sharpenesse of the aire you may judge of by this," wrote a visitor,

> for that water dropped downe or cast up congealeth into yce before it come to the ground. In the extremitie of Winter, if you holde a pewter dish or pot in your hand, or any other mettall . . . your fingers will friese fast unto it, and drawe off the skinne at the parting . . . you shall see many drop downe in the streetes; many travellers brought into the Townes sitting dead in their Sleds. Divers lose their noses, the tips of their eares, and the bals of their cheekes, their toes, feete, &c. Many times the beares and woolfes issue by

troupes out of the woods driven by hunger, and enter the villages, tearing and ravening all they can finde.

Spring brought surcease, but also widespread flooding as rivers, overflowing from the melting ice and snow, flooded the fields and turned the roads to mire. Yet by May, from such a thorough drenching of the ground, the countryside was transformed into one great garden of beauty and delight "so fresh and so sweete, the pastures and medowes so greene and wel growen," full of ecstatically singing birds (especially nightingales) that it could seem a vision of paradise.

"God is on high and the Tsar far off," goes a Russian proverb. Though not quite a "tsar," Vasily had been remote enough, ruling his kingdom from the Kremlin, then as now a stone battlemented triangle on a hilly terrace above the Moscow River. Surrounded by water—by the Moscow River to the south, the Neglinnaya River to the northwest, and by a wide, deep moat which joined them to the east along the edge of Red Square— it was an island fortress, a mile and a quarter in circumference, defended by monumental towers, advanced blockhouses, barbicans, drawbridges, and immensely thick walls up to sixty feet high. Its parapets bristled with heavy cannon; its serrated ramparts were cut with scores of gun-loops and embrasures. One tower, overlooking Red Square, soared to 200 feet; another, the massive northwest corner Arsenal Tower, included an underground reservoir fed by a spring from which water was also diverted to the moat by a secret canal. Altogether, the citadel was virtually unassailable—"fully as powerful as the castles of Milan and Metz."

Ivan III had made it so, with a brigade of Italian master-builders, engineers, and artisans of all kinds commissioned to transform Donskoy's white-stone edifice into an imperial palace. An extraordinary elite of Renaissance talent had assembled under his patronage. Perhaps the most versatile was Aristotele di Ridolfo di Fioravanti of Bologna, whose competence ranged from cathedral architecture to casting guns and bells. He set up a kiln for baking bricks, showed the Russians a new way of mixing lime so that, "when dried, it could not be cut with a knife," and contrived a machinery of ropes and pulleys for raising blocks of stone into place. Vasily III continued the construction, and by 1533 the Kremlin covered sixty-five acres, enclosed a complex of palace, office, and cathedral buildings, and was a town unto itself.

Its hub was Cathedral Square. Along one side stood the sovereign's residence, a five-story brick building that included an inner courtyard, a large veranda fitted with a folding lattice gate, a famous throne room or Golden Chamber, and an upper wing known as the *terem*, where in Asiatic fashion the women of the royal family and their attendants were chastely sequestered from common view. Connected to it was the gray-stone Granovitaya Palata or Palace of Facets, so called from the diamond-point rustication of its façade. Inspired by the Pitti Palace in Florence and the Palazzo Bevilacqua in Bologna, its principal feature was a seventy-foot-square throne room and reception hall supported by four cross vaults and one massive central pier. Adjoining the Palata was the small Cathedral of the Annunciation, paved in mosaics of jasper and agate and designed and built by architects from Pskov. Its cask-shaped roof with superimposed arch was uniquely Russian, though the ornamentation of its architraves and portals exploited Italian motifs. The high altar iconostasis or sanctuary screen was decorated with icons by two great masters, Andrey Rublev and Theophanes the Greek. Across from this church stood the red-brick Cathedral of the Archangel Michael, a large six-column, five-domed edifice where the grand princes were entombed. Built between 1505 and 1509 by Alevisio Novi of Milan, its Italianate façade of Corinthian pilasters, blind arcading, entablature and scallop-shell niches in the gables formed "a Renaissance catalogue of Northern Italian decorative detail." Within, the royal tombs were arranged in genealogical order to form "a sepulchral chronicle of the monarchy." Occupying another corner of the square was the Cathedral of the Assumption, the largest church in the Kremlin, where the grand princes were crowned. Erected under the direction of Fioravanti, its great central cupola was placed on four huge circular columns that also buttressed the vaulting of four smaller satellite domes. In this cathedral the last will and testament of the sovereign were kept in a silver casket, and the most precious icon of the realm, a portrait of the Virgin Mary believed to have been painted by St. Luke "from life."

Other historic buildings in the complex included the palace of the metropolitan; the Chudov Monastery, founded in 1358; the Convent of the Ascension, where royal princesses were interred; a bell tower fitted with a clock striking the hours; and the Oruzhenaya Palata or Armory, administered as a division of the Treasury. In the Treasury proper were housed the imperial regalia and wardrobe, court uniforms, gold and silver plate, and in separate vaults the sovereign's vast private inheritance of insignia collars in filigree, oriental carpets, gem-encrusted gospel covers, cameos carved on semiprecious stones, embroidered silk vestments, furs of every description, ornamental bonework, and a hoard of sapphires, diamonds, rubies, emeralds, and pearls. It is said of Ivan III that when he learned of a pearl that had once belonged to the wife of the khan of the Golden Horde, "he knew no rest" until he had obtained it for himself.

To the northeast of the Kremlin lay Red Square, as huge as it is today, and in the midst of it, opposite the Kremlin's Savior Gate, stood the *Lobnoe Mesto* or Place of the Brow, a circular limewood dais with a stone balustrade, from which the grand prince or metropolitan made proclamations or addressed the people, and where public executions were frequently carried out. When a foreign diplomat of importance was about to be received, all businesses in central Moscow were closed and crowds, deliberately swelled by people brought in from the suburbs, were assembled to impress the envoy with Russia's manpower might. But on an ordinary day Red Square resembled a Turkish bazaar. Collapsible trading stalls were set up in rows (one row for each kind of item) and not only Muscovites but merchants from as far away as Holland and Persia haggled over the merchandise. This included just about everything under the sun: sheepskins, caftans, kerchiefs, smocks and boots; pelts, mangy and sleek, from red fox and sable to the hides of domestic cats; bone for buttons; walrus tusks for the shafts of knives; vegetables and fruits, culinary delicacies such as gingerbread and, for the more discriminating palate, sweet melons grown in horse manure and straw.

In late fall the market moved onto the ice of the Moscow River, where butchers displayed their cows and pigs in little herds "frozen whole . . . skinned and standing upright on their feet."

Adjoining Red Square to the east was the merchant quarter or *Kitaygorod* ("Basket Town"), so called because woven baskets filled with earth like gabions had once reinforced a surrounding palisade. In 1534, this district, where many nobles, wholesale merchants, and foreign ambassadors lived, was surrounded by a masonry wall.

Beyond Moscow's bustling central zone were numerous suburbs, distinguished from one another by trade and class. Blacksmiths lived in the Blacksmith's Quarter, for example, armorers in the Armorer's, while the middle and lower classes in general were divided between *Belygorod* or "White Town," where the lesser nobility, courtiers, and retail merchants dwelt, and *Zemlygorod* or "Earthen Town" (surrounded by an earthen rampart) where semi- and unskilled laborers called the "black" people lived. Some "blacks" worked in the mills along the Yauza River, or as menials in the main armament plant, or pulled carts or carried lumber, or scrounged for mushrooms in the forests on the outskirts of town.

Beyond the suburbs Moscow was protected by a half-ring of semifortified monasteries—Novodevichy, Borovsk, and Zvenigorod, among others—some maintaining permanent garrisons, such as the great Trinity Monastery to the north which was "walled about with bricke very strong like a castle, with much ordinance of brasse upon the walles." Moscow was also graced by many churches, though it was not yet the city of "forty times forty" churches with gilded domes for which it was later famed. Nevertheless, every visiting foreigner was impressed by the city's size. It was frequently compared to contemporary London, and the comparison was apt. Like London it had about 50,000 inhabitants, stretched for five and one-half miles along the banks of a river, but from a distance, as viewed from the Sparrow Hills, appeared larger because of its many firebreaks, gardens and spacious yards. Overall, its circumference was about twelve miles. To feed the inhabitants, some 700 to 800 cartloads of grain rolled into the capital daily along the Yaroslavl road alone.

In 1533, the economy was growing. Agricultural production was prodigious, despite broad belts of varying vegetation and soil, and in the heart of the farm belt, across Vladimir, Nizhny-Novgorod, and Ryazan, the harvests were spectacularly abundant. A single acre might produce twenty to thirty thousand bushels of grain a year, and the ripening corn made a sea so thick that horses could not charge through it, "nor the quail fly forth."

There were also booming timber and fur industries, and through Muscovy's seemingly inexhaustible forests of spruce and birch, aspen, oak, and elm ran moose and deer, large black wolves, bear, fox, sable, marten, rabbit, squirrel, and other animals prized for their hides and pelts. The best black fox came from Vologda; the best squirrel from Perm, Vyatka, and Ustyug; the best sable was traded by the Samoyeds at Postozersk for kettles, bacon, and flour. The uplands were the home of splendid falcons and hawks; beaver flourished in the northern streams. On the southern steppes, wild boar stalked through the wormwood, antelope roamed on the grasslands, and the estuaries were aswarm with pheasants and swans. Fishing villages flourished everywhere. For those willing to brave the wild frontier, the Terek, Don, and Yaik rivers were a fisherman's paradise of herring, barbel, salmon, sturgeon, and carp. Beekeeping was big business outside of Tula; glazed tilemaking was inimitably and quietly pursued as a craft at a monastery near Pskov. There was also iron smelting at Serpukhov, and salt panning at Staraia Rus, Nizhny-Novgorod, and the great Solovetsky Monastery on an island in the White Sea. Salt could occasionally be obtained by trade with the Astrakhan Tartars, who scooped it out of great hills "cast up" by the Caspian Sea. One river that had its source in the White Lake district carried "sulphur in abundance down on its surface like foam."

In foreign trade, Muscovy exported to Western Europe raw materials such as timber, flax, hemp, pitch, hides, wax, honey, and furs, and imported finished goods such as cloth, linen, metal utensils, spices like saffron and pepper, and wine from as far away as France. Silk was imported from Transcaucasia and Persia, woven cloth from Bokhara, Khiva, and Samarkand.

But the economy was built on the backs of the peasantry.

There were three categories of landholding in Muscovy: *votchina*, or inherited patrimonial or Church estates; *pomestia*, or lands held in exchange for military or other government service; and state or crown land, which encompassed the remainder. The peasants worked it all, yet did not own a single acre: "Naught therof is ours," went a saying, "but the plowing and the rye." Nevertheless, they enjoyed a toiler's right on the land they tilled, and every autumn once the harvest was in, in the week before and after the feast of St. George's Day (November 26), a peasant might settle his accounts and move on.

But to settle his accounts was no mean task. He had to pay taxes to the state, a fixed tithe or quitrent to the landlord, and usually the interest on a loan required at the outset to purchase seed, livestock, and farming equipment. Sometimes that interest had to be paid in labor—tending to servitude. Ostensibly to lend the peasant a helping hand, but actually to bind him immovably to the estate, *kabala* loans (as they were called) eventually became a standard feature of peasant-landlord agreements.

More downtrodden still was the slave, who might be a former prisoner of war, a juridically insolvent debtor, or one born into bondage. Slaves had no legal rights and, like inanimate property, could be transmitted by will or dowry, bought or sold, used and abused by their masters at will. Some enlightened masters freed their slaves, of course, but only those who escaped from Tartar captivity were automatically emancipated.

Though an autocrat, the Muscovite grand prince was not all-powerful, and stood at the pinnacle of a social order made up of various classes with privileges to defend. In social rank, the mightiest were the boyars. They were the nobility, and advised the grand prince through the Duma (from *dumat*, "to think"), the chief legislative and administrative council of the realm. The grand prince set the Duma's agenda and presided over its deliberations, but he could not always control the debate. And he was obliged by tradition to select his Privy Council from its ranks.

The boyars made up a complex group. Some had been in Moscow service for a long time; others, as various principalities were annexed, had more recently flocked to the capital along with the princely families they had formerly served. The latter and their direct descendants comprised the hereditary, titled aristocracy of Russia, and formed the upper crust of the boyar class. But their pedigree itself did not guarantee their power. "Boyar" was the highest rank a grand prince could confer. It was therefore in his service to the monarch that a prince's authority tended to reside, and in his capacity as a boyar that his stature was affirmed. From the mid-fifteenth century on, more than one hundred and fifty princely families joined the Moscow court, and by and large their scions monopolized the highest civil and military offices in the state.

Nevertheless they formed a restless caste, for their eminence served but to remind them of the higher rank and dignity they had once enjoyed. Whereas the Muscovite grand prince was committed to strengthening the monarchy, they belonged to families that had once ruled elsewhere, and to some degree they lived in "the recollection of glories past."

Occasionally those glories seemed rather near to hand. A prince's submission to Moscow did not invariably mean a complete revolution in his fortunes, and he often continued to reside in his appanage as an hereditary landowner on a large scale, with a considerable court and military entourage.

The old nontitled Muscovite boyars, however, who had directly assisted in creating the new state, viewed their status in a different light. Whereas the former regarded themselves as the administrators of the realm "by right of origin," the latter owed their rise to the monarchy, and strove to see it maintained. This division in the class was compounded by genealogical subdivisions among the princes, some of whom were descendants of Rurik, others of Gedymin (the founder of the original Lithuanian royal house), while still others were direct or indirect descendants of lesser lines. A number of noble families were also of Tartar origin, and some of the Tartar princes were descendants of Genghis Khan. The descendants of Gedymin and Rurik were considered equal; those of Genghis Khan stood higher than all but the family of the Muscovite grand prince himself. This reflected not only a kind of cultural infatuation with noble ruling houses, but long-term imperial policy: for Moscow laid claim to both Lithuanian and Tartar land. Indeed, after the dissolution of the Horde, "thousands of baptized and unbaptized Tartars had merged with the ranks of men in service," so that coincident with Russian emancipation from the yoke, the Tartar element ironically "possessed the country's soul, not outwardly but from within, penetrating its flesh and blood."

What united this newly compounded but not blended aristocracy in general was its resentment against the compulsory character of state service. In appanage days, boyars had been free to "depart"—usually to serve another prince—and this right had facilitated the growth of the Moscow court. But by the reign of Vasily III, departure meant treason. To whom could a boyar depart except to a foreign power? Thus had the nobles flocked to their own cage.

Now, the respective rank of all these illustrious families in state service was regulated by a complicated system known as *mestnichestvo* (place order) based on two official books, the Genealogical Directory and the Service History Directory. Taken together they comprised a sort of "Who's Who in Muscovy,"[1] and the data they contained determined not only high appointments but where officials were placed at banquets or other court functions (such as weddings), or at receptions for foreign ambassadors.

In computing the qualifications of a candidate for a post, it was therefore lineage and family service history which counted most, not talent, competence, or proven worth. When one candidate stood against another, their ancestors did battle along their lines of descent. The grandson of a former chairman of the Boyar Duma (even if he happened to be an idiot) automatically enjoyed a stronger hand than the brilliant scion of lesser stock. One could not inherit an office, but one automatically inherited a relative claim.

In fact, no individual could be made to agree to hold an office either inferior to one his forefather had held or below that occupied by a man whose forefather had been less high-ranking than his own. An individual had to stand up for his "line"—not only its past but its future. If he accepted a rank inferior to that warranted by his pedigree, "he set a precedent that could damage the careers of his present and future relatives." "Precedence" disputes were frequent, while every time a new appointment was made, other officials within the same military or administrative unit were automatically promoted or demoted according to scale. This made steady promotion by merit virtually impossible and tended to kill initiative. In effect, a limited circle of men possessing the requisite hereditary service relationship to other officeholders maintained a mathematical grip on key civil and military posts.

Yet for all that *mestnichestvo* made a fetish of ancestral honor, it fundamentally expressed the priority given in Russian life to clan and family relations, as reflected, for example, in the enduring patronymic in Russian names. No one in sixteenth-century Russia had ever heard of the "individual" in the modern sense: Ivan was not "Ivan," but "Ivan the son of, and grandson of, and cousin to": kinship was inseparably a part of his identity. Little Grand Prince Ivan from the day of his birth was Ivan Vasilyevich—"the son of Vasily." This poignant bond embraced the whole Russian community, understood as one great combined family over which the grand prince presided as father of all. *Mestnichestvo* merely mapped the most eminent bloodlines on the family tree.

Nevertheless, it frustrated the grand prince in his power of appointment, and under Ivan III and Vasily III had caused him to rely increasingly on unofficial advisers. Moreover, since comparatively well-educated, literate men were needed for the new and more complex central administration developing in Moscow, he established the right to appoint qualified men of humble origin as *dyaki* or secretaries, and to promote them according to merit through the bureaucracy. Such assistants ranged from the lowliest underclerks of a sub-sub-department to the great state secretaries of the land. In between were the middling clerks attached to boyars, administrators, judges, and other officials. State secretaries, who administered the newly emerging *prikazi* or ministries, wielded a power comparable to that of senior members of the Duma. They qualified as "secretaries to the Duma," took part in its deliberations, and were, so to speak, cabinet-level appointees.

A minor nobility of "boyars' sons" and courtiers filled out the ranks of government personnel.

Provincial administration was given over to town and country district governors, whose principal responsibility was to preside as chief magistrates in the areas to which they were assigned. In lieu of salary, they "fed" off or derived their income from their locales by retaining a portion of the court fees and taxes they collected, and by levying food and other goods from the people in theoretically regulated amounts. Thus the system was called *kormlenie* or "feeding," and it was (all agreed) incipiently predatory, for appointees were more or less expected to recoup whatever losses they had incurred elsewhere in the service of the grand prince. Moreover, though judicial bribery was prohibited by law, there was no clear penalty for it; and as the governor's judicial revenues derived from litigation, which in turn derived from crime, the more crimes in his district, the higher his income. For certain officials, production of income had a clear priority over law and order, whereas to society—and the central administration—order and security were paramount and directly affected revenue that could be collected for the crown.

That revenue should have been considerable. Property taxes were assessed per *sokha*, meaning a certain number of houses or shops or a certain amount of arable land. Land surveys were made regularly, and entered into cadastral books. Money was also raised by numerous commercial taxes, including customs duties, the *tamga* or sales tax (a fixed charge or unit theoretically imposed on every sale made in the marketplace), and by a graduated sales tax on major purchases like a horse. A direct source of state revenue was the *myt* or highway toll, which a merchant paid when he transported goods past a fixed geographical point, such as a crossroads, ford, or city gate. The rest went into the pockets of the governors, invariably appointed from boyar ranks.

Yet to be a boyar was not necessarily to be rich. Some owned villages, hamlets, and large estates, and had a diversified staff of scribes, cooks, gardeners, falconers, and so forth; others were straitened by the expense of pursuing careers at court or of bringing their quota of troops into the field. A few were frankly destitute. One visiting dignitary discovered some boyars shamelessly grubbing among his discarded fruit and vegetable parings, "eating even onion peel."

Though *kormlenie* administration was the basis of the judiciary, legal theory and practice in Muscovy actually compared favorably with what could be found in much of Europe. Based on the *Sudebnik* or Law Code promulgated in 1497 by Ivan III (in turn founded on the ancient *Russkaya Pravda* ascribed to Yaroslav the Wise), it went a long way toward delivering Russia from the legal chaos of its Mongol past. There were higher and lower courts, procedures for empaneling a jury, for appeal, and for obtaining bail, a recognition of "conflict-of-interest" as applied to a judge, a scale of fines and punishments for various types of crimes, rules for litigation in both personal and property disputes, rules of evidence, and authenticating transcripts to assure that a rational format had been followed in conducting a trial. The victorious party received a document called a *pravaya gramota*, which consisted of the trial record and the court's final decision.

The chief town or provincial magistrates handled all but the gravest civil and criminal cases. These were referred to a central government court, or on appeal to the Duma, its Privy Council, or even the sovereign himself. To establish authority over far-flung hamlets, magistrates were assisted by a corps of mobile officials resembling bailiffs, who took suspects into custody or summoned defendants to trial. The central courts in Moscow, as well as bishops seeking to police distant monasteries, also had bailiffs wielding powers in their name.

Most lawsuits had to come to trial within three years. Litigants were expected to represent themselves, to produce what witnesses or evidence they could, and (instead of swearing on the Bible) to confirm their oaths by kissing the cross. Heavy fines were imposed for bearing false witness; an eyewitness who failed to come forward was also culpable under the law.

Court fees were substantial, and a case was brought at some financial risk. To discourage nuisance suits, the offending litigant had to pay the entire cost of the proceedings to the party deemed harassed.

Out-of-court settlements were common.

Occasionally, when there was no corroborating evidence—and the judge himself could not determine the truth—the issue might be decided in "God's court" by a duel, with a hatchet, dagger, or club. If the accused was deemed "incapable" (too old, too young, crippled, a woman or a priest), he (or she) was entitled to hire a proxy. For obvious reasons the accuser could not.

Torture was sometimes authorized to extract a confession, usually if a defendant was a "known criminal" or had a prior conviction. (Though the Mongolians had introduced torture into Russian legal procedure, it was High Church enthusiasm for the methods of the Spanish Inquisition that apparently contributed to its wider adoption.)

In Muscovy it was generally administered with the knout—a whip made of strips of leather "as big as a man's finger," like a cat-o'-nine-tails—or by wrenching at a rib "with a payre of hote tongs." Convicted thieves were whipped or had their heels crushed. For a third offense they were hanged. Delinquent debtors faced *pravezh*, or "the righter"—daily beatings with a cudgel on the shins and calves until the debt was paid. An irreparably insolvent debtor might be given to the plaintiff as a slave. Sedition, murder, arson, kidnapping, and espionage were all capital crimes, as was *podmet* (the planting of evidence in a frameup). Led to their doom with their hands bound together holding a burning candle, the condemned were variously hanged, beheaded, broken on a wheel, impaled, beaten to death, drowned, or burned in an iron cage. Women convicted of killing their husbands were "buried alive. Counterfeiters had molten lead poured down their throats. Those found guilty of sacrilege were torn to pieces with iron hooks." The word of five or six "respectable citizens" alone was sufficient to convict a man of even a capital crime. As anomalous as this may seem, in sixteenth-century Muscovy to find five or six men in one place willing to kiss the cross to a lie, at mortal peril to their souls, was probably rare.

To kiss the cross was about the most serious thing one could do. As Metropolitan Nicephorus had put it centuries before in his advice to Prince Vladimir II Monomakh: "First test your heart as to whether you can abide by your word, then kiss the Cross, and having given your oath once, abide by it, lest you destroy your soul."

The Russians were a religious people and hearkened to the Church as a mighty force in their lives. This was no less true of Vasily III (despite his divorce) than of the humblest peasant mumbling prayers at his toil. The German ambassador von Herberstein vividly remembered how Vasily III, on campaign, once stood trembling in his tent when the communion host accidentally fell on the ground. Nor could he be calmed until a priest had picked it up.

In the structure of the Russian Church, the whole realm comprised a single metropolitanate, so-called because the chief hierarch—the metropolitan—has his see in the capital.[2] From his own Kremlin residence, he presided over one of the largest Christian populations in Europe.

In doctrine, liturgy, and iconography the Russian Orthodox Church had remained fundamentally "Greek." It accepted the first seven ecumenical councils as the Seven Pillars of the Church, but believed Catholics had gone astray in their unlawful observance of fasting on the Sabbath, in dropping a week from Lent (so as to "allure men to their fold by the gluttony of feasting"), in rejecting the idea of a married priesthood, in using unleavened bread in the Eucharist (which in the symbolism of the liturgy as understood by the East was tantamount to denying the human nature of Christ), and in adopting without conciliar approval the word *Filioque* ("and from the son") with regard to the procession of the Holy Spirit in the language of the Creed.[3] Russians also denied the existence of Purgatory, yet believed in a sort of Limbo where souls awaited the last Judgment; used auricular confession "and thinke that they are purged by the very action from so many sinnes as they confesse by name"; held children to be sinless until the age of seven; believed in justification by works as well as faith; and fervently prayed to intercessory saints (especially the Virgin and St. Nicholas) because "like a prince of this world, God must bee sued unto by mediators about him."

In Russian Orthodox practice, baptism was by complete immersion thrice; the sign of the cross was made from right to left; services were conducted in the vernacular; and Communion was administered under both kinds, with the bread and wine mixed together and served to the communicant in a spoon. The Eucharist was linked to the sacrament of Penance, which was emphasized as "an annual purification or spiritual bath" that culminated in Communion as a sign of pardon and reconciliation with the Church.

Services were long (four hours on the average) with the congregation usually standing, and throughout the year the faithful were expected to abide by a very demanding calendar of fasts. Four long annual fasts together with the two regular fast days of each week—Wednesday and Friday (commemorating Christ's betrayal and crucifixion)—amounted to almost half the year. Nevertheless, even in "extreme sicknesse," according to a contemporary, most Russians observed the regimen "so strictly, and with such blinde devotion, as that they will rather die than eat one bit of flesh or egges."

Such habitual self-denial was of course monastic, and monasticism was the core of the Church. Though not materially suppressed by the Mongols, it had undergone a kind of spiritual death until its amazing and prolific revival in the fourteenth century, when after the founding of Holy Trinity Monastery by St. Sergius, it spread east to the foothills of the Urals and north to the White Sea. By the end of the fifteenth century, there were over 200 monasteries in Muscovy, each sheltering from 20 to 400 monks, with countless hermitages scattered through the forests of the north. By the mid-sixteenth century, a Protestant visitor could write: "Of friers they have an infinit rabble, farre greater than in any other countrey where Popery is professed. Every city and good part of the countrey swarmeth ful of them. For they have wrought (as the Popish friers did by their superstition and hypocrisie) that if any part of the realme bee better or sweeter then other, there standeth a friery or a monastery dedicated to some saint."

Most laymen also wore a cross about the neck and carried a rosary or "numbring beads," while icons adorned gables, doors, and posts and enjoyed the place of honor in every Muscovite home. "When one visits another," wrote von Herberstein, "and enters the house, he immediately takes his hat off and looks round to see where the image is, and signs himself three times with the cross, and bowing says, 'O Lord, have mercy.' " So dependent was their devotion, it was said, that if Russians could not find an icon or cross to stare at "they would not pray." Though Protestants regarded this as a "Popish" and "horrible excess of idolatry," even Catholics were appalled to see Muscovites "prostrating and knocking their heads to the ground before images, as to God himself." Moreover, although the internal adornment of Russian churches was fixed by tradition—with the Pantocrator (a figure of Christ as Lord of the Universe) placed in the cupola or dome, the Holy Virgin in the apse, pictures commemorating holidays in the central part of the church, and the Last Judgment on the wall facing the sanctuary— icons painted on wood gradually filled every niche and corner, enveloped every column, and covered every wall. Some eventually were made to form a standing screen, or iconostasis, that completely divided the sanctuary from the rest of the church.

Of course, even Orthodox Russia had its indifferent churchgoers, whose familiar type one contemporary bishop thus singled out for rebuke: "When you hear Scripture read or expounded, you stop your ears like an asp . . . you are hardly inside the church, before you yawn and stretch and cross one leg over the other and stick out your hip and fidget and make faces like a boor." One such cheerfully scrawled his defiance on a cathedral wall: "Yakim stood here and fell asleep but did not [in penance] dash his brow upon the stone."

Potentially more subversive were the wandering *yurydivy* or Holy Fools, popularly revered as saints, who went "starke naked" in the fiercest weather, "with their haire hanging long and wildely about their shoulders," and often self-encumbered "with an iron coller or chaine. These they take as prophets and men of great holines," noted a contemporary, "giving them a liberty to speak as Pasquils [court jesters] what they list without any controulment, thogh it be of the very highest himselfe"—meaning the grand prince.

Their seemingly irrational and impoverished ways, shameful or outrageous behavior sanctified by 1 Corinthians, stood in pointed contrast to both the pretensions of secular power and the worldly behavior and hypocrisy of many monks and ecclesiastics.

Monasteries, indeed, were hotbeds of every kind of vice, and the ignorance of the clergy was notorious. One Westerner remarked: "I talked with one of the bishops . . . where (to trie his skill) I offered him a Russe Testament, and turned him to the First Chapter of Saint Matthewes Gospel, where he beganne to reade. I asked him first what part of scripture it was, that hee had read? hee answered, that hee could not well tell. How manie Evangelistes there were in the newe Testament? He sayde he knew not. How manie Apostles there were? He thought there were Twelve." The advice of another hierarch to a group of novitiates—to look pious, with eyes lowered, neck bent, face pale, and "to cry often"—is superficial enough to be striking.

In Muscovy, rudimentary literacy was a real distinction where scarcely one in a thousand knew how to read. Public schools even of primary grade did not exist, and aside from private tutors hired by nobles, education was reserved for the clergy and conducted by monastic schools.

However, the notion that a book was scarcely to be found in all the land is mistaken. Some priests and *dyaki* were gifted scholars, translators, and literati, and one, for example, took a stab at translating Ovid. Despite the absence of printing, large monastic libraries had between 200 and 300 manuscript volumes, and though these were mostly of a liturgical or homiletic character—the lives of saints, ascetical treatises, and apocrypha—ancient Greek wit and wisdom were preserved in a fragmentary way in *Izborniki* or collections. Moreover, a knowledge of Byzantine canon law and legislation was to be had in the *Kormchaia* and the *Nomocanon*, two fundamental texts, while science was chiefly represented (as in the medieval West) by commentaries on the creation of the world.

The Russians made no distinction between Scripture and patristic literature. St. John Chrysostom the "Golden-Mouthed" and Ephrem the Syrian were the Fathers most revered, followed by St. John Climacus and St.

Basil the Great. The most popular work among the didactic or "Wisdom" literature of the Old Testament was the apocryphal book of Jesus, son of Sirach. The *Psalter* served as the first reader for a child or novice and as the common devotional book for laymen. The New Testament was divided into the Gospel and the Apostle (Epistles). Remarkably enough, the Old Testament was not completely translated into Church Slavonic until the end of the fifteenth century (500 years after the conversion of Russia to Christianity), when a Dominican monk in Novgorod compiled the first complete Russian Bible based on the Latin Vulgate.

Most Russians disparaged the Old Testament, believing that the Law and Commandments had been "made disauthentique and abolished by the death and blood of Christ." Accordingly, they refused to read publicly from the four last books of Moses (Exodus, Leviticus, Numbers, and Deuteronomy), and were reluctant to read from the Prophets, "as preceding the Savior and therefore pertinent only to the nation of the Jews."

Jews, in fact, were barred from the country. Though Ivan III had enlisted a couple as confidential agents, Vasily III had stressed to an Italian envoy in 1526 that he "dreaded no people more." Among other things he accused Jewish merchants from the Ukraine of importing "poisonous herbs." But the enmity was religious not racial, for the Muscovites were also a messianic people and refused to admit any rival in this sphere. Thus any deviation from official dogma was apt to be labeled "Judaizing" in order to stress the inherent heresy of un-Orthodox views.

More generally, the Russians were profoundly xenophobic, and even foreign technicians and artisans, lured to Muscovy for their coveted skills, often regretted coming, and occasionally met with an appalling fate. One doctor who abandoned a prosperous practice in Venice for the court of Ivan III rashly staked his life on a cure for the prince's eldest son. When his patient died, he was beheaded. Another who failed to cure a vassal Tartar prince was led under a bridge "and killed with a knife like a sheep." (Not surprisingly, medicine made little headway in Russia under foreign tutelage.) The same Fioravanti who served Ivan III so ably as cathedral architect, mint master, and military engineer was placed under house arrest as soon as he asked to go home. The renowned scholar, Maksim the Greek, summoned by Vasily III from Mt. Athos to correct the translation of certain liturgical texts, was tortured in chains after completing his task.

Foreigners in turn distrusted the Russians and on the whole despised them as brutish, dishonest, and vile. Some regional differences in character were alleged, but these were not flattering. Those who lived in Moscow, for example, were said to be more degraded and less courageous than those who lived in Novgorod and less refined than those who lived in Pskov. The commonest Russian supplication was, "Lord Jesus Christ, Son of the Living God, have mercy on us"; but when aroused and angry, "May a dog defile your mother."

Despite their calendar of punishing fasts, most Russians were reported to be "somewhat grosse and burley." The typical male was short, foursquare, flatheaded, and "mightily brawned," with gray eyes, a long, broad beard (carefully "nourished and spread"), short legs, and a big belly. "Bellies bygge that overhang the waste" were considered desirable in both sexes, and girdles were fastened low to give them prominence.

Men commonly wore shirts embroidered about the neck and fastened high with a pearl or copper clasp, kaftans belted with a sash, linen breeches ("hose without feet") and long, tight coats with narrow sleeves done up on the right with buttons. On their heads they wore fur kolpaks or triangular pointed hats "picked like unto a rike or diamond," and cleated ankle-high boots of red or yellow leather. Women wore linen gowns or long embroidered dresses, sometimes with pearls attached to the flounces, broad wool capes or fur shubas, kerchiefs, or velvet caps. Poorer Muscovites went about in rough blue serge or cow's hair gowns, sheepskin jackets, and buskins.

Muscovite women were heavily into makeup. They plastered their faces, necks, and hands with red and white dyes, painted their nails, daubed their eyebrows "black as jeat," and in a savage affectation that borrowed an ideal of beauty from the Tartars, blackened their teeth with mercury and even, somehow, the whites of their eyes. Visitors attributed their cosmetic preoccupation to the "bad hue of their skinne." One wrote: "I cannot so well liken them as to a miller's wife, for they looke as though they were beaten about the face with a bagge of meale." Whoredom was said to be rampant and many women "easily and for a small price allured to lechery." But, among the nobility at least, women were kept in relative seclusion—"seldom bydden foorth to any feastes," and "shut up with nothing to do but spin and sew." When "abrode upon some great consideration," they were expected to "diligently observe their walkes, and have an eye to theyr chastitie."

The more remote the region, the more freedom women had. One visitor encountered a group near Vologda wearing tall headdresses made from hoops of bark and sauntering gaily through the woods. He asked how they managed so lightly. They replied: "We pass through like the stag."

Muscovites tended to marry young. Girls were considered eligible at twelve, boys at fifteen—the legal age of manhood. No marriage was allowed within the fourth degree of consanguinity. Divorce and a second marriage were common; a third was allowed only for some extraordinary cause; a fourth was considered uncanonical.

In courtship, the man asked the father of the bride for her hand, and then, we are told (in a somewhat fanciful account)

> when there is love betweene the parties, the man sendeth unto the woman a small chest or boxe, wherein is a whip, needles, threed, silke, linnen cloth, sheares, and perhaps some raisins or figs giving her to understand, that if she doe offend, she must be beaten with the whip, & by the needles, threed, cloth, that she should apply her selfe diligently to sowe, and by the raisins or fruits that if she doe well, no good thing shalbe withdrawn from her, nor be too deare.

Weddings were solemnized much as in the West, with vows and a ring given to the bride, who then prostrated herself at the bridegroom's feet, "knocking her head upon his shoe in token of her subjection and obedience." In turn, the bridegroom "casteth the lappe of his gown over her in token of his duetie to protect and cherish her." Both drank from a cup, which the man crushed beneath his heel, as the ceremony concluded with guests merrily pelting them with kernels of corn.

Once the honeymoon was over, husbands were often tyrannical with their wives. "One common rule amongst them is, if the woman be not beaten with the whip once a weeke, she will not be good, and therefore she lookes for it" as proof of her husband's love. "Beat your shuba and it will be warmer, your wife and she will be sweeter," advised a popular proverb—not unlike the contemporary English rhyme: "A wife, a spaniel, a walnut-tree,/The more you beat them the better they be."

Cultural norms, however, are elusive. The swarthy prototype of the Muscovite male, for example, contrasted strangely with that of the Muscovite fop, who adopted effeminate ways and devoted himself overall to a life of epicurean lassitude. Depending on the fashion, he curled his hair, or wore it long, or fluffed it out with some sort of wig; plucked out unwanted body hair with tweezers, and sought "to make himself soft and glossy" with aromatic salves and oils. He might (according to some diatribes) wear perfume, rouge, and even lipstick, mince about in small, tight boots that pinched his toes, and talk in a supercilious and affected manner, "neighing like a horse."

Some, but not all, dandies were homosexual; but even among the burly peasantry the obsessive sexual "deviation" of the time was sodomy—"not only with boys but with men and horses." The clergy were constantly fulminating against it, and foreigners were amazed at how prevalent it was. One wrote: "This people live, flow and wallowe, in the verie hight of their lust and wickednes of the crienge Sodomiticall sines"; and another: "The whole countrie overfloweth with all sinne of that kinde."

Alcoholism, however, was already judged the great national vice. "Drinke is the joy of the Russes; we cannot do without it." So Vladimir the Saint was supposed to have told envoys from Islam in declining to embrace their faith. In this fundamental legend of Russian history, love of alcohol providentially intercedes to save the nation from an infidel creed.

But however the joy began, it tended among Russians to end in their cups. To quench their thirst some beggared themselves by pawning their valuables and clothing; others "dranke away their children" and "impawned themselves." "To drinke drunke," wrote one contemporary, "is an ordinary thing with them every day of the weeke . . . manie to the verie skinne."

Disorderly conduct led to periodic crackdowns on the sale of liquor, while the Church appealed for temperance. In a popular collection of aphorisms called the *Emerald*, the people were told: "Blessed are those who drink wisely. But if a fool is drunk and does not fornicate, even the dead must be amazed." Nevertheless, in Moscow and other great cities at least, the workday tended to end at noon when Muscovites trundled off to the local taverns. Drink could be had in great variety. Aside from imported wines that embellished court feasts, there were numerous native brews of wine and ale: a beer made of honey mixed with juniper berries strained through a hair sack; another of "honey and hoppes sodden together" aged in pitched barrels. *Kvas*, the cheapest and most widely consumed, was a black bread beer resembling penny ale. There were also raspberry, black cherry, gooseberry, and currant wines, and a birch-tree root concoction available only in spring. Vodka (a derivative of the Renaissance medicinal elixir *aqua vitae*) did not yet dominate the market, but was gaining. Finally, there was a drink of indeterminate composition consumed chiefly at meals for the prevention of flatulence, "to which their diet renders them prone."

Upper-class banquets were lavish. Dishes customarily included roast swan, spiced crane or geese seasoned with saffron or dressed with ginger and served with rice, pickled cucumbers and sour cream; hares with dumplings and turnips; confections of coriander, aniseed, and almonds, washed down with malmsey, Burgundy, Rhine and French white wines.

Needless to say, most Russians subsisted on humbler fare, such as onions, garlic, cabbage, and (so foreigners complained) "grosse meates and stynking fishe." These commonly contributed to dietary maladies, among which the Russians counted syphilis, which they blamed on imported wine.

Whatever their ills, Muscovites had few trained physicians to heal them, and relied primarily on faith, fasts, pilgrimage, works, and prayer. Some wore amulets (such as the elk hoof against epilepsy) or doted on icons of particular saints supposed to cure certain diseases. One physic, however, to which everyone subscribed was the riverside public steam bath: "You shal see them sometimes (to season their bodies) come out of their bathstoves all in a froth, and fuming as hote almost as a pigge at a spitte, and presently to leape into the river starke naked, or to poure colde water all over their bodies, and that in the coldest of all the winter time."

Such heroic therapy was thought to inure them to all physical hardship and temperature extremes.

Like Westerners today, many foreigners assumed the people were given to idleness and heavy drinking because they were oppressed. And this was plausible enough. The society was tightly controlled, and the capital set the style. At night it was governed like a district under military occupation: selected streets were cordoned off, barriers erected, log beams thrown down across the way. Watchmen took up their positions, and anyone caught wandering about was treated as a security risk. Trespassers were fined, whipped, or imprisoned; even noblemen were firmly escorted back to their homes.

In fact, throughout the land, day or night, virtually everyone was restricted in their movements in some way. "Formal written authorizations" were required to travel from place to place, and at various checkpoints documents had to be verified. If a Muscovite tried to go abroad without permission and was caught, he was usually killed—"that the people may learne nothing of other lands." Everyone was supposed to stay put—wherever they had last been recorded in the census—in their city or on their farm or tax-paying commune. Even a laborer looking for work away from home had to post bond that he would return. A stranger was automatically suspect—as a highwayman, runaway, deserter, or spy—and local officials were expected to "establish his identity" promptly and register his particulars in the appropriate book.

Not even important envoys or merchants were exempt from the rigors of constant surveillance. To and from the border they were escorted by gendarmes or *pristavs* (ostensibly to protect their persons and goods) who, in order to keep them "from knowing anything certain about the country," took them by a roundabout or confusing route. They were diligently prevented from any unauthorized contact with Russians not officially appointed for them to meet or with other foreigners with whom they might share information. Once in the capital, they were placed under a kind of house arrest. Ambassadorial residences were surrounded by tall stakes, and no one could come or go unaccompanied, not even a mere servant venturing out to water the horses in the barn. At night, armed sentries guarded the embassy gates and built fires in the courtyard to prevent anyone from slipping out under cover of dark.

Other governments, of course, kept a close watch on foreign missions, but the situation in Muscovite Russia was extreme. Nor can any "emulation" of Mongolian etiquette (which required visiting diplomats to be escorted, protected, housed, and fed for free) entirely explain it. Certainly visiting dignitaries did not experience it as a "courtesy."

Authoritarian regulations hemmed in the nobility too. The upper classes were laced with an ever-growing network of political informers, and it was understood that everyone had a "duty to denounce." This duty (to be ranked with serfdom in Russian history as an evil) had originated innocuously enough in interprincely agreements of the mid-fourteenth century, which bound both parties to have "common friends and enemies," and to keep each other informed "for good or ill." As the monarchy was consolidated and centralized in Moscow, and the other principalities absorbed, the contract degenerated into a one-sided loyalty oath on the part of the noble to the grand prince. Specific oaths were soon appended to a general pledge of allegiance. For example, one boyar might have to report anything he heard about "messages" or "poison"; another about "Polish-Lithuanian plots"; a third (if he belonged to a turbulent or ambitious family) about what his relatives were thinking. The servitors, friends, or peers of a noble all had "a personal stake in his continued good behavior," for they might be held accountable if he lapsed. In ways correlative to *mestnichestvo*, this system kept the nobility divided, for "boyars kept busy watching each other found it harder to unite in opposition to the sovereign's power." Eventually, through a process of ever-widening obligation, the whole population became bound by this "duty" until in the following century it became general law. Nevertheless, it was sufficiently entrenched in the life of the nation by 1533 for one political informer to complain bitterly from his cell: "What I heard, Sire, I reported in the way in which I served thy father. I could not plug my ears with pitch. Had I not reported it, but someone else had, I might have been tortured. For is that man worthy who has heard but will not tell?"

Yet this is not the whole story. In the "rude & barbarous kingdom" not everyone drank himself into a stupor, or beat his wife, or turned his neighbor in; not every noblewoman whitened, withered, and died like a gourmet mushroom in the sepulchral recesses of a *terem;* nor did every district governor plunder the local population given over to his care. Though in countless ways oppressed, many Muscovites were not only decent and industrious but liked to play, and found time to do so. Depending on the season, they went swimming, boating, skating, skiing, sledding, or horseback riding; wrestled and boxed; kept pets, grew flowers, gathered mushrooms, played cards or chess, or told fortunes with grains. There were swings, seesaws, and a kind of ferris wheel erected in a meadow on holidays, and street musicians who played wind, string, and percussion instruments and orchestrated the antics of trained dogs and bears. Occasionally the government sponsored gladiator-like sports spectaculars, when men armed with pitchforks fought it out with polar bears on the ice of the Moscow River or in a specially constructed pit. Everyone looked forward to the splendor of court and religious processions, sometimes accompanied by fireworks. On New Year's day (September 1), the grand prince and the metropolitan would ascend the *Lobnoe Mesto* together and bid farewell to summer as the metropolitan blessed and scattered holy water over both prince and people.

On Palm Sunday a large tree, hung with apples, raisins, figs, dates, and other fruit was bound upright fast to two sleds and drawn in procession as five white-robed boys stood on the branches and sang. A parade followed with candles, banners, and icons, a priest with a large lantern "that all the light should not go out," and the metropolitan on a horse, led by the grand prince himself on foot, holding a palm branch. Thirty men spread their caftans in the horse's path, and as the horse passed over them, would "take them up and run before, and spred them againe."

Every year on Good Friday a prisoner was released in commemoration of Barabbas; and every Easter Russians high and low would dye Easter eggs red and give one to their parish priest, and carry another about with them "for love, and in token of the resurrection, whereof they rejoyce. For when two friends meet during the Easter holy dayes, they come & take one another by the hand: the one of them sayeth, the Lord Christ is risen, the other answereth, it is so of a truth, and then they kisse and exchange their egs, both men and women, continuing in kissing 4 dayes together."

One great source of popular entertainment were the itinerant *skormorokhi*—actors, minstrels, mummers, and puppeteers—whose folk drama was the only organized theater Russia knew. The Church habitually denounced them, along with any kind of handclapping, folk music, or dancing, as evoking pagan passions or ideas. "A dancing woman," counseled the *Emerald*, "is called the bride of Satan. It is a sin and a shame even for her husband to copulate with her"; and at least one contemporary church mural depicted a wandering player as the Anti-Christ. But the people

knew better, and were defiant. The birthday of John the Baptist occasioned
all-night revelry—"games and masquerades, satanic songs and dances, hop-
ping and drinking, roaming along the waterside, splashing about, and," declared one sour cleric, "when the moon is full, people jump through bonfires and do other things disgusting to God."

The Russians also liked to swap tall tales: of the freakish tribes beyond
the river Ob, for example, who died every autumn and revived in the
spring; or of an astonishing creature called the "vegetable lamb" which
resembled a lamb in every respect, even to its hairy hooves, yet grew like
a plant on a stalk. The stalk was attached to its stomach, and when it had
devoured all the grass it could reach, it died.[4]

Like many Europeans, the Russians also believed some remarkable things
about the Lapps: that they could change their shape at will, bring the
dead back to life, and "by tying and untying three knottes on a stryng
like a whyp" control the weather and the tides. Mariners feared them,
especially off the North Cape; and in a related story (which seems some
sort of distillation of the Scylla and Charybdis myth) believed Lapland
women engendered dog-headed children by sipping water from the sea.

(Enterprising Russian merchants had in fact been trading with the Lapps
for years—as they had with the Samoyeds, who nevertheless fared no better
in common repute: for they "eate one another sometimes" and "if any
merchants come unto them, they kill one of their own children to feast
them withal.")

On any given evening, peasants in outlying villages might also be found
gathered around campfires or in low wooden huts to hear storytellers sing
or recite from memory the timeless folk and epic heroic tales. These *starina*
("what is old"), handed down by oral tradition from generation to generation,
father to son, told of the stalwart warriors of Kiev who with their mighty
sword-strokes had split their foes in two; or of Ilya, the cripple of Murom,
who triumphed over Nightingale the Robber; the comic adventures of Sadko
the Novgorod merchant, who used a cathedral bell as a helmet and its
clapper as a walking stick; or (a popular ghost story) of the wizard-prince
Vseslav of Polotsk, conceived by enchantment, who judged the people by
day, but by night raced as a wolf, from Kiev to Tmutorokan. And everyone
wept for love of valiant Prince Igor, the twelfth-century prince, who had
stood with the Russe against the nomads, declaring: "With you I wish to
lay down my head, and to drink of the Don in my helmet."

3.

Interregnum

The selfless dedication of Igor to his subjects was scarcely to be found among those who vied for power after the death of Vasily III. Over the next decade and a half Russia would be ruled by the faction-ridden aristocrats. In the words of Igor's lament: "Now brother said to brother: 'This is mine, and that is mine also,' and the princes began to say of little things, 'Lo! This is a great matter.'"

Everything Vasily had been afraid of came to pass. No one had listened. He had wasted his dying breath. Prince Yury, whose ambitions were undeterred by Ivan's birth, had begun canvassing the nobility for support even as Vasily lay dying, and a few days after his funeral made a bid to become Yury I. The plot collapsed immediately because those he thought he could count on doubted his prospects and turned him in. Starved to death in a dungeon, his body before entombment was rubbed down with oils "in an attempt to remove the marks left by chains."

Yury's challenge to the Regency Council proved much easier to thwart than that contemplated from the Duma, some of whose senior ranking members resented their exclusion from the new regime. From the beginning, relations between the two were strained.

Elena Glinskaya, Vasily's widow, also prepared to stake her claim. According to Russian law a widow was the rightful guardian of her children's inheritance, and "like Olga in olden times," writes one historian, "the grand princes' mothers continued to play important roles and influence their sons even when they became adults. Such precedents established Grand Princess Elena as guardian of Ivan and entitled her to administer the grand duchy as a matter of course." But such precedents were frail. One would have to go back to Olga herself to find an example in Russian history where a grand princess assumed power "as a matter of course," and only two others had even met with foreign envoys—the wives of Vasily I and Ivan III. Nor could a mother's right to dispose of her son's property be said to extend casually to the vast, imperial chain of possessions so tediously enumerated in the royal title. Though later official chronicles (composed to please Ivan) portrayed Elena as the designated regent, the whole drama of Vasily's deathbed scene suggests otherwise.

The strong man of the Regency Council was Mikhail Glinsky; the strong man of the Duma, Ivan Ovchina-Telepnev-Obolensky, whose family had held top positions in the government since the days of Vasily the Dark. Like Glinsky, Ovchina was a renowned and dashing soldier who had been Vasily III's last master of the horse. It was Ovchina who had patrolled outside the bridal suite, with sword drawn, on Vasily's wedding night. And perhaps he got a little closer than that. The grand prince was not long in his grave before he was reported to be Elena's lover. If Ivan had a secret father, Ovchina was probably the man. In any case, his competition with Glinsky was complicated by their mutual connection to Elena in other respects. While Glinsky was Elena's uncle, Ovchina's sister, Agrafena, was Ivan's dedicated nurse.

Elena's private life posed an obvious threat to Glinsky's authority. And he apparently upbraided her for it. As Vasily's speech to the boyars had made clear, he was regarded as an outsider, and when he committed himself to defending Ivan unto death, who aside from Yury was he supposed to be defending the infant against? Every disaffected boyar present must have wanted to protest aloud, "O Lord, surely it is not I?"

Though Glinsky had his supporters, the considerable bad blood between him and other nobles, especially Ovchina, dominated the court, and the contest between the Regency Council and the Duma was, in effect, decided by Elena's choice between the two men. Elena chose Ovchina, whose help she needed to come to power. In August 1534, Glinsky was arrested and charged with having sought to usurp the crown. Several other nobles were imprisoned as his accomplices. Two fled to Lithuania. The Regency as constituted by Vasily had lasted less than a year.

Like Yury, Glinsky was starved to death in a Kremlin tower. It was a cruel and perhaps unwarranted fate, but the coup unquestionably brought greater stability to the helm. Ovchina represented a satisfactory bridge between the Duma and the Regency Council, and though Elena herself had little training in governance, after an unsteady beginning she ruled with surprising competence for the next four years. In foreign affairs, she concluded a treaty with the king of Sweden which affirmed the principle of free trade between the two countries and bound the Swedes to neutrality in the event of war between Moscow and Lithuania; maintained cordial relations with the Austrian Empire, and good relations with the hospodor of Moldavia, an enemy of Poland; and promulgated a controversial but long-lasting currency reform by withdrawing from circulation denominations debased by clipped or counterfeit coinage, and by striking a new silver standard called the *kopeck*, after the image it bore of a knight on horseback carrying a spear (*kope*) rather than a sword. She also continued Vasily's vast program of building churches and monasteries in accordance with the notion of an Orthodox kingdom, while strengthening frontier fortifications and founding new towns. Ustyug, a major settlement, sprang up in the north. In the capital, an Italian architect, Peter Friazin, began a stone wall to surround the Kitay Gorod.

However, this little cameo of order was carved on a field of blood.

King Sigismund I of Poland-Lithuania, who had been following recent developments in Moscow with great interest, was encouraged by prominent Muscovite defectors (linked to Glinsky) to take advantage of what he supposed to be his enemy's disarray.

Sigismund was a formidable monarch—tall, powerfully built, energetic, and fearless—who bore himself as a half-barbaric warrior-king. He had broken the power, once and for all, of the Teutonic Knights in Prussia, converted their grand master, Albrecht, into a vassal duke, and secured access to the Baltic through Danzig. But he had lost Smolensk to Moscow, and in 1516 the Crimean Tartars had carried off tens of thousands of captives in one tremendous raid.

The loss of Smolensk had brought the Russians to within 250 miles of the Lithuanian capital of Vilna. Sigismund could not accept this, and for twenty years had waited for revenge. In the summer of 1534, when a longstanding truce between the two states expired, Lithuanian troops raided the environs of Chernigov, Briansk, and Starodub. The ease with which they carried out their exploits seemed almost too good to be true—and it was. The military and administrative chain of command, temporarily thrown into confusion by a flurry of defections and arrests, had been sorted out by late October, and renewed attacks by the Lithuanians near Smolensk were repulsed. Russian troops counterattacked to within thirty-five miles of Vilna. In 1535, they built a lake-island fortress at Sebezh in Lithuanian territory and attacked Mstislavl. In retaliation, the Lithuanians besieged, mined, and blew up Starodub. In February 1536, however, they failed to capture Sebezh, while the Russians managed to construct two important new frontier strongholds: Zavoloche in the district of Rzhev, and Velizh near Toropets.

Sigismund's military gamble had resulted in a net loss. He offered to negotiate and the Muscovites speedily agreed, for the Tartars had recently launched coordinated attacks against their southern and eastern frontiers.

Nevertheless, the negotiations were arduous, as each side haggled over preliminary details. The Lithuanians wanted the talks held in a no-man's land on the border; the Russians said this was unprecedented: the king's envoys had always come to Moscow. Eventually the Russians prevailed, and a high-level Lithuanian delegation arrived. Then they argued over how the war had begun, and tediously reviewed the whole history of their relations. Each side refused to be the first to present its demands. Again the Russians prevailed, and the Lithuanians made their statement. The Russians walked out.

In subsequent sessions the Russians demanded acknowledgment of Smolensk as their patrimony, preliminary to further discussions. The Lithuanians replied: "Our ruler will never accept any unequivocal formula acknowledging the loss of Smolensk." The Russians inquired what an "unequivocal formula" meant. The envoys explained: "If your sovereign intends to keep Smolensk he should hand over a comparable town"—meaning Novgorod or Pskov.

No permanent peace could be achieved, and at length a five-year armistice was hammered out to take effect on March 25, 1537. Beyond that the two sides could not even agree on a prisoner exchange.

Meanwhile Elena had been endeavoring to root out treason, and to consolidate her hold on the government had dealt ruthlessly with dissent. Under her administration, it is said, "no one came out of the dungeons alive."

After Glinsky, her most celebrated victim was Vasily's youngest brother, Andrey.

Perhaps the least enviable position in a dynastic crisis (next to being an infant monarch under the "protection" of ambitious men) is occupied by the brother of a dead monarch, since he is automatically seen as a rival to the crown. His benevolence (otherwise cherished as avuncular) is invariably taken for guile, his reticence for hatching of plots, his melancholy for hatred, and his boldest professions of loyalty for desperate attempts to conceal malicious designs. It could be said that he might as well immerse himself in plots, since secret intelligence is about the only way he can hope to anticipate the blow before it falls.

This didn't work very well for Yury—but then most historians agree he wore usurpation on his sleeve. But the fate of Andrey Staritsky is another story, and a classic case of how untimely uncles fare.

After Vasily's death, Andrey had served briefly on the Regency Council until Elena's accession obliged him to withdraw to his estates at Staritsa where, apparently, he wished to live in peace. Surely the demise of his two brothers weighed him down. He also had another life to lead. On

February 22, 1533, he had married Evfrosinia Khovanskaya, a descendant of Gedymin, and on January 9, 1535, they had celebrated the birth of a son, Vladimir. Though Evfrosinia was destined to prove mortally ambitious herself, her disposition before 1537 is quite unknown and cannot be fairly judged apart from subsequent events.

Andrey ought to have let well enough alone. But in anxious retirement, he sought reassurance of Elena's good will. Accordingly, he casually asked her to increase his holdings by a couple of towns—what a large monastery, for example, might acquire in a year. To his surprise she sent him instead a couple of racehorses and a little plate—"in memory of the deceased." He grumbled, and she got wind of it and asked for a meeting. From that moment on he knew he was a marked man. The metropolitan guaranteed his safety, but the conference went badly and he had to sign documents reconfirming his "duty to renounce" and prohibiting him from expanding his retinue.

He returned to his estates in gloom. Shortly thereafter he was summoned to Moscow to attend a session of the military high command about Kazan. Fearing arrest, he pretended to be ill. Elena dispatched a physician to ascertain if it was true and the man reported back that Staritsky had "but a mere spot on his thigh"—an odd remark in light of Vasily's fate. Twice more he was summoned, and twice more declined. Threatened with the confiscation of his estates, he protested that he "shouldn't have to come to court carried in a litter." Meanwhile, Elena's spies were telling her that he was surrounded by a great many people not normally present at his court. It may be so; but Staritsky was evidently more anxious than ever to convince Elena of his loyalty. In naive desperation, he threw away the one wild card he held—the large military guard it was his right as an appanage prince to command. In April 1537, he transferred most of it her service.

Elena seized opportunity by the forelock and sent a regiment under Ovchina to Volokolamsk and another toward Novgorod. Alerted, Staritsky assembled what troops he could and on May 2, 1537, rode hard out of Staritsa for Torzhok. From there he probably meant to cross into Lithuania, but a third column moved to interdict him, obliging him to turn toward Novgorod where anti-Muscovite sentiment, rekindled by recent disturbances over the currency reform, held out some promise of support. Preceded by a simple proclamation: "The grand prince is a boy. The boyars are in charge. Whom can you serve? I shall be glad to show my favor to you," he called the local gentry to arms. Some joined his band, but these were no match for the forces racing to meet him, and Novgorod shut its gates to his cause. This was the decisive development. Thereafter Staritsky's allies "melted away." As it was, his ranks were riddled with turncoats. One informer, trussed up and immersed in a lake with only his mouth and nose above water, named so many confederates that the prince cut short the interrogation because "it was impossible to hang them all."

Ovchina arranged a parley, promised Staritsky clemency for surrender, and escorted him to Moscow. Staritsky entered the capital on a Thursday; on Saturday he was dragged off to a dungeon and clamped in an iron mask. His wife and son were disinherited, and thirty prominent members of the Novgorod gentry from among the insurgents were hanged at fixed intervals along the main highway all the way from Moscow to Novgorod.

Thus far Elena had artfully played one faction off against another, and had managed to retain the loyalty of the Church hierarchy despite modest legislative initiatives against monastic landholding. Metropolitan Daniel and Archbishop Makary of Novgorod were among her closest advisers, and in a meeting between the three on January 9, 1535, she had empowered Makary to administer Novgorod on her behalf. Her confidence was not misplaced, for he had helped turn the tide of Staritsky's revolt and proved indispensable in securing local support for her currency reform.

Elena's position in fact had never seemed so strong. She had weathered several major trials, and although regarded, like her uncle before her, as a "sojourner" at the Moscow court, she had an outstanding general to protect her. Yet her repressions had multiplied her enemies, and Ovchina's power had also gone to his head. It was hard enough for the boyars to put up with a titled monarch, but he had lorded it over everyone, and they seethed with discontent.

On April 3, 1538, Elena was felled by poison. Six days later, Ovchina was locked in a little stone cell "behind the palace near the stables," and his sister, Agrafena, was shorn and exiled to Kargopol. With unseemly haste, Elena herself was buried without ceremony in nearby Voznesensky Convent. Such complete disregard for public feeling, not to mention the niceties due an eight-year-old sovereign upon the death of his mother, foreshadowed the callous days ahead.

In assuming the direction of state affairs, the Duma split into factions. Two rival coteries vied for power, one led by the princes Shuisky, the other by the princes Belsky. The Belskys, descendants of Gedymin who had transferred their allegiance from Lithuania to Moscow in 1482, were comparatively late arrivals in Muscovy but had married into the ruling house. The mother of Ivan Belsky, clan-head, was a niece of Ivan III. Generally speaking, they did not oppose the monarchy so long as the high position of the Duma and other aristocratic privileges were not infringed. Their natural allies were the nontitled Muscovite boyars and the clerical staff of the state bureaucracy.

The Shuiskys, on the other hand, belonged to the house of Rurik, and were competitive with the ruling branch. Like all the Moscow grand princes, they were descended from Aleksander Nevsky, and in fact belonged to the senior line. In Novgorod especially, where a Shuisky had been a popular governor during the last days of independence, the family enjoyed an anti-monarchist appeal. Their principal objective was "to strengthen the role of the appanage princely families in the government" and to somehow diminish the monarchy's power in favor of local autonomy.

Their paterfamilias was Vasily Shuisky, widely known as the "hangman of Smolensk,"[1] and the man who had acted with such dispatch in removing Ovchina from the scene.

Yet once a political distinction is made between the two factions, it is necessary to deny it. For in the seesaw conflict between them enmity, not principle, ruled. And this was understood by contemporaries. One wrote: "The hostility was based on personal gain and family advancement; each sought his own interests, and not those of the sovereign or the land." In their mutual scramble for advantage, they promoted their allies and relations into the hierarchy of the government, and almost from the beginning "began to quarrel over control of the state apparatus and to reward themselves and their followers with state lands."

The Belskys moved expeditiously to surround little Ivan with their own. He was now old enough to express opinions, or feelings, which had to be taken into account even if they lacked the power of law. Metropolitan Daniel and Fyodor Mishurin (the state secretary to whom Vasily III had entrusted the drafting of his will), and Mikhail Tuchkov, a powerful noble, among others threw in their lot with the Belskys; but the Shuiskys rallied to block several key appointments. On February 2, 1539, Daniel was defrocked and deported to the Monastery of Volokolamsk, where he had to sign a confession of incompetence. Tuchkov was banished, Ivan Belsky was remanded to a tower dungeon, while the lowborn Mishurin, who had dared to oppose a prince of the House of Rurik, was skinned alive and exposed on a block.

Ivan had looked upon Mishurin as one of his protectors. He didn't favor the Shuiskys, and would bitterly recall how they had "arbitrarily attached themselves to his person and 'acted like tsars.'"

As the Shuiskys took the helm, a succession of purges bred confusion and strife. As above, so below, where the lawlessness spread. Armed gangs of slaves from Tver, Yaroslavl, and elsewhere roamed the streets of Moscow, while in the countryside bandit chieftains divided up districts for plunder like warlords.

The Italian architect, Peter Friazin—who had married a Russian, converted to the Orthodox faith, and enjoyed a handsome estate—fled across the border from Sebezh into Livonia where he told the bishop of Dorpat: "The present ruler is a child. The boyars do as they please, behave unconscionably, and are at each other's throats. There is no order in the land. The state barely exists."

Andrey Staritsky's prophetic proclamation—"the boyars rule"—had come true.

In bidding for popular support, both the Shuiskys and the Belskys undertook grass-roots "reforms." The public was in a law-and-order frenzy, and in pandering to it both formulated experimental charters aimed at transferring certain criminal procedures from state-appointed governors to locally elected judges, to be assisted by district elders. Whereas a governor could initiate legal action only on a complaint, the newly established *guba* (police unit) chief was empowered to torture, punish, and even execute without trial. Though local officials were warned to "refrain from acts of private vengeance and never to harass or punish innocent persons," an exhortation to refrain cannot enforce restraint, as the prohibition against bribery among governors had shown. Abuses were rampant, but the experiment spread. Perhaps no charter was more pernicious than the one issued to the inhabitants of Galich:

> You are to establish a system of watchmen—a decurion for every ten houses; a fiftyman for every fifty, and a hundredman for every hundred. Whenever a traveller puts up at your domicile or enters it to buy salt or sell wares, you must inform the decurion of his presence. The decurion will inform the fiftyman, who will inform the hundredman. All these officials will examine and register such individuals. If an unknown person appears, who is evasive and refuses to give his name, they will apprehend and bring him before the town prefects and cooperate in an investigation to determine his identity. If you determine he is a respectable man you may register and release him. You and the town prefects are to torture severely any such persons found to be criminals. A representative of the crown, constables and leading citizens are to be present when torture is applied.

Despite the last provision, such legislation transformed the legal process into an inquisition. It meant that anyone reputed to be disreputable could

be arrested, tried on the basis of hearsay, tortured upon protest of his inno-
cence and, since torture was almost bound to produce a confession to crimes
real or imagined, arrest seldom led to anything but a pitiable end.

Vasily Shuisky died peacefully in his sleep, succeeded by his younger
brother, Ivan, as clan-head; and in 1540, the Shuiskys chose the progressive-
minded abbot of Trinity Monastery, Joasaf, to replace Daniel in the metropolitanate.

But however the Shuiskys thought Joasaf might serve them, he was not
their pawn. In July he exercised his sacred right of intercession and "acting
in the name of the grand prince" succeeded in freeing Ivan Belsky from
prison. Belsky's comeback was swift. Enlisting the support of the old Moscow boyar elite, "members of the state apparatus who detested the Shuisky
oligarchy," and Joasaf himself, he re-emerged as acting head of state. Immediately he moved to broaden his base by restoring Evfrosinia Staritsky and
her son, Vladimir, to their appanage domains.

As the power struggle continued, the Tartars took advantage of a breakdown in frontier defense. In 1539 and 1540, Kazanians ravaged the countryside about Kostroma and Murom, and "blood flowed like water." The undefended populace hid in forests and caves, and where once there had been
farms, wild bushes grew. Many monasteries were reduced to dust. "The
infidels lived and slept in the churches," wrote a chronicler, "drank from
the sacred vessels, mutilated the gilt and silver frames of the icons, put
burning coals in the boots of the monks, and defiled young nuns. Whomever
they did not abduct, they blinded, or dismembered. I write, not from rumors,
but of what I have seen and will never forget."

As the people bled for the motherland, it was not the government in
Moscow but political turmoil within Kazan itself which came to the rescue.
In revolt against their khan (a Crimean puppet who had been enriching
his bodyguard at the expense of local grandees and surreptitiously conveying
the state treasury out of the country), Kazanian dissidents solicited Moscow's
support. In response the boyars momentarily closed ranks and, preparing
to intervene, mobilized troops at Kolomna, to the south, and under Ivan
Shuisky at Vladimir on the eastern frontier.

The Crimean khan hurriedly brought his army north and on July 28,
1541, approached the Oka River defense line where, to his surprise, he
encountered the Russians massed on the opposite bank. The two sides
exchanged fire but the Russians refused to yield. The angry khan summoned
his advisers to his tent: "You told me the Russians were unprepared. I've
never seen so many soldiers in one place before." They reminded him

that when Tamerlane had invaded Russia with a mighty army he had been able to take only the fortress of Elets. This inspired the khan to emulate the legendary warrior and devastate one town in retreat. He chose Pronsk, which lay along his route. "We shall take it and treat it as Tamerlane once treated Elets, so no one can say the khan has utterly failed."

The Tartars approached Pronsk on August 3, but its defenders proved exceedingly valiant, as both women and children labored with the men on the walls. In a race against time, the khan hammered together some siege towers, but on the following day Russian cavalry appeared on the horizon and he was obliged to abandon the effort in disgrace.

Back in Moscow, however, the government again came apart. On the pretext of preparing to meet a new Tartar offensive from Kazan, Ivan Shuisky kept his regiments together in Vladimir through the fall of 1541, while secretly negotiating with anti-Belsky elements, including gentry militia in Novgorod. By Christmas his troops had been transformed into a rebel army. On the night of January 3, 1542, the gates of the capital were opened by his adherents and his forces were able to surprise and overwhelm the Kremlin watch. Belsky was seized at his residence and Metropolitan Joasaf was chased through the corridors of the palace to the bedroom of little Ivan himself, who awoke at six in the morning to find the hierarch trembling in terror by his bed. Not even this sanctuary was respected. Accounts of what followed diverge: either Joasaf was discovered, abused, and humiliated in Ivan's presence before being deposed and exiled to the White Lake Monastery, or he fled on through a secret exit, made it safely to Trinity Monastery north of Moscow, and was there saved by the abbot and a conscience-stricken rebel, Prince Dmitry Paletsky.

Belsky, exiled to the north, was murdered in May, and many of his appointees were deported to Tver and Yaroslavl, both Shuisky strongholds.

Like his elder brother before him, Ivan Shuisky now died peacefully in his sleep, to be succeeded by his cousin, Andrey. Vaguely implicated in Prince Yury's attempted coup nine years before, Andrey was otherwise notorious for his corrupt tenure as governor in Pskov, where he had accepted bribes, imposed disproportionately high fines for every offense, compelled artisans to perform services for him without compensation, and used slander rather than honest complaint to instigate lawsuits against the well-to-do. What could be expected of such a man as head of state? His first move was unquestionably a shrewd one—but ultimately his greatest mistake.

On March 2, 1542, he summoned Novgorod's Archbishop Makary to Moscow to replace Joasaf as primate of the Church.

Makary's elevation had broad appeal and the Shuiskys expected to profit by it. At one time or another, he had enjoyed the confidence and trust not only of Vasily III and Elena, but their interim successors, and had also managed, though an authoritarian pro-Muscovite, to be popular with the people of Novgorod. In short, each interest group or faction thought to discover in him their champion. But though unquestionably wily, elusive, and tough, he did not appear so. He displayed a "Christ-like tranquillity and gentleness," accepted his new appointment with genuine reluctance and, already sixty years old, seemed unlikely to attempt a strong or independent role.

Yet Makary was destined to survive another twenty years, and without faltering to pursue a mighty agenda of his own. It was Makary more than any other who would put an end to the boyar regimes, "retrieve the reins of the autocracy for Ivan," restore the dynasty to the helm, and "shape the official political and cultural world view of the Muscovite state." Both within Russian history and without, he must be counted one of the most remarkable men of the sixteenth century.

Oddly enough, few early biographical details—and apparently not even his full name—have survived.

Born of service gentry stock in 1481 or 1482, Makary had spent his novitiate at the Pafnuty Monastery at Borovsk, forty miles southwest of Moscow, and subsequently served as archimandrite of the Luzhetsky Monastery outside Mozhaisk, where he had access to a substantial library that fostered literary ambitions that would later come to the fore. In 1526, he evidently supported Vasily in his divorce, and in reward was appointed archbishop of Novgorod.

The post, if lofty, was a treacherous one. Novgorod's turbulent politics, continuing (if submerged) separatist tradition, variety of intellectual life, and strategic position on the western rim of the Muscovite state, had all proved too much for Makary's three immediate predecessors. Moreover, when he arrived in March 1526 the city was in the grip of an economic depression.

But Makary brought with him the favor of the grand prince, state subsidies, and renewal. Interest rates dropped along with the price of bread, and he embarked on a great building program that included a new and more formidable city wall, a new highway, a mill, and a bridge across the Volkhov River, and some thirty churches, half of them of stone. At the same time, he "ruthlessly purged nests of critics from his see," and forcibly converted non-Christians within his diocese. Priests were sent to outlying areas to stamp out paganism among the Lapps, Finns, and Chuds, and in 1534, he starved 149 Tartars to death in prison because they refused to convert.

In monastic life he was a vigorous advocate of the cenobitic rule. Before his time, we are told, "monks lived a communal life only in large monasteries; elsewhere each monk sat alone in his cell overwhelmed by the sorrows of the world." Makary emphasized community, and in a letter on the subject to Vasily III in 1526–1527 not incidentally also revealed his ardent and unequivocal belief in the monarchy: "Sire, thou art appointed Autocrat and Sovereign of all Rus, by the right hand of God on high; God selected thee to reign in his place on earth and elevated and placed [thee] on his throne, entrusting to thee the grace and the life of all Orthodoxy." Had Andrey Shuisky stumbled upon this letter in the Kremlin archives, he might not have been so eager to call Makary to the capital.

Belsky's murder had temporarily left the Shuisky faction without a formidable rival, but others were being created through the favor of the grand prince. Ivan was almost thirteen (two years short of the legal age of manhood), and the attachments he was beginning to form were not merely emotional ones. He began to make judgments (political and otherwise) about those around him, and the conscious favors he bestowed began to represent extensions of his power.

Mikhail Vorontsov, whom Vasily had kissed and forgiven the night he died, had a brother, Fyodor, to whom Ivan had begun to turn for advice. Vorontsov was a leader of the old Muscovite gentry and therefore epitomized the element standing in Shuisky's way. Andrey took note of his ascendance and determined to remove him from the scene. Instead of going about it the politic way, that is, by intrigue, he showed absolute arrogance and haste, and on September 9, 1543, as Grand Prince Ivan, Metropolitan Makary, and Vorontsov were conferring together in the palace refectory, burst in with some of his adherents and began to beat Vorontsov up. As they tried to drag him into another room to kill him, Makary successfully intervened, but not before Vorontsov was battered senseless and Foma Golovin, one of Shuisky's band, had trampled upon and torn Makary's robe.

Three months later, on December 29, Ivan stepped out of the shadows of his long minority and had Andrey Shuisky thrown to the dogs.

4.

The Education of a Tsar

The child, it is said, is father to the man. However much this maxim may be subject to debate, it is probably as good as any in exploring the character of the youth about to ascend the throne.

Much about Ivan's upbringing is profoundly obscure, except that it was continually beset by catastrophe. His father died when he was three; his mother by poison when he was eight; his nurse, Agrafena, was abruptly deported; and in the repeated defeat of his affections, everyone to whom he subsequently drew close was wrenched away from him by envious magnates. No sense of security could grow in him; what grew was a certain hopelessness that it could ever be achieved. As one boyar faction after another toppled from power, his life had never been out of danger, and rebels had not hesitated even to invade his room. It has been said—and surely it is true—that long before he was Ivan the Terrible, he was Ivan the Terrified.

Until the age of eight, most of his time had been spent in the *terem* wing of the Kremlin Palace, among Elena's ladies-in-waiting and the clicking looms of their embroidery establishment on the second floor.

After his mother's assassination, and the deportation of his governess to Kargopol, Ivan's immediate family consisted only of his deaf-mute brother, Yury, his maternal grandmother, Anna, and his two maternal uncles, Mikhail[1] and Yury Glinsky. Apparently they were forcibly prevented from forming a tightly knit family, and his intimate isolation as an orphan found scant relief. A quarter century later he would still bitterly remember how no one had bothered to give him "any loving care," how his mother's personal belongings had been rifled, and family treasures pilfered by boyars who stamped them with their own family seals to disguise the theft. He remembered, too, how one day when he and his brother Yury were playing in their father's bedroom on a rug, Ivan Shuisky had presumed to put his feet up on a chair and "leaning with his elbows on our father's bed, he did not even incline his head toward us, either as a parent or a master." Aside from the insult to his father's memory, what a difference a mere nod might have made! And "all my subjects did they make as servants unto themselves; and set up their own servants as grandees."

Ivan lived among strangers in a divided world. Officially, as the grand prince, "he played the leading role in the splendor of the court and church ceremonies, solemnly sat on the throne when receiving foreign ambassadors, and was outwardly accorded respect and adulation." But away from the spotlight, as he later claimed, he was neglected, inadequately clothed and fed, subjected to numerous other indignities and sometimes treated "like a beggar." He would never forget the humiliations he endured. In his letters and orations he repeatedly dramatized them, and the more exaggerated the idea of his own kingship became, the more outrageous in retrospect the transgressions seemed. Not only, he wrote, "was my will not my own," but "everything I experienced was unbefitting my tender years."

Yet the accident of royal birth had ensured that even had Ivan's parents survived, his playtime and domestic habits would have been abnormally circumscribed by royal chores. Sixteenth-century princes led precocious lives. Crowned grand prince at the age of three, Ivan ever since had been obliged to sit still for hours trussed up in little uniforms of stiff imperial brocade, and to move in a world minutely organized within the stifling protocol of a Byzantine court. Affectionate or protective parents, moreover, do not guarantee a happy adult, and the material privations Ivan later alleged must surely be taken in part as external correlatives for his emotional states. In any case, as Aristotle remarked, "men do not become tyrants to keep out the cold."

Quite apart from whatever temperamental peculiarities he may have possessed, however, Ivan's first conception of the high dignity of his office unfortunately derived in a deleterious way from the continuing spectacle of hypocrisy around him. Men who ignored or abused him in private behaved like fawning lackeys at official functions, while his first actual taste of power came in a corrupted form, as each boyar clique endeavored to use him as a pawn to eliminate its rivals. Yet throughout his childhood and adolescence it was the grotesque discrepancy between his actual helplessness and his nominal might that absorbed him. He could strike back at those he deemed his enemies only in his thoughts—yet as a monarch he could also take comfort in knowing that the scenes of savage justice or revenge he acted out in his imagination might one day come to pass.

Thus Ivan grew up morbid and excitable, mutely raving at the discrepancy between his title and his power. His natural timidity was warped and exaggerated into nervous terror by the revolting lawlessness around him, and the instinct of self-preservation began to dominate his conscious life.

Under various tutors he underwent a complex and contradictory development. The boyars had shown him how little life was worth, and in emulation of this school, he soon found surrogates for his rage. An *enfant terrible*, at the age of twelve he began torturing animals for fun, and dropped dogs off the Kremlin battlements "to observe their pain and convulsions." At fourteen, he gathered about him a gang of teenage thugs from among those brought in to be his playmates, and not unlike the Emperor Nero (who similarly mingled with the folk) he roamed the streets and squares of Moscow, roughing people up. In the rampaging of his youth, he tried to make up for the childhood license he had missed. The Glinskys (ascendant at last) did not restrain him, but on the contrary encouraged him to do as he pleased. Politically, however, they selected his targets, and "from this moment on," wrote a chronicler, "the boyars began to fear and obey the sovereign"—not as a monarch, but as a willing tool of revenge.

But as the government was reshuffled to fill the vacuum created by Shuisky's execution, the results were confused. Vorontsov was returned from exile and appointed to the Duma. On December 16, 1544, Prince Ivan Kubensky (a ringleader in the conspiracy against Belsky and Joasaf that had brought Shuisky to power, and one of those who had attacked Vorontsov) was deported to Pereyaslavl. The following May he was released, only to be deported again in October (1545), along with three associates. Meanwhile Vorontsov himself fell from favor for having presumed to take Shuisky's place; that is, for trying to dominate the government and distribute favors in the grand prince's name. No one was secure.

In the following May at Kolomna, as he was strolling on the outskirts of town, Ivan was importuned by some fifty Novgorod musketeers who wished to submit a petition. He told his attendants to clear the men out of the way. The Novgorodians reacted badly and began whacking his guard with their helmets and pelting them with mud. Ivan called for help; retainers came running; swords were drawn, clubs raised, and in a sudden skirmish Ivan's archers cut the men down.

Convinced that the incident had been an insurrection instigated by someone close to the throne, Ivan empanelled an investigatory commission (chaired by a lowborn dyak) that boldly fingered Kubensky and the two Vorontsov brothers, Fyodor and Vasily. All three went to the block.

In a solitary but curiously revealing glimpse of Ivan at this time, a chronicles entry records that (joining playfully in a bit of sympathetic magic), after sharing in the spring plowing at Kolomna and planting buckwheat seeds, he walked on stilts and decked himself out in a shroud. Yet there was another face to the young prince, more conspicuous perhaps to his tutors than the nation, which as he emerged from his minority seemed to justify the highest expectations for his impending reign. A big, strapping youth at sixteen, he looked every bit a monarch—muscular, broad-shouldered, and just under six feet tall, with a lofty brow, gray eyes, auburn hair, and a long, thin aquiline nose that could be traced to his Greek grandmother, Sophia. Moreover, his budding intellect was considerable—strong, supple, sardonic, even profound—and despite the alleged neglect of his adolescence, he had evidently been schooled according to a demanding curriculum that made him as versatile in his accomplishments as any Renaissance prince. He was (or was becoming) skilled as a musician, writer, and rhetorician; a connoisseur of icon painting; a fine horseman; and an expert in the military arts. Though (untypically of Renaissance princelings) he lacked Latin and Greek, these languages were known by few in Muscovy.[2]

Above all, in fact Ivan was bookish. Though he had learned his letters in the traditional way, by memorizing and reciting passages from the Breviary and the Psalter, he advanced quickly to a thorough study of the Bible, the church fathers, Roman history, Church history, and the Byzantine and Russian chronicles. He read about David, Solomon, Augustus, Constantine, and Theodosius; about his own great Russian ancestors, such as Aleksander Nevsky ("taller than any man on earth, with a voice like a clarion call, in visage like Joseph the Beautiful, in strength next to Samson, endowed with the wisdom of Solomon and the courage of the Roman King Vespasian"); and by extrapolation of what could be expected of himself because of the lineage to which he belonged. Inevitably, too, as he contemplated tales about "God's Anointed," he encountered allusions to "false councilors," and in an extremely subjective way applied it all to himself. In forming his own notions of governance, therefore, he had on the one hand the example of the boyars, and on the other the heroic literature; but he had no living figure to mediate between the two extremes. He had personally never witnessed a sovereign in action. He had his feelings about his own royal dignity, and about its violation, and a literary or iconographic idea as to what true sovereignty was.

In Makary he had a teacher who tried to unify his grasp of who he was supposed to be.

When Makary had arrived from Novgorod in 1542, he was already adorned "with the halo of literary fame." A bibliophile and archivist-compiler of unmoderated zeal, early on he had resolved to gather into one collection "all the books for reading in the Russian land." With a gifted editorial staff and a battery of scribes, he had compiled by 1541 the first edition of

The Great Menology, an encyclopedia of Christian literature in Slavic that filled 27,000 folio pages of script. Divided into twelve volumes according to a calendrical cycle of monthly readings subdivided for daily devotion, it contained hundreds of saints' lives, sermons, Biblical commentaries, paraphrases of whole books of Scripture, copious selections from the church fathers, the *Areopagitica* (a Christian Neoplatonic work of the sixth century ascribed to Dionysius the Areopagite), apocrypha, the works of Flavius Josephus, monastic statutes, and four translated Byzantine collections of sermons, maxims, laws, and homilies called the *Pearl,* the *Emerald,* the *Bee,* and the *Golden Chain.* Makary's compendium also included every anti-Catholic work translated into Slavic or composed in Russia up to that time, such as the sermons of Basil the Great against the Arian heresy and the famous legend of how Aleksander Nevsky had once dazzled ambassadors from the pope with his knowledge of theology. The whole Byzantine Greek inheritance was thereby shuffled together with Russian religious literature, while many new saints' lives were composed for the compilation, which was meant "to catalogue, exhibit and define" Moscow's cultural heritage.

Furthermore, in *The Great Menology* and subsequent analecta, Makary gathered together and made official a number of myths contrived since Moscow's emergence "to impart an authentic aura of antiquity and majesty to the kingdom and its rulers." Chief among these were the legend of St. Andrew the "first-called," the *Tale of the White Cowl;* legends concerning the imperial regalia; and the theory of Moscow the Third Rome.

Together they were to shape the world view of Russia for centuries—even down to the present day.[3]

The Legend of St. Andrew, Apostle to the Slavs (based on Eusebius' fourth-century *Ecclesiastical History*), had already appeared in the *Primary Chronicle,* which related that Andrew had sailed from Sinope across the Black Sea to the Greek city of Korsin, ascended the Dnieper and on the hills marking the future site of Kiev planted a cross, and prophesied: " 'The favor of God shall shine upon them. On this spot a great city shall arise, and God shall erect many churches therein.' And he drew near the hills, and blessed them."

Makary revived the legend to stress that notwithstanding Russia's late conversion, the origins of her faith were as ancient as those of the Latin and Greek Orthodox churches—in fact enjoyed a kind of priority because St. Andrew, "the first-called," had introduced Peter, his brother, to Christ.

At the same time, Russia's belated embrace of Christianity was inversely understood as a sign of special election—of the favored sonship of the Russian Church—by analogy to episodes in the Bible (with numerous folktale variations) where two older brothers are repudiated for the sake of the third and youngest son.

The theory of Moscow the Third Rome was akin to this in idea, and received its classic statement in a letter to Vasily III in 1510 from Filofey, a monk of the Lazarus Monastery of Pskov:

> Our ruler of the present orthodox Empire is on earth the sole Emperor of the Christians, the leader of the Apostolic Church which stands no longer in Rome or in Constantinople, but in the blessed city of Moscow. She alone shines in the whole world brighter than the sun. . . . All Christian Empires are fallen and in their stead stands alone the Empire of our ruler in accordance with the prophetical books. Two Romes have fallen, but the third stands and a fourth there will not be.

This theory in turn was closely connected to a document known as the *Tale of the White Cowl*, composed about ten years before, which traced the progressive transfer of a sacred vestment from Rome to Constantinople, the "Second Rome," to "radiant Russia," the Third. Its transfer or migration was symbolically understood as the migration of the true faith—from Rome to Constantinople to Russia—where "all the kingdoms will be united into one."

Notions about the migration of the faith were paralleled by myths about the migration of imperial power. To link Moscow to Rome, it was said that the House of Rurik derived from the Emperor Augustus himself, for "Rurik was a descendant of Prus," the emperor's (imaginary) brother, who had been sent by Augustus to the banks of the Vistula (Prussia) to help "organize the world."[4] To link Moscow to Byzantium, it was alleged that at the time of his conversion Vladimir I the Saint had been crowned by both Byzantine emperor and patriarch, and that Prince Vladimir II Monomakh had received his imperial regalia—the Russian crown (or *Shapka Monomakh*), a silk mantle of pearls and jewels called the *barmy*, a chain of Arabian gold, and a crucifix containing a piece of the True Cross—from Emperor Constantine IX Monomachus. (This, despite the fact that Vladimir II and Constantine Monomachus had ruled three-quarters of a century apart.) To bind the two stories together it was said that the regalia had been presented to Vladimir II in a sardonyx box "once prized by Augustus himself."[5] Thus, the dynasty of Rurik was traced by a fraudulent genealogy to the imperial house of Rome, while its inheritance of the Byzantine symbols of world empire were just as fraudulently traced to a chronologically impossible act. Nevertheless, such fantastic theories were to serve as the primary historical basis of Muscovite political claims.

What Russia had created for itself was not unlike what Pepin and Charlemagne, in reviving the Biblical kingship of David, had done for the Franks, who after their victory over the Arabs had begun to think of themselves as the new Israel or chosen people—and not incidentally, also claimed for themselves Trojan descent. The king became the priestly king, through his consecration with holy oil, like David the anointed of God. Jerusalem wandered to Gaul (long before Rome wandered to Moscow) where medieval rulership by divine right first emerged. Later "Jerusalem" (Christian Biblical universalism) and "Rome" (political world government) were combined in the Holy Roman emperorship of Charlemagne.

In Muscovy, rulership by divine right had managed to combine the pious absolutism of the Byzantine autocrat with the arbitrary despotism of the Mongol khan. But the trend was toward despotism, and to restrain it Makary laid especial emphasis on a fundamental Byzantine principle, accepted by the old Russia of Kiev but uncomfortably embraced by Moscow, of "symphony" between Church and State. "There are two great blessings," the Emperor Justinian had written, "the priesthood and the empire (*sacerdotium et imperium*). Each was established by God and has its own appointed task. But as they proceed from the same source they are also revealed in unity and cooperative action." Makary harped upon this idea, and took care in *The Great Menology* to include many texts that stressed not only the sovereign's high calling but his heavy responsibilities, and his obligation to respect the authority of the great Synods, Fathers, and traditions of the Church. In his own mind, at least, the state mythology he was helping to foster was subordinate to this ideal.

Ivan emulated the literary interests of the metropolitan, became thoroughly familiar with the great editorial work going on around him, and fell under the influence of the complex of ideas being elaborated by Makary and his chosen staff.

Such was the literary diet and indoctrination Ivan received. In the estimation of his contemporaries, he emerged an erudite young man of natural eloquence who through "an exceptional shrewdness and remembrance of God's writ" developed into a "rhetorician of lettered cunning." In the opinion of Russia's great historian, V. O. Klyuchevsky (whose judgment is widely shared), he became "one of the finest orators and writers of the century."

5.

Tsar Ivan IV

The whole purpose of Ivan's education had been to prepare him to be the pious ruler of an Orthodox realm. Makary determined the new and more lofty title he was about to assume, even as he judged that after the turmoil of Ivan's minority, it had become a practical necessity that he be recrowned.

In September 1546, Ivan began a round of the great monasteries and churches of his kingdom, as if to equip himself spiritually for his forthcoming coronation. From Trinity Monastery he went to Mozhaisk, Volokolamsk, Rzhev, and Tver, but after two months of pilgrimage and conspicuous piety it was a restless young sovereign who entered Novgorod with a bodyguard of 4000 troops on the morning of Sunday, November 14. Curious (if unenthusiastic) crowds turned out to greet him, but he treated them with contempt, and in revenge for the "insurrection" of the Novgorod musketeers, fined the city treasury. It is said he also desecrated the Cathedral of St. Sophia. According to the Chronicles, someone had told him of ancient treasure hidden in the choir loft. He subjected the cellarer and sacristan to torture, but they professed to know nothing about it. Ivan mounted the staircase himself, groped about, knocked here and there on the walls, heard something, and had his cohorts break in the paneling on the right-hand side. Out poured gold and silver coin.

Upon his return to Moscow on December 12, Ivan met with Makary, and after Mass in the Cathedral of the Assumption on the 14th, summoned a surprise meeting of the Duma. With Makary by his side, Ivan made three momentous announcements: first, that he had decided to marry; second, that he would choose a Russian, not a foreign, bride; and third, that he intended "to study the coronation formula of his ancestors," specifically that of Grand Prince Vladimir Monomakh and, in emulation of that prince, to be crowned Grand Prince and "Tsar," meaning Emperor. Etymologically, the word "tsar" derived from *caesar*, but had entered Church Slavic through the Greek as a translation of *basileus*, meaning "emperor." However, from the days of the Mongol conquest, Russians had applied it not only to the Byzantine emperor but to the Tartar khans. At the Moscow court only

Tartar descendants of Genghis Khan who had also been rulers in their own right were honored by the name. Not inappropriately, Ivan III had occasionally called himself "Tsar" after repudiating the Tartar yoke, for as one contemporary defined it, it meant "a king that giveth not tribute to any man." But he had not been so crowned.

The boyars were said to have wept at the "maturity" of Ivan's speech, and perhaps also in hopeful anticipation that one of their own daughters would be espoused. However, Ivan had already settled on Anastasia Roma-novna Zakharina, the niece of Mikhail Yurev Zakharin, one of Vasily III's trusted confidants, and the scion of an untitled boyar family which had long proved loyal to the princes of Moscow. No Zakharin had been seriously implicated in plots during Ivan's minority, but the choice displeased the class-conscious titled nobility. One remarked: "The sovereign offended us by his marriage, taking his boyar's daughter, his slave, for a bride. And we have to serve her as if she were our sister." They would have to serve her bloodline for a long time. Mikhail, the grandson of her brother, Nikita, was destined to be the first Romanov tsar; and a Romanov would occupy the throne until the Revolution of 1917.

Ivan was crowned Tsar and Autocrat of all of Russia in the Cathedral of the Assumption on January 16, 1547. He was anointed and invested with the regalia of office by Metropolitan Makary, who had conceived the entire ceremony, and who crowned him twice, first as Grand Prince "with our ancient titles," then as Tsar "according to our ancient custom." The regalia, which symbolized the unity of the monarch with his imperial ancestors, was jointly carried into the cathedral by a priest and a government official, to symbolize the unity of spiritual and secular power. On a red-carpeted dais, Ivan and Makary sat side by side on thrones. Makary proclaimed him "chosen by God, designated and given power by supreme design," and intoned a prayer of divine blessing for the coronation act: "King of kings and Lord of lords, who by the servant Samuel the Prophet, didst choose David and anoint him to be king over the people Israel, hear now the prayers of thine unworthy servant, and look down from Thy sanctuary upon Thy faithful servant Ivan whom Thou blessed and raised up as Tsar of Thy holy people, and hast redeemed with the most precious blood of Thy only-begotten Son."

In a vigorous precept, Makary emphasized the coequal powers of Tsar and Church, the role of the Church in Ivan's elevation, and the holy character of the imperial office. He exhorted Ivan to be good: "It befits thee either to be wise or to follow wise councilors; for verily, God is in them as in the throne." And he elaborated upon an admonition supposedly addressed by the Byzantine Emperor Basil I to his son Leo the Wise:[1] "Though an Emperor in body be like all other, yet in power of his office he is like God, Master of all men. For on earth, he has no peer. Therefore as God, be he never chafed or angry; as man, be he never proud. For though he be like God in face, yet for all that he is but dust, which thing teaches him to be equal to every man."

Following his anointment with myrrh, Ivan partook of Communion and then proceeded across the square to the Cathedral of the Archangel Michael to pay homage at the tombs of his ancestors. His brother, Yury, poured silver coins over his head and scattered them in his path.

On the Byzantine model, anointment symbolized the divine source of imperial power; the crown the ruler's imperial rank; the scepter, his temporal power for the protection of his land; and Communion the God-given nature of the empire. Perhaps the cape or *barmy* took the place of the Byzantine diadem to signify that the ruler was a soldier. Coin-scattering (which placed the wealth of the empire at his disposal) also formed part of the Byzantine rite. Omitted only was the public acclamation, which called for the emperor to be hoisted by soldiers upon his shield.

Thus did Ivan become the first tsar of Russia, and thereby officially laid claim to the mantle of the Byzantine emperor as Lord of the Orthodox Christian world. Use of the title became "general for both foreign relations and domestic proclamations from the date of Ivan's coronation," and recognition of its legitimacy by other powers became an *idée fixe* of his diplomacy.

On February 3, Ivan married Anastasia in the Cathedral of the Annunciation. A fortnight later the couple made a penitential pilgrimage to Trinity Monastery, forty miles to the north, going "the whole way on foot, in spite of the bitter cold."

6.

The Glinskys

Following the downfall of Kubensky and Vorontsov in 1546, the leading role in the government had been assumed by Ivan's two maternal uncles, the princes Yury and Mikhail Glinsky. Together with their mother, Anna, they had long remained in the background. Now their hour had arrived. They might have made the best of it; instead they made the worst.

In revenge for having been ostracized throughout Ivan's minority, and for family blood spilled, the Glinskys dealt ruthlessly with all who stood in their way. They sought to dishonor and disgrace numerous boyars who had once offended them, milked the public treasury for their own aggrandizement, and appointed district governors who were exceptionally predatory even among their kind. Ivan had been led to trust them fully by apparent community of interest and close ties of kinship, but their failure to restrain their minions from acts of lawlessness aroused widespread discontent. Bribery ruled, slander and rape. Now that Ivan was tsar and of age, they saw themselves as the final faction, fixed at the summit, in the ultimate turnover in power.

The abuses of district governors, in addition to their customary extortions, now went to almost unbelievable extremes. "In their double dealing and diabolical practices," testified a contemporary, "they even exhume newly buried corpses and thrust them, hacked up and bloodied with a boar-spear, into the houses of decent citizens, whom paid informers then charge with homicide."

Social protest began to show itself by arson.

Moscow was especially vulnerable, as a city of wood with resinous fir-tree pavements and log cabin-like houses typically built foursquare "without any lime or stone." Though built to "resist and expel all winds that blow," with low doorways, high thresholds, little casement windows, and moss pressed into every chink and seam, they were liable to rapid combustion, and "once fired burneth like a torch."

In city planning the Muscovites did what they could: by quartering smiths, metal casters, and other artisans who used fire in their crafts in outlying suburbs; by requiring firebreaks between the houses and outdoor cooking to be closely shielded by a bast screen, or by regulations prohibiting the burning of candles at night. But their chief weapon was a unique mass-production technology in housing, which used prefabricated lumber, variously tenoned and mortised, marked and numbered for assembly, enabling dwellings of almost any size to be bought, transported, and erected within a few days.

The lumberyards were busy. Throughout the spring of 1547, the capital was plagued by fires. On April 12, one blaze ravaged the warehouse district of Kitaygorod, where a tower, used to store gunpowder, exploded, blowing part of the city wall into the Moscow River. On the 20th, new fires destroyed the district beyond the Yauza River where the smithies and tanneries were concentrated. Suspects were executed, but the vandalism increased, as responsible protest was frustrated or ignored. The fate of the Novgorod petitioners was almost repeated on June 3 when seventy petitioners from Pskov caught up with Ivan at Ostrovka, one of his country estates, and tried to lodge a complaint against their governor, Prince Turontay-Pronsky, a Glinsky appointee. Perhaps they expected to find the prince transformed by his coronation. But he refused them a hearing, and showing an inclination to theatrical cruelty which he would demonstrate all his life, singed their venerable beards with a candle, splashed boiling wine into their faces, and had them stripped naked and stretched on the ground. He might have killed them if a courier had not arrived with word that a great bronze bell had fallen from a Kremlin tower. In superstitious alarm, we are told, Ivan returned to the capital at once.

Understandably, Pskov fumed at the shoddy treatment its delegates had received. Rebels seized the border fortress of Opochka. A regiment crushed the rising, but its sparks carried and dissident crowds gathered in towns throughout the realm. There was looting. Civil disorder spread.

Then, on June 21, at three o'clock in the afternoon, someone put a match to Moscow's Church of the Holy Cross and it went up like a torch. Though the day had dawned clear and calm, an unlucky wind arose and the flames leaped from roof to roof westward through the city in a rapid relay of fire. They reached the Kremlin and surged in sheets over the walls. As the wind made a whirlwind of the smoke, the blaze threatened the Cathedral of the Assumption, crumpled the roof of the palace, engulfed the Cathedral of the Annunciation, the Treasury, the Chudov and Ascension monasteries, the Armory and its warehouses, and the metropolitan's residence. Ivan and his court fled across the river to the village of Vorobevo, but Makary lingered in the Cathedral of the Assumption, desperately trying to salvage precious manuscripts and icons. He emerged heavy-laden, made his way to a secret passage that led to the Moscow River, but found it blocked by smoke. Soldiers tried to lower him over the battlements in some kind of wooden cage, but the rope broke and he was badly injured by the fall. Somehow he managed to reach the Novodevichy Monastery on the outskirts of town.

Meanwhile, central Moscow was gutted. Thousands were left homeless; two thousand died. "And every flower garden burned up," wrote a chronicler, "as well as all the vegetables and grass." For some time afterward heavy clouds of smoke hung over the city. Survivors searched hopelessly among the charred rubble for relatives and redeemable property. Everyone suffered some loss. A monk noted, "God punished us for our sins"—but soon the abject mood of the people turned to anger. As the Glinskys looked for scapegoats, their wheel of fortune turned.

Ivan paid a visit to the recuperating Makary on June 23, where an emergency meeting of the Duma was held. Several anti-Glinsky partisans (some with ties to the Shuiskys) left no doubt as to whom they blamed. Grigory Zakharin (Anastasia's uncle), whose own clan was now in the ascendant, accused the Glinskys outright of having started the fire. An investigation was launched, but the populace was already convinced that the grave-robbing, heartless Glinskys, especially "the old witch Anna," had brought about the catastrophe by witchcraft. Specifically, it was charged that they had plucked human hearts from corpses, soaked them in water, and flying over Moscow "like magpies," let them drip upon the town. And wherever the water dripped it burned.

Yury Glinsky heard the rumors, came to Moscow to reason with the mob, and was present on Sunday, the 26th, when as part of the investigation the citizenry was invited to Cathedral Square to answer questions put to them by certain boyars. Anti-Glinsky partisans worked the throng. "Who started the fire?" the crowd was asked. The people thundered back, "Anna the witch." The mood was savage, and Yury, grasping the situation at once, sought sanctuary in the Cathedral of the Assumption. The crowd pursued him into the parvis, dragged him out and killed him. He was not the only one. His bodyguard was stomped, and anyone associated—or assumed to be associated—with the Glinskys was attacked.

Meanwhile, Yury's brother Mikhail and their mother, Anna, had remained on their estates in Rzhev. The mob did not know this, and three days after Yury's murder massed before Ivan's temporary residence at Vorobevo on the outskirts of Moscow to demand their surrender. Some of the rioters were dressed in full military gear and threatened to kill the tsar if he did not comply. Ivan told them he was hiding no one, and had the ringleaders arrested; but sympathy for the rebels was widespread, and fugitives found asylum throughout the realm.

To restore order, Ivan confined Mikhail and Anna to their estates, vigorously began rebuilding central Moscow, circulated rumors of coming social reform and, at some calculated risk, allowed the usual precautionary summer mobilization against the Tartars to go forward as planned along the southern frontier. In the fall, he celebrated the marriage of his younger brother, Yury, to one of the princesses Paletsky, of titled boyar stock—perhaps to appease the nobility. Overall, he sought to create the impression of firm and continuing, calm authority at the helm.

7.

The Chosen Council

It was not an illusion. After the uprising of 1547, a government of compromise rapidly emerged made up of far-sighted individuals of both noble and gentry birth whose overriding goals were to consolidate the central administration and gradually reduce the political and economic power of the clans. These men had an eye for the great outlines of Muscovite policy, for the broad prospect of Russia's plowlands and pastures, thronged markets, and slowly emerging industries, and an instinct for what the people were thinking and feeling throughout the land.

During Ivan's minority, few men of character or ability could find advancement, but there now coalesced around him a remarkable coterie of favorites and councilors subsequently known as the *Izbrannaya Rada* or "Chosen Council." This council was not an administrative organ (like the Privy Council of the Duma) but an unofficial inner cabinet or "company of honestly-disposed advisors," who in the words of one probable member urged upon Ivan "what was best and needed to be done." The tsar, in turn, reputedly "felt such affection and friendship for them that he undertook nothing" without their advice and consent. Fundamentally, their program was based on the spiritual conception of the duties of a ruler, with the idea that he is answerable to God for his realm. Although Makary did not dominate the council, he almost certainly promoted its formation, and his coronation advice to Ivan "to follow wise councilors; for verily, God is in them as in the throne" was probably aimed at encouraging his submission to their direction. Moreover, there was a powerful consensus that whatever Ivan's potential, this was a tsar who had to be taken in hand. The same men who wished to exalt him also wished to restrain him, both for his own sake and the sake of the realm. Scholarship may wish to debate it, but it was obvious to his contemporaries that Ivan was profoundly sick. He was brilliant, but he was wild and cruel, and intermittently confessed as much even to the end of his days. This alone sets him apart from many a tyrant, and merits our close attention to his tragedy.

After the Moscow fire, he was near nervous collapse. Crowned, married, and almost overthrown within the space of six months, his palace in ruins, forced to place his own remaining family under house arrest, "there came to him a man," wrote a contemporary, "a priest by rank, Sylvester by name, a newcomer from Novgorod the Great, divinely rebuking him with holy scriptures in the terrible name of God." "Just as fathers scare their children with imaginary horrors to turn them from senseless or wicked games," so Sylvester told him of "miracles and apparitions," and "like a physician scraping at gangrene with a knife, as far as the live flesh, [so] he healed and purified his soul from leprous sores and rectified his depraved mind."

Though not quite a newcomer, Sylvester had originally been recruited by Makary in Novgorod to work on *The Great Menology*, and by 1540 had become a man of considerable influence. He had forged ties to both the Shuiskys and the Belskys, and during the Belsky administration had apparently helped to secure the release of Vladimir Staritsky and his mother from confinement. As a Church progressive he may have been close to Metropolitan Joasaf, but when Makary was called to take Joasaf's place, probably accompanied him to Moscow. Like Makary, he seems to have been adept at cultivating contradictory connections that assisted the advance of his career.

In the summer of 1547, he was appointed archpriest of the Cathedral of the Annunciation, which placed him in almost daily contact with the tsar. Entrusted with the cathedral's redecoration and repair, and with the creation of new palace frescoes for Ivan's edification, his power grew steadily until, in the resentful opinion of one colleague, he became "all-powerful. Everybody obeyed him and nobody dared to oppose him. . . . He gave orders to the metropolitan and the bishops . . . and the boyars and the dyaks . . . and the military commanders and members of the gentry and everybody else. To put it baldly, he directed both spiritual and temporal affairs . . . and was in complete command of both spheres, spiritual and temporal, as if he were tsar and metropolitan."

However exaggerated this account, there can be no doubt that Sylvester gained a kind of mastery over the mind and imagination of the tsar, and placed even the everyday organization of Ivan's life under his control.

The phenomenon of a spellbinding *starets* close to the throne was, as it happens, not without precedent, and of course had a notorious future. But though Sylvester might deliberately prey upon Ivan's credulity—"scaring me with bogies," the tsar would later say—he was no Rasputin, and more aptly to be compared with Vassian Patrikeev, a boyar-turned-monk who for many years served as chief adviser to Vasily III. "I was not so afraid of my sovereign," one of Vasily's courtiers recalled, "as I feared and hearkened to the monk."

Patrikeev's noble birth had facilitated his rise. In coming to power, Sylvester had taken the only route he could. As a married priest with a wife and son, he had no future in the ecclesiastical hierarchy; nor, because he was a priest and humbly born, could he ascend the political ladder by ordinary means. He had to rely on charisma. Yet he appears to have been a righteous man, and from certain remarks addressed to his son, we get some idea of the conduct he espoused. He was resolutely opposed to slavery, for example, to usury and dishonesty in commerce, and to all inequities under the law. But Sylvester's tyrannical side—which spooked Ivan for his own good—can also be glimpsed in his widely disseminated *Domostroy* or "House Order," a manual with advice on religious, dietary, disciplinary, and other matters that seemed designed to convert the whole of life into a ritual. Its maxims were phrased in rhythmical (and sometimes rhymed) prose suitable for chanting, and some were harsh: "Punish your son frequently, that you may rejoice later"; or "Give him no power in his youth, but crush his ribs while he is growing to save yourself from suffering and shame"; or "Save through fear." But generally speaking the context was more humane:

> Beatings should not be administered in the presence of others but in private in order to teach, and to say a word, and to show affection. . . . And for an offense, do not strike on the ear, nor in the eyes, nor with the fist under the heart, nor push, nor prod with a stick and do not hit with a stick either; . . . many injuries result therefrom. . . . Strokes of the whip should be inflicted carefully while the lesson is being taught; this is both reasonable and painful and awe-inspiring and healthy. And only for a great wrongdoing and fearful disobedience, should the shirt be taken off and a thorough beating administered while the hands are held.

Many a disciplinarian in Western Europe would have found such caveats indulgent.

Next to Sylvester, and eventually coequal in influence and perhaps in the tsar's affections, was Aleksey Adashev, a courtier of service gentry stock from Kostroma, whose father, Fyodor, was a government official. Originally brought into the Kremlin as one of Ivan's playmates (they were about the same age), and subsequently appointed to his personal bodyguard, in 1547 Adashev was promoted to chamberlain—a post only superficially analogous to that of *valet de chambre*—with responsibilities that made him Ivan's chief of staff. In time he would prove an exceptionally versatile minister, with a major impact on legal, Treasury, and foreign policy affairs. From 1547 on, his name appears on almost all important state documents.

Adashev's private character, however, may have surpassed his public renown. He was, wrote an admirer, "like unto the angels, so noble, decent and refined that coarse and mundane men would find it difficult to believe." Much given to fasting and prayer, he also secretly maintained and tended invalids in his own home whom he washed and fed, "many a time wiping their sores with his own hands"—even as he had once washed the tsar in his bath.

A third and equally precocious member of the Chosen Council was Ivan Viskovaty, a civil servant who had entered the government around 1537 as a clerk in the nascent Foreign Office. In 1542, he had drafted the armistice agreement with Poland-Lithuania and met with the king's ambassadors—responsibilities technically far above his rank. The Foreign Office, in fact, as it was then emerging into a highly organized, independent bureau, owed its creation largely to Viskovaty's initiative, and within two years of Ivan's coronation he would become Russia's first true foreign minister. As a *bolshoi dyak* or great secretary he enjoyed a seat on the Duma, and his name often appeared in conjunction with Adashev's on official documents. No Russian diplomat or statesman of the sixteenth century was more capable, or would be more widely admired both at home and abroad.

To complete the grand quartet (supreme within the council) Makary's role deserves to be restressed. It was to Makary that Ivan had gone with his court for advice on how to deal with the uprising and whether to repudiate the Glinskys, and Makary who may have thwarted an attempt by the Shui-skys to use the Glinsky affair to return to power. This had bought time for the Zakharins, Ivan's new relatives, to close ranks with other loyalists behind him, and for the Chosen Council to take a more definite shape. Before long, the cabinet was in place—"a gathering of Ivan's friends 'who wished him well.'" In supplanting the rapacious and arbitrary conduct of the boyars with a moral atmosphere conducive to enlightened policy, the council acted as Ivan's tutors to a degree that would not have been possible had he not already been "so accustomed to guardianship." It could almost be said that he entered upon a second minority. Nevertheless, though he relied on the council to help him rule, its very existence depended on his continuing favor, while there were two objective factors which imposed constraints upon it from the start. First, its initiatives had to take account of, and to some degree work through, the ruling institutions such as the

Duma, its Privy Council, and the synods of the Church. And this meant considerable compromise. Secondly, there were personality and other strains within the council itself.

Viskovaty resented Sylvester's autocratic presumptions, while Sylvester and Makary emerged as rivals. When Archbishop Feodosy, Makary's protégé in Novgorod, sent Easter gifts in 1548 to the court elite, the only person of importance he neglected was Sylvester. But in the beginning at least, the Chosen Council was presumably united by loyalty to the tsar.

The depth of Ivan's personal commitment to the council's ideals, however, are harder to assess. Ultimately, he proved a consummate politician. In pondering the degree of popular discontent the Moscow fire had illuminated, he seems to have realized four things: his own need for guidance; the need for reform; the importance of his public image; and the potential for using popular discontent as a weapon against the boyars.

8.

The First Wave of Reforms

Plans for the implementation of broadly conceived reforms, affecting local and central government, military and financial administration, the judiciary, and the Church community, were drawn up at the beginning of 1549. While the reformers, motivated on the whole by the desire for a more just and righteous society, could expect considerable opposition from many boyars, through his power of appointment Ivan somewhat modified the character of the Duma by the elevation of men on whose loyalty he thought he could count.

The legislative planning took place against a background of intellectual ferment—a kind of revival of inquiry (if not of learning) in Muscovite court circles—which presumably reflected the restless intelligence of the tsar. All topics were discussed—political, social, religious, and ethical: Church-State relations; the efficacy of the law; economic exploitation; corruption in monastic life; and the oppression of the poor—in public and private conversation, and in letters, pamphlets, treatises, and a number of petitions to the tsar.

A monk from Pskov, Ermolai-Erasmus, for example, drafted a memorandum which condemned the exploitation of the peasantry on boyar estates and called outright for the abolition of *kormlenie*. Another polemicist, who wrote a pamphlet against monastic landholding entitled "A Discourse of the Sorcerers of Valaam," [1] suggested that national assemblies be convoked every year to air complaints and to keep the tsar informed of abuses perpetrated in his name.

But the pamphleteer Ivan ultimately hearkened to most was the Lithuanian *condottiere*, Ivan Peresvetov, who had served in Hungary, Bohemia, Wallachia, and Poland before coming to Muscovy in 1538 with a patent for producing leather and iron shields of the "Macedonian type." In two petitions presented to Ivan in the fall of 1549, he advocated the emancipation of slaves, promotion according to merit in government and military service, a return to fair but rigorous justice in the Russian courts, and the creation of a standing army. His accent on building a class of military servitors was paramount. "Maintain a warrior," he advised, "as one keeps a falcon—always gladden his heart"; and in a challenge to *mestnichestvo* presumptions he reminded the tsar that both Caesar Augustus and Alexander the Great had disregarded wealth and origin in making high appointments.

Peresvetov cast his main petition in the form of a thinly veiled allegory in which he blamed the fall of Constantinople on the timidity of an emperor who, having ascended the throne at the age of three (like Ivan), came under the sway of a corrupt nobility and neglected justice and military affairs. Conversely, he extolled the example of Sultan Mehmet the Conqueror who, though an infidel, had ruthlessly swept from his path all who opposed his reforms. "When an emperor is mild and gentle with his empire," concluded Peresvetov, "its wealth declines and his fame decreases. When an emperor rules in terror and wisdom, his empire broadens and his name is known in all lands." Ivan's task was clear. "The true Christian faith of Moscow must be joined with Turkish justice, to create God's Kingdom on Earth."

Peresvetov's ideas were neither original with him nor arcane, but the manner of their presentation revealed an "occult" source. In his allegory he had mentioned that Mehmet the Conqueror had learned right governance from certain Greek "books of wisdom" discovered in the palace library of Constantinople—evidently referring to an esoteric work called the *Secreta Secretorum*,[2] which Ivan had (in Slavic translation) in the Kremlin library in

Moscow. This book, reputed to be the secret advice of Aristotle to Alexander the Great, contained precisely the advice Peresvetov declared Mehmet had found, and which he now urged upon the tsar. In particular, it harped on the need to rule by inspiring awe (*groza*), advised the sovereign to correlate the service of his nobles to their wealth, and to "test their loyalty by what each will suffer on your account." It also specifically recommended the institution of a foreign bodyguard, and ominously cautioned: "Do not fear things which are past and bloody, for this is the way of women and frivolous men."

Ivan, who either read the *Secreta Secretorum* or imbibed it in large draughts through Peresvetov, variously assimilated its "wisdom." The seeds were sown, and they grew. But Peresvetov's own immediate contribution to the early reforms may be doubted. He stressed social "justice," but something of the primitive intelligence he brought to the matter may be glimpsed in a refinement he proposed for judicial duels: "Let the litigants be left, unarmed and naked, in a dungeon where a single razor is hidden. Whoever finds the razor wins the duel, and has the right to butcher his opponent on the spot." As a mercenary, Peresvetov was probably good with a razor, and clever at guessing where one might be concealed. But if there was any wisdom buried in the *Secreta Secretorum*, he was probably not the one to find it.

Indeed, in a very different spirit Ivan had already convoked a "council of reconciliation" preliminary to launching his reforms. This gathering, sometimes called an Assembly of the Land, was a landmark event, for it pondered a new idea—the " 'land's affairs,' " meaning those of the nation as a whole, as distinct from the governing powers. To the opening session held in the throne room of the palace on February 27, 1549, attended by high state and church officials, the military high command, and selected members of the minor nobility and gentry, Ivan recounted, in a powerful speech, the tribulations of his minority, the abuses of the boyars (whom he called "usurers, bloodsuckers, and unrighteous judges"), and called upon them forthwith to rectify their ways. In a premeditated response the boyars declared themselves changed and contrite, and begged the sovereign "not to set his heart against them."

Ivan's speech, not incidentally, appealed so much to the popular imagination that a later Chronicle interpolation portrayed him as having delivered it on Easter Morning from the *Lobnoe Mesto* in Red Square.

The tsar also called for a fresh slate. Concerning provincial misrule, he said: "I cannot now redress all wrongs or undo all the taxes. But I beseech you to cease from enmity, the one against the other, and from all your strivings at law. In the future I shall judge and defend you as best I can, and root out injustice and restore what others have stolen." To lend credibility to his pledge, that afternoon he appointed Adashev head of a newly created Petitions Bureau, declaring: "Aleksey, I have raised you from low and humble station to be my assistant. You have not sought this position; I have conferred it upon you. I charge you to receive and examine carefully petitions from the poor and oppressed, without fear of the illustrious, but also without attention to the hypocritical tears of those paupers who, pretending to be righteous, calumniate the rich."

The next day his legislative program was launched when a "reformed" Duma cut deeply into the *kormlenie* system with a decree which prohibited governors from judging members of the minor nobility and petty gentry except in cases involving brigandage and homicide. Charters confirming this decree were dispatched to officials throughout the realm.

The assembly also endorsed the tsar's proposal to revise and expand the Russian Law Code, and formally established a system of government departments or ministries—chiefly, the Foreign Office, the Land Office, the Office of Military Affairs, the Bureau of Criminal Affairs, and the Treasury—which had been inexorably emerging since the time of Ivan III.

As the bureaucracy was consolidated, the Treasury was subdivided into various Taxation Chancellories, each headed by a boyar assisted by two *dyaki*. The bookkeeping was meticulous. "In every chancellory," we are told, "all affairs large and small were written down." Numerous underclerks, each equipped like any Western scribe with paper, inkpot and quill, made duplicate copies of all official documents, and cleverly ensured their integrity against tampering by writing across the inside binding where the document was glued. On the outside, the clerk wrote his own name and above it the date, in small letters. On the top of the first leaf, in large cursive, he wrote the name of the tsar. In the Tax and Treasury bureaus, where a small army of accountants did their sums with plum or cherry stones, all disbursements had to be countersigned.

Other initiatives followed. In November, Ivan issued a decree prohibiting the application of precedence (*mestnichestvo*) during military campaigns in order to allow him latitude over the appointment of commanders, though he judiciously appeased the great clans by declaring that whoever served "not according to genealogical rank" should "incur no prejudice" in other spheres to their ancestral claims. At the same time, to strengthen in one dramatic stroke the role of the gentry in the army and administration, it was decreed on October 3, 1550, that one thousand select personnel were to be registered in a special "Book of the Thousand" and settled on service tenure estates near Moscow, where they were to hold themselves in readiness for any administrative, diplomatic, or military tasks that might arise.[3] In a related development, Ivan established Russia's first standing army—the *streltsy* or musketeers, with a corps of 3000—under gentry command.

Even more momentous reforms were enshrined in the new law code which Ivan and his advisers had compiled for Muscovy by 1550. Though substantially based on its predecessor, among other things it confirmed the new curb on provincial governors, facilitated lawsuits against them or their agents in central courts, required the presence at all trials of district elders, and sought to curtail judicial corruption by making it a punishable crime. Judges caught with a bribe were to be fined "the sum at issue in the lawsuit plus all fees connected with the suit, thrice multiplied," and were liable to "whatever additional punishment the sovereign shall decree." Lesser officials who tampered with court records were subject to fine, whipping, and imprisonment.

Harsher retribution was meted out, in turn, to convicted felons. For example, not only bandits, but anyone who collaborated with them or harbored stolen merchandise were to be turned over to the authorities for execution, while the death penalty was prescribed for a new treasonable offense—surrendering a fortress to the enemy. On the humanitarian side, hired laborers denied their rightful wages were entitled to double compensation, and a real effort was made to curb the spread of slavery: by prohibiting the sale of children; by ordaining the emancipation of any slave who escaped from enemy captivity (Tartar or otherwise); and by imposing restrictions on *kabala* loans, to prevent the proliferation of indentured servitude.

A curious, but not incidental, feature of the code was its regulation of *beschestie* litigation, which established a scale of fines for offenses against "injured honor"—basically any kind of insult, from being cursed or slapped in the face to "being pushed off a bridge into a stinking moat." Damages were awarded to the victorious plaintiff specifically according to his place in the social scale—so that, for example, it was automatically more costly before the law to insult a boyar or a wealthy merchant than a peasant or a prostitute. Verbal affronts (called *lai* or "barking") were common pretexts for a suit, as when one man called another a jerk or a bastard—especially a bastard, because it impugned his lineage. In a society obsessed with *mestnichestvo*, this made perfect sense. On the other hand, even beggars, prostitutes, and witches were acknowledged to have honor, and women as a whole were entitled, within each class, to twice the compensation of men. Moreover, a great crown secretary, whose services were deemed invaluable to the state, might be entitled to the largest sum of all—"whatever compensation the Tsar shall decree"—suggesting that honor conferred by merit was beginning to compete with that rooted in pedigree.

Though *beschestie* litigation proved a lucrative new source of income for magistrates—where court fees regularly came to one-tenth the sum at issue—it probably restrained antisocial behavior, since offenders had to pay damages or face *pravezh*, while false accusers were subject to 100 strokes of the knout.

Finally, considerable attention was given in the code to the turbulent, complex, and potentially explosive problems of land tenure.

In Muscovy, as noted earlier, there were three categories of landholding: *votchina*, or inherited patrimonial or Church estates; *pomestia*, or lands held in exchange for military or other government service; and state or crown land, which encompassed the remainder.

Though the *pomestie* system—originating in the Mongol period on a very limited scale, but since vastly expanded under Ivan III and Vasily III—had come to form the basis of Muscovy's national defense, it had also long been apparent that the new gentry army could not be adequately financed by the resources of the crown alone. Not only was more land needed for the *pomestie* fund, but a wider distribution of landholdings to facilitate rapid mobilization on various fronts—against the Lithuanians, Baltic Germans, and Swedes to the west, and the Tartars to the south and east. But like his father and grandfather before him (for whom the land fund was also an issue), Ivan dared not attempt to expropriate the property of the boyars, for example, as a class (though they were the most likely target) at the risk of his own demise. The only other land reserve belonged to the Church. Accordingly, the possibility arose of seizing ecclesiastical property. In 1550, the Church owned about one-third of all arable land in Muscovy, comparable to what the Catholic Church had held in England before the dissolution of the monasteries under Henry VIII.

From the time of Vladimir the Saint, the Russian Church had enjoyed semiautonomous status and a number of special privileges. Ironically, that status had increased under the Mongols, who were impartially tolerant of all confessions, and who issued sweeping charters of immunity that protected Church property as inviolable and exempted both clergy and the peasants working Church lands from service and taxation. In return, the Church accepted the obligation to pray publicly for the khans. With the rise of Moscow, the growth of monastic wealth had continued largely unabated, and by the mid-sixteenth century it was cumulatively immense. Where did it come from?

From the lowliest peasant to the grand prince himself, Russians counted on the power of prayer. As death approached, they bequeathed money, goods, and land to monasteries to finance the liturgical commemoration of their souls. Grants were made with such regularity, in fact, that "if a man died without making a bequest to a religious body it was assumed he had forgotten to do so, and the oversight was remedied by his heirs." In time, "a fixed scale was worked out so that the testator could know how much clerical assistance for his soul his bequest would purchase." In addition to legacies and gifts, some monasteries increased their assets by investments, loans (typically at an usurious rate of 20 percent), and by foreclosing on mortgages. "Many an impoverished landowner," we are told, "was forced to sit by and watch his dwindling patrimonial possessions bought up by acquisitive, shrewd and often immensely wealthy abbots"—the real estate moguls of the time.

Other cloisters resembled wholesale-retail establishments, whose brethren were "as great merchants as any in the land of Russia, and doe occupy buying and selling . . . , and have boats which passe to and fro in the rivers with merchandise."

As a result, the holdings of certain abbeys were nothing short of stupendous. The White Lake Monastery, for example, owned 7 villages, 241 hamlets, and 145 settlements—about 67,500 acres of arable land. Trinity Monastery owned ten times that much, which made it the largest single landowner excepting the grand prince in Muscovy. Even a tiny community originally inspired by a hermit living in an oak tree had acquired, within a few generations, forty-five hamlets. All this was a far cry from the example set by Russia's St. Kirill, who wandered barefoot among beasts in the wilds for twenty years, subsisting on a diet of pine bark, roots, and grass, before consenting to live in a hut.

The growth of monastic "big business" was naturally accompanied by a decline in communal discipline and ascetic ideals. To begin with, the dogma of the efficacy of prayer for the souls of the departed encouraged the idea that repentance was not an urgent matter, while it turned monks into privileged, paid petitioners for the sins of the world. Many large donations even required an annual memorial banquet; and as the calendar grew crowded with festive obligations, fast days yielded to feast. Moreover, a fair number of those attracted to the cloister were looking either for sanctuary, business training, or simply a comfortable life. When a nobleman chose to or was obliged to withdraw from the world, he could, if he wished, often reconstitute within the monastery's walls the luxurious secular life he had known—with servants, stockpiled provisions, and so forth. Where admission entailed "a suitable donation," "impecunious aspirants" were accepted only to do menial tasks. The result was not a particularly devout brotherhood. "To speak of the life of friers and nunnes," wrote a visitor, "it needs not to those that know the hypocrisie and uncleannesse of that cloyster broode." In one monastery in Vyatka, an abbot who merely tried to prohibit late-night drinking was beaten senseless and thrown over the wall.

To add to the scandal, peasants were quite as brutally treated on monastic as other estates and punished as harshly in ecclesiastical as in secular courts. The need for Christian charity was also everywhere apparent—dramatizing Church neglect. Beggars, "so pinched with famine and extreame neede, that they begge after a violent manner," were aswarm in the land, while many others were driven to make bread from straw, or to survive, like St. Kirill, on grass, herbs, bark, and roots. Wrote one observer: "There is no people who live so miserably as do the Russian poor, while the rest care not how many die of famine or hunger in the streets."

The issue was joined. The question was: What was the social mission of monastic wealth? If, as was claimed, "the wealth of the Church belongs to the poor," why was its distribution confined to supplicants who congregated in churchyards? Moreover, by what religious tradition was the accumulation of monastic wealth and property upheld?

Two parties holding opposed views formed within the Church; and because the Russian Church was a state church, they also represented two political parties or camps. One group, which championed the status quo, was called the "Josephians," after Joseph Sanin of Volokolamsk, their original spokesman; the other, the "Non-Possessors" or the "Trans-Volga Elders," supported monastic divestiture and had their strongest following among the hermitages of the north. Their original, chief spokesman was Nil Sorsky.

The first great clash between the two parties, which had come at the turn of the century, had shaped the whole character of the ensuing debate.

Nil Sorsky (1430–1508), an alumnus of St. Kirill's White Lake Monastery and a Hesychast ascetic who had studied on Mt. Athos, believed monastics should return to their original profession of poverty and once again feed themselves by the sweat of their brow. He emphasized fasting, prayer, and breathing exercises as conducive to *hesychia* or "inner calm," preparatory to mystical illumination; and advocated the *skit* or small-group hermitage as a middle way between the large cenobitic communities and the solitude of the anchorite. He sought to reform the Church in spirit and pressed for the distribution of alms.

Nil's adversary, Joseph Sanin (1439–1515), was more preoccupied with the ceremonial aspects of piety, with the observance of Church ritual and the regulations which governed everything from seating arrangements to dress in the monastic community. In this, he was a product of the Borovsk Monastery south of Moscow and its austere abbot Pafnuty, who taught "obedience without reasoning." Joseph eventually succeeded Pafnuty as abbot before founding his own stern cloister in the forests of Volokolamsk. Whatever else may be said about him, he was not a hypocrite. Having forbidden his brethren contact with women, he refused even to see his own mother.

With regard to Church property, the Josephians emphasized the practical role of the Church in the accumulation of riches for the sake of organized public charity (seldom manifest), and the importance of monasteries as a training ground for hierarchs. Joseph wrote: "If the monasteries are deprived of the villages they own, how will it be possible for an honorable and noble man to take orders? And if there are no honorable monks, where will we find candidates for the metropolitanate, the archbishopric, the bishopric, and other offices? And if there are no honorable and noble monks, the faith itself will be undermined." In other words, the management of property was indispensable training for high office, and only a prosperous monastery could hope to attract suitable upper-class trainees.

The state naturally looked with favor on the Josephian stress on obedience to authority, while a preoccupation with ritualistic externals gave monastic life a certain kinship with the hieratic etiquette of court. Josephians were indeed staunch supporters of the growing autocracy, and helped elaborate the Church-State ideology on which the monarchy was coming to rest. But they opposed any attempt to secularize Church property. On this issue, the Non-Possessors were the state's obvious allies, as were many boyars who found themselves unable to compete with abbots for peasants and land.

The split within the Russian Church therefore bore some resemblance to the contemporary confrontation between the conservative wing of the Roman Catholic Church and the apostles of the Reformation in the West.

Both Ivan III and Vasily III had wavered in choosing sides. There is no doubt that either monarch would have been happy to secularize Church property if he could have gotten away with it; but the Josephians were the more powerful faction—they had the land—and they were aroused.

In the beginning, Ivan III had welcomed broad criticism of the Church on property and other issues, and accordingly had lent covert support to the so-called Judaizers, a varied group of dissidents who attacked Church corruption, in some cases espoused the dogma of Judaism, disputed the efficacy of the sacraments or denied the Trinity, disparaged icons, took a forbidden interest in astrology and astronomy, and employed the scholastic method of argument in defense of their beliefs. Some among them also disputed a widespread, apocalyptic conviction that the world was destined to end in 1492. Basing their own calculations on an astronomical work called the *Shestokryl,* the Judaizers confidently predicted the world's survival, and of course they were right. And because they were right many of their ideas gained immeasurably in prestige. Joseph of Volokolamsk wrote to the Bishop of Suzdal: "Now in homes, along the road, and in the market places, monks and laymen are all in doubt and anguish concerning the faith."

The Russian Church establishment therefore faced a triple crisis at the end of the fifteenth century: first, how to preserve its property as inviolate; second, how to accurately predict the end of the world and the Second Coming of Christ; and third, how to refute the Judaizers. All three were intertwined, for the Judaizers were also severe critics of monastic wealth.

The self-appointed savior of the situation was Archbishop Gennady Gonozov of Novgorod (1484–1504), a brilliant, literate, dedicated, but ultimately corrupt and sadistic hierarch whose enthusiastic sale of high ecclesiastical offices eventually led to his own downfall. Long before that, however, he had a profound impact on Russia's cultural life.

In meeting the challenge, Gennady turned (as Russia has so often done) to the West for "technical" assistance. His chief agent was Dmitry Gerasimov, a translator and interpreter in the ambassadorial service who had previously undertaken missions to Sweden, Denmark, and the imperial court in Vienna. In 1490, before the Doomsday date arrived, Gennady dispatched him to Rome to acquire polemical and other works that might assist the Church in its defense.

Gerasimov returned with a trunkload of books, including an exemplary selection of Catholic apologetics, and the *Tale of the White Cowl,* which he claimed to have translated from documents in the Vatican archives but had actually composed himself. He had also recruited a number of intellectuals, including Nicholas Bulev, the Renaissance magus who was later physician to Vasily III; and "the shadowy Croation Dominican priest, Benjamin, 'Slav in nationality but Latin in faith,'" who helped compile the first complete Slavic Bible, based on the Latin Vulgate.

Now, Gennady was out to get the Judaizers any way he could. But in

Russia persecution for heresy was rare. There was little precedent for it in Byzantium, where the usual punishment for witchcraft had been exile; and the Mongols hadn't known what heresy was. In the 1370s in Novgorod certain *Strigolniki* or "shorn ones" who had spoken out against simony had been drowned as heretics in the Volkhov River. But it was not until news of the Spanish Inquisition reached Muscovy that Gennady felt he knew what he was supposed to do. He wrote at once to the Metropolitan, Zosima: "See how the King of Spain has cleansed his own land!" and urged the adoption of a Russian Inquisition. "Our people are simple," he said. "They are unable to talk in the manner of books. Thus, it is better not to engage in debates about the faith. A council is needed in order that heretics be judged, hanged and burned." Such a council was convoked at his prompting late in 1490, but Ivan III (whose own metropolitan and secretary for foreign affairs were both Judaizers) did not countenance the vicious verdicts for which Gennady campaigned. No one was executed, though some of the accused were turned over to him for discipline, which gave him an opportunity to experiment with Spanish methods. As the party approached Novgorod, his victims were seated backward on their horses, with their clothing turned front to back, and crowned with pointed birch-bark hats and bast cockscombs bearing the inscription: "Behold the army of Satan!" As they passed through Novgorod, crowds spat in their eyes and screamed: "Here are the foes of God, the blasphemers of Christ!" and their hats were set on fire.

Most Non-Possessors wanted no part of this, but Joseph of Volokolamsk, Gennady's staunch ally, spread the alarm and not only managed to portray Judaizing as a threat to national security (by tracing it to a Lithuanian Jew by the name of Zakhar), but sought to link the Non-Possessors themselves to the "subversive" movement in order to stamp their views as heretical. This was not difficult to do because anyone who criticized the established Church could be called a Judaizer whether his convictions were Russian Orthodox or not.

A first test of strength came at a Church Council of 1503, when Nil Sorsky and Joseph Sanin clashed. Joseph demanded the execution of even repentant heretics. Nil replied: "Unrepentant heretics should be imprisoned, but the Church should receive the repentant with open arms, because Christ came to discover and save the lost ones." Joseph reminded Nil that the Apostle Peter had "struck Simon Magus blind with prayer" and that St. Leo the bishop had tied a sorcerer to himself and stood with him unharmed in the fire until he expired. Nil replied tactfully: "Do understand that there is a difference between the Apostles and yourself."

Nil won the debate but lost the case. The Non-Possessors were shown to be "soft" on heresy, and fear of being tarred with the same brush alarmed Ivan III and his allies. The move to secularize Church property was reluctantly abandoned, and after a Church Council in the following year several dissidents were burned at the stake.

The Josephian triumph had incalculable consequences for every aspect of Russian life.

At the Council of 1504, Joseph and his allies had assembled voluminous documentation in support of their position, including quotations from a document known in the West as the *Donation of Constantine*. Supposed to be the testament of Constantine the Great, by which he had bequeathed imperial rank and dominions to the pope, it established the first Christian emperor as the legal source for all temporal possessions and privileges of the Church. For seven centuries (until Renaissance philologists proved it a forgery) it was used by the Catholic Church in its struggles with secular powers. Ironically, just as it was being repudiated in the West, it was discovered and embraced by Russian Church apologists. And it would remain a powerful force in Russian history until Peter the Great.

Now, both the *Tale of the White Cowl* and Filofey's Third Rome Epistle—core documents in the mythology of the Russian Orthodox Tsardom—owed much to the *Donation*, and had originally arisen less as propaganda about Russian national destiny than as expedient fictions in the campaign mounted by the Josephians to protect Church property and privileges from the state. The cowl "of dazzling white representing the Lord's resurrection" symbolized the inviolability of such holdings, and was said to be "more honorable than an imperial crown." Filofey's epistle likewise admonished the sovereign: "Do not transgress against the precepts established by your predecessors—Constantine the Great . . . and other beatified saints of the same root as you."

For half a century thereafter the Josephians had dominated the Church. Though some Non-Possessors (like Vassian Patrikeev in the reign of Vasily III) had achieved prominence, Vasily's own flirtation with the idea of secularizing Church holdings had been discarded in exchange for Josephian support for his divorce.

But now Ivan IV had come of age. Though Makary was a Josephian, Sylvester and Adashev were not, while the tsar's personal interest in the growth of his military had begun to take precedence over what he had been taught about the inviolability of ecclesiastical estates.

To guide him, of course, Ivan had many inspiring examples from the Reformation—for example, in Sweden (an antagonist closely watched by the Kremlin) where on December 8, 1539, the king had promulgated "out of the plenitude of his royal power" Church statutes modeled on those of Henry VIII. Although in a sense it was unnecessary for Ivan to follow Henry's lead because "Makary had already nationalized the Church for him," it cannot have escaped his attention that although the Russian Church was perhaps *the* State Church *par excellence*, he was neither the declared head of it, nor had the State itself benefited from the arrangement in the customary way.

Therefore (in a measure also ominous to his nobles), in the autumn of 1550 Ivan commissioned a broad inventory of Muscovy's resources, including the registration of all classes of landholders and types of property, and in two articles of the new Law Code he sought to revoke all permanent tax immunity charters, and to regulate the alienation of ancestral estates so that monasteries could not acquire them with such ease. A third article restricted the establishment of new Church suburbs.

Makary vehemently dissented from these provisions and mustered his forces to thwart their enactment. His ire can well be imagined. He had orchestrated Ivan's coronation as "Orthodox tsar," and had since been laboring mightily for the spiritual glorification of the state. To begin with, in January 1547 and again in February 1549 he had convoked major Church Councils for the mass canonization of new saints on a scale without parallel in the history of Christianity. Russia had previously claimed just twenty-two saints in the five centuries since her conversion. In 1547, that number was doubled; and in 1549, increased again by seventeen. Many local saints were adopted as national saints to bring their adoration under central control, and some of the newly canonized were princes, preeminently Aleksander Nevsky. At the same time holy relics and icons from throughout the realm were deposited in Moscow's Cathedral of the Assumption to endow the capital with an aura of sanctity. In this the Third Rome was but emulating the Second (Constantinople), which had been revered in the eyes of the whole Orthodox East not only as the seat of emperor and patriarch, but for the "supernatural forces abundantly present within its walls."

With considerable political foresight, since his elevation to the metropolitanate Makary had also appointed Josephian hierarchs to the sees of Kolomna, Novgorod, Saraisk, Perm, Ryazan, Suzdal, Rostov, and Yaroslavl. Ivan, on the other hand, had recently appointed a Non-Possessor as archbishop of Ryazan, had installed a monk and radical reformer by the name of Artemy in the Chudov Monastery in the Kremlin, and at a private meeting with Makary on September 15, 1550, revealed his renewed determination to enforce the controversial articles of the code. Makary protested, assembled numerous documents "proving" long-standing imperial recognition of Church immunities—including, of course, the *Donation of Constantine*—and reminded him that even "unclean tsars," meaning khans of the Golden Horde, had abided by the precedent it set. Archbishop Feodosy of Novgorod sent Ivan a similar remonstrance.

Nevertheless, the tsar and his advisers sought the *imprimatur* of the ecclesiastical hierarchy on their initiatives, and accordingly in January 1551 a Church Council was convoked by Makary at Ivan's request to assess the new Law Code and to take up questions bearing on Church reform. The questions Ivan posed to the assembly established its agenda, and because its acts and pronouncements comprised one hundred articles, it was to be remembered as the *Stoglav* Council or Council of a Hundred Chapters.

In his opening address Ivan managed to place the Church on the defensive while sounding a conciliatory note. He quoted Genesis concerning the fate of Sodom and Gomorrah and told the hierarchy to set its own house in order (as the state was trying to do), and announced that in response to his appeal two years before, outstanding litigation connected with *kormlenie* abuses had been peaceably resolved. As in 1549, he spoke of his youth with a mixture of confession and accusation—how he was "orphaned" and "grew up neglected and without guidance, accustomed to the boyars' evil ways," committed "sins and iniquities beyond number," and even when he attempted revenge on his enemies "nothing turned out right." "I even tormented hapless Christians," he admitted, "until God unleashed the dreadful fires, my bones trembled and fear entered my soul. I grew humble and acknowledged my transgressions. I begged forgiveness and pardoned all."

On controversial matters before the council, he also left himself room for an honorable and pious retreat: "In your deliberations, reason out and confirm so that everything in our Tsardom conforms to divine law. . . . If I do not agree with you [in your righteous decisions], admonish me; if I fail to obey you, interdict me without fear, for the sake of my soul and the preservation of the faith."

Preservation of the faith was one aim of the council and some of its rulings in that regard were perhaps conservative to a fault. For example, in ritual it ordained the use of two fingers, not three, in making the sign of the cross (to symbolize the dual nature of Christ), and likewise condemned the triple alleluia as a Latin error. In icon-painting and music Byzantine tradition was upheld, and a committee was appointed to review manuscript copies of Church manuals and religious books to correct discrepancies due to careless transcribing. Folk music and drama were denounced as profane amusements; beards, "worn by the prophets, the apostles, and by Jesus himself," were declared an essential trait of Orthodoxy in men, and those who shaved were to be denied a religious burial. In a curious dietary edict the eating of "blood sausage" was prohibited.

Nevertheless, the council gave the reformers something to celebrate. It strongly condemned the sloth, corruption, illiteracy, drunkenness, debauchery, and ignorance of the lower clergy, and in answer to the tsar's ironic question, "Is it pleasing unto God that the treasures of the Church and of the monasteries be given in usury?" flatly repudiated the practice. Much of the Law Code and several sample charters for the reform of provincial administration were also ratified with alacrity. But with something like unanimity, the council rejected all encroachments on the inviolability of Church property and privileges and inserted into its digest of acts and pronouncements emphatic documentation defending its position. Only on the provision curbing the growth of Church suburbs did the council acquiesce, agreeing henceforth to seek the tsar's permission in acquiring land. As for the establishment of poorhouses to care for the indigent, the Church declined to volunteer its wealth to help subsidize them, or even to help ransom Russians from Tartar captivity, advocating instead a general tax. Ivan, who thought the Church in both cases should pick up the tab, went out of his way to solicit from ex-Metropolitan Joasaf, a Non-Possessor, his extraconciliar dissent.

Overall the tsar, who had hoped for consensus in compromise, was profoundly disappointed, and in May removed from office Archbishop Feodosy of Novgorod, Makary's most powerful ally. On June 18, he dismissed the Josephian bishop of Suzdal—though Makary promptly replaced him with another of like mind. Ivan did not relent. He designated the radical Artemy as abbot of Trinity Monastery (a key post within the Church) and demanded the return of all *pomestie* lands which had come into the Church's possession since the death of Vasily III.

Though the early reforms seemed to mark the beginning of sweeping changes throughout Muscovite life and to justify Ivan's growing reputation as a high-minded and enlightened ruler, they were scarcely revolutionary, and in coupling reaffirmations of former privilege with measures which tended to diminish vested powers, reflected considerable compromise behind the scenes. Every law that issued from the Duma was now to be introduced, "thus hath the tsar commanded *and* the boyars ordained," and a codicil to the Law Code itself required that any crown amendments had to be ratified, implying a constitutional limitation on Ivan's power. What the aristocracy gave up in provincial administration, it gained back in the central court system, which it supervised; and it enjoyed a new oversight role with regard to the work of the government ministries. The *mestnichestvo* decree and *bechestie* statutes both guaranteed continued recognition of pedigree. Finally, the Church had effectively rebuffed significant encroachments against its eminent domain.

The new legislation had in fact one overriding aim: to increase the revenue of the state—from the centralization of the judiciary with respect to major crimes (the most lucrative ones to try), and the elaboration of fines for *beschestie* suits, to the new laws bearing on tax immunities and the establishment of a new land tax unit (the great *sokha*) which weighed more heavily on Church property. Indeed, under Ivan's new Law Code, redress against an oppressive provincial governor could not be had unless a district kept Moscow furnished with up-to-date tax rolls, while penalties were to be imposed on anyone who underestimated the value of his taxable property. Impending, too, was a tax on vodka, and the opening of the first public *kabak* or tavern as a revenue venture, since the government now had a monopoly on the sale of alcohol. Finally the attack on Church property, though rhetorically directed against the monastic abuse of wealth, obviously aimed at the enrichment of the tsar's *pomestie* fund, out of which he paid his military salaries. It cannot be coincidental that during this period Adashev reportedly moved his offices into the Treasury. Military affairs formed a continuous background to the legislative debate. From revenue flowed military might. And part of the program of the Chosen Council was war.

part two

EMPIRE

9.

Military Affairs

Ivan presided over a considerable military machine. Its traditional core was the cavalry, increasingly supplemented (since the days of Ivan III) by musketeers, artillerymen, cossacks or frontiersmen, Tartars in Russian service, mercenaries, and an irregular infantry that included men to haul cannon, dig earthworks, and load and unload wagon trains. There were sappers, wasters, miners, and other "specialty" teams, expert at building or destroying fortifications and roads and at devastating the resources of the enemy— for example, crops. All in all, the tsar had at his disposal perhaps 100,000 troops—one of the great armies of the day, but far short of the 300,000 claimed by Muscovite propaganda,[1] which tried to create the impression that he had an inexhaustible reserve of manpower on which to draw. Russia, in fact, could not mobilize an army of 200,000 until the 18th century.

Roughly two-thirds of Ivan's army at any one time was on garrison duty along the Oka defense line to the south of Moscow "to repress the eruptions and depradations of the Tartars," or stationed along the Lithuanian, Livonian, and Finnish frontiers.

Every couple of years the government would carry out a census of its military servitors by district in order to determine their numbers and how many men and horses each could provide. Taxable property was the basis of conscription, with a quota of fully armed men and their mounts levied per *sokha*. A money indemnity was sometimes allowed in lieu of service.

In the marshaling of forces for a major campaign, troops were organized into five regiments, with the great regiment in the center, a right and a left wing, an advance and a rear guard. When proceeding against the enemy, whichever regiment happened to be attacked first became the vanguard in relation to which the rest were redeployed.

For the most part the Muscovites relied on numbers rather than skill in battle, and ran "hurling on heapes" in efforts to surprise and overwhelm the enemy. They avoided pitched battles in the open field, where they tended to fare poorly, but once dug in or barricaded up in a fort or town were incredibly tenacious in defense. They "bore cold and hunger without a murmur, died in their thousands on the earthworks, and never gave in till the last extremity." Their generals therefore made considerable use of portable defenses or movable forts, based on the technology of Muscovite housing. "Being taken into pieces" they could later be re-erected "without the helpe of any carpenter or instrument." Some were fairly elaborate; many

> nothing els but a double wall of wood to defende them on both sides behinde and before, with a space of three yardes or thereabouts betwixt the two: so that they may stande within it, and have roome ynough to charge and discharge their pieces and to use their other weapons. It is closed at both endes, and made with loope holes on either side, to lay out the nose of their piece or to push foorth any other weapon.

Most Muscovite cavalrymen wore light armor or woolen coats quilted thick enough to stop an arrow, and were typically equipped with a sword, a short Turkish bow, an ax in a bearskin sheath, a long dagger, and a "caestus" or club from which depended clusters of spiked iron balls. They rode Tartar-style with a short stirrup, feet drawn up high, and "executed their maneuvers with tremendous speed." Their small, unshod geldings, which possessed great stamina, were spurred on by little drums at the saddle-bow. Cavalry commanders had larger drums with which to signal deployments, and on great campaigns four horses yoked together supported huge drums on boards. A "horrible noyse" of trumpets, shawmes, drums, and shouting often heralded a charge.

The Muscovite soldier was incredibly tough. "When the ground is covered with snow frozen a yard thick," it was said,

> he will lie in the field two months together without tent, or covering overhead; only hangs up his mantle against that part from whence the weather drives, and kindling a little fire, lies him down before it, with his back under the wind: his drink, the cold stream mingled with oatmeal, and the same all his food: his horse, fed with green wood and bark, stands all this while in the open field, yet does his service.

One Westerner remarked: "How justly may this barbarous and rude Russe condemne the daintinesse and incense of our Captaines, who living in a soile & aire much more Temperate, yet commonly use furred boots and clokes. . . . I pray you amongst all our boasting warriors how many should we find to endure the field with them but one moneth."

The chief foe of the Muscovite was unquestionably the Tartar. And he was as mighty as any to be faced. Indeed, it would not be until the reign of Catherine the Great, after two and a half centuries of bloody struggle, that he would cease to be a fearsome fact of Russian life. If the popular notion (conveyed in many history books) were true, that the Tartars were basically tribal warriors who roamed the steppes and occasionally raided savagely into Muscovy and the Ukraine, the course of Russian history would be incomprehensible. Some were nomads (principally the Nogays, who had been an integral part of the Golden Horde as one of its tribal confederations), but most were gathered into four main khanates: Sibir, east of the Urals; Kazan in the Middle Volga; Astrakhan near its mouth; and the Crimea, north of the Black Sea. The seminomadic Kabardians and Circassians occupied land between the western end of the Caucasus and the Kuban River; the Nogays roamed largely to the east of the Volga along the banks of the Yaik River down to where it pours into the Caspian Sea.

They were a foe of many faces, occupied a vast territory (comparable in size to Muscovy itself) south and east of the kingdom, and their very diversity made them both hard to attack and impossible to contain—in the sense that Muscovy could work out a coherent, long-term border strategy with regard to her antagonists to the west. While there were conflicts among the Tartars which Kremlin diplomacy could exploit, conversely no durable peace could be made with them as if they were one. Yet at times they coalesced. And behind them stood the Ottoman Empire.

In addition, the khanates (or their capitals) were not just strongholds or enclaves to which the raiders could retreat, but had their own pretensions to statehood and even empire. As succession states of the Golden Horde they competed for control of its former lands. The situation recalled that of Russia just prior to the Mongol conquest, when it had broken into independent principalities ruled by rival branches of the House of Rurik. Only now the tables were turned. This presented opportunities for aggrandizement that were not lost on Moscow (herself a kind of Mongol succession state), as she emerged with the Crimea as a chief rival for hegemony.

At this time the Crimean khanate was one of the principal states in Eastern Europe, meeting all the criteria by which statehood is judged. It possessed a viable government with a central administration staffed by officials specializing in military, political, and economic affairs; a judicial system based on Central Asian traditions and Turkish-Islamic law; a social configuration with both a rural and an urban population; an economy based on trade; an educational system more advanced than that in Muscovy; architectural monuments; and a literature.

Like Muscovy, the khanate was ruled by a dynasty, the House of Giray, which belonged to the lineage of Genghis Khan. On that rock its historical legitimacy and political pretensions were based. Moreover the khans, like Muscovite sovereigns, governed with the advice and consent of a council made up of the leaders of the most important clans, which claimed hereditary possession of much of the land. Their claim had more weight, however, than that of the Muscovite titled nobility, for like the appanage princes of old, they commanded private armies. Though in theory the succession passed to the eldest son, a candidate could not succeed without majority clan support.

The palace of the khan was in the capital of the khanate, Bakchiseray. Built in the 1530s by Sahib Giray, it somewhat resembled the Topkapi Palace of the Sultans in Istanbul, though more modest in adornment and scale. It had three courtyards, the innermost (reserved for the royal family) furnished with a famous Golden Door.

Ethnically at least, the Tartars were basically of Mongol-Turkic mix. But to contemporaries, who looked at things historically, they were a mysterious people—either the Ten Lost Tribes of Israel, the "sons of Hagar," or the Gog and Magog of Scripture. Speculation that they were the lost tribes was based on Biblical passages in 2 Kings, Isaiah, and Revelation, on the apocryphal book of Esdras, on the *Jewish Antiquities* of Josephus, and on an etymological mistake, that the word "Tartar" signified "remnant." The "sons of Hagar" was basically an ethnic slur, as was the (Western) superstition—based on an etymological coincidence (Latin, *Tartarus* = Underworld)—that they were devils. Archaeology vaguely appeared to support the third conjecture, because Alexander the Great had reputedly built a continuous stone rampart north of his empire to contain the Scythians (with whom Gog and Magog were often identified), and it was known that a battlemented wall with towers extended inland from Derbend along the ridges of the Caucasus for miles.

The Russians themselves, however, were sure that the Tartars were "the sons of Hagar, the descendants of Ishmael." Their propaganda called them many other things besides, but a certain reluctant esteem—as captured in the following passage from one of the Chronicles—ever remained in the Muscovite psyche for these descendants of their former overlords:

The Ishmaelites are capable; they learn warfare from their youth; therefore they are stern, fearless, and fierce towards us, the humble. They have been blessed by their ancestors, Ishmael and Esau, who was full of pride, and they live by their arms. We are [descended] from the gentle and humble Jacob, and therefore we cannot oppose them, but humiliate ourselves before them, as Jacob did before Esau. Yet we defeat them with the arms of the Cross: this is our help in battles, and our support against our enemies.

In a composite description, the Tartars were of moderate height, with short legs, nimble bodies, broad, flat, tawny faces and "fierce, cruel looks." They shaved their heads but had wisps of hair on their upper lip and chin, spoke "very suddaine and loude, as it were out of a deepe hollowe throate," and when they sang, "you would think a cow lowed, or some great bandogge howled." Though strong and courageous, they were said to be "preposterously depraved," and though able to go for days without food, otherwise "gorged themselves beyond measure" on savage cuisine: such as raw flesh ("steak tartare") and the intestines of horses and cows washed down with "mare's milk soured" or "mylke mingled with bloude" drawn fresh from a horse's vein.

The seminomadic among them on the whole were the least belligerent. "We won't break the chicken's leg," they told the Muscovites, "if you don't cripple our colts." In wandering from place to place, they guided themselves by the stars—especially the Pole Star, which they called the "iron nail"—while a favorite curse among them was: "May you abide in one place continually like a Christian, and inhale your own stink."

But often war parties seemed to strike out of nowhere—eastward from Kazan, or riding "crouched like monkeys on greyhounds" from out of the feathergrass or wormwood steppes all the way from the Crimea 1000 miles away. Typically armed with a bow and arrow, short scimitar, spear, and iron darts, they tended to draw out their forces in a winding arc. On extended campaigns each warrior took two or three remounts to increase his range and speed. Skirting the main river crossings and picking their way along shallow ravines and intervening plateaus, they approached under cover of darkness in widely spaced bands, "but once into the target zone would coalesce, and move on like a whirlwind, detaching raiding parties thousands strong to turn the countryside around it into a wasteland." They burned settlements, seized crops, led away herds of cattle, and took captives—especially children, whom they bore off in great baskets like panniers. Many raids had no other purpose but mass abduction—to procure youths for the Turkish military corps, men to work the oars of Mediterranean galleys, women for Levantine harems, and slaves for Tartar estates. The traffic in Slavonic slaves, in fact, had long been multinational big business, from Kaffa and Constantinople to North Africa and the Middle East. While the Muscovites had been "gathering in" the Russian lands, the Tartars had been "harvesting the steppes."

In response, the Russians gradually created a formidable network of defense lines along their southern frontiers. Fortified towns, stockades, and watchtowers established at river junctions, fords, portages, and other strate-gic points were linked together in chains, and variously defended by castel-lated walls, trenches, earthworks, *abattis* made of brushwood, and log pali-sades. One line followed the Oka River from Nizhny-Novgorod to Serpukhov, before hooking south toward Tula; a second (in advance of the first) connected Ryazan, Tula, Odoev, and Lichvin. Between the strong-points, outposts of varying sizes filled in the gaps. To thwart the Tartar cavalry, certain heavily forested areas were left uncut, riverbeds spiked with pointed stakes, and bridle paths and other trails blocked by fallen trees. Farther out, into the hazardous woodland steppe between the Oka and the headwaters of the Don, lonely watchtowers scanned the far horizon as outriders patrolled the plains.

Partly to staff this effort and to garrison the major frontier towns, there was an annual spring mobilization of some 65,000 troops, assembled at various rallying points along the Oka, and drawn from every district south of Moscow. This army was divided according to Muscovite custom into five main regiments, with the principal regiment stationed at Serpukhov, the right wing at Kaluga, the left wing at Kashira, the advance guard at Kolomna, and the rear guard at Alexin. Thrown out in front of these was a sixth regiment or "flying column" which served as a body of scouts.

The social cost of such exertions was enormous. "If we consider," wrote the great and eloquent historian V. O. Klyuchevsky,

> the amount of time and resources spent upon this grim and exhausting struggle, we shall have no need to ask ourselves what the Russian people were doing when the West was progressing rapidly in industry, in social life, in the arts and sciences, and in trade. . . . Fate set the Russian nation at the Eastern gate of Europe and for centuries it spent its forces in withstanding the pressure of Asiatic hordes while Western Europe turned to the New World beyond the seas. . . . Outpost service, however, is everywhere thankless, and soon forgotten, especially when it has been efficiently carried out. The more alert the guard, the sounder the slumbers of the guarded, and the less disposed the sleepers to value the sacrifices which have been made for their repose.

10.

Kazan

Bakchiseray and Moscow confronted one another. Though the enmities between them were legion, in the 1550s the ripening apple of their discord was Kazan. And as a result (though he could not have known it) Ivan stood trembling on the edge of immortality.

Since the birth of Kazan as a state in 1436, the khanate had been the sometime antagonist and uneasy vassal of Moscow. Moscow dated its right to invest the khans with their title to 1487, when Ivan III had intervened in a dynastic struggle and installed his lackey, Mohammed-Amin. Mohammed later broke away, prompting an attack from Vasily III who in 1516 obliged him to reconfirm Moscow's right of investiture. The Kremlin immediately took advantage of this in its foreign relations and began to refer to Kazan as its patrimony. After Mohammed died without heir in 1518, Moscow replaced him with a thirteen-year-old Tartar princeling named Shah-Ali. In 1519, Shah-Ali, together with representatives of the Tartar nobility and clergy, signed an agreement recognizing Russian suzerainty.

These developments were hotly disputed by the Crimean Khan, Mohammed Giray, whose own candidate for the throne was his brother, Sahib. Sahib had considerable support within Kazan itself, and in 1521 he arrived with a detachment of troops and toppled Shah-Ali. This marked the real beginning of an attempt by the Crimea to dominate the khanate. Later that year, in a coordinated onslaught, Mohammed Giray crossed the Don as Sahib struck Vladimir and Nizhny-Novgorod. When the two Tartar armies converged on Kolomna, Vasily III fled northward and reputedly hid for several days under a haystack. Meanwhile the eastward colonizing drive by the Russians had also prompted local tribes (notably the Cheremis and Mordvinians) to look to Kazan for their defense. The Kazanians boldly

converted this defensive war into an offensive conflict and attacked the Russian frontier, ravaging dwellings and farmland and leading away prisoners. The war with the Cheremis which "went on without end" in the Trans-Volga region, not only depressed the economy of the farmers but obstructed routes of commerce and colonization. Communication between the center and the northeast (Vyatka and Perm) of the Muscovite state could be accomplished only by a detour far to the north. . . . It was with reason that the Russian people sang in their songs that "the city of Kazan is built upon bones, the stream of Kazan runs with blood."

Kazan was 425 miles from Moscow—almost as far to the east as Vilna to the west. Past military action against the khanate had proved inconclusive because, without forward bases of operation in hostile terrain, the Russians had been unable to hold their ground. To meet this problem, Vasily III in 1523 had founded Vasilsursk, a new Russian fortress about halfway between Nizhny-Novgorod and Kazan at the mouth of the Sura River. Its immediate utility was demonstrated the following spring when it served as a supply depot for a punitive expedition; and again in 1530 when Vasily bombarded Kazan itself. Meanwhile, Sahib had fled to Istanbul, to be succeeded by his thirteen-year-old nephew, Safa. In 1532, Moscow managed to replace him with another puppet, Jan-Ali.

In exile Sahib developed a close relationship with the sultan and dreamed of uniting all three Volga khanates—the Crimea, Kazan, and Astrakhan— under his rule. Unfortunately for Moscow, he was destined to prove a shrewd, energetic, and tenacious foe. He assassinated his chief rival for the Crimean throne in 1532, subsequently strengthened Crimean power in the Steppe, tied the khanate economically and culturally more firmly to the Ottoman Empire, built a solid relationship with the Nogays, undertook a number of campaigns in the Caucasus to bring the Circassians under his rule, and turned the Astrakhan khanate into a Crimean vassal state. When he finally died in 1551, his realm extended from Bessarabia to the northern Caucasus and represented a substantial increase in Crimean power. During Ivan's turbulent minority, Kazan, with Sahib's help, had also sought to reassert its independence, and upon the assassination of Jan-Ali, Safa was re-enthroned.

Despite Moscow's failure to maintain its client khans in Kazan, Kremlin officials continued to refer in contacts with foreign powers to the khanate as a subject state. In 1535, for example, a Russian envoy told the Lithuanians: "You know that Kazan has long belonged to our Sovereigns, who install the tsar there"—at a time when the tsar there (as the Poles and Lithuanians well knew) had been installed by the Crimean khan. Sahib, of course, saw everything in reverse: "Kazan is my *yurt* [patrimony]," he wrote to the Kremlin, "and Safa belongs to my royal house. Don't meddle in Kazanian affairs. If you do, watch out for me in Moscow!"

With the Russian government in disarray, the Kazanians in 1539 and 1540 had raided deep into Muscovite territory, as far as Murom and Kostroma, while the Crimeans attacked from the south. In the spring of 1542, Emin-Giray (Sahib's eldest son) besieged Seversk; and in December 1544 (with the Russian commanders, mired in a *mestnichestvo* dispute, neglecting to marshal their troops), Belaia and Odoev.

In April 1545, however, with Ivan nearing maturity, Moscow renewed its bid for control. A small river force advanced along the Volga, another from Vyatka down the Kama, with the two linking up near Kazan "at the same hour on the same day, just as though they had both come from the same estate." Though they killed as many Kazanians as they could, a third unit, belatedly advancing from Perm, was surrounded and exterminated.

Nevertheless, the Russian offensive had the effect of aggravating factional strife in Kazan. The Crimeans had been a heavy-handed overlord, and many Kazanians were even less enthusiastic about Bakchiseray than Moscow. Alerted that a coup was imminent, in December 1545 Ivan had gone in person to Vladimir on the eastern frontier to await the latest news. On January 17, 1546, Safa was overthrown. By June the Russians had reinstalled Shah-Ali, but in July Safa returned, toppled him from power and liquidated many of his supporters in a bloody purge.

Nevertheless, Shah-Ali was to prove the most resilient puppet ever fielded by Muscovite Central Asian policymakers. Though "most unwarlike," with an "effeminate and degraded constitution of body" and a goatish little beard, he was a descendant of Genghis Khan, and of all Tartar exiles continued to have the best dynastic claim.

After Ivan's coronation in January 1547, the tsar and his advisers made the subjugation of Kazan their paramount foreign policy objective. On this they were all united, while the degree of focus and concentration brought to bear on the problem would not have been possible without the continuing military stalemate with Poland-Lithuania, sustained by an uneasy truce, in the west.

In February, one of Ivan's most capable commanders, Prince Aleksander Gorbaty, led a reconnaissance expedition along the hilly right bank of the Volga to explore approaches of attack. In December, Ivan himself set out from Vladimir at the head of a large army. His artillery train followed in January (1548). In February, he proceeded from Nizhny-Novgorod to the island of Robotka, but an unseasonably warm winter swamped the roads and turned the ice on the Volga to pulp. As cannon were being dragged across, the ice gave way, and Russian losses were heavy. Bitterly disappointed and reportedly in tears, Ivan returned to Moscow.

In 1549, the armistice with Lithuania (where a new monarch, Sigismund August, was endeavoring to consolidate his position) was renewed. In a timely development for Moscow, a fresh succession crisis also arose in Kazan, when Safa Giray, apparently drunk, slipped in his stone bathtub and broke his neck. He was survived by his beautiful wife, Sunbeka, daughter of the Nogay chieftain, Yusuf, and a two-year-old son, Utemysh. Sunbeka appealed to the Crimea for help, but Muscovite service cossacks ambushed the envoys and delivered her letters to Ivan.

Ivan attempted a preemptive strike. Securing a pledge of noninterference from one of the Nogay factions, he advanced to Vladimir. Makary joined him there and addressed the officer corps directly, exhorting them to fight for Orthodoxy and not to get caught up in precedence disputes. Apparently Ivan's recent decree had met resistance, and indeed, when the troops reached Nizhny-Novgorod in January (1550), it had to be publicly repeated. By mid-February the army had come within sight of Kazan, but again unseasonable weather aborted the campaign.

The tsar decided to build a more advanced base. In the past, Russian troops had assembled at Nizhny-Novgorod (about 175 miles from Kazan) and reprovisioned at Vasilsursk, still 100 miles away. In May 1550, Russian troops once again encircled Kazan, sacked the outskirts in a sudden assault, withdrew to the mouth of the Svyaga River some thirty miles distant, and there on a thimble-shaped hilltop called the "Round Mountain," built the fortified stronghold of Svyazhsk. Erected in two months flat like a huge Tinkertoy set, its components, all carefully numbered and marked, had been floated down the Volga from Uglich.

The rapidity of its construction near Kazan naturally made a great impression on some of the local tribes, and in the summer of 1551 the right or highland-bank Cheremis, Chuvash, and Mordvinians swore allegiance to Moscow. The tsar reciprocated with charters confirming their tribal organization and exempted them from taxes for three years. The Kazanians appeared to capitulate, agreeing to the return of Shah-Ali, the extradition of Sunbeka and her son, Utemysh, to Moscow, the emancipation of all Russian captives, and the partition of the khanate. The highland bank of the Volga was to be annexed outright, with the Kazanians retaining the left—"the Meadowside and Arsk"—"the fishermen to fish in their respective halves."

All this was too much for most Kazanians to take. The point of the negotiations had been to preserve the khanate as a political entity and to prevent a crushing Russian attack. Their delegates had warned the Russians that they "must not do this, dividing the land"; and even Shah-Ali thought Moscow had gone too far.

Nevertheless, on August 16, 1551, he entered Kazan with a bodyguard of 300 Kasimov Tartars and 200 *streltsy*—the first time a Russian garrison had been quartered within its walls. Over the next several weeks, despite initial resistance, thousands of Russian captives were released and assembled for repatriation at Svyazhsk. "Just as in antiquity," wrote a chronicler, "when Moses led the people of Israel out of Egypt, so in our time our Orthodox Tsar led a multitude of Christian souls from captivity in Kazan."

The Biblical resonance was not inappropriate. In addition to those enslaved in the Crimea and elsewhere, it is said that in 1551 there were about 30,000 Russians held in Kazan alone. Popular feeling about their bondage was enshrined in Muscovite law, both in the Code of Ivan III— "And if a serf is captured by Tartar troops and escapeth from captivity, he shall be free"—and in the expanded provision of Ivan IV.

Any campaign against Kazan could therefore be regarded as a defensive war. Yet there were other, opportunistic reasons for regarding the khanate with covetous eyes. It was located at the junction of several main trade routes—the Volga route to the Caspian Sea leading to Bokhara, Khiva, and Samarkand; the Kama route to the Urals; and the old steppe caravan route to Central Asia—which Russian merchants hoped to control. Moreover, it may already have dawned on Ivan and his advisers that, with the Turks in control of the eastern Mediterranean, European trade with Persia and Central Asia might have to pass along the Volga—which the Russians as yet held only in the north. Finally, the fertile farmland of the khanate itself promised to richly replenish Ivan's *pomestie* fund. Indeed, Peresvetov had cynically remarked in a pamphlet that even if Kazan were a friendly neighboring state, she was too handsome a prize not to be seized.

In 1551, force seemed unnecessary. The new political arrangement was all the Russians could wish, and even Shah-Ali's unpopularity seemed to work in Moscow's favor, for the Tartar nobility decided they might as well just trade him in for a military governor. Unfortunately, Shah-Ali had several scores to settle first, and having invited some of his leading critics to a banquet, had them butchered in their seats. This discredited the Russian policy and started sentiment in another direction.

In February 1552, Adashev proceeded to Kazan with a regiment of troops to install the new governor. But Shah-Ali, perhaps suddenly mindful of his place in history, refused to participate directly in the abolition of the khanate, and in a fatuous bit of bravado rode out of the city before their arrival, still a khan. Once the gates closed behind him insurgents seized control. As the Russians approached, the Kazanians feared an impending massacre, and during the stand-off offered the throne to Prince Yadigar of the Nogays, who instigated uprisings among the Chuvash and Cheremis and hemmed in the Russian garrison at Svyazhsk. The whole political arrangement came apart.

In April, Ivan resolved to take Kazan by storm. He stripped his frontier defenses, widened conscription, and in an all-out effort threw the bulk of his army into the campaign—archers, cavalry, *streltsy*, cossacks, and service Tartars, backed by 150 cannon, against a garrison of some 33,000 Tartar warriors in Kazan. A tightening Russian blockade frustrated Yadigar's attempt to bring in reinforcements, but within his means he brilliantly organized the city's defense.

Ivan's army proceeded in two columns from Kolomna to Svyazhsk (one through Nizhny-Novgorod, the other through Murom), linking up at a ford on the Sura River before advancing to Svyazhsk. A third, a supply train with heavy artillery, advanced from Nizhny-Novgorod down the Volga. Contingency plans were wisely drawn up for a rapid redeployment of troops, if necessary, to meet a Crimean challenge on the southern frontier.

Adashev planned the campaign, but Makary inspired it, and it was permeated with his anti-Tartar fanaticism and ideology of Holy War. As archbishop of Novgorod, it will be remembered, he had starved 149 unconverted Tartars to death in his diocese, and in a send-off oration to the troops invoked the names of the Virgin and all the Russian saints. Perhaps without being cynical it can also be supposed that the possibility that Kazan might suffice to replenish Ivan's *pomestie* fund—thus diverting attention from Church land—added something to his zeal.

Meanwhile, Muscovite propaganda had begun to build up a tripartite legal, historical, and messianic claim to the territory. The legal claim rested on the precedent of investiture and the several contracts (signed by Muscovite puppets) reconfirming it over the years; the historical, on a passage in the *Primary Chronicle* which averred that local tribes had once paid tribute to the Russians of Kiev, and that Vladimir I had also conquered the region—making it twice over an ancient patrimony of the crown; and the messianic, on the obligation of Orthodox Christendom to crusade against the heathen.

Sylvester was behind Makary on this 150 percent. In a letter to Ivan in 1550, he placed the coming conquest of Kazan in a world-historical context that linked it to the slaughter of Sennacherib's army under the walls of Jerusalem at the hand of the angel of the Lord; to two major victories won by the Byzantines over the Turks prior to the fall of Constantinople; and to Ivan III's confrontation with the Golden Horde on the banks of the Ugra River in 1480. Thus, the anticipated Russian event was seen to crown a series of victories "won by the people of God against the infidel."

Sylvester went further. In a startling encomium based on passages from the Psalms, he proclaimed the universal supremacy of the Russian Empire: "And Thou shalt be blessed, and Thou shalt have dominion from sea to sea and from the rivers unto the ends of the universe, and all temporal tsars shall fall down before thee and all nations shall serve Thee." Makary had been content in his coronation prayer to hope that Ivan might subdue "all barbarian nations," but he never imagined the Russian Empire exceeding the Russian plain. Sylvester idealized the tsar as a kind of Messiah, subduing the world, and it is therefore to Ivan's moral disciplinarian (ironically enough) that we owe the first explicit prophecy of Russian world domination.

Meanwhile, in the real world of the Kazanian war, an epidemic of scurvy together with a complete breakdown in military discipline had created a dangerous situation in Svyazhsk. Thousands of former Tartar captives, including women and pubescent girls and boys, had crowded into the frontier town and were going wild over their freedom. The Russian garrison, surrounded by hostile tribesmen and facing impending battle, was in a desperate *carpe diem* mood. Moscow might be the "New Jerusalem," but Sodom and Gomorrah were assuredly in Svyazhsk. A horrified Makary got wind of the debauchery, and on May 25 an archpriest raced out of Moscow with flasks of holy water. When he got to Svyazhsk he made a fiery speech in the town square exhorting the troops to remember that they were involved in a crusade. Meanwhile, Ivan had withdrawn to Trinity Monastery to pray before the relics of St. Sergius, whose assistance he invoked in memory of Dmitry Donskoy.

On the morning of June 16, he set out from Moscow to join his troops. Anastasia, grief-stricken to see him go, secluded herself in the *terem* "like a swallow in its nest," we are told, "or a bright star going under a cloud, and stayed there and shut all the windows and would not look upon the light of day until the tsar should return victorious."

There was much for her to fear. When Ivan reached Kolomna on June 21, he was immediately informed that the Crimean Tartars (under their formidable new Khan, Devlet Giray) were besieging Tula. Three detachments from Kashira, Rostislavl, and Serpukhov converged to repel the attack. Devlet retreated, but Ivan lingered nervously for almost two weeks before proceeding northeast through Vladimir to Murom. There on July 13, he received a long letter from Makary designed to strengthen his resolve. It reviewed the causes of the war, and after the fashion of *The Great Menology* grandiloquently flattered the tsar by comparing him to Constantine the Great, Vladimir I the Saint, Vladimir II Monomakh, and Aleksander Nevsky, among others. After such a buildup it must have come as something of a shock to find himself sternly admonished to avoid the abominations of Svyazhsk. In a terse reply he promised to do his best.

On August 13, he reached Svyazhsk, where discipline had been restored, and from there wrote to Yadigar promising clemency in return for surrender. He received no reply.

Having refreshed themselves in their fortress sanctuary, the troops crossed to the left bank of the Volga, forded streams and tramped over brushwood paths till on August 23 they emerged onto a broad, smooth meadow which stretched for about a mile before Kazan.

Kazan was a major metropolis, almost the size of Vilna, built on a hill, with vertical escarpments to the west, steep pathways leading up to it from the east, and high walls of oak beams reinforced from within by hardened mud and gravel. Encircling it entirely was a deep moat filled from the Kazanka River, which flowed below the acropolis to the west. The immediate suburbs were cut by a large ditch, across huddled streets and long avenues leading to heavily fortified gates. From where the army was encamped along the Volga, minarets, mosques, and a white-stone inner citadel could be seen in silhouette against the sky.

There were roughly five ways to subdue a fortified city: to starve the inhabitants into submission by a lengthy siege, scale the walls, breach them with battering rams or artillery, tunnel beneath them, or blow them up. The Russians came prepared to do whatever was necessary.

Ivan deployed his main regiment to the east and south, the vanguard to the north, the rear guard and left wing to the west, and the right wing to the marshy ground south of the Kazanka River. Despite such impressive preparations, an eerie quiet enveloped Kazan itself. "We saw the citadel standing as it were empty," recalled one general. "No one could be seen, nor a single voice heard."

Shah-Ali (technically commander in chief after Ivan as the khanate's erstwhile head of state) acted as "a special adviser" to Princes Ivan Mstislavsky and Mikhail Vorotynsky, the two generals in actual charge. No one was likely to tangle with Mstislavsky in a *mestnichestvo* dispute. He was of triple royal descent and could trace his genealogy back to Gedymin, Rurik, and Genghis Khan. His grandfather, Prince Kudaikul of Kazan, had married the sister of Vasily III, and his mother was their daughter. He was therefore also Ivan's cousin and one-fourth Tartar.

However, as he was exactly Ivan's age (twenty-two), the tsar probably looked to more veteran heads for overall guidance—while everyone looked to Rasmysl, the head of the sappers' unit and a Danish engineer.

In a rousing field speech to his officers, Ivan exhorted them to remember their Christian brethren in bondage and, promising to look after the families of all who fell, to be willing to lay down their lives for the faith. Behind him fluttered his mighty standard, which bore an image of Christ "not made by human hands." In addition to his own great pavilion and another which served as the headquarters of the high command, three large church tents were erected, dedicated to St. Sergius, the Archangel Michael, and St. Catherine the Martyr.

The Russians began to build a network of trenches to link their gun emplacements, and erected earthworks to protect their infantry. Behind great wickerwork baskets, eight feet in diameter, packed with earth, they placed their heavy guns.

The first skirmish took place on August 25, when a regiment fording a muddy stream to the west was rushed by Tartars from one of the city gates in a bold sortie. Momentarily routed, the Russians regrouped and drove the enemy back.

Almost immediately violent weather caused concern. Rains deluged the encampment and sank artillery barges; food and ammunition was lost; high winds tore up the soldiers' tents. Tartar cavalry, concealed in the forest of Arsk northeast of Kazan, ambushed Russian supply lines, in charges coordinated with sorties from the fortress by signals from the towers. Army rations were tightened. The men "lived on gruel."

Prince Aleksander Gorbaty (Ivan's best general) undertook to clear the Tartars from the woods. As he approached an *abattis* erected between two swamps, his cavalry dismounted and split into two groups, one mounting a frontal assault, the other hacking its way through the forest to attack from the right. As the Tartars fled, Gorbaty pursued them to their stronghold in the town of Arsk itself, plundered it for supplies, and roamed the countryside ransacking Tartar estates.

Meanwhile, the Russian artillery, "operating from both concealed battery positions and a moveable wooden tower" had surprisingly little effect. The ramparts were too elevated to be pounded with sufficient power, at least from where the forward trenches were cut, so that the shells fell upon the suburbs, which were blasted to smithereens. Several infantry assaults were repelled by the Tartar archers, whose stealth and marksmanship made it impossible for those in the front lines to get any sleep or enjoy a peaceful meal.

In frustration, at one point Ivan had all his Tartar prisoners tied to stakes within earshot of the walls. He thought their piteous cries might induce the defenders to surrender, but instead they riddled their brethren with arrows, shouting: "Better to die at the hands of true believers than of infidels."

Meanwhile, the continuing rough weather so beleaguered the troops that they began to attribute it to witchcraft. One general testified that as soon as the sun began to shine, wizened old men and women would appear on the city walls, shout something, lift their robes and fart in the Russians' direction. "Then straight away the wind would rise, and clouds would come with tremendous rains, but only over our army," so that even a few intelligent officers were spooked. In response, Ivan's coronation crucifix containing a sliver of the True Cross was hurriedly brought from Moscow, and great tubs of holy water were sanctified with it as priests fanned out through the camp to sprinkle it everywhere. "And from that hour onwards," we are told, "all trace of the pagan magic disappeared."

Nevertheless, the siege dragged on for five weeks. Increasingly, the army looked to Renaissance technology—specifically mining, in combination with gunpowder blasting—to work the wonders for which every Russian prayed.

And indeed, during all this time Rasmysl and his sappers had been digging away.

After a Tartar turncoat disclosed that the Kazanians obtained their drinking water from a nearby spring reached by an underground passage, Rasmysl located it, undermined it, and blew it up. Part of the city wall came crashing down. The Russians failed to fight through the breach, but by the end of September two corner towers had also been undermined and forty-eight barrels of gunpowder rolled down the long tunnels into place. Meanwhile, the moat was stuffed with earth and trees to facilitate a charge. Everything awaited the blast. Winter was coming on. The Russians could not remain much longer in the field.

On October 1, the troops were told the assault would come at dawn. That evening, Ivan was so overwrought that he "distinctly heard" the church bells ringing in the Simonov Monastery in Moscow.

After a brief, fitful sleep, he buckled on his armor, went to the church tent of St. Sergius, and prayed before the icons. Meanwhile, as legend has it, Rasmysl lit two candles—one above ground to time the blast, the other below, next to the powder charge. The first burned out more quickly in the open air. When no blast ensued, Ivan supposedly reacted with fury— but in fact, he was far from the scene.

He was at the morning service, where he tarried almost to disgrace. The two explosions reputedly punctuated the liturgy: "Your enemies shall bow down to you" coinciding with the first; then, "There shall be but one fold and one Shepherd," as the second shook the air. Breaches were made in the east and south walls, and Russians by the thousands hurtled through. Ivan lingered. A boyar rushed in: "Sovereign, the moment has come." Ivan replied: "Prayers are weapons. We must complete the service." Time passed; another appeared: "The assault is faltering. Sire, you need to be seen." And this was true. At first the defenders had been routed from the walls and towers, and in desperate hand-to-hand combat in the streets, steadily forced to give ground. Whereupon the Russians, believing the contest won, began to plunder the town. As looters emerged with their spoils, even those pretending to be dead or wounded jumped up and joined in the sack. Before long, as many were leaving the city as had entered it, and when the Tartars saw this, they regrouped and counterattacked.

Where was the tsar? "He kissed the miraculous picture of St. Sergius, drank a little holy water, swallowed a morsel of host, received his chaplain's blessing, spoke to the clergy, prayed for their pardon, claimed their blessing," and at last reluctantly emerged from the tent and called for his horse.

He was terrified. Though a considerable part of the army had been assigned to guard him, when he was told the fight still raged, "his face changed, for he had hoped that Christianity had already prevailed." His generals, however, abruptly ordered the tsar's standard to be raised within view of the battle, and taking his horse by the bridle, placed him near it "whether he liked it or not."

The Russian cavalry elite, held till then in reserve, entered the fray, as anyone caught with plunder faced death on the spot. The tide turned. At length the Tartars saw that their cause was lost. Hastily arranging a field truce, they surrendered their khan, Yadigar—as a point of honor, so that their own valor would not cost him his life. "And the rest of us," their representative said, "are going to drink with you the last cup." And so they did, as the Russians "swooped swift as famished eagles and hawks upon the ruins" and hunted the Tartars down like hares. Many fought their way across the Kazanka and into the forests and swamps where they were stalked by the Russian light cavalry. "No quarter was asked and none given. The flower of the Tartar nobility perished on that day."

In the conquered city, Ivan ordered a *Te Deum* sung and planted a great cross where the standard of the khan had flown. The Muscovite dead were buried; Tartar corpses were bound at the ankles, hung upside down from logs, and floated down the Volga. Messages, however, were sent to all the subject tribes—the Chuvash, Votyaks, Mordvinians, Bashkirs, and Cheremis—promising peace and security in return for their submission. Two tribes (the Votyaks and the Highland Cheremis) accepted these terms with alacrity. On October 4, Ivan made a solemn, ceremonial entry into Kazan, where he selected a site for the city's first Christian cathedral and laid its foundation stone.

Gorbaty, a man of broad capacities, was appointed governor, but along with Adashev and others he warned that a major military presence would be required to effectively administer the khanate and pacify the countryside. Ivan himself, they said, might have to remain until spring. But the tsar violently rebelled at this advice: Anastasia was expecting a child, and his own nerves had been stretched to the snapping point. His officers were also eager to go home, for most of the troops were not regulars as in a standing army, but special levies mobilized at their expense. The troops were just as impatient to depart.

Only a fragment of the army—3000 *streltsy*, 1500 crack cavalry, and several Cossack detachments—were given to Gorbaty to garrison both Kazan and Svyazhsk. Under the circumstances it was little more than a police force.

Ivan returned by boat up the Volga to Nizhny-Novgorod, where he was greeted wildly; and to Vladimir, where he received word that Anastasia had given birth to a son. He named him Dmitry (probably after Donskoy), and in his joy gave the messenger the cloak off his back. At Trinity Monastery he knelt in grateful prayer with former Metropolitan Joasaf, and on October 29, "clothed as for bright Easter Sunday, in armor and silver raiment, with a gold crown on his head," made his triumphal entry into Moscow. The whole population turned out to greet him. Thousands massed along the banks of the Yauza River for a distance of four miles, while others climbed to the rooftops or onto the battlements and towers.

Makary's welcoming speech compared him to many heroic worthies, including Donskoy, and rejoiced that God through Ivan had destroyed "the dragon in its lair."

Ivan's address (preserved only in summary) quoted Job and Isaiah in comparing the recent Tartar captivity of the Russians to the Babylonian and Egyptian captivity of the Hebrews.

The conquest of Kazan had a tremendous impact on the Russian psyche. In folk tradition, ballad, and song, it eclipsed both 1380 and 1480 in the story of the overthrow of the Tartar yoke, and in reality transformed Russia into a multinational empire.

Despite Ivan's personal timidity at the critical moment of the siege, he underwent a kind of apotheosis. Henceforth the epithet *grozny* begins to be attached to his name. The word, mistranslated as "terrible," actually means "dread" or "awesome," denoting majesty. If we wish (at this stage of his career) to translate it conventionally, it can only be as in the "terrible swift sword" of heavenly wrath revered by Americans in "The Battle Hymn of the Republic." That, indeed, in the eyes of his people, was the holy sword he brought to Kazan. To commemorate his victory, a gigantic icon, known as "The Church Militant" or "Knights Blessed by the Almighty," was painted for the Cathedral of the Assumption depicting him at the head of an army that included all the Russian princely saints and the heavenly host led by the Archangel Michael. Sodom, symbolizing Kazan, was shown in a circle of flames opposite the Heavenly City, surrounded by angels, symbolizing Moscow the Third Rome. The Russian people—"onward Christian soldiers" advancing in triple rank—were the "new Israel." Above Ivan, three angels held Monomakh's Crown aloft.

This icon (today in the Tretyakov Gallery in Moscow) made a handsome supplement to the canopied throne carved for Ivan out of walnut and limewood, and covered with gilded bas-reliefs depicting the life of Vladimir Monomakh. Related iconography adorned the Kremlin palace and cathedrals. In particular, the frescoes in the Golden Hall or throne room of the palace, executed under the personal direction of Sylvester as part of the great work of restoration after the Moscow fire, depicted young Ivan "as a righteous judge and fearless warrior," generous to the poor, like the Biblical conqueror Joshua in his conquests (vividly portrayed) and Solomon in his wisdom. On the wall opposite his throne was placed the legend of the Indian prince Josaphat and the hermit Barlaam (a Byzantine Christian romance based on the life of Buddha) showing Barlaam (probably a portrait of Sylvester) in sacerdotal robes exhorting the young ruler to follow the true way.

The truly courageous way at least might have been to stay in Kazan. But as a family man, national hero, and monarch who now had a male heir,[1] Ivan was disposed to relish his triumph without being reminded of new challenges and hard work ahead. He set off for Trinity Monastery to have Dmitry baptized—though not by Makary, perhaps signifying a continuing chill in their relations—while ordering a plenary session of the Duma in his absence "to deliberate on the affairs of Kazan and to go further into the question of *kormlenie*." According to Viskovaty, the first item got short shrift, as the boyars neglected to tackle problems having to do with pacification of the khanate. Meanwhile, as Adashev had feared, the tribes in the Kazan region on both sides of the Volga rebelled. The Votyaks and Cheremis refused to pay tribute, and on two occasions in the spring of 1553, Russian troops sent against them were massacred. Prince Semeon Lobanov-Rostovsky, a powerful noble, spoke for many when he remarked: "The tsardom has been impoverished by the Kazan campaign, and it will not be possible to hold Kazan anyway." In their deliberations, the boyars concentrated on how to recoup their losses. Their ingenuity in this regard, however, was abruptly interrupted by an event that shook the tsardom to its core.

11.

The Crisis of 1553

Later in his career, with a world of experience behind him, Ivan would have occasion to expound on "the varyable and daingerous estate of princes and that as well as the meanest they are subject unto change, which caused us to suspect owre own magnificence." But in 1553, though he knew something of variability and danger, he could not have known how much there was to suspect. And unfortunately, what he was about to learn he would never forget.

In early March, he developed a fever which progressed so rapidly it was feared he would die. Within a few days "he hardly recognized those around him." During a lucid interval, Viskovaty gently but firmly reminded him of his will, and Ivan amended it to designate the infant tsarevich, Dmitry, as heir. Viskovaty authenticated the document with his signature, but advised the tsar to oblige the nobility, and especially his cousin Vladimir Staritsky (whose father, it will be remembered, had died in prison under Elena), to swear allegiance to the child. To Ivan's anguished astonishment, a significant number refused. The result was turmoil.

Some who demurred did so (as they thought) for the sake of the state, which they doubted could survive another long minority; others, because they detested the comparatively lowborn Zakharins, Ivan's in-laws, who would presumably emerge as regents; still others yearned to see the dynasty fall. Ivan's deaf-mute brother Yury was not considered a realistic candidate. But many regarded Ivan's cousin Vladimir Staritsky, energetically promoted by his mother, Evfrosinia, as acceptable, because he in part seemed incapable of authoritarian rule.

Viskovaty, Adashev, and seven members of the Duma's Privy Council[1] (including Prince Dmitry Paletsky, whose daughter was married to Ivan's brother, Yury) promptly swore allegiance to the tsarevich. Two other members of the Council[2] pleaded indisposition but were apparently in touch with Evfrosinia, while Paletsky, despite his pledge, secretly indicated to Vladimir that he would not oppose his accession—provided his daughter and son-in-law were assured of an appanage estate. In the words of Viskovaty, whose handwritten interpolations in one of the Chronicles preserve an extraordinary record of the crisis, Paletsky had begun negotiating with Vladimir "as with one who would be tsar."[3] Other powerful nobles joined the rebel camp,[4] but the unseemly haste with which the Staritskys endeavored to consolidate their advantage provoked a reaction. As they openly began to canvass for support, and even to distribute money to military servitors as a down payment for their loyalty, those devoted to Ivan—who were understandably convinced that a legitimate regency was preferable to a weak, illegitimate monarchy—began to close ranks. Literally constituting a bodyguard, they refused to allow Vladimir into the presence of the tsar.

In a stunning development on March 11, Sylvester intervened on Staritsky's behalf. "Why do you not let Prince Vladimir go to the tsar?" he said to Ivan's protectors. "He wishes more good to him than you do." Though speaking as if to reconcile the different factions, he had reason to fear a regency, for his power over the tsar had incurred the antipathy and jealous resentment of Anastasia and the whole Zakharin camp.

On the morning of March 12, the tsar rallied and insisted that each member of the Duma publicly repeat the loyalty oath before the Privy Council. Prince Ivan Shuisky (the son of the hated Vasily Shuisky of Ivan's minority) protested, and Adashev's father, Fyodor, recently promoted to boyar, complicated the situation further by declaring, "We are ready to kiss the cross to thee, sovereign, and to thy son, Dmitry, but we refuse to serve the Zakharins. . . . Thy son is still in swaddling clothes . . . and we have already suffered much from the boyars during thy minority." In other words he did not regard the Zakharins as strong enough to hold the boyar factions in check. At this point, in a reprise of the deathbed scene of Vasily III, "there was great trouble and noise and much debate among the boyars, for they did not wish to serve a babe." As each party argued its cause, "there was shouting and cursing."

Ivan now summoned all his remaining strength to take control. He told the dissidents: "If you do not swear allegiance to my son, Dmitry, that means you have some other sovereign," and told Fyodor Adashev and his adherents: "I order you to serve my son, not the Zakharins, according to your conscience." Next he urged those who had shown themselves unequivocal in their support to flee abroad if necessary with his wife and child to save them; and finally, he reminded the Zakharins, who had been intimidated by the boyars and may have felt themselves somewhat denigrated by the tsar, that their interests coincided with his own: "And you, why are you so downcast, or are you hoping that the boyars may spare you? The boyars will discard you first of all. You must die for my son and for his mother, and you must not allow the boyars to insult my wife."

Ivan's masterful performance crushed the incipient rebellion. Most of the boyars meekly filed into the antechamber to take their oath (administered by Prince Vladimir Vorotynsky, with Viskovaty holding the cross), though Prince Ivan Turontay-Pronsky, a Staritsky partisan, resisted, and Staritsky himself at first refused. He was hauled before the tsar, who told him: "I don't know what will become of you. And I'm not interested," and turning to his loyalists, sighed: "I am unable to do anything myself. Let your deeds be in the spirit of your oath." Viskovaty and Vorotynsky bluntly told the prince that unless he swore allegiance he would never leave the palace alive. But though Vladimir acquiesced, his mother Evfrosinia later declined three times to append the family seal to his bond. She cursed at Viskovaty and said: "What kind of bond is it, if it is an unwilling one?" And "from this time there was great enmity between the sovereign and Prince Vladimir,"[5] wrote a contemporary, "and among the boyars there was confusion and turbulence; and heavy days came upon the realm."

12.

Vassian Toporkov Versus Maksim the Greek

Ivan never recovered from his revelations. He had discovered how faction-ridden the ruling circles remained; that some of his closest friends and associates hated his family; and that not every member of the "chosen" council had been prepared to choose him. Whom could he really trust? What difference had it made that he was now a crowned tsar and conquering hero, celebrated in Muscovite propaganda as "coequal with the apostles," if in his hour of need so many had hastened to desert him, perhaps even to plot his death? A sudden illness in a monarch is always a suspicious occurrence, especially if he has thrown his weight behind reforms. Indeed, though much of the opposition to Ivan's testament was "loyal," there were some—Lobanov-Rostovsky, for example—who were genuine rebels to the crown. In the following year he was arrested for passing state secrets to the Lithuanians and condemned by the Duma to death. Brought to the block, he was apparently reprieved at the last moment and remanded to a dungeon in the north.[1] Other partisans of Vladimir were likewise tried and convicted, but the dissident circle as a whole was too varied to confront. A quarter century later, with anger still fresh, Ivan would charge: "I was born to rule by the grace of God. . . . I grew up on the throne. What qualifications did Prince Vladimir have to be sovereign? Where did he stand in the order of succession? His only claim was treacherous support." And this was basically true.

The tsar had barely recovered his strength when in May (with fateful resolve) he kept a vow made before the Kazan campaign to make a pilgrimage of thanksgiving with his family to the White Lake Monastery in northern Russia. En route he paused at Trinity Monastery, where he conversed with Maksim the Greek.

Maksim (born Michael Trivolis in 1475) was a man of truly Renaissance education. Muscovy had probably never seen his like. Before entering Russian service, he had studied philosophy, rhetoric, and classical literature in the great universities of Italy, and had worked in Venice for Aldus Manutius in the publication of Greek manuscripts. In Florence, at the Platonic Academy of Lorenzo de' Medici, he had mingled with the leading humanists of the age, including Michelangelo. Of a powerfully religious bent, he also came under the influence of Girolamo Savonarola, the Dominican friar and radical Church reformer burned at the stake in the Piazza della Signoria in Florence in 1498. Maksim became a Dominican monk himself, in emulation of his hero, but in 1505 converted to Greek Orthodoxy and withdrew to the monastery of Vatopedi on Mt. Athos where he blissfully immersed himself for a decade in the manuscript collections of two Byzantine emperors. However, not even Vatopedi's remote seclusion guaranteed sanctuary from the world, and in 1516 emissaries from Grand Prince Vasily III had come to the Holy Mountain in search of a scholar equipped to translate the Greek commentary on the Psalter into Russian. Maksim was enlisted, arrived in Moscow in March 1518, and "took control of the splendid collection of Greek manuscripts preserved in the Kremlin library." Though he discharged his commission superbly under difficult conditions (his imperfect Russian obliged him to rely heavily at first on collaborators), a former disciple of Savonarola was not likely to keep silent about ecclesiastical corruption. He spoke out, and in sometimes violent rhetoric worthy of his mentor accused the clergy of preying upon the poor "like some sort of bloodsucking beast, and from the dry bones attempting to suck out the marrow, like dogs and ravens."

This did not go over well with the Josephians, but during his Non-Possessor phase Vasily III had tolerated Maksim's outspoken views. In the 1520s, however, the grand prince underwent a change of heart, retired his progressive metropolitan, Varlaam, and replaced him with Daniel, who immediately launched a witch-hunt. In the winter of 1524–1525 Maksim and two like-minded acquaintances, Fyodor Zhareny and Ivan Bersen-Beklemishev, were arrested and tried for treason. Bersen, a boyar who had recently been expelled from the Duma for speaking his mind too freely, and Zhareny, his confidant, both admitted to subversive conversations, but Bersen also testified that Zhareny had told him he'd been promised clemency if he slandered Maksim at his trial. In the middle of this inconvenient revelation the official transcript breaks off. Shortly thereafter Bersen was beheaded and Zhareny had his tongue cut out.

Russia's first political show-trial came to an ignominious end.

In May, Maksim was tried anyway and condemned for grammatical mistakes in his liturgical translations, on the grounds that they were heretical adulterations of the text. He was also condemned for having attempted the translations in the first place—the mission for which he had been drafted—because it implied that the original translations were faulty, even though "our saints prayed according to these books and were saved." His opposition to monastic wealth was similarly denounced because "our sainted martyrs did not oppose it." Helpless to repudiate such charges, Maksim was sentenced to life imprisonment in the Volokolamsk Monastery, where he was cruelly tortured, laden with chains, denied books and writing materials, and given a government informer as a cellmate.

Arraigned again in 1531 for having had "evil thoughts about the grand prince" and for not reporting a subversive conversation he had had with the Turkish ambassador (a fellow Greek), he was relocated to the Otroch Monastery in Tver.[2]

Over the years, however, Maksim had gradually been vindicated. At Otroch he had once again been allowed to read and write;[3] and one of his disciples, Isaak Sobaka, condemned in 1531 for no other reason than that he had served as Maksim's scribe, re-emerged under Metropolitan Joasaf as abbot of the Simonov Monastery in Moscow, and later as head of the Chudov Monastery in the Kremlin. In 1546, the patriarch of Constantinople appealed for Maksim's release; and in 1548 Makary himself told him: "Though we cannot help thee, we devotedly kiss thy bonds as if thou wert one of the saints." In 1551, his long imprisonment came to an end upon his transfer to Trinity Monastery, where under Artemy, the Non-Possessor abbot, he received friends and disciples, including Prince Andrey Kurbsky, to whom he taught the rudiments of Greek. In that year Maksim's unimpeachable corrections in the liturgical texts gained official acceptance and were adopted without fanfare by the *Stoglav* Council. Everyone seemed to realize that this was a man whose name would not die.

Maksim's personal contact with Ivan had been slight. Some years before he had sent him a rather patronizing letter on the principles of good government (in which he spoke to him as though he were a newly converted barbarian), and perhaps Ivan now wanted to show Maksim what a great Christian he was. Ushered into his cell, he finally met the remarkable old man, now seventy-eight, crippled by arthritis and almost blind.

Ivan told him about the pilgrimage he was about to undertake. To his chagrin, Maksim criticized it as useless: "God is everywhere, He accomplishes all things. He sees all things with his sleepless eye," and urged the tsar instead to demonstrate his piety by looking after the widows and orphans of those who had fallen at Kazan—as in fact he had promised to do. Indignantly, Ivan brushed the proposal aside. Maksim waxed prophetic: "If you neglect them and continue on this journey, your son shall die and not return alive." Kurbsky, Mstislavsky, Adashev, and Ivan's own confessor, Andrey, were all reportedly witness to this exchange.

Defiantly proceeding north, Ivan stopped at the Pesnoshsky Monastery of St. Nicholas, where he sought out a very different sort of Elder, Vassian Toporkov, formerly bishop of Kolomna and one-time protégé of Metropolitan Daniel. Though Toporkov was a Josephian, even Makary detested him, and upon his accession to the metropolitanate had dismissed him for "cunning and cruelty." Whatever his offenses, his surname (meaning "little ax") was said to be apt. Ivan, brooding over the recent succession crisis, asked him: "How can I rule well and hold my magnates in obedience?"— a not inherently ignoble question. According to Kurbsky, Vassian replied: "If you wish to be an autocrat, you cannot have councilors around you wiser than yourself or you will have to obey them." Ivan took this in. In Kurbsky's punning remark, it became "a big ax to cut down glorious men."

Toporkov's twisted advice unfortunately combined in an ambiguous way with the sound and sensible counsel (to which Ivan was later devoted) once given by Metropolitan Nicephorus to Vladimir Monomakh: "Attend to all matters yourself. Rely not upon your steward or your servant. When you set out to war, depend not upon your captains. Post the sentries yourself, and only after you have posted them at night at every important point around your troops, then take your rest. But arise early. Do not put off your accoutrements without a quick glance about you, for a man may perish through carelessness in the twinkling of an eye."

Battlefield precautions are not necessarily appropriate to everyday governance, but they seemed increasingly warranted by the hazards of Ivan's life. We cannot but sympathize with him. Maksim's dire prediction came true. As Ivan and his party were boarding boats to take them down the Sheksna River, Dmitry's nurse stumbled near the landing stage and pitched the child into the water.

The heir around whom all the recent furor had swirled perished in the twinkling of an eye.

13.

Art and Heresy

Makary remained conspicuously absent from the scene. The confrontations at the *Stoglav* Council had been bitter, and subsequently he had been preoccupied with how to reduce the influence of Sylvester, who had spearheaded the campaign against Church estates. In Viskovaty, who had been chafing under Sylvester's overlordship, he discovered a volatile ally.

Makary's objective, like that of Joseph of Volokolamsk fifty years before, was to stamp the Non-Possessor movement with heresy so that Ivan IV as Orthodox tsar could not proceed with the land reforms to which the movement was linked.

An opportunity soon arose which Makary (with unusual daring) exploited to the hilt.

Sylvester had recently been consorting with a freethinker by the name of Matvey Bashkin, an up-and-coming member of the minor nobility enrolled in the Chosen Thousand. Like Sylvester, Baskin held progressive views, but also voiced opinions apparently influenced by contact with Lithuanian Calvinism. His confessor, Simeon, Sylvester's colleague in the Church of the Annunciation and a Non-Possessor himself, found them so extreme that he felt obliged to call them to Ivan's attention. Ivan referred Simeon to Makary, who had Bashkin arrested and "confined in a shed in the Kremlin courtyard." In June 1553, an investigation conducted by two monks, Gherman Polev, abbot of the Monastery of the Dormition in Staritsa, and Gerasim Lenkov of the Monastery of Volokolamsk, scrutinized Bashkin's writings for Orthodoxy and found them wanting. Viskovaty also denounced him, and Sylvester himself began to say, "heresy is abroad in Moscow," to put Bashkin at arm's length.

Meanwhile, Feodosy Kosoy, a runaway slave who had gained a considerable following by his attacks on the organized Church and the oppression of the peasantry, had been similarly accused, along with Artemy, whom Ivan had recently appointed abbot of Trinity Monastery. This was a dramatic and extremely dangerous development, for it was said of Artemy that "the tsar loved him greatly and talked with him many times."

On October 25, 1553, Makary convoked a Church Council Against the Heretics, attended by both tsar and Duma, and packed it with Josephians. Their numerical advantage increased when the Non-Possessor bishop of Ryazan, rising in protest, collapsed from a stroke. Though there was sufficient "evidence" to convict Bashkin and Kosoy, some of the counts against Artemy were absurd. For example, he was charged with a journey he had once made to Neuhausen in Livonia for a dialogue on the differences between the Catholic and Orthodox creeds. The council thought "he ought to have known all the advantages of the Orthodox faith over the Catholic without discussion."

Nevertheless, all three were variously tortured and condemned to life imprisonment for rejecting the Trinity, the miracle of Christ's redemption, and icon worship. Artemy was placed in solitary confinement in a cell of the Solovetsky Monastery on an island in the White Sea.

Sylvester did not emerge unscathed. In October 1553, with Bashkin under arraignment, Viskovaty had charged that Sylvester, Artemy, and Simeon all belonged to the same cabal. Specifically, he asserted that the new icons in the Cathedral of the Annunciation, executed under Sylvester's care, reflected Bashkin's ideas, communicated to Sylvester through Artemy. "Bashkin consulted with Artemy and Artemy with Sylvester. And the priest Simeon is the spiritual father of Bashkin and was instructed to speak about and to justify their association out of fear." In November, Viskovaty repeated his accusations in greater detail in a memorandum submitted to Metropolitan

Makary. Ironically, Simeon and Sylvester were thus caught in the net they'd thrown. Makary turned Viskovaty's memorandum over to Ivan, who summoned Viskovaty before the court.

Viskovaty was a man of conservative political and religious convictions. He believed in a hierarchical organization of society; and he believed in hieratic art. "I am horror-struck," he once said, "when the small is equated with the great. If everything becomes equal, then no distinctions in rank will remain." A pious and knowledgeable art connoisseur, he accurately discerned in the new icons painted for the Cathedral of the Annunciation and in the new palace frescoes, un-Orthodox innovations, especially in concrete representations of the divine nature of God. The *Stoglav* Council had forbidden icon painters to "invent" or to paint "out of their own understanding," especially with regard to the Divinity: God the Father was not to be portrayed, "for we only have the description of Christ Our Lord in the flesh." Sacred tradition had already established what was permissible, in the standard images of the Savior, the Virgin Mother of God, and the saints. Timeless and powerful, these images "allowed the illiterate faithful to comprehend the Christian drama and recognize the figures of their visions." On such *terra firma* did Viskovaty take his stand.

What had been frescoed on the walls of the Golden Chamber was like nothing he had ever seen:

> Upon the gates of Heaven were Chastity, Reason, Purity, and Right: on those leading to Hell, Lechery, Unreason, Wrong, and Uncleanness. Then came the circle of the Earth with waters, winds, &c.: the fiery circle of the Sun and the circle of the Moon: the Air in the shape of a Maiden: the circle of Time winged with the four seasons: the circle of Creation: the Year in the form of a Man: Death with a trumpet in his hands. . . .

and so on. Such mystico-didactic, allegorical iconography was alien to Russo-Byzantine tradition and obviously reflected influences from the Renaissance West. Instead of the truths of the Gospels, he found Old Testament "types" or "shadows," which had been superseded by the reality of the Incarnation. "Let the glory of Our Lord Jesus Christ's human form not be diminished," he warned, or idolatry would arise from venerating "images more than truth." He called attention to unapproved interpretations of sacred texts, the use of untraditional texts, naturalistic portraiture, and an un-Orthodox stress on contemporary history and settings. "And when I behold these things," he declared, "I am seized with terror of contamination and every sort of cunning."

Specifically, Viskovaty took exception to God the Father portrayed according to the vision of Daniel as a gray-haired elder, the "Ancient of Days"; to Christ depicted with wings, like an angel, at Creation, because it demeaned him; to the representation of the Holy Spirit as a dove; to the Lord in imperial garb; and to an image of a warrior Christ, in armor and sword, sitting atop a cross. In other icons he found evidence of Latin heresies: in a *pietà* composition, where Christ's palms were closed (as if to deny his offer of healing and salvation to the world), and in another where "The Word," inscribed on the Cross, implied that Christ had suffered in divine as well as human form.

However, he tactfully refrained from criticizing the overtly political murals in the throne room of the palace that depicted, for example, the conversion of Russia under St. Vladimir and the legendary coronation of his descendant, Vladimir Monomakh, even though both were based on secular sources.

In answer to Viskovaty's accusations, Sylvester claimed that his links to Artemy and Bashkin were exaggerated and that he hadn't consulted with either about the frescoes. He reminded the court that it was Simeon who had discovered Bashkin's heretical ideas in the first place, and that he and Simeon together had told the tsar about them in July 1553. Moreover, it was through the tsar that he had met Artemy two years before. This attempt on Sylvester's part to seek sanctuary behind the throne created anxiety all around.

Simeon, however, now detached himself from Sylvester. Yes, it was true he had been the one to discover Bashkin's heresy, but he had told Sylvester about it in February or March, not July; and Sylvester had urged him to keep quiet because, as Bashkin's confessor, it would be "improper to relate" what he knew.

Sylvester's motives, however, may not have been pure. Bashkin and Sylvester were both close to the Staritskys, and all through the spring, as uncertainty about Ivan's health continued, it still appeared that Vladimir might become tsar. It was not until summer that his cause was obviously lost; and this may explain why Sylvester suddenly "changed his mind about the sanctity of the confessional and denounced Bashkin and Artemy before anyone could use his political mistake to denounce him." He was, after all, a master politician as well as a priest.

But Viskovaty had gone too far. Makary had encouraged him to link Sylvester to Bashkin and Artemy, but he had not expected, and could not condone, his attack on the new art. The frescoes represented but one of many official projects undertaken (after the fashion of *The Great Menology*) to glorify the Russian tsardom, while both Makary and Ivan had helped select the icon painters and approve their themes. Viskovaty had managed to call everyone's orthodoxy into question. Provoked, Makary warned him: "You started with a crusade against the heretics, and now you turn to pseudo-philosophizing about the icons. Take care not to be caught as a heretic yourself."

Viskovaty, in turn, was placed under investigation, as Makary prepared a learned brief to rebut his charges. He cited numerous church fathers to disprove that only icons on the themes of the Crucifixion, the Mother of God, and the saints were permitted, and claimed that rule one of the Seventh Ecumenical Council justified the dramatization of canonical writings. He upheld the pictorial rendering of prophetic visions, and explained that "The Word" in the image of the Cross meant only that the invisible person of God was present, not crucified. To justify the image of the "warrior" Christ, he quoted: "He shall put on righteousness as a breastplate and true judgment as a helmet" (Wisdom of Solomon 5:18–19 in the Septuagint); and showed that the allegory of virtues and vices had been inspired by Biblical proverbs. Nevertheless, he conceded that he could find no authority for depicting the Holy Spirit as a dove; that he knew of no precedent for the image of the Lord as David, in imperial garb; or for that of a crucified Christ with closed palms. And he ordered those icons corrected.

As character witnesses, meanwhile, Viskovaty had called in Vasily Zakharin and Mikhail Morozov, both related to Ivan's wife, Anastasia, and probable enemies of the Staritskys and Sylvester; while it is likely that Ivan's growing affection for his foreign minister, on whom he had leaned so heavily in March, was also felt.

The council found Viskovaty guilty of blasphemy, not heresy; compelled him to recant his charges; and after hearing his appeal for mercy, on January 14, 1554, imposed penance upon him for three years.

Sylvester was acquitted. But as a result of the trials, political alignments within the Duma were significantly affected. The Staritskys and their allies had been exposed twice over as a danger to both State and Church, while the position of the Zakharins was enhanced. Sylvester had been compromised and, in the wake of the trials, the whole Non-Possessor movement was checked. Under cross-examination, Bashkin had implicated many Trans-Volgan hermits in his heresies, and over the next five years they were hunted down by constables throughout the north. Hundreds of monks and elders were dragged from their cells and hauled before tribunals as the dungeons of Muscovite monasteries were filled with those awaiting trial or already condemned. The Russian Inquisition Gennady had once dreamed of had finally come to pass.

The conservative Viskovaty, on the other hand, manifestly suffered no political disgrace. He retained his high state rank in the bureaucracy, continued as a member of both the Duma and the Privy Council, was a frequent guest at the weddings of the court elite, and in negotiations with Sweden and Denmark in 1554 was described, together with Adashev, as one of "the [two] close and trusted counsellors of the tsar."

14.

On to Astrakhan

Infighting eventually afflicts every executive cabinet, and the triumph of one individual or faction does not necessarily entail another's fall. Sylvester's acquittal apparently enabled him to maintain a firm, if diminishing, grip on state affairs, even as he also kept Ivan more or less convinced that "if I did not acquiesce [to his advice], it would lead to the downfall of my soul and the destruction of the Tsardom." Moreover, Ivan remained apprehensive that certain advisers might meet in secret behind his back and take independent action—"deeming me incapable of judgment"—which later prompted him to charge: "In word I was sovereign, but in fact I ruled nothing," since they had "taken the splendor of my power away." Ivan's actual situation, however, is to be distinguished from his own description of it, as belied by all the evidence of his active and intelligent involvement in a broad range of affairs. Certainly by 1554, as private disagreements gave way to public confrontation among his advisers, the informal cabinet that helped him to govern had begun to come apart. And as the reins of power gradually slipped from other hands, he skillfully gathered them in.

Meanwhile, the birth of Ivan's second son and heir, Ivan Ivanovich, on March 28, 1554, strengthened his position and perhaps fueled his determination to hold on to Kazan.

An all-out effort was made. To the massacres of 1553, the Russians had retaliated in kind. In Svyazhsk, 112 rebel tribesmen were hanged; and in the winter of 1553–1554, huge punitive expeditions carried out a scorched-earth policy with indiscriminate slaughter and devastation. In the summer of 1554, natives struck back with large-scale reprisals aimed chiefly at Tartar collaborators. This brought another Muscovite army into the field, which rampaged through twenty-two districts, followed by three more brutal campaigns in 1556. Russian colonization was pushed, with tax exemptions and other enticements, as tribal territory was gradually occupied and dotted with forts. Many Tartars were also deported into the Russian interior, while a vigorous program was launched for converting the infidel.

The newly created post of archbishop of Kazan, in fact, ranked second only to that of Novgorod, and considerable land and revenue within the khanate were allotted to help subsidize the missionary work. Utemysh Giray, the former infant khan, and Yadigar, his successor, both converted and in the winter of 1553 were thrice immersed in the icy Moscow River and emerged as Christians.[1]

It was, not incidentally, chiefly the need to rapidly furnish the khanate with accurate religious texts, free of discrepancies due to scribal error, that finally brought printing to Russia one hundred years after Gutenberg. Ivan had written to Christian III of Denmark for a master typographer and equipment, and in 1552 one Hans Meissenheim (later expelled as a Lutheran agent) arrived and established a small printing press in the Church of St. Nicholas in the Kremlin. There he expertly trained the deacon Ivan Fedorov and his assistant Peter Mstislavtsev. The first book to roll off the press (in 1564) was the *Apostol,* in Maksim the Greek's edition.

Gury, one-time abbot of the Volokolamsk Monastery, was appointed the first archbishop of Kazan. In declining health, he "accepted the see as a cross," yet bravely served for eight and a half years, presiding justly over his diocese, and without coercion brought some 20,000 "infidels" to Christ.

Ivan saluted his exceptional piety in a grateful letter to him on April 5, 1557, in which he also singled out Makary for praise.

The conquest of Kazan had broken the power of the Tartars in the middle Volga region, and by opening the way south plunged the Russians directly into Astrakhan politics. All the surrounding tribes saw Russia as the power to appease. Bashkiria, a Nogay territory to the east of Kazan, gradually came under Russian domination, driving the Nogays southward between the lower Volga and the Yaik. The horde itself split into two camps: the Great Nogays, allied to Moscow, and the Little Nogays, who migrated toward the Kuban River and linked their fortunes to the Crimea. In the northern Caucasus, Circassians and Kabardians sought Moscow's protection. In 1555, the khan of Western Siberia, east of the Urals, acknowledged Ivan's suzerainty—although Siberia was still a long way from being under Moscow's control. Persia and Central Asia likewise became part of Russia's immediate political world.

Devlet Giray, the Crimean khan, was understandably agitated and sought by whatever means possible to hold on to the wandering tribes. In 1555, he contemplated an attack on the Circassians, but Ivan sent a regiment south to give him pause. The regiment met up with a raiding party galloping toward Tula and pursued them, but in a battle at Sudbishchi 100 miles to the south suffered a terrible defeat. In a moment of hysteria, Ivan called it "a disaster for Orthodox Christianity."

The Russians were soon to reconfirm their strength. Two opposing candidates were put forward for the Astrakhan throne. One was the khan in power, Yamgurchey, supported by Devlet Giray and the Little Nogay chieftain, Yusuf; the other, Derbysh-Ali, supported by Moscow and Yusuf's Great Nogay brother, Ismail. Ismail encouraged Ivan to intervene, and wrote to his brother: "Your men go to trade in Bukhara, and mine to Moscow. Were I to fight with the Tsar, I might end up with nothing—not even shrouds for the dead." Meanwhile, Russian propaganda had begun to build up a claim to Astrakhan by erroneously identifying it with ancient Tmutorokan,[2] which had belonged to Kiev in the time of Vladimir I.

In an attack coordinated with Ismail's troops, the Russians sped down the Volga, fought their way past poorly fortified outskirt defenses, and occupied the city on May 21, 1554. Yamgurchey and his partisans fled; Derbysh-Ali was installed as khan; and Nogay fratricidal strife reached awesome proportions. Then, in April 1555, Derbysh-Ali defected to Devlet's side. The Russians launched a second flotilla down the river, recaptured the city, and subsequently built a new metropolis, with a large and permanent garrison, on a midriver island one mile to the south.

To imperial myth had now been added mighty imperial fact. "Tsar of Kazan" and "Tsar of Astrakhan" were adopted into the tsar's litany of titles and the conquests were assiduously used by the government in pressing for foreign recognition of Ivan's title of tsar. While the forged genealogies and Third Romism of Muscovite theorists had been previously disregarded (if not scorned) abroad, the Russians had now incontrovertibly subdued two states ruled by descendants of Genghis Khan.

In talks with Poland in 1556, the campaign for recognition was pressed. In 1557, Ivan dispatched a letter to the patriarch of Constantinople asking for confirmation of his title as "tsar of all Russia," and in 1561 received a flattering reply which addressed him as "tsar and Orthodox sovereign of the whole Christian community from the East to the West as far as the ocean." In return the patriarch expected donations. And he got them.

When the patriarch of Alexandria got wind of Ivan's generosity, he dashed off a letter to him too. "It is written in some Greek books," the patriarch declared, "that a king will come from the Orthodox country of the East; with God's help he will conquer many kingdoms, and his name will be glorified in East and West like that of Alexander, King of Macedonia, in ancient times. He will ascend the throne of Constantinople and rescue us from the infidel Turks." This sufficed to garnish a handsome subsidy for the Orthodox Church in Egypt.[3]

No one, however, was prepared to acknowledge Ivan's descent from Caesar Augustus. The patriarch of Constantinople flirted with the idea in a thank-you note, but would say no more than that he knew Ivan belonged to "a really royal lineage and blood," and would remember him in the commemorative diptychs, as with the emperors of old.[4]

In the West, the conquests were eventually used by Muscovite diplomacy to encourage the idea that the tsar might make common cause with Europe against the Turks. This excited the Vatican as well as the patriarchs, and as early as 1550 (before the conquest of Kazan) Pope Julius III had evidently addressed a letter to Ivan as "supreme Lord and Emperor of all Russia, Grand Duke and Prince." The papal mission to Moscow, however, had been interdicted by the king of Poland, because the "all Russia" in Ivan's title might be construed to encompass Lithuania.

Ivan in fact had no interest in a Turkish Crusade, and even as he communicated one set of sentiments to the West, he was careful to declare a policy of tolerance toward Islam. Repeatedly, his envoys assured the sultan that the tsar was not his foe. There were many unconverted Tartars in Russian service, as well as baptized Tartar nobles at the Russian court. And to keep them coming, it had to appear that a change in allegiance did not necessarily require a change in faith. A copy of the Koran was kept in the Kremlin to facilitate the swearing of oaths by Moslems, while Tartar chieftains were not averse to quoting the Gospels in appealing for peace.

Muscovite imperial pretensions were also being enshrined in massive productions of official court historiography akin to *The Great Menology:* especially, *The Book of Degrees*, a comprehensive compilation and thoroughgoing revision of the Chronicles from the official Muscovite point of view; the *History of the Empire of Kazan* (completed 1566), which set forth the fate of Kazan from its founding to its conquest by Ivan; the *Chronicle of the Beginning of the Tsardom*, confined to Ivan's reign; the enormous 20,000-page *Nikon Chronicle* adorned with 16,000 miniatures, which began with the creation of the world, connected Russian history with the universal historical developments of antiquity, and ended in 1552; and the so-called *Tsarstvennaya Kniga* or *Imperial Book*, a somewhat more secular survey. Altogether these voluminous historical and religious treatises represented an attempt to organize, catalogue, and interpret the national heritage in a definitive way.

The *Book of Degrees* epitomized the others, and amounted to a wholesale rewriting of Russian history. Its fundamental myth was that Russia had been ruled from the beginning by a family of saintly princes presiding over the kingdom in harmony with outstanding representatives of the Russian Church. The Mongol conquest was blamed on envious magnates who had grasped at the power which God had placed in the hands of a single sovereign; and Russia's subservience as "wilful humiliations designed to spare the people and expiate their sins." Beginning with Donskoy, the sins were evidently expiated, and God's favor restored. But no inkling was given that Russian princes had ever collaborated with the infidel. The antagonism between Moscow and other principalities was also heavily edited out, as local developments were portrayed as organically antecedent to the history of the united Muscovite state. That state, moreover, was exalted as a divinely ordained empire standing at the pinnacle of history and ruled by a dynasty that could be traced to Augustus himself. The book's title typified its insufferably bombastic style:

> This is the Book of Degrees of the Imperial Genealogy of the Illustrious God-ordained Scepter-Holders Who Ruled in Piety the Russian Land; Who Like the Groves of Paradise, Were Planted of God by the Water Springs and Given to Drink of Orthodoxy and Made to Grow in Wisdom and Grace. . . . And Many From the Roots and From the Branches by Manifold Efforts Like Golden Steps, Erected a Rising Unfaltering Staircase to Heaven, and by it Ascend Humbly to God.

The entry about Yaroslav the Wise began: "Of a noble root the fruitful and unwithered branch, of an imperial stock a seed productive of Russian autocrats, was this Great Prince Yaroslav." And that devoted to Ivan I "Moneybags" Kalita: "This noble, God-appointed heir and blessed inheritor of the noble realm of the God-loving Russian empire, Grand Prince Ivan Danilovich, called Kalita, grandson of blessed Aleksander, was the tenth degree from the apostolic St. Vladimir I, thirteenth from Rurik." Ivan IV was revealed to be the seventeenth degree from St. Vladimir I and the twentieth from Rurik. His birth was treated as miraculous, but his power as a sovereign and his limits as a mortal were perhaps pointedly circumscribed by the quotation from Basil (Agapetus) that Makary had built upon as a subtext in the coronation rite. Nevertheless, the book "so embellished its material stylistically as to produce the effect of one continuous high-flown and flowery panegyric."

Another amazing compilation of sorts was St. Basil's Cathedral, commissioned by Makary to commemorate the conquest of Kazan. Designed by the brothers Barma and Postnik Yakovlev, architects from Pskov, it was originally called the Church of the Intercession of the Virgin; later, the Cathedral of St. Vasily (Basil) the Blessed, after a Holy Fool. In its combination of Byzantine, Russian, and Oriental elements the church at once became, and has remained, the most celebrated in the realm.[5]

With eight distinct, domed, satellite chapels encircling the main sanctuary, its unique configuration and appearance have challenged the prose of art historians. One of the most evocative describes its steeples as "banded together like an immense bundle of fantastically shaped plants," and the variegated shapes of the cupolas as "faceted, like pineapples," or "reminiscent of Oriental turbans"—though its flamboyant use of colored tile was not added until the seventeenth century.[6] In its sheer clutter and extravagance, however, the cathedral was unquestionably connected in style with the new official historiography and art. It was yet another of Makary's productions; and to glorify the tsardom was its theme. For each chapel was dedicated to a saint whose feast day coincided with an important victory over the infidel.

Indeed, a remarkable consistency binds together Moscow's whole encyclopedic program of synthesis and consolidation as an expression of national destiny. In this light, the physical gathering of the Russian lands, paralleled politically by the gradual concentration of all boyars and appanage nobles at the court of Moscow, had their religious equivalent in the canonization of local saints into one great national pantheon. Similarly, the collection in the capital of holy relics and icons from throughout the realm coincided with the gathering of "all the books for reading in the Russian land" into one great Muscovite compendium, followed by the compilation and blending of local chronicles into a spurious if unified national history.

One may wonder, in fact, if even Stalin was to exercise a more totalitarian grip on Russia's cultural life than the court of the first tsar of the tsardom the Revolution helped to overthrow.

15.

A Hammer for Lapland

Ivan's triumph over the two Tartar khanates had aroused his neighbors to the west. Lithuania had the most to fear; but the first to test his strength was Sweden, along the Russo-Finnish frontier.

Sweden held Finland as a subject province (as Denmark held Norway), and this was not really disputed by the tsar. The line of demarcation had been fixed by the Treaty of Noteborg in 1323, and most of the border conflicts since had been provoked by the Swedes. But the treaty left much to be desired. While the Varanger Fiord had been designated the boundary in Lapland, elsewhere certain unmapped rivers, supposed to trace the frontier, were found to divide and merge as they twisted and coiled among the deep forests and many lakes of Karelia. Near Olea stood a great stone monolith on which three boundary marks were cut: a lion for Sweden, a cross for Russia, and a hammer for Lapland.

Sweden bore Russia a long-standing grudge. A century before, when the Scandinavian union of the three kingdoms (Denmark, Sweden, and Norway) had collapsed, Denmark conspired with Muscovy to reunite them under Danish rule. Finland may have been Moscow's promised reward. In 1492, Ivan III (obviously skeptical of the Apocalypse) had built Ivangorod opposite Narva as a beachhead on the Baltic, and in 1493 signed a mutual aggression pact with Denmark. As the Danes prepared to invade Sweden, Russia opened a second front and bombarded Vyborg in the summer of 1495. Vyborg held out, but in February 1496 the Russians threatened Abo. In April, a third Russian army crossed the White Sea to the Kola Peninsula and raided the northeastern shores of the Gulf of Bothnia. In retaliation, a Swedish armada of seventy boats, attacking across the Gulf of Finland, sacked Ivangorod. With Swedish forces thus dispersed, the Danes in July of 1497 marched all the way to Stockholm, where an insurrection toppled the regent, Sten Sture, and enabled them to recover the Swedish crown. However, they could not hold it; the people of Norway and Sweden rose in revolt; and after Sten Sture was reinstated in 1501, the independent Kingdom of Sweden was born.

These were two great issues between the nations. A third devolved upon a matter of diplomatic protocol. By tradition, Sweden had negotiated its Russian treaties with the governors of Novgorod, because prior to the concentration of power in Moscow, the principality of Novgorod had been the area power with which to deal. Now that the governor was merely the tsar's lieutenant, royal Swedish envoys expected to be escorted to the capital. Vasily III had rejected this as an affront to his dignity; and Ivan IV followed suit. Ivan pointed out that Gustav Vasa (king since 1523) was not an hereditary monarch but a merchant's son, whereas the Novgorod governors were the "sons of kings." Politically, this put Sweden on a par with a dependent principality.

Ivan, not incidentally, suffered comparable humiliation in his turn. Though he called himself Tsar and Autocrat of vast dominions, in the diplomatic pecking order at the courts of Europe he was seen to be "on a par with the Italian princes, below the Electors of the Empire but above the dependent dukes and republics." However pretentious the battery of his titles, it is worth asking whether a scheme which placed him below the elector of Brandenburg made any sense.

His specific territorial claims were actually more objective than most. Sigismund August of Poland, for example, styled himself "by the grace of God, King of Polonia, Great Duke of Lithuania, Russia, Prussia, Massovia, and Samogetia"; and King Edward VI "our most dread and soveraign Lord by the Grace of God King of England, Fraunce and Ireland," even though the only part of France England held was Calais, and in Ireland effectively governed only suburban Dublin.

Tensions between Sweden and Muscovy built. In the early 1550s, Gustav Vasa encouraged illegal homesteading on the Karelian Isthmus, and to justify the settlements produced a forged treaty showing the border considerably farther to the east. In tacit acknowledgment of how provocative this was, he scrambled to secure armed assistance from Livonia. The Kremlin archives, however, were nothing if not compendious, and to refute Gustav's claims a great tome containing the whole history of Russo-Swedish agreements was promptly produced from a dusty crypt.

Inevitably, a series of skirmishes culminated in a major outbreak of fighting. Gustav refortified the castle at Vyborg and dispatched musketeers to Kivinebb. On March 11, 1555, several hundred Finnish hornbow marksmen launched a surprise attack on skis and routed a much larger Russian contingent at Joutselkai. A few months later, the Russians repulsed a combined land and sea assault against Noteborg.

Ivan prepared to invade Finland, and concentrated his troops in Novgorod for a strike at Savolax. Gustav in turn proclaimed a *levée en masse* throughout Finland, rearmed his infantry with halberds and pikes, and for the first time in Swedish history brought light artillery into the field.

On January 12, 1556, the Russians poured across the border, overran Kivinebb, and bombarded Vyborg where the garrison had already been depleted by a typhus epidemic. Before Gustav could marshal reinforcements, the Russians withdrew, devastating the Karelian Isthmus in their wake. Gustav, stunned, immediately appealed for a truce, and in March 1557 humiliated himself at Karajakallio where he signed a forty-year treaty with the governor of Novgorod. This notable document reconfirmed the old boundaries (to be more precisely drawn by a joint commission), and contained a commercial coda giving Swedish merchants the right to trade through Muscovy to Central Asia, and their Russian counterparts right of transit through Sweden to Spain, France, England, Lübeck, and Antwerp. Ivan well understood that he was now master of the water road from northwestern Europe to Turkestan and Persia. And he was determined to turn it to account.

16.

"A Thousand Kingdoms We Will Seek From Far"

Ivan's grasp of his international position had been immeasurably enhanced by the momentous if wholly unexpected "discovery" of Russia by the English. Sooner or later Russia's comparative isolation was bound to fall victim to the great age of exploration, whose brave and stalwart mariners and adventurers fanned out across the globe in frantic competition to discover new worlds. The Cape of Good Hope had been rounded in 1488, the West Indies revealed in 1492, the Indian Ocean crossed in 1498, and the Americas (New India) identified as a separate continent in 1513 when Balboa forced his way through the steaming forests of the Isthmus of Darien and stumbled upon the Pacific Ocean. But outside of itinerant merchants of the Hanse, the German diplomatic service, some Venetians, and perhaps a few Eastern European specialists in the Vatican secretariat, few Westerners had any real conception of what the world of Muscovy was. Her immediate European neighbors had clear propaganda reasons to stress whatever was savage about her, and clear strategic reasons for not wishing to see her admitted to the civilized company of nations. Almost mysteriously she had seemed to emerge as a nation-state, then suddenly as a great colonial empire. Even as Ivan's cavalry was storming Kazan, far away in England the learned cosmographer Sebastian Cabot and the mystic mathematician and alchemist John Dee were plotting an expedition to find the Northeast Passage to China or "Cathay," unaware that Russia lay along the route.

Thus it was that on August 24, 1553, an English ship, the *Edward Bonaventure*, wandered utterly lost to the mouth of the Northern Dvina and cast anchor in St. Nicholas Bay.

In exploration, the English had done poorly and were scrambling to catch up. The Spaniards and Portuguese had doubled the southernmost capes of both hemispheres and had met at the Spice Islands on the opposite side of the globe. They were tramping through Canada, Florida, and Brazil; and were already fighting for supremacy in the Caribbean, Central and South America, and parts of Africa, Arabia, India, Malaysia, and Indonesia. The French were in America and the Dutch were beginning to develop their great merchant marine. The English had discovered Labrador.

English merchants were understandably agitated, and as tactfully as they could suggested their monarchs show more initiative. Other governments were handsomely funding expeditions. England was scarcely spending a crown. In 1527, the merchant Robert Thorne wrote to Henry VIII: "There is left but one way to discover, which is into the North: for that of the foure partes of the worlde, it seemeth three parts are discovered by other Princes." Optimistically he supposed God had reserved the fourth unto England as a northern realm.

How difficult this would prove no one could have guessed. Mercator's great globe of 1541 conjectured the distance as "short and easy," and that once the North Cape had been rounded the coast would slope gently down into the Pacific Ocean. Instead, of course, it thrust impassably upward toward the North Pole, and would not be accurately charted until the twentieth century—and then only with the help of icebreakers and planes.

The English, however, were highly motivated in their quest. Like their continental confreres, they had become addicted to spices (for medicinal purposes as well as cuisine), just when the Turks, ensconced in Asia Minor as well as elsewhere, had intercepted the land spice route, evicted the Genoese and Venetians from their ancient trading stations in the Levant, and with their galleys in the eastern Mediterranean patrolled the outlet from Alexandria. The Turks were thus in a position to impose prohibitively heavy tolls on whatever trade could be had, and had cut deeply into the dwindling supply of "trans-Sahara"[1] gold, which furnished coin of the realm. Even if one could get past them in Asia Minor (after running a gauntlet of Moslem corsairs in the Mediterranean and surviving travel by caravan across the Syrian desert and down the Euphrates Valley), the only way to India from Basra was by primitive native craft through dangerous, turbulent seas "which involved a degree of 'roughing it' discouraging to even the hardiest of men." Considering the time, cost, and inevitable tribulations of such a journey, to and fro, no fair markup price could be practical. The Spanish and Portuguese had managed to discover independent sources of supply. The English had not.

England was also facing a more general import-export crisis, as the price of foreign commodities rose sharply while the demand for English products (especially woolen cloth) "waxed cold and in decay." Finally, like Portugal and Spain, England dreamed of empire—"A thousand kingdoms we will seek from far," the poet Michael Drayton wrote, "And those unchristened countries call our own, /Where scarce the name of England hath been known." But it was commerce, not religion, which furnished the inspiration, and in reflecting upon this a century later the poet John Milton remarked that the discovery of Russia "might have seemed an enterprise almost heroic if any higher end than excessive love of gain and traffic had animated the design."

Perhaps only Dee and a few others had a higher end in view: to find, beyond gold and spices, a "Commoditye farre passing worldly Treasure"— occult wisdom.[2]

Henry VIII had been too busy with his wasteful foreign wars to listen to Thorne, but in 1553, after the accession of young King Edward VI, Sebastian Cabot in London formed the "Mysterie and company of the Merchants Adventurers for the discoverie of Cathay and divers other lands." He found an immediate and enthusiastic backer in the duke of Northumberland, and before long other dignitaries and great lords of the realm took shares. Three small ships were newly trimmed for the expedition—the *Bona Speranza*, the *Edward Bonaventure*, and the *Bona Confidentia*—and Cabot composed a broad set of ordinances and instructions for the voyage, including a probably futile ban on drunkenness and "filthy tales," and baleful advice to look out for "naked swimmers" who might "covet their bodies for meate."

The captain general of the expedition was Sir Hugh Willoughby, a valiant soldier who in 1550 had beaten back a French assault on Scotland's Fort Lawder after casting all the pewter in the fort into shot. His pilot general was the "incomparable" Richard Chancellor, Dee's protégé, who had designed for himself "the best quadrant in England." King Edward gave them his blessing and furnished a letter of introduction to all rulers "in all places under the universal heaven" which elegantly linked commerce between nations to a Divine Plan for universal accord: "The God of heaven and earth greatly providing for mankinde, would not that all things should be found in one region, to the ende that one should have neede of another, that by this meanes friendship might be established among all men, and every one seeke to gratifie all."

The three ships weighed anchor on May 11 and having come to Greenwich (where the king and his court then were), "courtiers came running out, the privy council at the windows, the rest on the battlements and towers." The common people "flockt together, very thicke upon the shoare" as soldiers, dressed in watchet or sky-colored cloth, fired a salute, which came ringing back in echoes from the hills.

After an anxious month at Harwich waiting for the weather to clear, the ships crossed the North Sea to Norway, but off the Lofotan Islands met "such flawes of winde and terrible whirlewinds . . . that we were not able to beare any saile." Night brought no abatement. A thick fog rolled in and the ships were dispersed. Though Willoughby's *Speranza* managed to link up again with the *Confidentia* at dawn, Chancellor's *Bonaventure* was nowhere to be seen.

But it was Willoughby and his eighty-three companions who were doomed. He made his way along the Lapland coast toward the White Sea, where near a tongue of land called Svatoy Noss, he was driven back by a whirlpool. Forced in line with breakers treading northwest, on September 18 he spotted the rocky black edge of Nokujeff Island and sailed into the bay. There he waited patiently for the wind to change. He waited until the days roared in with frost; and then the moon began to wane. He sent out scouting parties in every direction, but the island was found to be desolate. Daylight steadily diminished; their rations soon dwindled; after November 25, the sun disappeared. One year later Russian fisherman would discover them (so it was said) "platter in hand and spoon in mouth" frozen to death in their ships.

Meanwhile, in August Chancellor had returned to the Norway coast and put in at Wardhouse, their appointed rendezvous in case of emergency. Beset with premonitions of their fate, "If the rage and furie of the Sea have devoured those good men," he wrote sadly in his journal, "I must needs say they were men worthy of better fortune, or if the crueltie of death hath [otherwise] taken holde of them, God send them a Christian grave and a Sepulchre." But after a week (as it was still midsummer), he resumed his perilous voyage, and holding a steady course, "sailed so farre, that hee came at last to where hee found no night at all, but a continuall light and brightness of the Sunne shining clearely upon the huge and mightie sea." On August 24, 1553, he came to the mouth of the Northern Dvina and disembarked on Russian soil.

Chancellor had no idea where he was; but the local fishermen "prostrated themselves before him, offering to kisse his feete," and later officials arrived who were perfectly polite. Messengers were dispatched from Kholmogory, the nearest substantial town, to Moscow 1000 miles away, and on the 23rd of November Chancellor and a few members of his crew set off in sleds for the capital. After traveling by way of Vologda and Yaroslavl (a journey of 1500 miles), they were enthusiastically greeted in the Kremlin by Ivan, whom they found so imposingly enthroned that "our men beganne to wonder at the Majestie of the Emperour: his seate was aloft, very royall, having on his head a Diademe, or Crowne of Golde, his robe all Goldsmiths worke, and in his hand a Scepter garnished, and beset with precious stones: and there was a Majestie in his countenance proportionable with the excellencie of his estate." At a ceremonial dinner in their honor Ivan brought out "rich and very massie" gold plate and ostentatiously changed his crown twice— so that they saw him wear three crowns in one day. By the cupboards stood two men "with napkins on their shoulders" (like modern maître d's), each holding a gem-encrusted cup which they filled repeatedly with wine. From time to time Ivan "drank them off at a draught."

The tsar sat apart, crossed himself with every bite of food, and sent bread from his own table as a gift to various guests. Whenever he did so, all stood up as his long title was loudly proclaimed. At the end of the banquet, in a ritual demonstration of his prodigious memory, he addressed every one of his two hundred guests by name "in such sort that it seemed miraculous for a Prince otherwise occupied in great matters of estate."

This is the first objective glimpse of Ivan that we have. He was twenty-three at the time, and his majesty and poise may be judged the more remarkable since his government was then in the throes of the heresy trials.

The English of course were meant to be impressed, especially by Muscovy's wealth and might. The nobility paraded about in such costly armor that, Chancellor wrote, "I could scarce beleeve it," but the tsar "above all measure: his pavilion is covered with cloth of gold and so set with stones that it is wonderfull to see. I have seene the Kings Majesties of England and the French Kings pavilions, which are fayre, yet not like unto his." Among other things, he was told that the tsar could bring into the field two or three hundred thousand men, and that at any given time he had 40,000 stationed along the Livonian border, 60,000 facing Lithuania, and 60,000 more against the Tartars on the southern frontier. Though Chancellor considered Muscovy deficient in the art of war, he believed her individual soldiers second to none. "Now what might be made of these men," he wrote, "if they were trained and broken to order and knowledge of [modern] war? If this Prince had within his countrey such men as could make them to understand such things, I do believe that 2 of the best or greatest princes in Christendome were not able to match with him, considering the greatnes of his power."

Nevertheless, Chancellor was repelled by many aspects of Russian life: the adoration of icons, ignorance of the clergy, abject servility of the people, and "as for whoredome and drunkenesse there be none such living: and for extortion, they be the most abominable under the sunne." On balance, he concluded, they were "ignorant Barbarians."

Chancellor's large and relatively impartial intelligence lend his observations weight, but he could also be wide of the mark. Though he accurately described the *pomestie* system, for example, various customs and the geography of the Russian north, his précis of Russian law was comically askew: The plaintiff, he writes, initiates a suit, and then an officer "fetcheth the defendant, and beateth him on the legges." If the man cannot furnish surety "his hands are tied to his necke, and he is beaten all the way, till he come before the Judge." The judge asks him (in the matter of debt) "whether he oweth any thing to the plaintife. If he denies it, 'How canst thou deny it?' saith the Judge, the defendant answereth, 'By an othe.'" If the matter cannot be resolved "they fight it out."

Shakespeare's portrait of the Muscovite ambassadors in *Love's Labour's Lost* ("In shapeless gear, . . . /their shallow shows and prologue vilely penn'd,/And their rough carriage so ridiculous") indicates the general reputation Russians were destined to enjoy in England. Yet in the context of the continental Renaissance, at least, the English were also still comparatively rude. They had military engineering but little architecture, except for the palace building begun by Henry VIII; and in medicine evinced an amazing faith in laxatives, comparable to the Russian faith in baths. Like the Russians they went in for bear-baiting as an organized sport, and sodomy was also a vice of official concern. In 1533, Parliament had passed "An Act for The punishment of the detestable and abominable vice of buggery, committed with mankind or beast," and made it a capital crime. Bloody Mary repealed the statute[3] (along with much of Henry's Reformation legislation), but under Elizabeth I Parliament would revive it. Russia was not an absolutely alien world.

Yet whatever resemblances might be drawn, differences eclipsed them. England was a constitutional monarchy; and the public conscience expressed itself in a general concern for "social betterment." The nobility subsidized almshouses; the gentry involved itself in poor relief; the great merchants of London, Norwich, Bristol, and other towns engaged in schemes to assist the unemployed, and lent money at marginal interest to young apprentices starting a trade. A great national effort in education led to the founding and endowment of schools. And to the free and fantastic efflorescence of the arts in England nothing in Russia could compare.

Chancellor's preliminary trade discussions with Ivan were gratifying: need met need. Russia sought manufactured goods, England a large, new, diversified market. Both appreciated that commerce past the northern coast of Europe would be subject neither to the Sound dues levied by Denmark nor the tariffs imposed by the Livonian and Hanseatic middlemen who dominated Baltic trade. And so with a kind of zest otherwise unthinkable in dealing with a still strange and virtually unknown foreign power, Ivan in his missive to King Edward written in February 1554 welcomed English ships to his White Sea port and hoped that an agreement could be struck to extend "ffree markett with all free lyberties through my whole dominion with all kinde of wares." He dated his letter Anno Mundi 7062, appended a translation into Dutch, and to the astonishment of Chancellor sealed it upon wax with what looked like "the broad seale of England, having on one side the image of a man on horseback in complete harnesse fighting with a dragon," in the manner of St. George.

Good King Edward, however, was not to enjoy these salutations. On July 6, 1553, he had died of consumption after a reign of just six years, and England plunged toward turmoil. In a coup engineered by the duke of Northumberland on the 10th, Lady Jane Grey (daughter of the duke of Norfolk and coincidentally Hugh Willoughby's grand-niece) was proclaimed queen. Nine days later "Bloody" Mary entered London, toppled Jane Grey from the throne, and imprisoned her in the Tower. Northumberland's head rolled from the block. Civil war ensued, fiercely fueled by religious strife and by Mary's resolve to marry the Catholic King, Philip of Spain. England's very existence as an independent nation seemed at stake. Crosscurrents of rebellion swept the land. The prisons "were filled with persons of rank," and even as the blood of Sir Hugh was freezing on the Lapland coast, Lady Jane's was shed on the scaffold. In July 1554, Mary went through with her marriage to Philip and attempted to enforce the wholesale reconversion of England to Catholicism. Persecution produced heroic martyrdom, with many beleaguered Protestants imminently expecting the Second Coming of Christ.

In the midst of such disorders, it is not surprising that Chancellor's startling announcement of the discovery of Russia aroused little public interest, and perhaps seemed a comedown from the expectations for Cathay. However, Russia was better than Labrador, and the commercial prospects he unfolded were certainly not lost on the Catholic queen. She issued a charter to the Muscovy, or Russia, Company on February 26, 1555, drafted a letter to Ivan expressing her hopes for a mutual trade agreement, and sent Chancellor back in May with two ships, the *Edward Bonaventure* and the *Philip and Mary*. He was accompanied by two very capable company agents, Richard Grey and George Killingworth, the latter a London draper whose spectacularly long, thick yellow beard amazed the Muscovites.

At the Kremlin they had found Ivan preoccupied with "preparations to warre" with Sweden, but negotiated an agreement with Viskovaty and a delegation of Muscovite merchants that was all they could have wished. Principally, it allowed the English to trade tax-free ("without any customs, duties, tolls and impositions") wholesale and retail in Moscow itself, and selectively throughout the realm; to hire local labor (shippers, packers, etc.), with legal jurisdiction over their own personnel (to adjudicate all "causes, plaints, quarrels and disorders betweene them moved" by fine and imprisonment); and promised prompt and equitable justice from the tsar himself in all cases involving disputes between Englishmen and Russians. Finally, it stipulated that no merchant's goods were to be held hostage for an underling's offense, no matter how grave; and no Englishman was to be imprisoned for debt if he could find "sufficient suretie and pawne."

Ivan, enamored of the English, soon became rather familiar. At one festive dinner in their honor in October, he doted on Killingworth's long, flowing beard (which extended over the table and onto the floor), and at one point "tooke it into his hand & presently delivered it to the Metropolitane, who seeming to blesse it, sayd in Russe, this is Gods gift."

Chancellor equipped four ships for his return—the *Edward Bonaventure*, the *Philip and Mary*, and the newly refurbished *Bona Speranza* and *Bona Confidentia*, which the Russians had graciously retrieved from their Lapland cove. These were loaded with a fair sampling of what Russia had to offer—wax, train oil, tallow, furs, felt, and yarn—and (as royal gifts for the king and queen) twenty sable pelts with teeth and claws, four live sables with collar and chain, and a white gerfalcon with a gilded lure.

What Ivan really wanted in exchange, aside from assorted manufactured goods, neither Chancellor, Killingworth, nor Grey were empowered to discuss. Grave political issues were involved which required negotiation at a higher level.

Ivan understood this, and in March 1556 appointed Osip Nepea, governor of Vologda, Russia's first ambassador to England. With sixteen compatriots, he set sail with Chancellor in mid-July.

17.

Hanseatic Merchants and Red Cross Knights

In the mid-1550s, two great foreign policy objectives were hotly debated within the inner councils of the Kremlin. Most, if not all, of Ivan's cabinet and a clear majority of the Duma advised the tsar to consolidate his conquests of Kazan and Astrakhan, aggressively retrench and refortify the Oka defense line, and undertake an all-out campaign to put an end to the perennial Tartar raids from the south. A series of reconnaissance patrols and trial expeditions was planned to culminate in the march of a vast Muscovite host, under the personal command of the tsar, across the Wild Field to strike the Crimean Tartars in their lair. Such a campaign, launched from Tula across 700 miles of steppe—a remorselessly inhospitable vast stretch of plain—would have been extraordinarily difficult, especially without a network of navigable rivers to facilitate the transport of troops and matériel, and without advance bases like Vasilsursk or Svyazhsk to serve as supply depots, refueling stops, and fortified sanctuaries in the event of retreat. Moreover, an aggressive military action on that scale was almost certain to provoke a response from the Ottoman Turks. Yet in other respects the plan seemed opportune. Kazan and Astrakhan were in Russian hands, the Crimean Tartars had been intimidated, and their Nogay allies decimated by drought and disease. The Crimeans were also riven by factions, and in 1556 one of their grandees, Tokhtamysh, a grandson of Khan Ahmad of the Golden Horde and the second cousin of Shah-Ali (a grandson of Ahmad's brother, Bakhtiar) fled to the Little Nogays. In July 1556, Ivan wrote to Ismail, their chieftain: "We need Tokhtamysh for our state affairs," and wrote also to Tokhtamysh himself, inviting him to Moscow. In December he came, perhaps as the projected Muscovite candidate for the Crimean throne. Meanwhile, in 1556 and 1557 respectively, the dyak Rzhevsky, military commander of Chernigov, and Prince Dmitry Vishnevetsky, a Dnieper cossack chieftain, explored attack approaches to the Crimea and carried out successful raids to the shores of the Black Sea. Vishnevetsky, an anti-Tartar fanatic, had established a Cossack stronghold on the Dnieper island of Khortitsa as a base of operations; and though a Lithuanian, he was furnished by Ivan with a training camp, money, and supplies. In February 1559, a double expedition was launched—Vishnevetsky down the Don with 5000 troops, and Daniel Adashev (Aleksey's brother) with 8000 down the Dnieper. Vishnevetsky won a skirmish near Azov; Adashev captured two Turkish ships, sailed into the Black Sea, landed on the Crimean Peninsula, and attacked several camps. Khan Devlet Giray pursued him back up the Dnieper but failed to catch him. The khan surmised that these were but preludes to a full-scale invasion.

Ivan himself, however, backed by a rising corps of new advisers, had his eyes on Livonia, a rich, strategically placed, but composite and dissolving state to the west, roughly comprising modern Latvia and Estonia, plus Courland and the islands of Dago, Oesel, and Loon. The case for intervention in Livonian affairs was strong. Among Moscow's rivals, Denmark "dreamed of expanding her commercial interests throughout the entire Baltic area," Sweden "of consolidating the position she had already acquired in the northern part of the country," where the coastal ports were economically tied to Finland, while "both Sweden and Poland wished to gain control of all of Livonia in order to check the ambitions of Moscow, which had emerged as a new and vital factor in the Baltic power equation." Conversely, Russian acquisition of Livonia would enable her to attack Lithuania from the north as well as from the east, curb the growth of Swedish might, break a *de facto* Western blockade on certain specialized goods sought by Moscow, eliminate the Livonian middlemen and their punitive tariffs from the scene, and give Russia a real seaboard, beyond her small coastal outlet at Ivangorod, with all that that was bound to mean for the development of commerce and industry. If Russia failed to seize the prize—coveted by every one of the Baltic powers—Poland, Sweden, or Denmark surely would.

Pomestie economics were a motivation too. The conquest and pacification of Kazan had been hard, but a campaign against the Crimea was even less prepossessing—"to the mass of military servitors, the most uninteresting imaginable"—since it would be impossible to settle in the Crimea itself, and in the waste steppes of south Russia there was nothing to be appropriated. On the other hand, an invasion of Livonia promised the swift acquisition of already well-organized and cultivated farms and estates, ready-furnished with slaves and serfs.

Adashev, Viskovaty, Sylvester, and others were evidently not blind to the Livonian option, but believed they could open the trade and perhaps secure a Baltic port by diplomacy, threat, or (if necessary) by a very limited war. It was a question of how best to use Muscovy's resources. The split went deep, and in the breach the dragon's teeth were sown.

Officially, Livonia was defended by the *Fratres Militiae Christi* or Brethren of the Sword, a medieval chivalric order founded in 1202 by Bishop Albert of Riga and affiliated after 1237 with the Teutonic Knights. Like the Knights of Dobryzn on the lower Vistula, formed by a Cistercian bishop at about the same time, they were an efficient body of cavalry to aid and abet the arduously slow baptism of the native population. The Knights of Dobryzn wore a star on the hilt of their swords in commemoration of Bethlehem; the Livonian Knights a Red Cross on their mantles and shields.

All these knights, including the Black Cross or Teutonic Order, were variously linked to the so-called Northern Crusade which had been launched by the pope, and which came to serve, in effect, as the cutting edge for German colonization, which after the founding of Lübeck in 1143 spread along the entire southern coast of the Baltic Sea.

In theory the mission of the Knights was conversion, and with a sort of anticipatory penance, they endeavored by stern privations to make themselves fit for their holy work. On the one hand, the Brethren took a triple vow of poverty, chastity, and obedience, and on the other committed themselves "to fight with a pure mind for the supreme and true King." The militarized language of the cloister (echoing Ephesians) facilitated the transition from cleric to man-at-arms, and comfortably enveloped their fusion in the mission of the warrior-monk. But though St. Augustine's doctrine of

"Just wars avenge injuries" had furnished some rationale for the three great crusades to Palestine to recapture the Holy Land and its sacred shrines (the "patrimony" of Christendom), the war against "the heathen of the North" remained anomalous. The only charge against them was that they happened to be there—and didn't believe in Christ.

The original ten knights to gather in Albert's household had probably not been conceived as the nucleus of a subjugating army, but to hold the fort at Riga while his priests proselytized in the field. However, as the bishop expanded his control over the Dvina Valley, their numbers grew in order to garrison the strongholds—fortified monasteries, stone blockhouses and hill-forts, which formed the nuclei of future towns—to rivet their gains. There were reverses, of course: rebellions in Latvia (1212) and in Estonia (1223); and in an immortal engagement on April 5, 1242, Aleksander Nevsky defeated the Knights on the ice of Lake Peipus. Employing tactics reminiscent of Hannibal's at Cannae (and not incidentally anticipating Red Army tactics at Stalingrad), he caught the galloping iron triangle in a pincer movement and shattered its power. Nevsky's victory put an end to German expansion eastward, but within Livonia (as in Prussia, under the Teutonic Knights) the Germans built up a kingdom for themselves as an outpost of the Holy Roman Empire.

After the see of Riga was raised to an archbishopric in 1253, the rule of Livonia was divided among five powers: the archbishop; his three bishops of Courland, Oesel, and Dorpat; and the Brethren of the Sword. The bishops and knights enfeoffed secular vassals, and the archbishop chartered a community of burghers at Riga. In time the principal towns became a third and coequal force in the centrifugal division of authority.

Livonia prospered through its involvement in the Hanseatic League, a loose confederation of north German towns and overseas merchants, which had its headquarters at Lübeck. It controlled the vital overland trade route across the base of the Danish peninsula, and coordinated a huge commerce flowing to the east as far as Russia and west even to Ireland. Well over a hundred towns belonged to the League at its height, including Oslo in Norway, Stockholm in Sweden, and Cracow in Poland, which lay on the famed "amber road" into the Balkans. In addition, there were major overseas "factories" (warehouse markets) or *Kontore* (counters) at London, Bruges, Bergen, and Novgorod, together with key if lesser depots scattered from Iceland to Spain. Until the end of the fifteenth century, the League absolutely dominated the commercial life of northern Europe.

From the rich hinterland to the south and east were drawn raw materials such as grain, timber, pitch, tar, train-oil, potash, charcoal, wax, honey, hemp, flax, and furs; while from the relatively more industrialized west came manufactured goods in exchange, such as textiles, implements, and rope. Livonia in particular served as the chief artery of Muscovite trade.

The League, however, was not a true political federation. A representative assembly of its members met periodically at Lübeck, but with the rise of authentic nation-states in the region, whose economic and political coherence it could not hope to match, its power was gradually broken, and in a predictable scrimmage for self-advantage its members began to stab each other in the back. The misguided destruction of the German *Kontor* at Novgorod by Ivan III also contributed to the League's decline, but the critical development was the resurgence of Denmark, which expelled the League from its territory and seized control of the gateway to the Baltic, the Danish Sound.

By the sixteenth century the League was in a shambles, and the Livonian economy reflected the disarray. Riga collaborated with Reval to block Narva from membership, and sought to set up its own merchants as the exclusive middlemen for Russian trade. This naturally antagonized Lübeck, whose own merchants had formerly bartered directly with the Russians in Novgorod.

Ivan followed the squabble with angry interest. Regardless of who prevailed, the aim was the same: to squeeze the commerce with heavy transit dues. Especially during Ivan's long minority, the burghers had exploited their advantages to the full, while Russia continued to face a Western embargo aimed at repressing her technological development. In a famous incident in 1547, a German entrepreneur, Hans Schlitte, had recruited 123 Western technicians—engineers, architects, physicians, jewelers, and so forth—to serve in Muscovy, but en route through Lübeck he was arrested and his experts admonished and dispersed. All this was happening, too, at a time when unhindered trade with Europe "might have insured Muscovy a favorable balance of trade." It must be said in fact that whatever the machinations of his policy, Ivan apparently made a peaceful effort to secure a coastal outlet, for as late as 1557 he offered Narva the right to establish a *Kontor* across the river in Ivangorod. Narva should have been grateful. But with a kind of ruinous greed, her burghers insisted on the same monopoly Ivan was trying to surmount.

Meanwhile, the lives of the Livonian Brethren had long since ceased to be exemplary. Once content to serve as the "poor soldiers of Christ," they had acquired large estates, hired mercenaries to do their fighting, kept concubines, and pitilessly wrung from the subjugated peasant population of Livs, Letts, and Estonians the wealth they needed to subsidize their luxuries and wars. It is not at all certain that the local population was converted, but it is quite beyond doubt that they were forcibly baptized, butchered, or enserfed.

Throughout the land, ethnic enmity was aggravated by class hatred. Non-Germans were excluded from positions of influence, and after 1500 no one could acquire property who did not already own it. As the establishment grew fat, the typical peasant "counts himself happy," wrote a contemporary, "if he has a bit of bread with his mush, and clean water to drink." Nor were the prosperous content among themselves. The archbishop and the grand master quarreled constantly, and both vied for power with the free-market towns. The Protestant Reformation gnawed away at the ruling classes from within. Livonia's whole reason for being, in fact, disappeared. Originally created as a province of the Holy Roman Empire for the conversion of the heathen under the auspices of the Roman Catholic Church, it was now a mostly Protestant state belonging to an Empire which had ceased to exist. In 1556, in tacit acknowledgment of the emptiness of his titles, Charles V abdicated and divided his realms. Thereafter, the Empire meant little more than a loose federation of the different princes of Germany, lay and ecclesiastical, under the presidency of the House of Austria.

During the confrontation in the 1550s between Sweden and Russia, Gustav Vasa had dispatched a secret agent to Livonia to assess what could be expected from his ally. The agent's report (an up-to-the-minute picture of the situation) must have made old Vasa's eyes roll. Instead of "knightly labor" he had found "much eating and feasting, pomp with costly gems and gowns"; and rather than sturdy warriors, an amazing number who were either alcoholic or physically deformed. He supposed "no mustering had been held in Livonia since time out of mind" and revealed that instead of investing in new armaments or fortifications, the Knights had been smuggling money out of the country into safe overseas accounts.

Moscow's planned intervention naturally occasioned a propaganda blitz. Rival powers in the region also put forth their claims. That of the Germans, incidentally, was neither more nor less old than that of the Danes, who under Waldemar the Magnificent in 1238 had conquered part of Estonia. At about the same time, the Swedes had crossed the Gulf of Finland to secure a beachhead on the Estonian coast. Poland, on the other hand, relied on hoary legalities that established the king as a mediator in Livonian affairs in the event of internal political disputes. But insofar as all such claims had meaning, the Russians carried the day. The *Primary Chronicle* documented that various local tribes had once paid tribute to the Russians (or Varangians) of old, and in 1030 a hill-fort, Yuriev (which evolved into the Livonian town of Dorpat) had been founded by Yaroslav the Wise—two centuries before Bishop Albert established himself at Riga. The first Christian missionaries to proselytize in Livonia had come from Kiev not Riga, and even into the sixteenth century many Livonian towns were familiarly known in Russia by translated Slavic names: Narva as Rugodiv, for example, or Wenden as Kess.

Aside from putting their archivists to work to manufacture titles to the deed, each power sought to locate and court within the country potential allies. Denmark reminded the burghers of her control of the Sound; Poland endeavored to persuade the archbishop of Riga to follow the example of his brother, Duke Albrecht of Prussia, and secularize his "diocese" and enfeoff it to the Crown.[1] Sweden lobbied her cause with Narva and Reval. Russia looked for, and found, expectations of deliverance among the peasantry, based on Ivan's reputation for humbling his lords.

Finally (a factor not to be overlooked), the persecution of Russian merchants in Livonia and the desecration of local Orthodox shrines had fired up the Russian population. "Just wars avenge injuries," so Augustine had written: but times had changed. If the medieval concept of Holy War had meaning for any power in the region, it was no longer to be read in the Red Cross of the Livonian Knights, but in the doctrine of the Third Rome and the banner of the Russian Orthodox Christ. Like Pope Urban II, Ivan was spellbound by the Old Testament God of Hosts and by the military feats of Joshua, Samson, Judas Maccabeus, and Jephtha. Biblical notions of personal election and national destiny had accompanied his eastward march against the infidel, and had glossed his bloody road to Kazan. In Livonia, he faced the apostate Latins, the heretic Lutherans, and the apocalyptic expectations of a downtrodden native population that was prepared to welcome him as a redeemer with open arms. And what a prize he had to gain! A port on the Baltic, a "window on the West"!

A pretext was ready to hand. In 1503, after a border war with Moscow, the grand master had "ransomed the Order from capitulation" with a fifty-year treaty entailing an annual tribute (revived from "of old") to be paid by the bishop of Dorpat. This was supposed to be for certain rights in a territory called the "Honey Meadow"—a belt of wild country between Neuhausen and Pskov. Once upon a time it had been paid in the form of ten pounds of honey. In 1503, it had been converted into a token monetary sum. The Livonians had never bothered to pay it and the Russians had not pressed. Then, in 1554, the treaty expired.

The Livonian ambassadors came to Moscow to renew it for thirty years.

Ivan offered to renew it for fifteen, and then only on condition that (1) the Orthodox in Livonia were allowed freedom of worship, (2) Russian merchants were allowed freedom of trade, and (3) the accumulated debt in tribute was paid in full within three years. This was now fixed at one mark for every inhabitant, with arrears amounting to 50,000 crowns.

The ambassadors professed confusion: what tribute was this? Adashev, who met with them, said: "Your ancestors came to Livonia from beyond the seas, and thus invaded the patrimony of the Russian grand prince. Much blood flowed, and to stop it his forebears in exchange for tribute allowed you Germans to remain. You may not wish to remember this, but it is so."

The Livonians acquiesced, promised to pay, and were compelled to sign a nonaggression pact with Moscow that prohibited them from entering into any anti-Muscovite alliance with Poland. The treaty was nothing but a tactical delay. Everyone knew it—and everyone knew they knew. The border war with Sweden had begun, and Ivan needed time. But he had not failed to tell the ambassadors that he understood what a tiny country Livonia was, and that, though he was not thirsty for blood, he would person- ally come for the tribute if he had to —and as sure of it as if he already held it in his hands.

As expeditiously as he could, Ivan secured for himself considerable free- dom of action. Within the next three years, he had "pacified" Kazan, com- pleted the annexation of Astrakhan, concluded an armistice with Poland (August 6, 1556), and imposed a truce on Sweden (1557). In 1556 and 1557 he had also raided into the Crimea, to further contain the Tartar threat from the south.

Thus, the "Livonian option" formed a continuous background to all the famed initiatives of Ivan's early reign. Those initiatives may even be seen as the deliberate and systematic prelude to what ensued.

Meanwhile, in Livonia the work of self-destruction went on. While Ivan and Gustav Vasa were burning each other's homesteads, Sigismund August of Poland advanced his scheme of linking a secularized Livonia as a vassal duchy to the Polish crown. The archbishop of Riga, Wilhelm of Hohenzol- lern, who thought his brother had done rather well for himself in Prussia, was provisionally chosen to be the future duke. But he was not very popular. Wilhelm von Fürstenberg, the new grand master of the Livonian Order and a kind of old-fashioned knight, opposed the Polish plot, and the result was civil war. The archbishop sent a coded appeal to his brother for 10,000 troops, but it was intercepted and he was arrested for treason. At about the same time, one of Sigismund's envoys was murdered by the grand master's son. The king now intervened, citing (as legal justification) two documents: one, from 1354, in which Emperor Charles IV had appointed the king of Poland protector of the Riga See, the other from 1392, in which the pope had named the king mediator in disputes between the archbishop and the Order. Faced with an attack by Poland, von Fürstenberg capitulated, and on September 5, 1557, at Poswol, signed an interim agreement which imposed a Polish-Lithuanian protectorate on Livonia and committed the Order to an offensive and defensive alliance against Moscow—in explicit violation of the Russo-Livonian accord. Though the pact furnished the practical and legal basis for the king's further intervention in the event of war, it made Russian wrath inevitable. It could even be said that it forced Ivan's hand, to prevent Poland from bringing the whole area within her sphere of influence. Sigismund, however, gambling that a Russian onslaught was almost certainly impending, perhaps hoped the pact would give Ivan pause.

Thus was the stage set for the Livonian War, one of the longest and most complicated wars in Eastern European history.

18.

The Second Wave of Reforms

The Livonian War was to dominate Ivan's foreign relations for the remainder of his reign, and it is in the context of his preparations for it that the so-called Second Wave of Reforms must be viewed.

In 1553, it will be remembered, the Duma had neglected Kazanian affairs, despite imminent tribal uprisings, and had turned instead with enthusiasm to the subject of *kormlenie*. In the intervening years, the government prepared to abolish the system entirely—a development usually understood as the natural and enlightened culmination of the Law Code reforms of 1550.

But these reforms, which imposed restraints on the system, had in no obvious way aimed at its abolition. On the contrary, they had modified and corrected *kormlenie* administration so as to enable it to continue as a viable form of provincial government. Ivan himself had declared that the code, as written, was to stand "for centuries." Such an effort at putting the system on a more solid basis would scarcely have been made if the purpose at the time had been to prepare the way for its demise.

Between the first and second wave of reforms, something had happened. Revenue had increased but (as Lobanov-Rostovsky had anticipated even before the exertions required to complete the pacification of Kazan), not enough to offset the expenditures of recent campaigns. The brief border war with Sweden had been fierce. The Astrakhan venture, and Moscow's attempt to expand its control along the Volga, were continuing strains. The result, evidently, was the bankruptcy of the Central Treasury.

The new reforms emerged in part as another revenue scheme, while the boyars arranged for themselves in the process handsome compensation for giving up their *kormlenie* posts.

The time for this was ripe from every point of view. To begin with, the *kormlenie* governorships of old were no longer the sinecures they'd been. Over the years, the average term of office, territory of jurisdiction, and latitude of action had all been gradually reduced as local revenues had come under closer scrutiny and the magistrate had to reckon with district representatives at every step. Even if he discharged his responsibilities with reasonable competence, a flurry of lawsuits tended to follow him out of office. A new administrative era was inexorably dawning, and the boyars were determined not to be left out. At the same time, residual hatred of the old order conveniently enabled the Duma to draft its new legislation with popular support.

A number of experimental charters, each framed as a response to a local petition, replaced the district governor with a council of locally elected officials. In compensation, the boyars, "coveting wealth"—not justice—in Viskovaty's illuminating phrase, arranged to collect a regular salary from the State Treasury, where the local revenue (once fed upon by them) was now to be deposited safe and sound. To ensure the money got there (and that there was plenty to go around), they granted their replacements a negligible salary and made malfeasance in office punishable by death—a penalty no governor had ever had to face.

What the local community got out of the arrangement was increased self-rule and a kind of tax break, for a portion of the property of convicted felons was credited against the "quitrent" of the district, or its collective tax. That quitrent, however, which replaced the fees and subsistence allotments formerly collected by governors, was considerable (on the average, about a hundred rubles per annum) and represented no discernible amelioration in the economic burden of the folk. Moreover, other revenues traditionally due the tsar still had to be paid in full. Nevertheless, with a fine political flourish, Moscow called the new impost a "redemption tax."

What Moscow got out of the arrangement, in addition to increased revenue, "was the free services of officials who knew local conditions more intimately, and who presumably had a greater personal interest in maintaining law and order than their predecessors." Moreover, high-ranking military servitors, formerly dispersed to administrative seats throughout the realm, were now free to devote their attention more fully to military affairs.

After an experimental period, in 1556 Ivan, "out of pity for the people," he said, declared the new reform general for the nation—except along the frontiers, where military governors remained.

But the boyars paid a price for their gains. In 1550, Ivan had told the *Stoglav* Council that he had undertaken a comprehensive census "to measure and record all resources . . . so I shall know who has been granted what, who needs what, and who renders service on the basis of what resources." Now, six years later, this bore fruit in a decree (issued on September 20, 1556) that established for the first time an explicit and proportional connection between landholding (of whatever kind) and military service. Henceforth anyone who possessed an estate had to provide a fully equipped, mounted man-at-arms for every 400 acres of arable land, with an additional horse for distant campaigns. Any landowner who provided more than his quota was entitled to a cash subsidy; in lieu of service, a landowner had to pay a substantial fine. "Thus," goes a Chronicle summary attributed to Adashev, "nobles and warriors owning much land but performing little service hold their patrimonies against the sovereign's wishes. The sovereign has taken steps to equalize holdings, has surveyed them, has given each his due, and has distributed the surplus among those who lack." Active service was to begin at age fifteen and continue until death or incapacitation. Upon a man's demise, his estate, with all its obligations, was to pass to his sons who, if their divided inheritance came short of the service norm, were entitled to additional land grants and perhaps a monetary salary. Outstanding soldiers could expect a bonus.

Such salaries had to come out of the State Treasury. Obviously both reforms were intertwined. In short, the new system of provincial administration, which replaced *kormlenie*, was designed to pay the debt "for campaigns recently undertaken or upon which the tsardom was about to embark."

19.

"To Subdue and Conquere His Enemies"

Russia's budding trade relations with England were important for her war effort, but they failed to develop as rapidly as Ivan hoped. On the return voyage in 1556, not even Chancellor's expert knowledge and incomparable quadrant could secure the fleet from mercurial weather and the turbulent arctic seas. The *Bona Confidentia* "was seene to perish on a rocke" off the coast of Norway; the *Bona Speranza* vanished without a trace; and the *Bonaventure*, after four months' stormy passage, reached the Bay of Pitsligo on November 7 only to be "dashed to pieces by a tempest on the Aberdeenshire coast." Chancellor, in a valiant effort, sacrificed himself to save Nepea, but seven other members of the embassy drowned. Whatever cargo washed ashore was thoroughly picked over and plundered by the "ravenous" Scots.

The *Philip and Mary* alone survived the voyage, but did not wander into the mouth of the Thames until April 18, 1557.

Nepea, detained for two months in Scotland by an official inquiry, finally reached the outskirts of London on February 27. A mounted escort of "fourscore merchants with chaines of gold and goodly apparell" rode to meet him, and on the following day he was treated to a fox hunt. Afterwards "divers lustie knights, esquiers, gentlemen and yeomen" accompanied him into London proper, where the lord mayor and the city aldermen all in scarlet conducted him to a house in Fenchurch Street. Ivan, rumored already to be "the most rytch prynce of treasour that lyvethe this day on earthe, except the Turk," was well represented by his ambassador whose sumptuous wardrobe included a "nyght cap sett with perles and precious stones."

On March 25, Nepea was presented to the king and queen, and began a round of conferences with their advisers; on England's St. George's Day (April 23), he participated in a service in Westminster Abbey, and on the 29th was honored at a banquet at the Draper's Hall.

Although his dignified solemnity was praised at court, the London merchants sensed trouble ahead. One wrote to a colleague in Moscow: "Hee is very mistrustfull, and thinketh everie man will beguile him; therefore you had need to take heed how you have to doe with him, or with any such, and to make your bargaines plaine." Nepea for his part had reason to be wary. What he had really come for was armaments. What Mary granted was the right to trade with England on the same terms "as other Christians"—a not very generous or even useful concession since the only ships Russia possessed were two-masted *lodia* or flat-bottomed coasting sloops with twenty oars for river navigation. Nevertheless, these privileges were fulsomely set forth in a Latin epistle to the tsar drafted by the rhetorician Roger Ascham.

Behind the scenes, however, Nepea had apparently secured the right to hire technicians, including shipwrights, and a few may have returned with him to Russia in the summer of 1557, perhaps in the guise of Russia Company personnel. Also on board were two coopers to fashion casks for the export of tallow and train-oil; seven rope and cable makers; a furrier; an apothecary; a doctor; and a crossbow maker to scout for yew trees. Their custodian was the new English envoy to Russia, Anthony Jenkinson, who also conveyed two gifts from Mary for the tsar: a suit of parade armor and a pair of lions.

Jenkinson was a most remarkable man—exceptionally capable and fearless, and a great adventurer in an age when many lesser men deserved to be called extraordinary. Still in his thirties, he had, as ad hoc envoy and merchant, already traveled through Flanders, the Netherlands, Germany, Italy, Portugal, and Spain, "sailed through the Levant seas every way," been to Rhodes, Malta, Sicily, and Cyprus, tramped through Greece into Turkey (where he had met the sultan), "passed over the mountains" to Damascus and Jerusalem, and had visited, along the coast of northern Africa, Tripoli, Tunis, and Algiers. On November 4, 1553, when Chancellor was casting anchor in St. Nicholas Bay, Jenkinson was at Aleppo in Syria, to witness "the manner of the entering of Solyman the Great Turke with his armye" into the city, "marching toward Persia against the Great Sophie."

He had survived uncounted perils. Now under his guidance, the four ships he commanded made it safely past the Lofoten Islands, not far from where Willoughby's course had gone fatally astray, steered around a whirlpool that formed a roaring cataract (where a whale was seen to perish with "a pitifull crie"), and survived Svatoy Noss, a headland known for its riptides at the western entrance of the White Sea. Over his head a rainbow appeared in the heavens, "like a semicircle, with both ends upwarde," which seemed to signify divine aid.

From St. Nicholas, Jenkinson ascended the Dvina fifty miles to Kholmogory, lingered to examine the rope walk and the spacious warehouses the company had under construction, then, venturing farther upstream, explored the alabaster rocks and "Pyneaple trees lying there since Noes flood"— probably fossilized logs of fir or larch. After roaming with surprising freedom about the Russian north (sometimes camping out in the wilds), he finally reached Moscow in December, where Ivan's court was aswarm with Tartar chieftains, "men of warre to serve against his enemies," and other signs of a military buildup. In a striking gesture of trust, the English were invited to watch the Muscovites at artillery practice on the outskirts of the capital, which proved something to behold. Two large houses, with targets marked on the sides and filled with earth, were erected at one end of a large field, along with man-sized blocks of ice, two feet thick, ranged in a quarter-mile row. A large and varied arsenal—"faire ordinance of brasse of all sortes"—was brought out, including "canons double and royall," mortars that "shoote wild fire," and six great bombards, all escorted by musketeers marching precisely "five and five," each "carying his gun upon his left shoulder, his match in his right hand." Twice the cannoneers let loose their barrage, "beginning with the smallest and so orderly untill the biggest and last," reducing the houses to smithereens. With equally devastating fire, the musketeers at a signal "began to shoot off at the banke of ice, as though it had bin in any skirmish or battel, and ceased not untill they had beaten it all flat on the ground."

"Now what might be made of these men," Chancellor had wondered a few years before, "if they were trained and broken to order and knowledge of [modern] wars?" The answer was becoming clear.

Perhaps to offset the impression, however, that Ivan was a warmongering prince largely surrounded by barbarians, Jenkinson and his compatriots were also invited to witness him at the pious blessing of the waters (an annual ritual) on the Moscow River, where he stood bareheaded in the bitter wind over a large hole cut in the ice; and on another occasion heard him exalt Metropolitan Makary "to be of higher dignitie then himselfe; for that, saith he, he is Gods spiritual officer, and I his temporall." Moreover, at a royal banquet in their honor, it was observed that near Ivan "was set a Monke all alone" (perhaps Sylvester) "in all points as well served as the Emperour."

The combination of impressions had their effect. One Englishman concluded:

[The tsar] is no more afraid of his enemies than the Hobbie [larkhawk] of the lark. Not onley is he beloved of his nobles and commons, but also held in great dread and feare through all his dominions, so that I thinke no prince

in Christendome is more feared of his owne than he is, nor yet better beloved.
. . . Hee delighteth not greatly in hawking, hunting, or any other pastime,
nor in hearing instruments or musicke, but setteth his whole delight upon
two things: First, to serve God, as undoubtedly he is very devoute in his
religion, and the second, howe to subdue and conquere his enemies.

In fact, Ivan loved hawking, hunting, and music. As to whether or not he
served God one dare not surmise, but that he delighted in conquest is
quite beyond doubt.

20.

The Collapse of Livonia

In November 1557, Russian troops began to assemble on the Russo-Livonian
frontier. On January 22, 1558, they advanced from Pskov and crossed the
border in three columns near Neuhausen. Over the next several weeks
they cut a wide swath through the country with an army that included a
vanguard of 7000 Tartars and 1600 tracking dogs. The general staff was a
composite group: Daniel Adashev, Aleksey Basmanov, and the Crimean
defector Tokhtamysh in the vanguard; Prince Andrey Kurbsky in the rear
guard; with overall command given to Shah-Ali and Ivan's uncle, Mikhail
Glinsky, whose disgrace of a decade before had apparently been erased.
   "And we went through their land," remembered Kurbsky, "fighting on
a front of more than forty miles." On the 23rd, they stood at the gates of
Livonian Marienburg; on the 26th, at Wesenberg. Without attempting to
take the towns, they devastated the northern quarter of the country all
the way to the Gulf of Finland. Mikhail Glinsky was particularly random
in his looting, carting off works of art, bullion, and gold and silver chalices
for the Imperial Treasury.
   In March the Russians came to the port of Narva and began to bombard
it. This was one prize they meant to seize.
   The Livonians appealed for a truce, hastily collected the overdue tribute,
and dispatched an embassy to Ivan as reinforcements hurried to Narva from
Fellin and Reval. The mood of the garrison, thus strengthened, changed

from despair to reckless defiance and shots were fired across the river into Ivangorod, killing a Russian soldier. Ivan canceled the negotiations, rejected the tribute, and resumed the siege. Taking advantage of an outbreak of fire in the town (later attributed to a miracle), the Russians stormed the fortress on May 11, seized the heavy guns that stood on the outer walls, and turned them against the defenders. Under the protection of their fire, they inexorably advanced. After the port capitulated, it was reported that on the previous evening drunken Livonians had broken into the house of a Russian merchant and had flung two icons onto his flaming hearth. "And all that fire struck upwards, and immediately the top of the room caught fire, but there were no traces of fire where the icons had been thrown."

Livonian morale cracked. Syrensk fell on June 6; Neuhausen (after a month-long siege) on June 30. In July the Russians beleaguered Dorpat, where the bishop and others were in clandestine contact with the Russian camp. After reinforcements failed to arrive, the city offered to surrender in return for the preservation of its traditional liberties. This was accepted by the commanding Russian general, and subsequently confirmed by Ivan, who also granted the burghers free trade privileges in Novgorod, Pskov, Ivangorod, and Narva. Resistance dissolved; "the idea of submission took hold." To foster it, the Russians readily exchanged prisoners and prohibited their troops from molesting the population. "A serious effort" was even made to improve the lot of Estonian peasants by supplying them with bread, seed, cattle, and horses, and by converting confiscated estates into communes.

By October 1558, the Russians had captured some twenty fortresses and towns, controlled eastern Livonia, and by their occupation of Narva transformed the world of Baltic commerce almost overnight. Workmen constructed a breakwater and enlarged the harbor installations, as traders from as far away as Antwerp and Marseille, long frustrated by the Livonian middlemen, hastened to trade directly with the Muscovites. In Russia the price of Western imports fell sensationally, as Narva promised to become the chief emporium of East-West trade. At Reval the merchants wept openly onshore as they watched the ships go by. Meanwhile, English shipwrights sent to Muscovy in response to Nepea's embassy began laying the foundations for a Russian merchant marine. In time, they built dockyards not only at Narva, but at Nizhny-Novgorod on the Volga, and later at Vologda and Kholmoghory on the Northern Dvina. At Narva a few merchant vessels were swiftly converted into warships.

A French Protestant in Wittenberg prophetically wrote to the theologian John Calvin: "If any power in Europe is destined to grow it is this one."

In crisis, the Livonian Knights elected a new grand master, Gotthard Kettler, who immediately sought to sell his country to the Poles. However, Reval and the surrounding provinces of Harrien and Wierland preferred to place themselves under Danish protection, and appealed to Denmark's King Christian III to cut off the Narva trade at the Sound. Before he could do anything, Russia invaded again in January 1559, swept through southern Estonia toward Riga, and crossed the Western Dvina into Courland, plundering at will. Christian III dispatched an embassy to Moscow and Ivan, on the advice of Adashev and others, reluctantly agreed to a six-months' armistice, from May to November 1559. However, he also insisted that the back tribute be paid regardless, and that the grand master himself or his adjutant come to Moscow to acknowledge his suzerainty.

In their negotiations the Danish envoys claimed Livonia as a protectorate of their king. Viskovaty scoffed at this and questioned the legitimacy of the embassy itself, since the Livonians, as the tsar's "subjects," had no business appealing to a foreign power. He reminded them of the Russian founding of Dorpat, the history of the tribute at issue, and produced two weighty old tomes with records "beyond the memory of man" to substantiate his tale. Ivan himself was so displeased by Danish presumptions that he facetiously refused the king's gift of a beautiful clock on the grounds that he "believed in God and would have nothing to do with planets and signs."

The German emperor (Livonia's nominal overlord) also sent a delegation, but it was so low-level and ill-equipped that Ivan almost refused to acknowledge it. He scornfully told the envoys that instead of worrying about Livonia, the emperor ought to be trying to regain Hungary from the Turks. Meanwhile, the Imperial Diet raised such a pitiful sum of money for Livonia's defense that Kettler's representative was said to have declined it.

Kettler went to Vilna, not Moscow, as the rest of Livonia began to deliver itself up piecemeal to its Baltic neighbors.

On August 31, 1559, he signed an agreement with King Sigismund August that made Livonia a Lithuanian protectorate, and by September, without much coaxing, the archbishop of Riga was persuaded to go along. Lithuanian troops immediately occupied land along the Western Dvina from Riga to Dünaburg. It deserves to be noted, however, that Sigismund in this instance acted only in his capacity as grand duke of Lithuania, not king of Poland, since the Polish Diet as yet did not wish to commit its resources to the cause. As dual monarch, he had two disparate kingdoms to hold together (and ultimately to unite); and he shrewdly discerned that it was premature to arrange or otherwise enforce a similar treaty between Livonia and Poland because this would come about almost automatically, and on the best possible terms, in reaction to the developing threat from Moscow. His Livonian policy, indeed, was subordinate to his overall strategy for union—to demonstrate to Lithuania and Poland that they needed each other to survive.

Though Sigismund was not yet prepared for a military confrontation with Ivan, in writing to him to protest Russian aggression, he seemed to mock the premise of Viskovaty's lecture to the Danes: "You call Livonia yours. But how was it that the war between Moscow and Livonia at the time of your grandfather was brought to an end by a truce? What ruler concludes a treaty with his subjects?"

In October 1559, an emboldened Kettler broke the cease-fire with Moscow and besieged Dorpat, just as a Crimean raiding party attacked from the south. Fearing a coordinated campaign, Adashev and Sylvester sent an urgent message to Ivan at Mozhaisk, where he had gone with an ailing Anastasia on pilgrimage. The couple hurried back to the capital in a blizzard, only to discover that their exertions had been unnecessary. The garrison in Dorpat had repulsed the Knights; the Tartars vanished into the steppe.

Meanwhile, Christian III of Denmark had been succeeded by his young and ambitious son, Frederick II. Frederick immediately bought the island of Oesel from its bishop (who absconded with the episcopal treasury) and traded it to his younger brother, Magnus, for Holstein, a far more valuable property. Magnus, led to believe that he could build up a dominion of his own in the eastern Baltic, landed on Oesel in the spring of 1560, crossed over to the mainland, purchased the castle of Sonnenburg, and bought out the bishop of Reval. Unfortunately, the alacrity with which he had become a little king himself went to his head, and he recklessly undertook a campaign to extend his authority along the littoral.

Now, at this time, a number of the south-central provinces which today form part of Sweden belonged either to Denmark or to Norway, which was subject to the Danes. Thus Denmark controlled the southern Baltic and every one of its outlets—the Great and Little Belt, as well as the Sound. Sweden, on the other hand, held only a narrow strip of coastline a few miles wide at the mouth of Gota Alv to the west. Her dominions therefore opened toward the east where, across from the Gulf of Finland, she now beheld a Danish duke trying to stake his claim.

Fearing encirclement by her historic foe, Sweden began to concentrate on acquiring Reval. Meanwhile, Russian operations in Livonia in the spring and summer of 1560 resulted in the complete military collapse of the Order. Marienburg fell in February; Weissenstein was besieged in March, where in a nearby battle one hundred and seventy German officers were captured. In April, the Russians surrounded Fellin—with three stone inner citadels, wide, deep moats, some 450 cannon in mint condition, and houses sheathed in lead—probably the strongest fortress in Livonia. But morale was desperately low; and though von Fürstenberg, the garrison commander, tried to rally his men by promising them the whole of his private fortune, after a three-week siege their will to fight was spent.

The fall of Fellin occasioned the second major miracle-legend of the war, which attributed the victory to Our Lady of Pechery, an icon copied from Our Lady of Vladimir and belonging to a monastery near Pskov.

At about this time, Ivan (perhaps inspired by Sigismund's use of Kettler) began testing the idea of setting up a puppet Livonian regime. His first candidate was the captive von Fürstenberg, Kettler's predecessor. But the knight refused to cooperate. Ivan told him, "Do you not see that we have the power?" to which he replied, "I have sworn an oath to the Holy Roman Empire and I will live and die by it." Ivan accepted this, and eventually settled him comfortably in the town of Lyubim in Kostroma, northeast of Moscow.

From Fellin the Muscovite army advanced on Ermes. In May, Aleksey Adashev departed for the front with a train of heavy artillery; on August 2, the Landmarschall of the Order, Philip von Bell, boldly sauntered out of the fortress to challenge what he supposed to be a modest Russian incursion. Almost at once enveloped by the Muscovite host, he was captured by Adashev's squire and his troops were annihilated.

In captivity the Landmarschall charmed and impressed the Russian generals, who commended him to the tsar. But Ivan, "who had already begun to be fierce and inhuman" (or at least tired of valiant Livonian knights) had him tortured and executed.

With the demise of the Order, Latvian peasants rose in revolt against their German overlords; farmers volunteered to help the Russians as scouts; various elements within the ruling elite scrambled to ingratiate themselves with the invader before it proved too late. Some fortresses capitulated without a fight. Pro-Russian sentiment among the Livonian populace was strong as the invader roamed unhindered over the countryside.

Nevertheless, as long as the two principal harbors of Riga and Reval remained outside his grasp, Ivan was not likely to be recognized as ruler of the country; while the Russian victories served to spur the active intervention of other powers. Lithuania mobilized; Reval, disappointed with Denmark, turned to Gustav Vasa of Sweden for some arrangement that would bring the city under his protection. And though Gustav died before he could respond, his son and successor, Erik XIV, immediately occupied the city. Ivan anticipated war between Poland and Sweden; Sigismund, war between Sweden and Russia. Denmark awaited the results of another embassy to Moscow, while the German Empire made ineffectual pronouncements from afar. In the suspended animation of these powers, Erik, swept west along the coast in the fall of 1561 and took Padis, Leal, and Pernau. These strongholds could be protected and resupplied by his navy, which now operated out of a powerful triangle of bases at Stockholm-Abo-Reval. Indeed, if the Volga could be called a "Russian river," and the Sound a "Danish strait," Erik could almost claim the Gulf of Finland as a "Swedish stream."

The next twist was inevitable. By a treaty concluded at Vilna and signed in March 1562, both the Order and the Archbishopric of Riga were secularized, Kettler was made hereditary duke of Courland, to be held as a Polish fief, and Riga and its environs submitted directly to King Sigismund, who styled himself accordingly "Sovereign of Livonia."[1]

Russia immediately countered by recognizing Danish claims to Oesel, Courland, and part of Estonia, and by a Russo-Danish accord of economic cooperation that promised to frustrate efforts by other Western powers to mount a Narva blockade. On September 15, 1562, Viskovaty left for Copenhagen at the head of a large delegation.

But he could scarcely reverse the trend of events. The partition of Livonia into four occupied zones—with Russia holding the eastern portion, Denmark staked out on Oesel, Sweden in possession of Reval and northern Estonia, and Poland-Lithuania occupying the southwest—meant that by the latter part of 1562, instead of a weak Order and a disinterested Empire, Ivan faced three comparatively strong opponents, who were all bound to forestall further Russian conquests.

21.

Turning Point

Ivan blamed the swiftly developing complications in the war on the untimely truce he had been persuaded to accept in 1559. He believed (and tactically speaking he was probably right) that it had arrested Russian momentum and allowed the enemy to regroup. He held Adashev, Sylvester, and others responsible, and unfortunately his simmering feud with these advisers coincided with a fatal decline in the tsaritsa's health.

By all accounts, including his own, Ivan's marriage to Anastasia had been a happy one. In sickness or in health, his "little heifer," as he once affectionately called her, was often by his side, and their arduous, postnuptial midwinter trek together on foot to Holy Trinity Monastery had proved emblematic of their solidarity in love. Together they had six children—Anna, Maria, Dmitry, Ivan, Evdokia, and Fyodor (born May 31, 1557)—but only Ivan and Fyodor survived past the age of two.

Tradition ascribes to Anastasia beauty, wisdom, and grace. Ivan "being young and riotous," it was said, "she ruled him with admirable affability and wisdom." One contemporary relates that she was "benign and bore no malice towards anyone"; another, that she was "honored, beloved, and feared of all her subjects" for her "holiness, virtue and government." Formulaic as such eulogies may sound, a huge crowd apparently turned out to mourn her at her funeral.

Oddly enough, though one might have supposed Adashev and Sylvester her natural allies, they ostracized her, apparently for some indiscretion— Ivan said bitterly, for "one single little word."

What remarkable word that was we cannot know. But the crisis of 1553 had revealed a profound antagonism between certain Chosen Council members and her family, and doubtless Anastasia shared in Ivan's resentment at any interference in their domestic life.

That life, however exalted, had not been an easy one, for aside from the ceremonial demands of being a tsaritsa, relentless parturitions coupled with nearly continual grief from losing her children gradually sapped her strength. The program Ivan prescribed for her recovery, under Sylvester's guidance, may be divined from the therapy recommended in the *Domostroy:* "If God send any disease or ailment down upon a person, let him cure himself through the grace of God, through tears, prayer, fasting, charity to the poor, and true repentance." The pilgrimage by the couple to Mozaisk in October 1559 (where Ivan received word the Livonians had broken the truce) typified the cure. Unduly alarmed, and notwithstanding Anastasia's fragile condition, they had hastened back to Moscow through snow and freezing rain, as the truce violations flared and expired. Anastasia, however, never recovered, and fell into the grip of some wasting disease. Rashly, Sylvester tried to explain her decline as a divine chastisement for Ivan's "disobedience" to the council (or rather, its antiwar faction) in pursuing the Livonian War. Immediately, however, he realized he had gone too far and sought sanctuary in the White Lake Monastery. Subsequently Ivan supposed his wife had been poisoned, or bewitched, and accused Sylvester of complicity.

Adashev's influence was also fading fast. Though the tsar was loath to do without his considerable gifts, he was unwilling to abide his advice, and in the summer of 1560 appointed him governor of Fellin, a post of semiexile. Unfortunately, Adashev's tremendous popularity there, combined with his original opposition to the war, convinced the tsar that he was an enemy sympathizer even though his reputation for justness might have done much to convince the Livonians of Russian goodwill. Ivan's fear of subversion, however, was uppermost, and in July it was exacerbated by another Kremlin fire that forced Anastasia's evacuation to the village of Kolomenskoe, where she died on August 7, 1560.

In late September a joint council of Church and Duma convened to try Sylvester and Adashev on various trumped-up charges, including witchcraft. The assembly was packed with their opponents (Vassian Toporkov among them), and neither was allowed to appear on his own behalf. This brought a protest from Makary, even though he was about to behold the annihilation of the most powerful Non-Possessor faction remaining in the realm. He declared: "They ought to be brought here to face their accusers, and we ought to hear what they have to say."

His opinion was disregarded. Adashev, taken in chains to Dorpat, was either poisoned or committed suicide there in December. Sylvester, deported to the Solovetsky Monastery, died an unknown death.

Others close to them, such as Aleksey's brother Daniel, were summarily executed, and Dmitry Kurlyatev, a probable member of the Chosen Council (but one of the last to take the oath of allegiance in 1553), was later murdered at the tsar's behest.

Despite his personal bereavement at Anastasia's loss, Ivan at once began to consider how a second, foreign marriage could assist his affairs of state. His threefold aim was to advance his prospects in Livonia, enhance his international prestige, and preempt an untimely contest among boyar families hoping to promote one of their nubile relations to be his bride. Accordingly, deputations were sent to Lithuania, Sweden, and Circassia: to Lithuania (speaking politically) in order to check the king's Livonian policy and perhaps facilitate new gains for Muscovy on the frontier; to Sweden, to encourage a satisfactory arrangement in Estonia and security on Russia's northwestern flank; and to Circassia to obtain additional Tartar allies in the Caucasus against the Crimeans.

A Lithuanian marriage had the most appeal but was clearly far-fetched. Sigismund August had two unmarried sisters, Anna and Katerina; and though Ivan's envoy hoped to court the latter, the king allowed him only a fleeting opportunity to peep at her one Sunday out of a little window across from the cathedral where she attended Mass. The Swedes proved equally unenthusiastic; and on August 21, 1561, Ivan married the Circassian Princess Kucheney, rechristened Maria, whose father had already sworn allegiance to Ivan in 1558, and whose baptized brother, Mikhail, was fighting at the head of a Tartar contingent in the Livonian War.

Ivan's foreign marriage may have spared the court prenuptial intrigue, but Maria, not unlike Elena Glinskaya, was soon resented as an outsider by the aristocracy as a whole, and her allegedly wild, cruel, and dissolute behavior established a very different atmosphere at court. An ominous and prophetically inscrutable note was also struck when as a security measure Ivan decreed that on the day of his wedding "no person (certeine of his householde reserved)" was to be allowed into the streets.

Historians customarily divide Ivan's reign into two parts: the first, "good" period—extending from his coronation to the death of Anastasia and the fall of the Chosen Council—as distinguished by far-sighted foreign policy initiatives and enlightened domestic reforms; and its bloody, tyrannical sequel, with all that has yet to be unfolded in our tale. In this, historians take their cue from Ivan's earliest biographers and from Ivan himself, who sometimes blamed his subsequent cruelties on Anastasia's death. "If only you had not taken her from me," he would write, vaguely accusing the Chosen Council, "there would have been no sacrifices to Cronus." However, Ivan's documented inclination to cruelty was already long-standing, while his policies can scarcely be so plainly characterized. If a division must be made, it might (with much qualification) be said that the early part of Ivan's reign was largely preoccupied with the religious duties of a divinely ordained monarch, as reflected in the program of the Chosen Council; the second, obsessed with the dimensions of his secular power. Unfortunately, this corresponded on the one hand with his willingness to be guided and on the other with his "emancipation," so that in all things his will was at last his own. Ultimately, Ivan theologized his power in a way that gave eschatological sanction to his tyranny.

Giles Fletcher the Elder, sometime English ambassador to Russia and a close student of Ivan's career, was to write in *The Rising to the Crowne of Richard the Third*:

Blood and revenge did hammer in my head,
Unquiet thoughts did gallop in my braine:
I had no rest till all my friends were dead,
Whose helpe I usede the kingdome to obtaine.
My dearest friend I thought not safe to trust,
Nor skarse my selfe, but that perforce I must.

He wrote of Richard, but he wrote of Ivan too.

As sovereign Ivan had every right to disband the Chosen Council and to dispense with, and even execute, its membership; but in doing so he afterward acted, and reacted, as one who had overthrown a legitimate government and usurped the throne. Though certainly by 1557 (if not before) Ivan was master at the helm, he had governed so long under guidance that he was psychologically assailed by a kind of insidious doubt as to the legitimacy of what he had done. And in subsequent anguished (and belligerent) reaffirmations of his "divine rights" as a monarch can be heard a kind of protesting too much. Though no one in Russia really questioned his lineage, like any usurper he seems to have felt the need almost to prove his royal line; while in his contest with the hereditary aristocracy, the fact that the House of Rurik, as ennobled by a bogus mythology, was repudiated by the rest of Europe, added a psychological twist to his frantic search for security. Formerly afraid of advisers meeting behind his back, after 1560 Ivan "lived in great danger and fear of treasons," wrote one contemporary, "which he daily discovered, and spent much tyme in the examinacion, torteringe, and execution of his subjects."

Forestalled by the military stalemate in Livonia, the tsar tried to advance his interests there by resuming Muscovy's perennial war of conquest along the Lithuanian frontier. This time the target was Polotsk, a key border fortress on the Western Dvina and, historically, the "gateway to the Kingdom." On November 30, 1562, Makary (who opposed the Livonian War but shared his monarch's obsession with "gathering in" the historic Russian lands) received Ivan in the Cathedral of the Assumption to bless the campaign, while a Muscovite army of 50,000 assembled at Mozhaisk and marched to Veliky Luki, the staging point for the attack. From there, the troops fanned out through the woods, but in a near fiasco they became entangled with the supply train. Enraged, the tsar on some pretext slew a prince in his own retinue with a mace. The Lithuanians, however, failed to take advantage of the confusion—apparently refusing to believe the Russians were coming. Suddenly they were there. Heavy artillery smashed the outer fortress walls, forcing the garrison to retreat to the upper citadel, where the guns, now advanced to within the perimeter of the town, relentlessly bombarded the defenders. Fires broke out which could not be quenched. On February 15, 1563, Polotsk surrendered.

Muscovite propaganda justified the campaign on a number of grounds, including the tsar's sacred obligation to extirpate the "Lutheran heresy" from Russian soil. Ivan didn't find many Lutherans in Polotsk, but he did find Jews, who faced death if they would not convert. Three hundred heroically refused and were drowned in the Western Dvina.

Sigismund's failure to relieve the siege may be connected to a crisis developing at the time among the other Baltic powers. That crisis had its germ in Sweden, where Erik XIV, a brilliantly endowed but tragically unhappy monarch, whose self-torturing ways were to inspire Shakespeare's *Hamlet*, had become embroiled in a mortal duel with his brother Johan that threatened the very destruction of his realm.

Erik's three half-brothers—Johan, Magnus, and Karl—had each inherited an independent duchy. Though bound by their father's testament to remain faithful to the crown, they were "not warmly attached to one another," to put it mildly, and even before his coronation Erik had persuaded the *Riksdag* or national assembly to radically curtail their powers. There was a kind of suppressed ferocity in the formal proclamation which the royal herald read out: "This be known unto all loyal inhabitants of Sweden, that *one* is our king, the illustrious Prince and Lord Erik XIV; and though ye may see more crowns than one, ye must not think that they be royal. *One* is king of the Swedes, Vandals and Goths."

Nevertheless, Johan as mighty duke of Finland pursued his own foreign policy, and imagining (like Denmark's Magnus) that he could carve out a principality for himself from the Livonian mess, had conducted secret negotiations with Kettler even as Erik was evicting the Knights from a string of Estonian ports. When Kettler submitted to Poland, Johan followed his lead and sought a Polish bride. Erik, on the other hand, decided on a policy of accommodation with Moscow and pursued the hand of Elizabeth of England, crowned in 1558. Erik at first had better luck. Though he was prepared, if necessary, to assassinate Robert Dudley, the queen's reputed paramour— or challenge him to a duel, in a scenario that cast his fainthearted adviser, Nils Gyllenstierna, as proxy—by the summer of 1561 his prospects seemed so bright that as he set sail for England, London woodcuts already showed him enthroned by Elizabeth's side. Stormy weather, however, defeated his connubial hopes as he zigzagged for weeks about the *Skaggerak*.

Other such disappointments followed as throughout his reign Erik's failure to find a suitable, strategic match—despite subsequent approaches to Poland, Saxony, Mecklenburg, Hesse, and Scotland—contributed to political disarray within his realm. But it was the marriage of Johan to Sigismund's sister, Katerina, the recent object of Ivan's designs, that had a critical impact on state affairs.

Sigismund promoted the marriage, both to restrain Erik's rapprochement with Moscow (which also dismayed the Danes), and to link Poland to Sweden's naval power. But when Erik wavered, Johan defied him and hurried to Vilna in October 1561, where he celebrated his marriage to Katerina and lent Sigismund a small fortune, for which he received in pledge seven castles in Livonia. One of them, Weissenstein, was surrounded by Erik's troops. Obviously, Johan's technical possession of it was Sigismund's last best hope for its defense. Erik took it anyway and got the *Riksdag* to condemn his brother for treason.

Johan and Katerina sought refuge in Abo Castle on the Gulf of Finland. Erik stormed the citadel on August 12, 1563, captured the couple and interned them in Gripsholm. Scores of Johan's confederates were hanged, and Finland was "confiscated" for the crown.

Sigismund immediately forged an alliance against Sweden with Frederick II of Denmark in an agreement that abrogated the Russo-Danish accord—and the day after Abo capitulated, a Danish herald delivered Frederick's declaration of war in Stockholm.

Frederick quartered the Three Crowns of Sweden in the Danish shield. Erik, in response, incorporated the Danish Three Lions in his standard.

Thus began, as a "sideshow" to the Livonian War, the Seven Years' Northern War (1563–1570)—a remarkably futile conflict that sapped the strength of all belligerents to no gain. Russia, with nothing to lose, remained aloof from the fighting while opening her Baltic harbor to all nations, as the contradiction of interests between her various antagonists repeatedly frustrated efforts to mount an effective embargo on the Narva trade.

Ivan was now "at the apex of his power. He had an outlet to the sea at Narva, held much of the eastern half of Livonia, and had hewn for himself a commercial and military road to the Western Dvina," which flowed directly to Riga, the largest Livonian port on the Baltic. Moreover, the Northern War had neutralized the potentially disastrous coalition against him in the West.

Heroic iconography expanded across the walls of the Kremlin palace and cathedrals. In 1563–1564, a gallery joining Ivan's residence to the Cathedral of the Annunciation was adorned with haloed portraits of Moscow sovereigns from Daniel I through Vasily III, and in 1564–1565, the whole Russian imperial house (beginning with Caesar Augustus) was frescoed on murals and pillars in the Cathedral of the Archangel Michael. At this time, Ivan also devised a new State Seal, recasting the insignia of his forebears into a Seal of Empire. On one side a dragon-slaying knight in armor—representing Moscow—was centrally and impressively depicted on the breastplate of a double-headed eagle. The eagle's heads were spanned by a single crown, and the whole image encircled by twelve territorial medallions or seals, arranged clockwise to correspond to their sequence in Ivan's title. A thirteenth seal, surmounting them all, depicted a three-beamed cross with the skull of Adam on Calvary. The three beams stood for the Three Romes of Christian history, and the cross itself (established by the *Stoglav* Council in answer to Ivan's eighth question, "What should the form of the Cross be?") for the Orthodox Christian Empire. On the reverse, likewise encircled by twelve territorial seals,[1] was depicted a unicorn, signifying the power of the righteous (Deuteronomy 33:17 and Psalm 92:10), and perhaps universal dominion: "And his horns are like the horns of unicorns: with them he shall push the people together to the ends of the earth." The two inscriptions read: "The banner of Christ gives honor to the Christians," and "Jesus Christ, the King of Salvation, reigns—Calvary leads to Paradise."

Yet, another reality was unfolding behind the scenes. To begin with, Ivan's Livonian intrigues were not panning out. In the fall of 1563, he made contact with a certain Count Artz who controlled the castles Sigismund had pawned to Johan for his loan. Erik and Sigismund both claimed them, but Artz offered to sell them to the tsar; and on November 8, 1563, confirmed the deal. Unwilling to tolerate their loss, the Poles captured Artz, brought him to Riga, and had him publicly torn apart with iron hooks. None of the castles fell into Ivan's hands. Disappointed, he plotted revenge. In January 1564, after negotiations with Poland had concluded, according to tradition, with an exchange of insults and impossible demands, Russian troops from Polotsk and Smolensk converged on Minsk to the south. But near Vitebsk one regiment was ambushed and, driven south toward Chasniki, wiped out on the banks of the Ula River. Units marching to meet it were annihilated near Orsha.

These setbacks took place against a background of deepening domestic turmoil and personal loss. On November 24, 1563, Ivan's brother Yury died, and one month later, the venerable Metropolitan Makary.

Toward the end of his life Makary had exerted little influence over the tsar, but in May 1563, he interceded with him on behalf of Vladimir Staritsky and his mother Evfrosinia, who had been denounced and arrested. Though a trial was averted, Staritsky's retainers were disarmed and replaced by Kremlin spies; and in August, Evfrosinia took the veil.

On December 3, Ivan visited the dying hierarch. They reminisced together about the metropolitan's long and illustrious career, but despite the lingering affection between them, when Makary asked (on the 21st) to be allowed to die at the monastery of his novitiate, Ivan refused. On December 31, Makary was dead.

His successor, promptly chosen by the tsar and confirmed by a Church Council in February 1564, was Afanasy, Makary's protégé and the archpriest of the Chudov Monastery. Formerly called Andrey, he had been the tsar's confessor since 1550, and (it is conjectured) chief editor of the *Book of Degrees*. As metropolitan, he would be the first to don the white cowl "with the cherubim sewn on each shoulder."

The mantle was to prove a heavy one to wear.

22.

Sacrifices to Cronus

The Chosen Council and its allies had constituted a bridge within the government between various factions and interests, especially in mediating between the nobility and the tsar. It had helped to strengthen the monarchy, but it had also helped restrain it. As a composite group, made up of lord and gentry, lowborn and high, its art of government had combined striking initiative with broad compromise. In the wake of its demise came polarization and strife. Long-standing issues between the sovereign and his nobles over their respective rights and prerogatives were resurrected anew. Ivan stood upon his lineage and divine right to rule; they idealized the vanished era of their independent princedoms, while having before them the "progressive" example of contemporary Poland, where the magnates, in a "democracy of nobles," had so reduced the style and power of the king as to make him almost a first among equals.

Though inconceivable in Muscovy, such a spectacle sharpened the aristocracy's awareness, by contrast, of how much their dignity had declined.

Nor was the end of that decline in sight. Like other sixteenth-century monarchs, Ivan had allied himself with the rising gentry, who shared an interest in breaking down the bastions of wealth and privilege in favor of a strong centralized state. As a youth, he had helplessly watched certain families "wax mightie and enlarge themselves," but once enthroned had begun "by degrees to clip of their greatnes, and to bring it down to a lesser proportion." With the help of the Chosen Council, he transformed their holdings into service tenure estates; obliged many to find peers willing to guarantee their loyalty by posting bond; confiscated all property bought or sold by princes during his minority, on the grounds that they had neglected to secure the throne's permission; and in 1562 decreed that the land of anyone without male heirs was to escheat to the tsar, "who would provide a life portion for the widow, dowries for the daughters, and prayers for the deceased." He encouraged precedence disputes; "made advantage [among the aristocrats] of their malice and contentions, the one against the other, by receiving devised matter [slander] and accusations of secret practise and conspiracies to be intended against his person and state," so that in punishing individuals for treason, he "cut them off with the good liking of the rest."

But though Ivan enjoyed a kind of tyranny over individuals, in ruling jointly with his boyar and Church councils he increasingly chafed over the limitations of his power. Particularly with respect to the imperatives of precedence, no slow promotion of comparatively lowborn gentry through the ranks could, within his own lifetime, replace the boyars in sufficient numbers so as to place the administration of policy under the direction of a true civil-servant class. This situation was intolerable to him—for autocratic, not "progressive," reasons: he wanted people who would do his will.

Accordingly, he began to surround himself with sycophants and flunkies—men who, "kissing his fingers and wallowing at his feet, flatter and placate him in every way." Clergymen began to "show too much indulgence to him," wrote a dissident. "No one intercedes, but all seek to get rich. And if any man is faithful to the Lord and speaks the truth, he is imprisoned, tortured, and killed." He grew more licentious, was apparently drinking heavily, and in keeping with a certain developing addiction to masked balls, began to show his talent for theatrical executions. One victim, Prince Mikhail Repnin, a member of the Duma, had publicly rebuked him for his unseemly behavior. A few days later, as Repnin stood in church during an all-night reading of the Gospel, he was slain "at the very altar like an innocent lamb of God." That same night another noble, Prince Yury Kashin, was slain "on his way to Matins."

At about this time, Prince Dmitry Obolensky (the scion of a venerable house) reproached Fyodor Basmanov (the son of Aleksey Basmanov, one of Ivan's generals) for his homosexual relationship with the tsar. Fyodor "went in tears" to Ivan about it, and shortly thereafter Obolensky was invited to a banquet where Ivan pressed him, in a friendly manner, to down a carafe of wine—"to show how he valued the tsar's health." He drank what he could, but not enough. Ivan helpfully suggested he descend to the wine cellar to select a vintage of his choice. By prearrangement, assassins lay in wait among the casks.

In more edifying diversions, so the Chronicles recount, he once got his Privy Council drunk as scribes secretly recorded the jokes, songs, obscenities, and other things they said. The next morning he showed them copies and "the modest men marvelled" at what they read. Nor could Ivan refrain from occasionally unmasking flunkies for what they were. After two members of the Russian nobility, Osip Shcherbatov and Yury Boriatynsky, were obtained from Poland in a prisoner exchange, Ivan threw a banquet for them, gave them gifts, drank their health, and asked them about the situation in Poland. Shcherbatov replied honestly, but Boriatynsky, "who wanted to be considered an expert on Polish affairs, made all sorts of reckless allegations"—for example, that "the Polish king was timid, and so fearful of the power of the Prince of Muscovy that he did not know which way to turn." After the banquet, Ivan went up to Boriatynsky and said, "Come now, tell me again how much the Polish king is afraid of me." As Boriatynsky began to repeat himself, Ivan shouted, "Liar!" and beat him to his knees.

Ivan was right. The king was not afraid. He was waiting. And beyond the issues of autocracy versus privilege, or the tsar's alarming personal behavior, the prospect of fighting a large-scale and protracted war in the west, while having to contend with the Tartar threat from the south, more objectively animated the conflict between the tsar and an increasingly broad cross-section of the establishment. For though in his struggle for Livonia Ivan may have had history on his side, insofar as he anticipated the Baltic Wars of Peter the Great, that did not make his policy wise, or the time of its prosecution right. The war was a tremendous gamble, technologically feasible as a limited, but not unlimited, war. On the one hand, despite continuing Western attempts at embargo, Russia had considerable armament expertise, the latest weaponry and equipment, first-rate cannon foundries in Moscow, and natural resources that were enviable. Copper and tin had to be imported, but in northern Russia, iron was mined, refined, smelted, and forged, and as the war continued, production increased, with English metallurgists helping industrialists like the Stroganovs to locate new deposits of the ore. Saltpeter was produced in quantities sufficient for export beyond domestic needs, and it is worth observing (in an age that continues to be obsessed by the idea of Russia's perennial technological dependence on the West) that the development of advanced weaponry was probably indigenous. The Russian musket, though crude, was unique; and the largest bombard of the sixteenth century was the "Great Mortar of Moscow" which had a 36-inch bore, weighed over 14,000 pounds, and could fire a stone projectile weighing a ton. In the Kazan campaign, Ivan had proven his familiarity with time-honored military technology like siege towers and sapping, in combination with up-to-date methods of trench warfare and the use of explosives. Moreover, he had stockpiled his cannon and munitions as assiduously as any Renaissance king. In his principal arsenal, the great "artillerie house at Musko," one contemporary beheld "all sorts of great ordnance," and declared: "No prince of Christendom hath better store."

All of Ivan's cannon, incidentally, were embossed with double-headed eagles and bore proper names. When any were captured, he "immediately ordered new ones cast with the same names and symbols, to show that fate could take nothing from him that he could not replace."

Nevertheless, the character of the Muscovite army reflected priorities other than the arms race. At least until 1558, the principal enemy had been the Tartar, against whom heavy artillery was virtually useless. The large cannon was a siege weapon. Only one Tartar city had ever been near enough to bombard, and that was Kazan. But mobile steppe warfare was a continuous reality, and even after the development of field artillery, which the Russians were not slow to acquire, the bows and sabers of the cavalry militia decided the outcome in the feathergrass and plains.

Ivan's military expenditures took this into account, as did those of Sigismund August, who also had to face the Tartars in the Ukraine.

Western Europe had nothing like the Tartars with which to deal. Nor, for that matter, did the Turks, whose military machine was the most sophisticated and modern in the world. What the Turks and the West had in common was a numerical and strategic emphasis on the new infantry, equipped with handguns and pikes. The opposite was true in the army of Ivan IV, where the ratio of cavalry to infantry was never less than three to one. Though his standing force of *streltsy* or musketeers grew from 3000 to about 10,000 during his reign, it was impossible for him to simultaneously maintain a massive cavalry militia along the steppe frontier, and a modern infantry army on the Western front.

By and large Ivan tried to make up the difference with mercenaries. On the eve of his invasion of Livonia it was noted that he "retaineth and well rewardeth all strangers that come to serve him, and especially men of warre." Eventually he acquired entire regiments of Scandinavians, Germans, and Scots. Together with the Tartars, they comprised perhaps a fifth of his total force.

Doubts about the wisdom of the Livonian War (which now included war with Lithuania) had not perished with Adashev, Sylvester, and others, and by the end of 1563 both the Church hierarchy and the Duma had broken with Ivan on his conduct of both foreign and domestic affairs. Ivan surmised treason, especially after the two staggering defeats at Chasniki and Orsha, which seemed to suggest that the Lithuanians had been tipped off in advance.

It may have been so. The recent executions and repression had confused and demoralized officials of the army and administration, and Lithuania, the perennial sanctuary of the disaffected nobility, began to beckon with open arms. Among the first to defect was Andrey Kurbsky, a great prince and boyar of the Yaroslavl line who had been loyal to Ivan in the succession crisis of 1553 and had accompanied him that summer on his ill-fated pilgrimage to the monasteries of the north. A probable member of the Chosen Council circle, he had also been Ivan's sometime intimate companion, for it is apparent from their subsequent correspondence that they had discussed everything together from women to theology.

A scholarly intellectual (like Ivan) with a particular feeling for Church literature, Kurbsky had made his mark as a soldier, both as a hero of the Kazan campaign and in the Livonian War. His service record was second to none. He had been gravely wounded twice (in 1552 and 1554) fighting the Kazanians and Cheremis; in 1556 had directed the mobilizations at Kaluga and Kashira on the southern frontier; and in January 1558 had commanded the rear guard in the invasion of Livonia. That summer, together with Daniel Adashev, he also led the vanguard in the siege of Neuhausen, which fell on June 30, after three weeks. In the winter of 1558–1559, he was back at Kaluga; and in the spring of 1560 at Dorpat, where Ivan had sent him "to put fresh heart into my troops." From Dorpat he went to Veliky Luki, early in 1562, to help prepare for a sweep into Lithuania, and in June carried out a successful raid on Vitebsk. In August, however, he was defeated in the Battle of Nevel, where, according to a Polish chronicler, a large division under his command was pathetically routed by a much smaller force. Nevertheless, in the campaign of 1562–1563 against Polotsk, Kurbsky commanded the rear guard. In March 1563, however, the tsar shook up his military high command and Kurbsky was abruptly "banished" to Dorpat as "governor," an assignment indicating disgrace. We know its meaning in part because Mikhail Morozov, Kurbsky's successor there, was revealingly taunted by another émigré: "Your governorship is no better than my monkhood was [after I was forcibly tonsured]. You were governor for five years in Smolensk, and now your Sovereign has presented you with Dorpat. And your wife and child have been taken hostage, and you have no salary, but must survive on loans." During his brief tenure there Kurbsky too survived on loans, probably obtained through his friend, the Elder Vassian Muromtsev, of the Pskov-Pechery Monastery. At this time he wrote several letters to Muromtsev condemning the new corruption at court and, as he put it, the "threatened thunderings from Babylon" (meaning Moscow) against him, which Muromtsev understood to mean "the evil plans of the Grand Duke to kill him." After the failure of the Artz plan (which he had negotiated), Kurbsky knew his fate was sealed, for his name was omitted altogether from the new list of military appointments. Secretly, he opened negotiations with King Sigismund, and waited for his safe-conduct to arrive.

On April 30, 1564, it came. With twelve others he fled across the border to the Lithuanian outpost of Wolmar, where he was met by at least three other prominent émigrés: Artemy, the former "heretical" abbot of Trinity Monastery who had escaped from prison a few years before and in exile had proved a rock of the Orthodox faith; and two former artillery captains, Timofey Teterin and Mark Sarykhozin. From Wolmar he rode to Vilna, where Sigismund welcomed him with open arms. To show what other defectors could hope for, the king immediately enriched him with several large estates.

Meanwhile, at Wolmar, Kurbsky had dashed off a letter to the tsar accusing him of murdering his best generals ("the commanders given to you by God"), of witch-hunting ("falsely accusing the Orthodox of treachery and magic"), of torturing his subjects with "red-hot pincers, needles driven under the nails,"[1] white-hot pans and stoves, and of profaning his holy Orthodox churches with the blood of martyrs. He reminded Ivan, too, that he had sacrificed his entire youth to his service—"in far-distant towns have I stood in arms against your foes, suffered many wants and illnesses and wounds, and little have I seen my parents, and my wife have I not known"— yet had been marked for destruction. In closing, he appealed for the intercession of the Virgin, the Saints, and the elect, including his own sainted ancestor and paternal grandfather to the ninth degree, Prince Fyodor Rostislavich, "whose corpse remains imperishable, emits sweet odours, and pours forth miraculous healing streams, as you, O tsar, know well."

There is a legend that Kurbsky entrusted this fierce indictment to his faithful servant Vaska Shibanov. Shibanov delivered it to the tsar, who at once transfixed his foot with the iron tip of his staff, and leaning on it ordered him to read the letter aloud. In fact, Shibanov had been caught at the border and executed; but the legend accords with the ferocity of Ivan's reaction and the reputation he had begun to acquire.

Stunned, Ivan drafted a remarkable 28,000-word rebuttal that included a defense of autocracy and intimate revelations about the unhappiness of his childhood. In passing, he displayed an extraordinary command of Biblical and patristic quotation worthy of his mentor, the bibliophile Makary, but mingled them in an eccentric way with learned allusions to Greek mythology and other material in a tumult of impressions, images, and ideas. Although his method was to "prove through Scripture, so that the quoted Scripture stood in the forefront," the mélange was delivered in a highly distinctive style—witty, sarcastic, sometimes rambling and self-consciously rhetorical, yet also marked by daring paradoxes and connections, combining "the lofty language of the liturgy with the coarse but succulent diction of the streets." Nothing quite like it had ever been seen in Russian literature before.

"Your epistle has been received and clearly understood," Ivan began after an invocation to the tsardom. "You have put adder's poison under your lips. You thought your epistle was filled with honey, yet is it found to be bittterer than wormwood, according to the prophet who says: 'Their words were softer than oil, yet were they drawn swords.' "

He compared Kurbsky to Judas, denied he had planned to kill him, disparaged him as a general, ridiculed his swarthy "Ethiopian face" with its "pale blue eyes" (Aristotle in the *Secreta Secretorum* had warned Alexander to beware of advisers with pale blue eyes), and called him a "stinking hound." Quoting St. Paul ("Let every soul be subject unto the higher powers. For there is no power ordained that is not of God. . . . Whosoever, therefore, resisteth the power, resisteth the ordinance of God,") to prove Kurbsky's sacred obligation to serve him, he implied that even if he were a tyrant, it had been a sin for Kurbsky to rebel. In obvious retaliation for the condemnation of Anastasia for "one little word," he now claimed that because of "one small angry word" (i.e., "treason"), Kurbsky had destroyed not only his own soul but retroactively those of his forefathers. This was *mestnichestvo* with a vengeance.

Though Ivan was prepared to acknowledge his own fallibility—"I am only human; for there is no man without sin, only God alone"—his need for self-justification was greater that his impulse toward repentance, and he surged forward into a Biblical portrait of the true autocrat that rendered his formulaic humility meaningless.

Is this then "contrary to reason"—to live according to [the demands of] the present day? Recall to memory Constantine, mighty even amongst the tsars; how he killed his son, begotten by him, for the sake of his kingdom. And how much blood was spilt by your forefather, Prince Fyodor, in Smolensk at Easter time! Many other things too you will find in the reigns of the tsars. And what about David, the elect of God? When he was refused entrance to Jerusalem, he ordered the slaying of the inhabitants, of the halt and the blind. And [therefore] is it ever befitting for tsars to be perspicacious, now most gentle, now fierce; mercy and gentleness for the good; for the evil, fierceness and torment. If a tsar is not like this then he is no tsar. For he "is not a terror to good works, but to evil." Would thou be not afraid of the power? Do that which is good. But of that which is evil, be afraid; for he beareth not the sword in vain.

One is hard put to discover in this passage any distinction between the tsar and God Himself.[1] With considerably more discretion, Ivan proceeded to develop a lesson on the different responsibilities of priestly and royal power:

Who placed you as a judge or as one in authority over me? Or will you answer for my soul on the day of the Last Judgment? In the words of the apostle Paul: "How shall they believe without a preacher, and how shall they preach, except they be sent?" Now, you will never find a kingdom which does not fall to ruin when ruled by priests. . . . Thus the Greeks destroyed their kingdom and became tributaries of the Turks. Do you counsel us to this destruction? Did God, having led Israel out of captivity, appoint a priest to have command over men, or numerous governors? Nay, he made Moses alone lord over them, like a tsar; and he forbade him perform priestly offices, but bade his brother Aaron fulfill them, though forbidding Aaron to assume [administrative] authority over the people; but when Aaron did assume [it], then did he lead the people away from God as well. Take heed of this, that it is not befitting for priests to assume the authority of tsars.

So much for Sylvester. Ivan continued:

It is one thing to save one's own soul, but it is another to have the care of many souls and bodies: it is one thing to abide in fasting; it is another to live together in communal life. Spiritual authority is one thing—the rule of a tsar is another. To abide in fasting is like being a lamb which offers resistance to nought. . . . But in the communal life, even if one has renounced the world, one still has regulations and cares, and punishments too. If one does not heed this, the communal life will be destroyed. Spirtitual authority, because of the

blessed power within it, calls for a mighty suppression of glory, honor, adornment, supremacy, and other such things unbefitting for monks; but the rule
of a tsar, because of the folly of wicked and cunning men, [calls for] fear and
bridling and extreme suppression. Consider then the difference. . . . Is it
befitting for a tsar when he is struck on the cheek to turn the other? Is this
the supreme commandment? How shall a tsar without honor rule his kingdom?
Yet to turn the other cheek is befitting for a priest.

And he reminded Kurbsky that in contravention of Biblical wisdom "the
intention" of the Chosen Council had been "that I be sovereign in name,
but co-reign with the priest."

Ivan excoriated the pretensions of the nobility with equal finality. "The
beginning of our Autocracy is of St. Vladimir," he wrote. "We were born
and nurtured in the office of Tsar, and do possess it, and have not ravished
what is not our own. From the first the Russian Autocrats have been lords
of their own dominions, and not the boyar aristocrats. . . . Hitherto the
Russian masters were questioned by no man, but were free to reward and
punish their subjects; and they did not litigate with them before any judge."
According to this revised standard version of Russian history, present as
well as past, the true autocrat was not only independent of any overlord,
but of any institutional restraint—free to choose his own advisers and elevate
whomever he pleased, without having to account for his actions to either
the Duma or the Church.

From such autocratic heights Ivan plunged into a review of his childhood
privations and constraints, recalling the boyar rule of his minority ("was
that sweet?") and his subsequent domination by "that cur" Adashev, whom
he had "raised from the gutter," and by Sylvester, whom he had taken
into his service "for the sake of spiritual counsel and the salvation of my
soul." But the priest had "trampled his own vows under foot" and like
Eli the Priest had been "carried away by power. . . . And so Sylvester
joined Aleksey in friendship and they began to hold counsel in secret and
without our knowledge, deeming us incapable of judgment." Even after
his coronation, he said, he was treated as a child, supervised as to his
bedtime, his footwear, clothes, and so forth, by the "Council of Dogs."
Passing over in silence such early achievements as the Law Code and the
conquest of Kazan, he condemned Adashev and Sylvester for having opposed
the Livonian War "on every possible occasion," and for accepting "the
cunning [truce] suggestion of the Danish king" which had given the enemy
"a year to prepare themselves." Meanwhile, the boyars, affecting submission, had returned to their "cunning ways."

In a most remarkable passage he explained Kurbsky's defense of Adashev and others according to a psychological interpretation of classical mythology:

> Man made gods the advocates of his passions, so that sin might be reckoned not only irresponsible, but even divine, taking refuge in the objects of his worship as his apology. And there are countless foul Hellenic deeds, for their gods were worshipped by them according to their passions—fornication and rage, incontinence and the lusts of desire. And insofar as anyone was possessed by a passion, so did he choose for himself a god like unto it and he believed in him—as [for instance] Heracles for fornication, Cronus for hatred and enmity, Ares for rage and murder, Dionysus for shrieking and dancing—and other gods too, accordingly. . . . And thus do you, because you are a traitor, exalt treachery.

Ivan threw down the ultimate challenge: "As judge between us you place Christ our God, and I do not shrink from this judgment. For there is nought hidden from the fire of the eyes of him, who knows all things secret and concealed."

Ivan had idols of his own, of course, and aside from inadvertently confessing (at a later date) to his adoration of Cronus, he betrayed himself in a striking "Freudian" slip. Though he had psychologized Kurbsky, in one passage he identified the threefold nature of the soul (by convention, "thinking, feeling, and willing") as "reason, anger, and lust."

Dating his letter the fifth day of July, Ivan sent it by special passport in the care of Grigory Pleshcheyev, a confidential messenger, to Ozerische in Lithuania before the planned start of a summer campaign on July 22. Pleshcheyev waited there for Kurbsky's reply, which was promptly composed and entitled "Short answer of Prince Andrey Kurbsky to the extremely bombastic epistle of the Grand Prince of Moscow." It began:

> I have received your grandiloquent and big-sounding screed, and I have understood it and realized that it was belched forth in untamable wrath with poisonous words, such as is unbecoming not only to a tsar who is so glorified, but even to a simple lowly soldier; and all the more so, [as] it was raked together from many sacred discourses with much fierceness, not in measured lines or verses, as is the custom for skilled and learned men. . . . Your epistle is prolix beyond measure, whole books being included and whole proverb collections and epistles! And there are passages about beds, and body-warmers, and countless other things—as it were the tales of crazy women—so barbarically written that even simple people and children would read it with astonishment and

laughter, all the more so in a foreign land, where some are learned not only in grammar and rhetoric, but in dialectics and philosophy.

Kurbsky, whose own fine style was conservative Church Slavonic, did not appreciate Ivan's original literary gifts, but he did appreciate that Ivan had considerable literary pretensions, and thought he could hurt him most by putting them down. (At the same time he was so confident of Ivan's learning that in the course of their continuing correspondence he sometimes broke off after beginning a quotation with, "for you know the rest by heart.")

Finally, turning to politics, Kurbsky said: "I do not understand what you want from us. . . . Already you have killed . . . not only princes who trace their descent from great Vladimir, and robbed them as your predecessors never did, but . . . we have given you the shirts off our backs."

In late September 1564, Sigismund August tried to recapture Polotsk. Kurbsky served as commander of the advance guard and brought a cavalry detachment of 200 men equipped at his own expense into the field. Ivan rushed fresh units to the front, but in the process stripped his southern defenses—as the king had guessed he would. In a coordinated attack, Devlet Giray broke through the Oka line and rampaged across Ryazan. Effective resistance could not be mounted until Aleksey Basmanov, turning his local estate into a command post, managed to raise a relief force to rout the Tartar squads. Yet the king inexplicably failed to exploit his advantage. Passive after a first assault, his army retreated from Polotsk on October 4, and toward the end of November the Muscovites, in a retaliatory strike, overran Ozerische.

Meanwhile, Ivan had been unable to quell the mounting domestic dissent. Dmitry Obolensky's murder had temporarily galvanized the opposition, and despite contemporary complaints about the fawning clergy, a number of high officials, led by Metropolitan Afanasy himself, confronted the tsar. Afanasy, Markary's protégé and originally an archpropagandist for the state, carefully framed his rebuke. Alluding to Ivan's childhood sadism, he said: "No Christian Tsar has the right to treat human beings like animals"; and to his persecution of certain noble houses (the Obolenskys, for example, who continued to suffer, he reminded him of "the righteous dooms of God, Who avenges the blood of innocents into the third generation."

Ivan appeared to take this to heart. In mid-November of 1564, he spoke openly at court of abdicating in favor of his sons—while secretly conferring with advisers as to how to enforce his dictatorship by novel means. Those means were not anything the Duma could be expected to approve, short of institutional suicide. An Italian merchant who met him exactly at this time remembered Ivan walking with slow dignity, leaning on a crozierlike staff, escorted by four stout courtiers carrying large silver axes on their shoulders. In this sacerdotal pose there was but the subtlest hint of the sinister initiative about to plunge the state toward anarchy and dissolution.

Ivan III.

Vasily III.

The Cap of Monomakh (R. C. Howes, *The Testaments of the Grand Princes of Moscow*, © 1967 Cornell University Press).

As part of the coronation ritual, gold coins are showered on Ivan IV.

MUSCOVY, 1505 — 1533

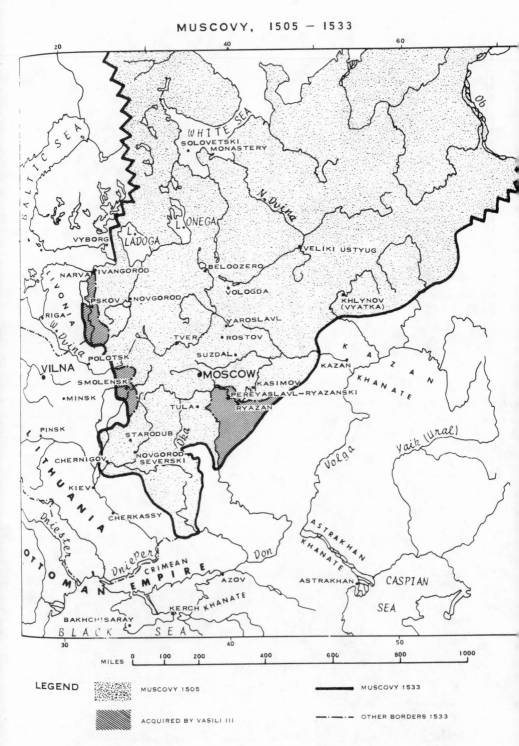

Map of Moscovy, 1505-1533 (A. F. Chew, *An Atlas of Russian History*, © 1967 Yale University Press).

Ivan IV holding a banquet.

Russian cavalry.

Under this banner of Christ, Ivan IV conquered Kazan (Sovfoto).

Ivan IV advancing against Kazan.

Blessing of Kazan.

Ivan IV as Conqueror of Kazan.

Ivan Fedorov, the first Russian printer, in his shop (Sovfoto).

Gustav Vasa (Nationalmuseum, Stockholm).

Finnish raiders bombard the Russian
coastal settlements while a rider
warns the Moscovite prince.

John Dee (Ashmolean
Museum, Oxford).

Sebastian Cabot.

Manuscript portrait of Maksim
the Greek.

The throne of Ivan IV (Sovfoto).

Ivan IV.

Queen Elizabeth I (National
Portrait Gallery).

Map of the Theater of the Livonian War
(George Vernadsky, *The Tsardom of
Moscow*, © 1969 Yale University Press).

Smolensk.

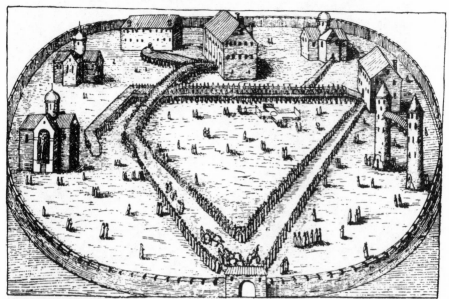

Aleksandrova Sloboda.

Metropolitan Philip.

A diplomatic audience at Aleksandrova Sloboda.

Vasnetsov's famous portrait of Ivan IV (Sovfoto).

Erik XIV (Nationalmuseum, Stockholm).

Johan III (Nationalmuseum, Stockholm).

The Great and Little State Seals of Ivan IV (G. Stökl, *Testament und Siegel. Ivans IV*, © 1972 Westdeutscher Verlag).

Selim II, the Sot (Lord
Kinross, *The Ottoman
Centuries*).

Stefan Batory.

Suleyman I, the Magnificent (Lord
Kinross, *The Ottoman Centuries*).

Ivan IV. Late sixteenth-century portrait (Nationalmuseum, Copenhagen).

Detail of Repin's famous depiction of Ivan IV cradling his mortally injured son (Tretyakov Gallery, Moscow).

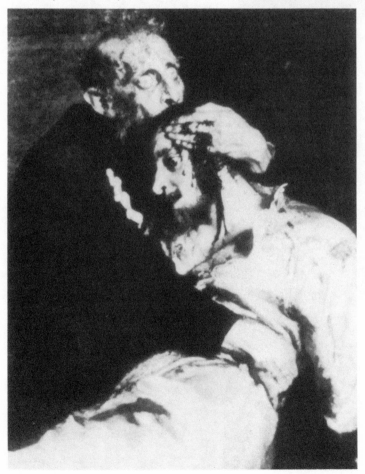

Henry of Valois, duke of Anjou (G. Slocombe, *A History of Poland*).

Antonio Possevino.

Yermak (Sovfoto).

Sir Jerome Bowes.

Ivan IV as portrayed in a fresco in
the Novodevichy Monastery.

Ivan IV's son Fyodor, who succeeded
him as tsar.

Yermak's emissaries laying the conquest of Siberia at the feet of Ivan IV (Sovfoto).

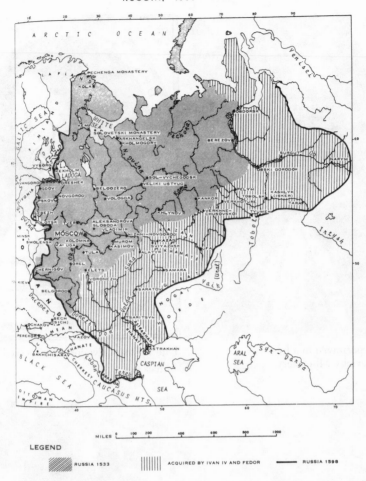

Map of Russia, 1533-1598 (A. F. Chew, *An Atlas of Russian History,* © 1967 Yale University Press).

The head of Ivan IV as reconstructed by a Soviet specialist from his disinterred remains (Sovfoto).

part three

SCHISM

23.

Satan's Band

To impress upon the nation the extremity of his frustration and resentment, Ivan followed through with his threat. At the end of 1564, he abdicated, and did so too in a manner that was both theatrical and deliberately mystifying to all but his inner circle. Hundreds of sleds, assembled in Red Square, were loaded with treasures from the royal vaults, and with icons, relics, and other precious items from churches and monasteries about the capital. On Sunday, December 3, after attending service in the Cathedral of the Assumption, he departed for the village of Kolomenskoe south of Moscow with a substantial retinue, largely drawn from the Chosen Thousand.

From Kolomenskoe, where he celebrated the feast of St. Nicholas the Miracle Worker, Ivan made his way to Trinity Monastery, where he remained for several days conspicuous in his devotions. On the 21st, he proceeded to Aleksandrova Sloboda, a former hunting lodge and sometime summer residence sixty miles northeast of Moscow. The Sloboda was transformed into a fortified camp. Meanwhile, Moscow was gripped by alarm as the tsar had failed to designate anyone in his absence to a caretaker regime. "In doubt and despair," we are told, state officials had "no idea of the road he would follow."

The road he followed led through abdication to a new tsardom. On January 3, 1565, a courier arrived with a letter addressed to the metropolitan and the Duma which gravely indicted the whole ecclesiastical and secular establishment for treason, embezzlement, neglect of military service, theft of the sovereign's land during his minority, and other crimes. The Church was specifically faulted for interceding on behalf of the tsar's enemies. "Wherefore the Tsar and Grand Prince, not wishing to endure these many acts of treachery, has abandoned the Tsardom with a heavy heart and now travels whithersoever God may lead him."

Yet knowing full well that the people looked to him as their shield against the rapacity of the nobles, he sent another letter, too, by another messenger, which largely belied the poignant pathos of his complaint. Addressed to the merchants and commoners, whom he exempted from his anger and disfavor, it was publicly declaimed to large crowds in Kremlin Square, and in whipping up antiboyar sentiment reminded the populace of the oppression they had suffered under *kormlenie*. The crowd began to agitate and flow, like water coming to a boil.

To prevent an uprising, Pimen, archbishop of Novgorod, was dispatched at the head of a delegation to plead with Ivan for forgiveness, and to beg him to return to Moscow "to govern as he pleased, and to punish traitors at his discretion."

"We are but poor and inconsolable sheep," Pimen told him. "We are now without a shepherd, and the wolves, our enemies, surround us. . . . In the past nations have been conquered and left without rulers; but that a mighty sovereign should abandon his loyal subjects and his tsardom—such things are unheard of, and not to be read in books. Let the Tsar proclaim the names of those whom he knows to be traitors, and let him punish them as he likes."

This momentous concession struck at the very heart of the Orthodox Church, for it abolished what was most precious in its advisory role to the tsar: the voice of mercy. Metropolitan Afanasy would have nothing to do with it and adamantly remained in Moscow.

Ivan feigned resolve not to return. In a meandering accusation, he recalled anew the turmoil of his childhood, the humiliations to which he had been subjected, and the threat to his birthright by the boyar regimes. And some of these boyars, he pointed out, were still around. He also charged that Anastasia had been poisoned and that (but for the grace of God) he might have been murdered too.

Over the next four weeks, the terms of his resumption of the throne were negotiated in his camp. The decree which emerged openly transformed him into a despot. It allowed him absolute power over the life and property of any disobedient subject "without advice of council"; and gave him his own separate court and administration staffed from top to bottom by hand-picked personnel. A part of Muscovy was also to be carved out for the tsar's special jurisdiction, while the rest of the country was to remain under the former administration, Ivan presiding over all. To finance the new bureaucracy, he required an indemnity from the state of 100,000 rubles—an astronomical sum at the time.

Ivan's abdication and re-enthronement as "free tsar" (in the Mongolian sense) took place when he was just thirty-five years old. But to "smash everything is something to grow gray over," and the nervous strain of it had visibly ravaged his appearance. When he returned triumphant to the capital in mid-February, his eyes were glazed and most of his hair had fallen out.

In Ivan's new tsardom, the nation-at-large was called the *Zemshchina* or "Land"; Ivan's court and the territory it ruled, the *Oprichnina* or "widow's portion"—that which a princess customarily received upon a sovereign's decease. There was a measure of ironic self-pity in the term, connoting as it did defenselessness in bereavement. But in practice it was pitiless, and its might was absolute.

In the beginning the territory under *Oprichnina* jurisdiction comprised some twenty towns and their environs; eventually, by "a generall schisme and publike division of the realm," about a third of the empire. Thus, wrote one *dyak* some years later, "in his hatred and wrath did he divide his single people into two halves. He split his entire realm as with an axe."

It took time for the *Oprichnina* to reveal itself, however, and to some degree it evolved or changed. Originally conceived as a kind of land reform to expedite the military service decree of 1556, with the new gentry servitors employed directly under the tsar himself in an expanded "court," its correlative objective was apparently to undermine the hereditary aristocracy as the major political force in the state. In a sense it was probably meant to serve as a large-scale demonstration of the kind of Muscovy Ivan wanted to rule, and this is surely what he meant long afterward in his testament (of 1572) when he said that in the *Oprichnina* he had created the "pattern" for his sons.

However, its evolution hideously distorted its ends.

The *Oprichnina* became a state-within-a-state. It was an instrument of Ivan's will which paralleled the traditional bureaucracy of the "Land"—with its own ministries, treasury, council and so forth—but which actually existed to implement (not check, balance, or modify by legalities or counsel) Ivan's desires. Within it he need face no inconvenient lecturing from a hierarch on moral or Christian imperatives, or concern himself with the welfare of the Land, whose government he had theoretically left in capable hands. Who could accuse him of abandoning the realm? It continued as before, entrusted to two aristocrats in whom the tsar appeared to have complete faith: Ivan Belsky and Ivan Mstislavsky. "These two men and I," he declared, "are the three pillars of Muscovy. The three of us hold all power."

Belsky, a boyar since 1560 and a direct descendant of Gedymin, had held a number of high positions in military and civil service, and with Pimen and Mstislavsky had served as a chief negotiator in the delegation to Aleksandrova Sloboda. Mstislavsky, whose illustrious pedigree has already been described, had been a boyar since 1549. One of the first to swear allegiance to the tsarevich in 1553, he had also wholeheartedly supported the Livonian War.

To staff his new court and administration and (as was soon apparent) to enforce the expropriation of land, Ivan assembled a sort of Praetorian Guard. Weirdly foreshadowing Hitler's SS, these *Oprichniki*, as they were called, donned black uniforms, displayed enigmatic or morbid insignia, and regarded themselves as a new form of religious sect with their own rites and customs. Whereas the SS sported a death's-head badge and a runic double-S flash, the *Oprichniki* rode on black horses and carried at their saddlebow a dog's head and broom as symbols of their determination to guard, day and night, the safety of their master and to sweep away all his enemies. No social contacts between them and the rest of the population were tolerated. Anyone could enlist, regardless of race, religion, or social origin, so long as he was willing to pledge himself to complete obedience to the tsar, and to execute faithfully all his orders. Their oath was almost a transcription of Matthew 10:37: "He that loveth father or mother more than me is not worthy of me: and he that loveth son or daughter more than me is not worthy of me."

The "elect," it seems, were being assembled. The Last or "Terrible" Judgment had begun.

Among the *Oprichnina*'s charter members were Aleksey Basmanov, Mikhail Cherkassky, Afanasy Viazemsky, and Peter Zaitsev—all, incidentally, aristocrats. Cherkassky, the Tartar chieftain, was the brother of Ivan's second wife and himself married to a Zakharin. In 1563, he had served as one of the tsar's sublieutenants on the Polotsk campaign, when Viazemsky was transport commissioner. Viazemsky had been a confidant of Ivan's since 1560. In the *Oprichnina*, he scrutinized candidates for admission and presumably administered to the initiates their loyalty oath. Zaitsev's early career anticipated his later notoriety. In January 1542, when in the ebb and flow of the boyar regimes the Shuiskys had made a comeback, he had assassinated the elder Prince Ivan Belsky in Beloozero. Subsequently elevated to boyar in 1550, he served briefly in Polotsk after its capture until his appointment to the *Oprichnina* Council in March 1565. Like Zaitsev, Basmanov was a seasoned veteran of Muscovite intrigue. However, he was also an outstanding general, belonged to a venerable branch of the House of Pleshcheev (an old Muscovite boyar family, like the Zakharins), and had been a boyar since 1544. His son, Fyodor, was Ivan's occasional homosexual paramour.

The first casualties to fall before Ivan's unlimited right of execution were Prince Aleksander Gorbaty, his adolescent son Peter, and the boyar Peter Golovin. Gorbaty, a Suzdal prince, hero of the Kazan campaign and afterward governor of Kazan, had been close to both Sylvester and Kurbsky. Golovin had been Kurbsky's comrade-in-arms. Both were accused of "all kinds of evil things" against the tsar and his family—a charge that sufficed, in the dawning day of Ivan's new reign, to destroy them. On the basis of similar evidence princes Dmitry and Ivan Kurakin were forcibly tonsured, and several other court officials deported to Kazan. Henceforth upon "the slightest suspicion, or on any pretext, men of the highest standing were arrested, deported, or put to death." Often their friends and families shared their fate. Whereas denunciations for treason had formerly arisen mostly from quarrels among the aristocrats themselves (enabling Ivan to "make advantage of their malice and contentions"), the tsar, it was said, now "ennobled and countenanced all the rascalliest and desperatt souldiers he could pick out, to affront the chieff-nobilitie."

Also known to have been executed at this time were Prince Simeon Lobanov-Rostovsky (a genuine traitor), Prince Andrey Rostovsky-Katyrev, and a saintly old cleric, Feodorit, apostle to the Lapps during Ivan's minority. In 1557, Ivan had sent him to Constantinople to obtain the coveted decree recognizing his title as tsar. In reward, Ivan offered him money, a velvet-lined fur coat, and virtually any ecclesiastical office he might wish. Feodorit declined them all, but later interceded for Kurbsky—an act which clinched his fate.

From among the slain, martyrs began to emerge. One, a certain Gorbachev, followed his father to the block, and, taking his severed head into his hands, thanked God "for having considered them both worthy to die innocent." Another, Dmitry Shevyev, "sang from memory all day long the canon to our Lord Jesus Christ and also the *akathist* hymn to the Blessed Mother of God," as he was slowly impaled on a stake.

This is not impossible. History affords numerous instances of incredible gallantry or courage in the face of unbearable pain. A contemporary Englishman, John Stubbs, condemned to lose his right hand for a pamphlet which had offended the queen, was hauled into the marketplace at Westminster where sentence was carried out with a butcher's cleaver and mallet. No sooner was his right hand severed, than Stubbs pulled off his cap with his left, waved it in the air, and cried, "God save the Queen!" Under Charles I one of Cromwell's "iron followers," executed at Charing Cross for regicide, was hanged, cut down alive, promptly disemboweled and presented with his own entrails. In the madness of his agony, he rose up wildly and punched his executioner in the face.

In England, at least, such punishments had followed due process. In Russia a kind of judicial terrorism began to hold sway. Torture, once an instrument of the code, began to dominate it; hearsay permitted a judge "to begin to pull a person's joints out and break his bones, to lacerate his body with the knout and burn him with fire." Peresvetov's anecdote about how the Sultan Mohammed dispensed with corrupt officials begins to describe the pitiless new procedure of the law: "He did not accuse them, he simply ordered them flayed alive and said: 'If they grow new skins, the fault shall be forgiven them!' And he bade to be inscribed on their skins, 'without such terror, justice cannot be brought into the realm.' "

Gradually, the *Oprichnina* acquired the wealthiest part of the state: the industrial middle, most of the north (remote from the Tartars), together with the chief trade routes and their flanking network of market towns. In the central provinces, *Oprichnina* holdings were interspersed with *Zemshchina* land in a crazy-quilt patchwork improvised to prevent the *Zemshchina* from comprising an integrated or continuous realm. Thus Russia was subdivided twice over, as the lands allotted to the new regime formed a wedge from north to south, dividing the nation-at-large in two. The borderlands and front-line towns—Novgorod and Pskov, Veliky Luki, Smolensk, and Seversk—were left to the *Zemshchina* to defend.

In Moscow, a suburb was taken, with the Neglinnaya River serving as the boundary line. All those to the west were evacuated. Ivan himself moved out of the Kremlin to an *Oprichnina* palace in the occupied zone.

Estate holders throughout Muscovy who happened to live in the reserved districts were evicted to make room for Ivan's new servitors. Although large-scale resettlement and deportation, as used by Ivan III in the conquest of Novgorod, Vasily III in subduing Vyatka and Pskov, and Ivan IV in the pacification of Kazan and parts of Livonia—not to mention his experiment with the Chosen Thousand—were by now almost a familiar feature of Muscovite policy, nothing so wrenching had ever been attempted before. Some resettlements were orderly; but others were abrupt, harsh, and without pretext of equity. In exchange for vast estates, a magnate might get a small *pomestia* plot on a distant frontier or a patch of arid soil. Those not assigned land to begin with had to search for it themselves and stake their claim. Because many boyars were uprooted from their home bases of power, local military organization and criminal justice were thrown into disarray, as administrators were dispersed and replaced by inexperienced *Oprichniki* who knew nothing about the district to which they were assigned. In ways that eventually surpassed the worst days of *kormlenie*, they took a purely mercenary interest in how justice was pursued. Nor was the plight of the peasants under them improved. Most *Oprichniki* hoped to get rich quick or live high while the phenomenon lasted. Their rapacious conduct as landlords dealt devastating blows to the economic viability and legal status of the peasants and destroyed traditional manorial relations without putting anything stable in their place. "Many beautiful estates," wrote a contemporary, "were quickly neglected and ruined as if an enemy had passed through."

It is probably not coincidental that at this time Russia's first Colonial Department, administering Kazan, was upgraded to *prikaz* or ministry status. Henceforth much of its work was taken up with the logistics of deportation, as the land under its jurisdiction became a place of exile for both dissidents and prisoners of war. In the absence of a unified prison system, the headquarters of the *prikaz* itself contained cells for temporary incarceration of offenders. "Kazan" anticipated "Siberia."

24.

English Interlude

Commercial relations with England remained unaffected at first by the domestic turmoil—though xenophobic tendencies showed themselves in other ways. Symptomatic of Muscovy's regression, her solitary printing press was smashed by a superstitious mob aroused by the "guild" of professional scribes headquartered in the Armory, which saw its livelihood slipping away. Perhaps Josephians were behind it, for the two printers, Fedorov and Mstislavets, both Non-Possessors, were accused of "Lutheran heresies." Escaping to Lithuania, they joined Artemy and others in contributing to a great Orthodox revival.

Though in some ways the Russian economy was prospering through the new flood of imports, its base was showing strain. To keep the war effort going, "both merchants and peasants," wrote a contemporary, "are burdened with enormous taxes, extorted from them by unmerciful bailiffs. When one lot has been collected, others are being levied, a third is being sent for, and a fourth is being thought out." Each peasant commune also had to produce one to three men to haul artillery and to sign a notarized guarantee that the men sent would remain with the guns unto death. In gradually increasing numbers, commoners had begun to "flee beyond the frontiers" into the wilds.

Ivan counted on the English to shore up his strength. After Jenkinson had met with Viskovaty in 1558 to discuss an expanded trade agreement, the Russia Company had been digging in. Its three principal agents, Richard Grey, George Killingworth, and Henry Lane, operated out of Moscow, Vologda, and Kholmogory. Soon a fourth agent was established at Yaroslavl.

Organized as a joint-stock company (the first of its kind to be fully incorporated in England), it traded as an entity, meaning that its members were not to trade individually for themselves or anyone else within the area of the company's monopoly. All members were shareholders and by definition shared in the fortunes of the company as a whole. In the hierarchy of its organization, there were agents, salaried clerks, stipendiaries, and apprentices, most maintained at company expense. Though only a few were also employees of the English government, company and state affairs were closely intertwined. After Queen Elizabeth's accession in 1558, some of her chief ministers—including Sir Francis Walsingham and Sir William Cecil, Lord Burghley—had a financial interest in the venture, and whatever privileges the company sought from Ivan were usually first expressed in a memorandum to Lord Burghley, who "laid the matter before the Queen."

Compared to the traffic at Narva, English-Russian trade by the northern route was modest, for the voyage was difficult and the port of St. Nicholas icebound from autumn to spring. Theoretically the shipping season lasted from May to October, but ships had to leave England no later than June if they hoped to manage a round trip, which meant returning from Russia by early August. The voyage out averaged more than a month, homeward about two.

Nevertheless, the northern trade, on which England had a monopoly, was alone secure from blockade.

The first stopover upon arrival was Rose Island, at the mouth of the Dvina, where the company had a mansion set in a pinewood clearing, supplied by a freshwater spring. Red rose and damascus, violet and wild rosemary grew in luxuriance about the grounds.

After goods were unloaded, most were sent up the Dvina to Vologda, thence to Yaroslavl en route to Moscow. English exports included broadcloth, kerseys, raisins, prunes, almonds, pewter and salt (oddly enough)— nine and a half tons of salt, for example, in 1560. In exchange the company imported wax, tallow, flax, train oil, furs, tar, and hemp.

At Kholmogory the merchants had their principal dwellings, warehouses, offices, and a great ropewalk where hemp was combed, spun, tarred, and laid into cable. Another complex almost as large stood at Vologda, 700 miles upstream.

With Russia to preoccupy it, the company had more or less given up its attempt to round the north of Asia to Cathay. In 1556, Stephen Burrough, Chancellor's one-time shipmate, had sailed past the White Sea, and continuing eastward until he "went in over the dangerous barre of the Pechora," cast anchor near Vaigach Island. There he made the acquaintance of the Samoyeds, whose extensive reindeer culture he was the first to describe. However, he did little to improve their reputation. In exchange for a mirror and a couple of pewter spoons, a local fisherman led him to their "bloodie idols," facing "bloody blocks . . . the tables whereon they offer sacrifice." But his discovery of the head of a unicorn (presumably a narwhal) also suggested the proximity of Cathay, and he therefore pressed on, through polar mist and rain, until on August 22 he was nearly crushed by an iceberg at Nova Zemlya. No further attempt would be made until 1580, when Arthur Pet and Charles Jackman failed to get past the pack ice of the Kara Sea. Pet barely made it back alive; Jackman went down with all hands off the Norway coast. For many years their observations represented the extreme eastern limit of what was known of the Arctic coast.

A somewhat more rewarding, but no less hazardous, undertaking from which Ivan also hoped to benefit was the company's exploration of a trade route through Russia to Central Asia, India, China, and Persia. Entrusted with letters "unto sundry kings and princes," Jenkinson had set out on April 23, 1558, from Moscow with a Tartar interpreter and two companions for Astrakhan.

At Astrakhan he saw what Russian conquest had wrought. The Nogays were treated as outcasts, and the city horribly ravaged with famine and disease. "I could have bought a thousande Tartar children, of their own fathers and mothers," he surmised, "a boy or a wench for a loaf of bread. But we had more need of victualles than any such merchandize."

Instead they bought a boat, sailed boldly into the Caspian sea, and "sette up the redde crosse of St. George in our flagges, for honour of the Christians, which I suppose was never seene in the Caspian Sea before." Sailing eastward along the coast of the Mangishlak Peninsula, they disembarked and joined a caravan of a thousand camels bound for Turkestan. When Mangishlak tribesmen harassed them, Jenkinson wisely sought out their chieftain who lived in a field "in a little rounde house made of reedes covered with felt." On the 11th of October he reached Urgenj on the Oxus, where he delivered a letter from Ivan to the governor, and was told by some holy men who wrote "certaine Characters" in bone dust and blood on the ground to beware of thieves ahead. Shortly thereafter he was ambushed by Turcoman tribesmen looking for loot and Christians to enslave. Drawing his wagon train into a circle and making skillful use of a handful of muskets, he beat off the attack, but over the next several days his party was forced to eat their own camels, with only brackish well water to drink. On December 23, they staggered into Bokhara—the first Europeans to enter the city since Marco Polo three centuries before.

Though welcomed by the local khan, Jenkinson failed to interest him in a trade agreement since the inhabitants were too poor to buy English commodities. He planned to push on to China (again like Marco Polo) but since it had already taken him nine months to get to Bokhara, and he was told it would take him nine more to get to Peking, he abandoned the idea.

After wintering in Bokhara, Jenkinson departed for Russia on March 8, 1559—as ever, his guardian angel by his side: one week later the city was savagely sacked by troops from Samarkand. For two months he trekked through waste wilderness, then, in a kind of improvised ship, with broadcloth sails and an anchor made out of a cartwheel, battled stormy weather on the Caspian Sea.

Yet he did not return to Moscow empty-handed. Accompanied by envoys from Bokhara and Urgenj, twenty-five Russians liberated from Turcoman captivity, and a Tartar girl he would later present to the queen, he also had with him a generous sampling of merchandise and two gifts Ivan would prize: a yak's tail and a Tartar drum.

Back in London, Jenkinson prepared a valuable map of his travels that was included in the great Ortelius Atlas of 1570. Among other things, it corrected at least two important errors in the current knowledge of geography by showing that the axis of the Caspian Sea was greatest north to south, and that the Don did not branch from the Volga.

No Englishman was to cross the same terrain for another 300 years. Though Jenkinson's travels had shown that overland trade with the Orient was out of the question, trade with Persia for silk, spices, and other luxuries appeared more promising. Accordingly, in the summer of 1561, he set sail again from England, this time with goods to test on the Persian market and with letters addressed from Elizabeth to the shah. Ivan furnished him with safe-conducts, entrusted him with a secret mission, and arranged that he be accompanied by the Persian ambassador as far as Astrakhan. From Astrakhan (in the spring of 1562) he was escorted by fifty gunners on two brigantines across the Caspian Sea to Derbend, where he met with the local governor, Abdullah Khan, a small, fierce, but surprisingly friendly man who entertained him royally in his richly carpeted pavilion. Abdullah promised duty-free trading privileges for the English within his own jurisdiction and provided Jenkinson with a military escort to Kazvin, where the reigning Persian monarch, Shah Tahmasp, had his capital.

The shah, however, was hostile. When Jenkinson tried to present the queen's letters to him (written in English, Latin, Italian, and Hebrew) the shah said, "We have none within our realme that understand those tongues," and demanded to know if Jenkinson was a Mohammedan or an unbeliever. Jenkinson said he was a Christian. "What is that?" he asked an aide, who told him Christians believed in Jesus Christ. "Dost thou beleeve so?" asked the shah. "Yea that I doe," replied Jenkinson. "Oh thou unbeliever sayd he," and expelled him from the tent. As Jenkinson left, sand was scattered behind him to obliterate his tracks.

Subsequent expeditions to Persia met with mixed success, but eventually the changeable shah agreed to negotiate a wide grant of privileges for English trade in return for "all sortes and colours of London clothes," chain mail, handguns, suits of armor, brushes "not to be made of swines hair," and "a mill to grinde corne in the field as they goe." The English (always on the lookout for weaponry as well as spices) wanted to know how the Persians forged their thin but durable armor, and were gratified to find (after the forests of Russia proved disappointing in this regard) many yew trees at Shemakha fit for crossbows.

A formal agreement was impressively written out in characters of azure and gold, and the Russia Company optimistically changed its name to the "Companie of English merchants Adventurers for Russia, Persia and Mare Caspium, with all the landes and countries adjoyning to the same."

But the company's privileged status in Russia was in jeopardy. In 1564, Raphael Barberini, an undercover agent for a consortium of Antwerp merchants and uncle to the future Pope Urban VIII, had managed to obtain a letter of recommendation from Queen Elizabeth to the tsar by telling her that some Englishmen in Russia owed him money. Apparently not eager to see the company used as a sanctuary for fugitive debtors, she wrote in good faith to Ivan, on June 23, 1564, that "though an Italian [he] is dear to us."

Her affection was misplaced. Barberini's purpose was to discredit the English trade by convincing Ivan that the commodities he was receiving were actually not English but German and Dutch, and that just like the Hanseatic and Livonian scalpers, the English were jacking up the prices and skimming a profit off the top.

Ivan may not have wished to disbelieve him, for in addition to wanting to press the English for better terms, regular trade with Denmark and other countries remained one of his principal aims. The Russo-Danish treaty of 1562, for example, had provided for Russian warehouses at Copenhagen and Visby, and Danish warehouses on Russian soil. Thus Barberini easily secured the privileges he sought, hurried home to Antwerp, loaded a sizable ship with goods, and set sail for Narva in summer of 1565. By prearrangement, the Danish king gave him free passage through the Sound. On board were a number of items Ivan had specifically requested, including armor, turkey cocks and hens, kidney beans, cauliflower, pumpkinseeds, "good wine but not too sweet," thick paper for printing, and marcasite for the composition of type. (Evidently, he had set up a press at Aleksandrova Sloboda for his own use.)

Queen Elizabeth was naturally mortified, and on May 4, 1566, dispatched Jenkinson (who had lately been chasing pirates off the coast of Scotland) to set things right.

Her gracious but ironical note[1] to Ivan began, "We understand that Your Majesty holds our letters in such esteem that, out of respect to their contents You grant more favours to our subjects and even to foreigners, out of courtesy to Us, that We ourselves ask for them. This happened last year, when we recommended to you a certain Italian, named Raphael Barberini, not as a merchant, but as a traveller." Explaining too that Barberini had misrepresented himself, she charged that he had meant all along to "deface her subjects trade."

25.

The *Zemsky Sobor* of 1566

From the beginning Muscovite diplomacy had sought to conceal the *Oprichnina* from the outside world, and before Lithuanian envoys arrived for important discussions in the spring of 1566, the Russian negotiating team was instructed to deny it existed. They were also to explain that the tsar was now living in a new palace, surrounded by his loyal subjects; and that those not so loyal lived farther off. To calm the domestic waters a bit, Ivan pardoned some of the disgraced, but on May 19, Metropolitan Afanasy resigned anyway in protest and withdrew to the Chudov Monastery, destroying the appearance of a united front. When Jenkinson arrived on June 11, he immediately became aware of the new institution, which was clearly being felt as a domestic calamity. On June 26, 1566, he wrote to Lord Burghley:

> This Emperor of Moscovia hath used lately great cruelty towards his nobyllyte and gentlemen by puttynge to death, whyppynge, and banyshynge, above four hundred with confyscation of Lands and goods for small offence, and specyally toward four of theym, viz., one wurryed with beares, of another he cutt of[f] hys nose, hys tonge, hys eares, and hys lyppes, the thyrde was sett upon a pole, and the fourth he commanded to be knocked in the head, and putt under the yse in the Ryvar. His Majestie is now buyldinge of a castell which wylbe fowre square and two thousand four hundred fathom in compas. A fort most strange and sumptuous, having dayly in number above ten thousand men. The stones for the sayd buyldynge ar fetched five hundred mylles.

This was the *Oprichnina* Palace in Moscow, located "a gunshot away" (as one *Oprichnik* quaintly put it) from the Kremlin on a square of high ground to the west, where some of the original Chosen Thousand had been settled, and where the anti-Glinsky insurrection in 1547 had begun. If there was a hotbed of antiboyar "populist" sentiment in Moscow, it was there.

Encompassed by white-stone and red-brick walls, the palace had three gates, each surmounted by a double-headed eagle with extended wings carved out of oak and painted black. The gates to the south and east were sheathed in lead; the north gate facing the Kremlin was covered with iron plates and flanked by a sculpted pair of snarling lions with mirrors set in their eyes. Archers and musketeers continually patrolled the walls.

The principal buildings of the compound had stone column supports, but Ivan's own residence was beautifully chiseled, carved, and planed out of fir wood, with a porch next to a low stretch of wall where he liked to dine and "catch the sun and breeze."

Nevertheless, Moscow could never be secure enough for him, and he also began to construct a separate, Kremlin-like fortress in Vologda—roughly midway between Moscow and the port of St. Nicholas—from where he could flee north if necessary, with family and treasure, to English ships on the White Sea. Urgently built over the course of several years, the Vologda citadel, with great towers and ramparts, had its own Cathedral of the Assumption, and was defended by 300 cannon and an army of musketeers.

As the lull in the Livonian War continued, fighting on the Lithuanian front had heated up, though recent action was inconclusive. Veliky Luki had been assaulted by Lithuanian troops commanded by Kurbsky, but the Muscovites refortified Usvyat and built Sokol, a new fortress, on the Drissa River just twenty miles from Polotsk. The most urgent item on Sigismund August's agenda was to unite his two kingdoms into a single realm, a task exacting every morsel of his strength. He desperately wanted peace, and the Lithuanian delegates accordingly arrived equipped with serious proposals. To begin with, they were prepared to cede part of Livonia—namely, Dorpat, Narva, and several lesser towns—to Ivan without contest. It was not a concession to be ignored, for it recognized much of what Ivan had obtained and gave him precisely what he had sought at the beginning of the war. But in the arrogance of victory, he insisted on territory west of the Dvina (to within a few miles of Vilna) and also the port of Riga, to which the king could scarcely consent.

To intimidate the envoys as the talks got under way, Ivan in a striking and unexpected move convoked a National Assembly (*Zemsky Sobor*) to confirm support for his objectives in the war. Such an assembly was almost unprecedented, except for the less diversified gathering summoned in 1549.

But it was not democratic. Made up of representatives of the Duma, the upper clergy, the gentry, the state bureaucracy, and the merchant class, it merely resembled the assemblies to which the Lithuanians were accustomed, in a kind of parliamentary dumb-show or "constitutional seduction." All of its 374 members were Muscovite officials, selected by the crown, gathered at its pleasure, and obliged to deliberate on subjects of the sovereign's choice. They were not there so the tsar could learn their opinions—their opinions were already known, and were known to agree with the tsar's. They were expected to proclaim their support and transmit the will of the government to localities.

On another level, however, the *Sobor* showed Ivan's common sense, for in order to prolong a costly and difficult war, he needed a public consensus among leading members of his nation. By giving representatives from the gentry (automatically excluded from the Duma) numerical dominance in its deliberations, he also acknowledged their incontestable political and military importance in sustaining the state.

The *Sobor* met from June 28 to July 21. Each "estate" made its recommendations separately; all backed the tsar's negotiating demands and called for vigorous prosecution of the war. There was but one cautiously dissenting voice, and predictably it belonged to Viskovaty, who suggested that Russia refrain from demanding Riga so long as the Lithuanians also agreed to "leave Riga alone." His recommendation was ignored.

Such "policy-making" by acclamation (which mimicked the rule of una-nimity in the Polish Diet)[1] no doubt dismayed the Lithuanians, for whatever they thought they knew about the *Oprichnina*, it had apparently not divided national sentiment with regard to foreign policy. They left Moscow in gloom, convinced they were faced with a long and bloody war.

Yet Ivan's intransigence in 1566 was to prove the greatest foreign policy blunder of his career. And its immediate domestic repercussions were dire.

In bringing so many officials together, Ivan had risked a coming together of dissent. Disparate elements met, conferred with one another, and con-cluded that the tsar might agree to abolition of the *Oprichnina* in return for their moral and financial support of the war. Having given him this, in the words of a contemporary chronicle, "they petitioned him orally, and handed him a signed petition [in mid-July] saying it was improper for such a thing as the *Oprichnina* to exist."

Meanwhile, a successor had to be found to Metropolitan Afanasy, who had laid down his pacificatory office in despair. The ecclesiastical component of the *Sobor* met as an authentic Church Council and after voting on secular issues, approved Gherman Polev (archbishop of Kazan since March 12, 1564), after his nomination by the tsar.

Gherman, a strict disciplinarian of the faith and a former prosecutor in the Bashkin case, had signed his name to the assembly's resolution endorsing the Livonian War; but he deplored the *Oprichnina* and apparently lost no time in admonishing the tsar, in private, to stop the persecutions and give the experiment up.

Ivan, taken aback, secluded himself with his inner circle. His acolytes vehemently reminded him of his days of bondage to Sylvester and Adashev, and insisted that Gherman was trying to revive them. Fyodor Basmanov is said to have hugged Ivan about the knees and begged him to continue to be free.

Two days later, Ivan went to Gherman and said, "You have not yet been elevated and already you are trying to bind me," and ordered him out of the metropolitan's residence before he could unpack.

To the bitter disappointment of Novgorod's Archbishop Pimen (who cov-eted the post) Ivan next nominated Philip, abbot of the Solovetsky Monas-tery, who had just arrived from his White Sea island parish as the assembly prepared to disband. Though he was also a risky choice—a Non-Possessor who administered one of the largest and wealthiest monasteries in the em-pire, yet the man to whom Makary had entrusted Sylvester's imprisonment—in deference to the memory of the venerable Makary, Ivan was apparently not yet prepared to see a toady in the metropolitan's see.

Born Fyodor Kolychev about 1510 of untitled but distinguished boyar stock, Philip had been strongly drawn as a youth to the Moscow court. His grandfather had served Ivan III as envoy to the Crimea, governor of Novgorod, and fortress commander in Ivangorod; his uncle had been an adviser to Andrey Staritsky; and his father tutor to Ivan's brother, Yury, during Ivan's minority. In 1537, however, several Kolychevs had taken part in Staritsky's revolt and been hanged on the road to Novgorod.

Neither Fyodor, an up-and-coming young courtier at the time, nor his father had been implicated, but two months later as he stood listening to the Gospel in church, "he realized he could not serve two masters" and that very night fled the capital with little more than the clothes on his back. Making his way anonymously by a circuitous route past the tributary lakes and swamps of Lake Onega, into ever more desolate terrain, he arrived at last at the Solovetsky Monastery, the northernmost cloister of the realm, located just within the Arctic Circle on a wild island in the White Sea.

Despite its growth as a community since its founding a century before, many monastics still found its polar isolation almost too much to bear. The rough-clad brethren were called to worship not by the resonant peal of copper bells from the towers of gilded cathedrals, but with an old stone hammer and gongs, and knelt before an altar slab of granite and a large irregular cross carved out of walrus tusks.

Fyodor, who arrived under an assumed name, was accepted as a novice, tonsured, rebaptized Philip, and eventually prepared under the tutelage of a *starets* or elder for the post of ecclesiarch, the monk who supervises the ritual of the liturgy. Over the course of several years, his exemplary piety, obvious intelligence, and devotion to the rigorous monastic routine repeatedly brought him to the attention of the abbot, who came to regard him as his likely successor. At length elected, in 1544, he unexpectedly declined and withdrew for three years into the forest as a hermit. Elected again in 1547 (the year of Ivan's coronation), he accepted, and soon revealed the extraordinary administrative capacities that would bring him his first renown. Over the next several years, he set the brethren to clearing fields for cultivation, established a dairy farm, a mill, and a workshop for making leather and fur apparel, and developed a saltworks which eventually grew to vast proportions, producing 3500 tons of salt annually by 1565. Great storage bins had to be erected to house the monastery's grain. To drain the swampland and bring water into the monastery from surrounding lakes, he built dams, an artificial reservoir, roads, and a network of canals. One of the canals, for sanitation, passed directly beneath the cloister itself. He also erected a hospital for pilgrims, new dormitories, and a fortresslike cathedral crowned with five cupolas, and furnished with a great copper bell weighing over 6000 pounds. In the island's harbor he planted majestic crosses atop artificial mounds as beacons for ships at sea.

During Philip's tenure, the monastery's stupendous expansion trans- formed it into one of the great industrial complexes of the empire. It owned many villages and hamlets along the White Sea coast, and in return for the "privilege" of working and subsisting on its land, peasants had to donate considerable labor and produce on terms that were typically stiff. Yet it remained a community where monks also worked the land, and where agri- cultural and industrial labor was consecrated to God. Philip himself contin- ued to reside in a humble wooden cabin where he sought to preserve intact the spirit of his vows.

Of all this no tsar could fail to take note. Ivan sent gifts: money to help finance construction, silk robes and satin shrouds to enrich the vestry, and two gold altar crosses adorned with rubies and pearls. To Philip personally he sent one of his favorite books, Flavius Josephus' *The Jewish Wars*.

If there were others Ivan might have turned to in 1566, Philip's life bore the circular stamp of destiny, as three decades after fleeing the court of Moscow in such desperate haste, he was summoned to return—"to wear the white cowl, and the martyr's crown."

Nominated for the metropolitanate on July 20, like Gherman before him Philip felt obliged to urge Ivan to abandon the *Oprichnina* and "concentrate on bringing unity to the land." The tsar vehemently insisted that the *Opri- chnina* was his "court," and therefore his private affair. But he could not afford to force another holy cleric to decline. Uneasily, the two men came to terms. Philip publicly signed a document in which he pledged not to interfere in the tsar's "domestic" arrangements, but pointedly did not for- swear his right to intercede.

What did this mean?

From the beginning, the spiritual independence of the Church and the loftiness of its moral truth had been epitomized by its "custom of intercession on behalf of the disfavored and the accused." That intercession was seldom disregarded, especially when attempted by the metropolitan, the second most powerful figure in Muscovy. Yet, except for a certain resurrection of its dignity under Makary, the office of metropolitan had long been in decline. Under Ivan III it had become politicized, as the appointment and deposition of Zosima, for example, had followed the fortunes of the grand prince's campaign against Church property. In the following reign, Metropolitan Varlaam, a man of Non-Possessor sympathies, had enjoyed the support of Vasily III until 1522, when he was deposed because of his "constant intervention in favor of persons who had incurred Vasily's disfavor." Varlaam was succeeded by Daniel, whose notorious record as a marionette was to be unrivaled in the history of the Russian Church. Sigismund von Herberstein, the German ambassador, memorably described him in 1525 as "a man of about thirty years of age, of large and corpulent frame, with a red face, who, so as not to be thought more given to gluttony than to fasting, vigils and prayers, used on all occasions when he had to perform any public ceremony, to expose his face to the fumes of sulphur to make himself pale." Another contemporary, the boyar Beklemishev-Bersen, said of him: "He does not instruct. He does not concern himself with anyone. He does not intercede. I don't understand. Is he the Metropolitan, or just a plain monk?"

During Ivan's minority, the office became a plaything of court factions. Daniel, deposed by the Shuiskys, was exiled to the Volokolamsk Monastery and forced to sign a document in which he confessed his moral and physical unfitness to continue in the post—"an abasement which even Zosima had been spared."[2] Joasaf, elevated in his place, tried to assert his moral independence but was publicly beaten and defrocked. Only with the appointment of Makary in 1542 did the office regain a measure of its clout. Initially a creature of the Shuiskys (or so they thought), Makary brought to his responsibilities exceptional political acumen and a strong, spiritual sense of Russia's national destiny. In glorifying the Church, he had tried to furnish a living example of its majesty, and energetically revived the right to intercede. He interceded constantly, in fact, as if to re-educate both tsar and nation as to this unique privilege in the metropolitan's role. His protégé Afanasy, however, had been unable to follow his lead; and after him Gherman had lasted as metropolitan but a day. The recent failure of the Church to intercede and remonstrate with Ivan about his overall behavior had also formed the core of Kurbsky's complaint to Muromtsev, while previous intercessions had also been the foremost target of Ivan's abdication letter to the establishment in 1564. It was *the* issue because ultimately the Church was the only power that could limit the tsar's tyranny. No one really questioned the tsar's right to punish the disobedient—or even to execute. But the right of the Church to appeal for mercy—a mercy which was above the law—was also inviolate. "Executive clemency" cannot fathom its meaning: it referred to a principle higher than any secular prerogative. Moreover, every hierarch had a sacred obligation, as stated in the *Epanagoge*, a Byzantine law manual with which every metropolitan was familiar, "to speak the truth to the emperor and fearlessly defend the dogmas of the faith before him." In fact, this very injunction was paraphrased and elaborated in the metropolitan's own consecration vow—"not to be silent before the tsar in matters of truth. And if the tsar or his magnates attempt to force us to speak other than the holy laws, then we shall not listen to them, and we must not obey even if death is threatened." Makary had reminded Ivan of this in their early struggle over the secularization of Church property; and the tsar himself had acknowledged it in admonishing the *Stoglav* Council: "Do not be silent. Correct me without fear." Even Joseph of Volokolamsk, the arch Church apologist of autocracy, had ventured: "You should not obey a king or prince who is himself overruled by unclean passions, or who causes you to perform dishonorable and deceitful acts, even if he should torture you or threaten you with death. The prophets, the apostles and all the martyrs confirm this, for they gave up their lives to infidel kings, rather than submit to them."

In the fullness of his understanding of all such matters, Philip bravely accepted the metropolitanate and was invested with the office on July 25 in the Cathedral of the Assumption. On the floor of the nave a large double-headed eagle with extended wings had been drawn, and at the midpoint of the liturgy Philip was led from the altar to stand on this image, as he donned the white cowl—"representing the Lord's resurrection"—and received from Ivan himself the primate's staff.

As metropolitan, he then completed the liturgy himself.

26.

The Tsar at Chess with Elizabeth and Erik

Ivan's maneuvering in international relations inevitably began to reflect the derangement of his domestic policies. Perhaps Sergey Eisenstein meant to suggest this, as well as the complexity of Ivan's strategic thought, when in his cinematic biography he showed the tsar at chess silhouetted against the gigantic, distorted shadow of an astrolabe with its intersecting bands encircling his head.

Relations with England preoccupied him. The "honeymoon" was over and his courtship of Barberini suggested the trouble the Russia Company was in. Part of it (and the lesser part) was disciplinary. Most of the stipendiaries were very young men out on their own for the first time, and because the English enjoyed such favored status, were tempted to revel in the vices strewn in their path. They hung out in taverns, debauched themselves with prostitutes, and embezzled company money to get themselves up in silk and velvet so they could "ride and goe like Lordes." Though servants themselves, they kept servants of their own, along with "superfluous burdens like dogges and beares." London ordered a crackdown. "If they do not amende," read the directive, "ship them home." Jenkinson was empowered to do just that, but other problems appeared beyond the company's control. At Narva, a port potentially far more prosperous than the roadstead of St. Nicholas could ever hope to be, Ivan welcomed ships from all nations, including those operated by English merchants not affiliated with the company. In 1558, for example, six ships at most disembarked at St. Nicholas, while fifty-seven English and thirty Scottish ships entered the Baltic through the Sound. The possibilities for barter at the new international crossroads also tempted certain merchants within the company itself to trade individually, thus breaking the franchise rules.

The company claimed it had a flat monopoly (granted by the queen) on English-Russian trade. Unaffiliated merchants claimed that when the charter had been issued, Narva was not yet a part of Russia. Therefore, it didn't apply to that city. The company reminded the government that it had pioneered the White Sea route with considerable suffering and loss, and that it had helped build up the English Navy, both through its import of cables, cordage, tar, hemp, wax, and flax and by fostering shipping and seamanship through its promotion of the merchant marine. On both counts, its contributions had indeed been valuable, along with others tactfully unmentioned in its service as a diplomatic pouch. The Privy Council was swayed. Seeking both to reward the company for its efforts and to protect the monopoly, it ruled that no other "should henceforth be permitted to trafique to the Narve out of this realme," and reinforced the edict by Parliamentary Act.

The interloping trade, however, could not be stopped completely, in part because Ivan favored it as an additional source of supplies. Barberini was the sort of man he wanted to meet. As the company strove to retain its monopoly, Ivan, "feeling the mounting costs of the war and fearing diplomatic isolation, hoped to bring down prices of imports by flirting with rival merchants" (English and foreign) and "to woo Elizabeth into an alliance, by promising expanded trade benefits." At the same time he could not afford to provoke her too far, for the northern route alone was safe from interdiction, even if the mariners had to brave the shoals and stormy seas.

After reading Elizabeth's letter of concern about Barberini and the state of English-Russian trade, he expressed sympathy, granted Jenkinson's request that the company be allowed to establish new warehouses at Narva, Dorpat, Kostroma, and elsewhere, and to transport its merchandise duty-free to Central Asia. But in turn he demanded that Elizabeth send him, as a sign of goodwill, "technical experts to bolster his war machine." Specifically (letter of September 16, 1566), he requested fortress architects, prospectors ("such as are cunning to seke out gold and silver"), metallurgists, plus a doctor and an apothecary, among "craftsmen to be sent owt of Englande." Promising to pay them handsomely and to reward Elizabeth too, "out of ower great goodness," he also pledged (rather self-consciously), "when [the craftsmen] are willing to goo home ageyne we will lett them goo." What other monarch would have had to promise this?

Ivan deemed his communiqué too urgent to await the White Sea thaw, and since "the Baltic had become an unsafe avenue for English shipping, above all for an envoy of Elizabeth," due to "intense patrolling of the sea lanes leading to Narva in order to halt suspected military supplies from reaching Muscovy," Jenkinson was obliged to travel overland at some considerable risk through Europe to the North Sea. He delivered Ivan's letter to the queen in December, and returned to Russia in the summer of 1567 with exactly those craftsmen Ivan had sought (including Humphrey Lock, an outstanding military engineer) and a letter from Elizabeth dated May 18 appealing for confirmation of English trade privileges and help in cracking down on maverick English merchants—"obscure destitute men . . . deceived by false beliefs and misled by a desire for gain"—who were slandering the company monopoly as a confinement of trade.

Ivan's prompt reply (September 1567) thanked her for the technicians ("We prayse God alone, singing with holy words"), hoped for "everlasting love" in friendship between them, but hedged on her appeal. Instead of rewarding her out of his great goodness, he challenged her to break diplomatic relations with Poland, on the grounds that Polish *agents provocateurs* had recently been stirring up ill-will between their merchants, and insisted upon a "great messenger" or fully accredited ambassador (not another merchant-envoy) be sent from England so that high affairs between them could be discussed at the appropriate level. Those affairs were spelled out in the following extraordinary demands:

The Emperour requireth that the Queens majestie and he might be (to all their enemyes) joyned as one; ffriend to his friends and enemy to his enemyes, and so per contra. And that England and Russland might be in all matters, as one; that the Queens majestie would lycence maisters to come unto him which can make shippes, and sayle them, and suffer him to haue owt of England all kynde of Artillerie and things necessarie for warre. Further the Emperor requireth earnestly that there may be assurance made by oath and faith betwixt the Queens majestie and him, that yf any misfortune might fall or chance upon either of them to goe out of their countries, that it might be lawfull to either of them to come into the others countrey for the safegard of them selves and their lyves.

And he gave Elizabeth until "St. Peter's day next"—June 29, 1568—to reply.

A kind of brinkmanship also began to affect Ivan's diplomacy on the Livonian front, where he closely followed the progress of the Northern War. Despite Erik's early initiative, Frederick appeared at first to have Sweden entrapped. Sjaelland, Skane, Bornholm, Gotland, and Oesel formed a chain of Danish strongholds across the Baltic, while Jamtland and Harjedalen put the Danes within striking distance of the Gulf of Bothnia, which divided Sweden from southern Finland. Erik's solitary access to western seas—and western salt—was Alvsborg.

He met the challenge with vigor and audacity, refortifying Alvsborg to safeguard his gate to the Atlantic, Vyborg to protect his back door in Finland, and Reval to secure his foothold in Estonia. Rearming his infantry (which he reorganized into units modeled on the Roman cohort and legion) with pikes, halberds, and body armor, he also took the strong navy Gustav Vasa had bequeathed him and made it "unsinkable" by giving his warships a double hull packed with iron ore at the waterline. Legend credits him with the invention of broadside tactics. History incontrovertibly records that his ships were bigger, better, and stronger than any in the northern seas, and that under two brilliant admirals, Jacob Bagge and Klas Kristersson Horn, they dominated the Baltic, and even patrolled the Sound. Indeed, Erik was able to impose a toll of his own in the Gulf of Finland and a partial blockade on Narva. In June 1563, his navy seized a fleet of thirty-two Danish merchantmen returning from the Russian port, and in 1566 the entire Dutch salt-fleet of fifty-two ships, with enough cargo to supply the whole of Sweden for a year. Though the Danes finally took Alvsborg in 1565, the Swedes triumphantly offset that loss by capturing Varberg, as Erik laid plans for a drive on Oslo.

Nevertheless, all these hard-won and spectacular achievements could not be considered out of jeopardy until—or unless—either Poland or Russia were secured as a firm ally. Though the Swedish Navy had remained supreme in the Baltic, the Danes had proved superior on land. Their answer to Klas Horn was Daniel Rantzau, a brilliant general, who drove Erik back from the North Sea and evicted his troops from Norway. Plans were drawn up for the invasion of Sweden itself. An alliance between Sweden and Poland was out of the question, however, as long as Johan and Katerina were incarcerated, yet Erik dared not release them because of Johan's certain challenge to his throne. That left Russia.

Katerina's marriage to Johan had humiliated Ivan (for what was a duke of Finland compared to a tsar?), and because of Johan's solidarity with Sigismund, his sexual jealousy was aggravated by political hate. Erik had been conciliatory of late, yet Ivan understood well enough that it was only because of the Northern War that his goodwill was coveted in Stockholm. *Mutatis mutandis*, he regarded Erik, Johan, and Sigismund equally as his deadly enemies. And it was therefore with a certain vindictiveness perhaps peculiar to himself that he concocted a triple revenge: in one move, to obtain a hostage against Sigismund, Johan's humiliation, and Erik's disgrace. This was the kind of chess move Ivan lived for.

Accordingly, in 1565 he offered Erik peace on the Russo-Finnish frontier, recognition of Swedish sovereignty in northern Estonia, and a full alliance—in exchange for Johan's wife.

Erik at first ignored the gambit. Then Ivan began to press. On the one hand, Erik was tempted, for he was determined, as he wrote, "not to sacrifice my state for the Duke of Finland"; on the other, he sincerely scrupled to commit a godless act. "What God hath joined may no man put asunder": Katerina and Johan really were in love. Katerina wore a ring engraved: "Till death do us part."

He vacillated, increasingly, and in his vacillation considered fratricide; and though he couldn't bring himself to do it, the impious idea ate steadily away at his mind. Meanwhile, the two abnormal and not altogether dissimilar monarchs continued their correspondence. They had, in fact, a number of things in common: a taste for theological learning, a mystico-historical belief in their own royal lineage, a reputation for personal cowardice and (au pair, as these things go) extreme ruthlessness in dealing with the shortcomings of subordinates. Both, it is fair to say, were also incipiently paranoid.

But "even paranoids have enemies," and in 1567, with the tide of war turning against the Swedes, Ivan invited Erik to send envoys to his royal compound at Aleksandrova Sloboda, to negotiate a treaty "between equals."

With his own pretensions to ruling by "divine right," this mattered to Erik rather too much. Katerina was all Ivan asked. Erik gave in, and over the opposition of his own royal council empowered Gyllenstierna to yield Katerina—if that's what it would take. That's what it took. The notorious treaty was signed on February 16, 1567, at the Sloboda, and in May a Russian embassy arrived in Stockholm for its ratification.

The weight on Erik was tremendous. He recoiled within himself at the shame he was bound to incur in the eyes of posterity, yet hoped to eclipse it by the name he would earn for having preserved and enlarged his kingdom, which seemed to depend on his disgrace. Either way he faced a national catastrophe, for as king his personal ignominy would stain the realm.

Under the circumstances, he did perhaps the only decent thing: he went insane.

27.

Conspiracies

Ivan had reacted badly to the petition submitted to him after the *Sobor* of 1566. While the signatories had hoped to induce him to abandon the *Oprichnina* in return for their support of the war, Ivan was convinced that his tentative concessions earlier that spring had been read as a sign of weakness: people were beginning to raise their voices in dissent who would never have dared to raise them before. As soon as the Lithuanian embassy departed, he launched into reprisals, and over the next several months tortured, imprisoned, mutilated, or executed most of the petitioners. The *Oprichnina* was significantly expanded, as the entire district of Kolomna was appropriated for his guard, its ranks engorged with 500 new recruits, and fortress construction in Vologda and elsewhere accelerated at strategic locations on *Oprichnina* land.

Perhaps to allay some tincture of guilt after concluding his treaty with Erik, Ivan trekked north on a pilgrimage to the White Lake Monastery where, "overcome by dark and gloomy thoughts," he confided to certain elders his burning desire to become a monk. He fell upon his knees and the abbot blessed him. In gratitude the tsar donated 200 rubles to finance the preparation of his cell.

Ivan's renewed talk of abdication gave rise to rumors, which rippled around the court. Naturally, they increased the malaise in government circles and prompted even some of Ivan's loyalists to explore new arrangements that might enable them to survive. If the first abdication had led to the *Oprichnina*, what might the second one bring?

With both Lithuania and Moscow preparing to resume the war, Sigismund August moved to take advantage of the domestic discord and sent secret invitations (cosigned by the Lithuanian hetman, Grigory Khodkevich) to four prominent *Zemshchina* boyars—Ivan Cheliadnin, master of the horse, and princes Ivan Belsky, Ivan Mstislavsky, and Mikhail Vorotynsky—inviting them to defect. Although these letters were dutifully turned over to Ivan (and the courier who delivered them promptly impaled on a stake), Sigismund had rightly guessed that the tsar would have to wonder why the four had been singled out, and whether, perhaps, the king knew something about them that he didn't know. No protestations of loyalty would suffice. The nobles would know this too, and be uneasy. At the very least it would stir up trouble between Ivan and those on whom he chiefly relied.

The heaviest suspicion fell on Cheliadnin, in whose care the letters had been sent. He had been among those to negotiate directly with Khodkevich the summer before, and it is not impossible that the two had come to some understanding. This would have been a blow as stunning as Kurbsky's flight. Of untitled boyar stock, whose family had served the grand princes of Moscow since the early fourteenth century, Cheliadnin had been master of the horse since 1547, and in the crisis of 1553 had firmly supported the tsarevich Dmitry. During Ivan's absence from the capital, he had occasionally governed in his place, and during the *Oprichnina*'s first year had presided over the *Zemshchina* Council that administered Moscow. But Cheliadnin also represented the opposite of what the *Oprichnina* stood for. Though a fabulously wealthy landlord, he was said to be incorruptible, and enjoyed the reputation even among enemies of being "the only honest judge in Moscow."

Ivan kept his suspicions to himself, but rode from Vologda to Aleksandrova Sloboda, where he dictated sarcastic and abusive replies for each correspondent (except Cheliadnin) to send. Cheliadnin was invited to draft his own.

Impersonating Belsky, Ivan began with a parody of Kurbsky's second epistle: "We have carefully read your letter and we understand it well. You have written in the manner of a procurer, swindler and scoundrel.

. . . You should know that the will, the mercy and the hand of God uphold the autocracy of our Tsar, and bless us who are his worthy councillors. We cannot be destroyed by a little gust of wind." As Vorotynsky, Ivan denied the existence of the *Oprichnina* and the execution of any but outright traitors. Apostrophizing Khodkevich, he wrote: "You whelp of the devil! Our tsar is a true Orthodox ruler and wisely directs his country; he favors the good and punishes the bad. Traitors are merely executed here as elsewhere." As Mstislavsky, Ivan repeated his theories of rule by divine right and his legendary descent from Caesar Augustus. Cheliadnin wrote on his own behalf: "I am already old. Were I to betray my sovereign, it would be like breaking my heart, and I would die. I am not young enough to serve you as a soldier. . . . And I have not been trained to be a court jester."

These letters were never sent. In August, Lithuanian troops attacked and destroyed the new frontier island fortress of Kopiye on Lake Susha, forty-five miles from Polotsk, and in September routed a Russian force nearby. In late October, Sigismund marched with a large army (more than 20,000 strong, equipped with artillery) to Radoshkovits on the Lithuanian frontier. In mid-November, Ivan abruptly canceled the scheduled fall campaign and returned to Moscow. Alleging that his artillery had not been delivered to the front on time, he executed his new transport commissioner, Kazarin Dubrovsky. In fact the campaign had been aborted because he had "uncovered" a broad-based conspiracy linking Cheliadnin with his cousin Vladimir Staritsky.

On Ivan's insistence, the hapless Staritsky went to Cheliadnin to ask him, as if in confidence, for a list of those on whose support he could count. Cheliadnin apparently obliged, and thereby betrayed some thirty colleagues. Who knows how many had really joined together in a plot? Cheliadnin may merely have been giving his opinion. But insofar as Ivan was concerned, they all might as well have sworn a blood oath of tyrannicide. Nevertheless, his fears were not unfounded and Polish sources indicate that a plot, coordinated with Sigismund August, did in fact exist: namely, to kidnap Ivan during the fall campaign and hand him over to the king at Radoshkovits, where Sigismund indeed seems to have waited in vain until January 1568 for the coup d'état.

Muscovy sped toward catastrophe.

Despite his professed desire to become a monk, Ivan had Archbishop Gherman murdered in Moscow on November 6, 1567, and after his discovery of the plot to abduct him, unleashed a reign of terror. One eyewitness later recalled:

It was a pitiful and sorrowful spectacle of slaughter and killings. Every day ten, twenty or more *Oprichniki* concealing large axes under their cloaks, rode about the streets and alleys. Each detachment had its own list of boyars, dyaki, princes and leading merchants. No one knew what his own guilt or alleged wrongdoing was supposed to be. No one knew the hour of his own death or even the fact that he had been condemned. Everybody went about their affairs as if nothing was the matter. Suddenly a band of killers would descend.

✦The luckiest were forcibly tonsured or exiled to Kazan. One boyar, Peter Shchenyatev (a member of the Staritsky faction in 1553, afterward governor of Polotsk) saw the reprisals coming and withdrew to a monastery. This did not save him. He was dragged from his cell, needles were driven under his nails, and he was roasted in a large iron pan. Another prince, impaled on a stake "which came out at his naeck, languished in horrible paine for fiften houres alive, and spake unto his mother brought to behold that wofull sight, . . . the Emperour saying, 'such as I favour I have honoured, and such as be treytors will I have thus done unto.' "

Except for a handful of cases it is impossible to know—or even to conjecture—what Ivan's grudges were. By the late 1560s, he had clearly become obsessed with threats to his personal security. There was no consistent social profile to the victims or consistent criteria of selection for the *Oprichnina* other than Ivan's favor. The social makeup of the *Oprichnina*, in fact, was almost identical to that of the country as a whole, and included scions of some of Russia's most eminent aristocratic families. The purges had no discernible social goal. The issue was treason, most of it imaginary. Yet just as the thirst for blood grows with its satisfaction, so (contrariwise) "the more Ivan indulged in repression, the more alienated his subjects became, until he was finally confronted with a situation he was powerless to control." If the original purpose of the *Oprichnina* troops had been to enforce the confiscation of estates, especially those of the nobility, such estates in the end comprised a relatively small proportion of what was expropriated. The majority of Ivan's victims were not nobles at all, but ordinary gentry. Eventually *Oprichniki* executed one another. Thus "they prepared the whip and the birch with their own hands, and all those brightly painted devil-masks before which the spiritual and secular orders bowed down."

Just as the lawless boyar regimes of Ivan's minority had bred crime by example in the realm, so the conduct of *Oprichniki* fostered arbitrary and degraded behavior throughout Muscovite life. And this was destined to remain true for some time. "For as [the common people] are verie hardlie and cruellie dealte withall by their chiefe magistrates and other superiours, so are they as cruell one against an other, specially over their inferiours and such as are under them. So that the basest and wretchedest that stoupeth and croucheth like a dogge to the gentleman, and licketh up the dust that lieth at his feete, is an intollerable tyrant where he hath the advantage. By this meanes the whole countrie is filled with rapine and murder." Though Chancellor had once noted Ivan's reputation for settling controversies "with the utmost fairness and partiality," by 1560, when Ivan refused to allow Sylvester and Adashev to defend themselves at their trial, official disregard of the law had already been given sanction. By 1568, Ivan's own great Law Code had been openly pushed aside. "Fear not the law, fear the judge," warned a contemporary Russian proverb; and once in prison even for a misdemeanor a man might languish "until his hair hung down to his navel." Just about everyone in the system received kickbacks, from magistrate to bailiff, and it is said that a petitioner or litigant couldn't even get into court without paying off the guard. In the government, too, nothing was accomplished without money changing hands. "One hand washes the other" became a common expression. A tenth of all emoluments was reputedly skimmed off the top.

Moreover, Ivan explicitly prohibited *Zemshchina* courts from convicting *Oprichniki* of any crime! In the gleeful if understated recollection of one of his guards: "This caused the spirits of the *Zemshchina* to sink." A long-standing if parenthetical anomaly of Muscovite law—trial by combat—became more prominent. Hired fighters abounded, yet no one was willing to risk his life in a losing cause. Those hired by *Zemshchina* litigants, having taken the field fully armed, would often just fall to the ground and exclaim, "I'm guilty."

A large number of *Oprichniki* were German and Tartar mercenaries. A perhaps not untypical example of those enrolled was Heinrich von Staden, a Westphalian who in his teens had been expelled from school for stabbing a fellow student with an awl. A few years later, when he left home, his family was so glad to be rid of him that one relative took a thorn bush to wipe out his tracks in the dust. At Riga he witnessed the execution of Count Johann von Artz, who for collaborating with the tsar was "torn to pieces with hot tongs." This did not dissuade Staden from seeking service in Muscovy, where he had heard the mercenary pay was very good. And in the *Oprichnina* he made a great career.

This is how he remembered one excursion: "We came to a place with a church. My servants went inside and plundered it. Nearby was the estate of a prince in the *Zemshchina*. When his people saw [us], they fled. I shot one immediately and quickly went throught the gates as they threw stones at us from the upper floor. I ran up the stairs with an axe in my hand, and was met by a princess who wanted to throw herself at my feet. Seeing my angry face, she turned to go back into the room. I struck her in the back with the axe and she fell through the doorway. Then I sprang over her and greeted her ladies."

Even as the guard attracted criminals, criminals masqueraded as *Oprichnik* bands and molested with impunity whomever they encountered. In time, local action against them became hopeless, as the *Zemshchina* inhabitants lost the ability to distinguish between bandits and the tsar's own men. Gangs of thugs rampaged over the countryside, sometimes organized on a paramilitary basis, and ambushed traveling merchants or raided farms at harvest time. *Oprichniki* also roamed as far north as the coast of the White Sea. Meanwhile, as the burdens of taxation and obligatory service inexorably grew, officials were helpless to check the flight of the peasantry into the wilds.

What Pushkin once remarked about the reforms of Peter the Great could almost be applied to Ivan's in reverse: "The later laws were created by a broad mind, full of wisdom and kindness. The earlier decrees were mostly self-willed and seemed to have been written with a knout."

28.

The Martyr's Crown

Aside from the slow, dignified walk and pious eating habits Ivan habitually displayed for foreign visitors, what was his daily routine really like? Any answer to this must contain a large measure of conjecture, but as often as not, it seems he could be found at Aleksandrova Sloboda, the "capital" of the *Oprichnina* kingdom, sixty miles northeast of Moscow. His compound there included an inner stone citadel, a *terem* palace, warehouses, barracks, ministries, dungeons, and a new masonry church dedicated to the Virgin, with a cross ostentatiously etched on every brick. Wooden causeways criss-crossed the central court over marshy ground, and the whole was encircled by ramparts and a moat. Various approaches were guarded by stone block-houses, and two high watchtowers surveyed the surrounding countryside. Roadblocks and overlapping patrols enforced the tsar's edict that no one was to enter or leave the town without his consent. At the main checkpoint, two miles to the south, identification passes were issued and verified. Beyond the town, the roads quickly vanished into dark forests.

In this retreat, freed at last from all constraints, Ivan "let it all hang out."

In a profane parody of monastic life, he assumed the role of abbot over a community of *Oprichniki* brethren, with Viazemsky cast in the role of cellarer, and Malyuta Skuratov (a rising favorite married to Viazemsky's sister) sacristan. The brethren went about in dark cassock habits and cowls of rough black serge, and divided their time between exhausting church services and atrocities.

The monastic "rule" was strict. Everyone was awakened at three in the morning for matins, which lasted until dawn. During the service, Ivan sang, read, or prayed—sometimes with such fervor that he bruised his brow from beating it on the ground. Occasionally he would confer with his advisers and "often the bloodiest orders were dictated at matin-song or during Mass," which followed at eight. At ten the brethren gathered for their first repast of the day. During the meal, Ivan stood and read occasionally from the lives of the saints or some other edifying work. Leftovers were distributed in the marketplace to the poor. The remainder of the afternoon Ivan spent on affairs of state, or in the company of a favorite, or in hunting forays in the woods. Not infrequently, however (and he "was never so happy as then in countenance and speech"), he would descend into the dungeons to observe acts of torture. "Blood often splashes his face," goes one eyewitness account, "but he does not mind; indeed he is delighted, and to indicate his joy he shouts, 'Hoyda, Hoyda!' "—a Turkish word resembling "giddy-up" or "let's go," used by Tartar horsemen to urge on their steeds. In-vigorated by such excursions, he occasionally convened the brethren for an orgy, though on most days he "liked to execute before the eight o'clock bell" which called the community to evening prayer. After ves-pers, three blind storytellers, reciting by turns, lulled him to sleep with their tales.

Peter the Great in a later age, with comparatively harmless variations, mimicked Ivan's confraternity in his Jolly Company and Drunken Synod, which had a "Prince-Pope, All Rowdiest and Most Mock Patriarch of Moscow," with twelve cardinals, a suite of bishops, abbots, and abbesses, all bearing scandalous nicknames. Peter himself assumed the rank of archdeacon. Their first commandment was never to go to bed sober.

Fortunately Peter, who often supposed himself to be following in Ivan's footsteps, had other lights to guide him on his way.

"The strict and orderly regulation of Ivan's ecclesiastical-torture chamber," one historian has pointed out, "destroys the common notion that his religiosity was a state of radical vacillation between sin and repentance." On the contrary, within his daily routine Ivan was evidently able to "combine without strain atrocity with religious piety," and through a rigid attachment to ritual externals, without regard for their inner meaning, confuse customs with dogmas of the faith. This last was a Josephian legacy. Moreover, the beauty of the liturgy evoked "a sense of excitement in Ivan which incited in him a craving for the shedding of human blood, just as the excitement of voluptuousness incited him in the same direction." By a law of progression, "the passions thus excited and the sensations they dulled united in a cry for constantly stronger and more startling effects."

Ivan's theatrical executions and other histrionic behavior may be linked to this, along with the pious ferocity with which he beat his forehead on the ground, "causing his brow to be full of boines and swellings, sometimes to be black and blew, and often to bleed." Perhaps to prove the Roman imperial blood in him, he also showed an increasing tendency to cast some executions as large-scale sporting events. Thus, for example, though reputedly kind to the poor (maintaining, it is said, some 200 paupers at his own expense), he one day decided to separate out the counterfeit mendicants from those in genuine need. Proclamation was made that all "beggars and cripples should resortt to receav the Emperors great almes" at his Sloboda, and "owt of som thowsands that came," one contemporary records, "700 of the most villest and counterfeit wear all knockt in the head and cast into the great lake, for the fish to receav their doll therof: the rest most febliest wear disperst to monnestaries and hospitalls to be relieved."

On another occasion, we are told, Ivan herded seven "rebellious bigg fatt friers" into a high-walled amphitheater, and having furnished them with spears, led each one, trembling, out into the center of the ring to face by turns seven "great wild, fierce and hungrie beares, lett lose, rainginge and roaringe up against the walls with open mouthes." The first bear, "scenting the frier by his garments, made more mad with the crie and shouting of the people, runs fearsly at him, catches and crushes his head, bodie, bowells, leggs and arms, as a cate doth a mous, tears [him] in peces and

devours him for his prey." And so on with the others, till all the brethren
were dead.

Into Ivan's arbitrary world, Metropolitan Philip intervened. He admonished the tsar in private, paraphrasing Basil (Agapetus): "If you are high
in rank, then in body you are just like any other man, for though you may
be honored with God's image, you are still God's 'subject.' He who truly
can be called a ruler, rules himself; he is not controlled by passions but is
victorious over passions through love." Ivan was not accustomed to hearing
the second half of this text, and Philip's erudite insistence on remembering
it in full was not welcome. As a result the tsar "kept away from the hierarch
and avoided encounters with him. In the admonitions of the metropolitan,
he seemed to hear the hateful voice of the seditious boyars."

Then, on March 22, 1568, Philip publicly upbraided the tsar in the Cathedral of the Assumption. As the metropolitan was celebrating the Eucharist,
Ivan and a troop of *Oprichniki* entered the cathedral in their black robes
with high hoods over their heads "like Chaldean boors." Three times the
tsar approached Philip to receive his blessing, but the hierarch refused to
acknowledge him. Certain boyars in the congregation exclaimed: "Holy
Metropolitan!" but Philip said: "I do not recognize the Orthodox tsar in
this strange dress." Fear swept the cathedral. "We are offering here the
pure bloodless sacrifice for the salvation of men," the metropolitan continued. "But outside this holy temple the blood of the innocent is being
shed, and there is no mercy in Russia for the righteous." Looking directly
at Ivan, he added: "Have you forgotten, O Tsar, that you too are dust
and will need forgiveness of your sins?" Ivan responded: "It would be
better for you to be in accord with us," to which Philip replied: "Where
is my faith if I am silent?" Ivan struck his iron-tipped staff against the
rostrum: "We shall see what your strength is." Philip, who knew full well
what the tsar could do, showed what his faith was: "I too am but a passing
stranger on this earth. But I must tell you the truth, even if I have to die
for it. I am not grieving for the innocent among your victims—they are
God's martyrs. I am grieving for your soul." Ivan exclaimed: "In the past
I was humble before you. Now you shall come to know me!" And on the
following day, he began to execute members of Philip's staff.

Following Afanasy's example, Philip moved out of the metropolitan's
residence in the Kremlin to the Monastery of St. Nicholas the Elder. But
he refused to resign his office. Ivan withdrew to Aleksandrova Sloboda to
prepare a case against him, and sent an investigative commission to the
Solovetsky Monastery to corroborate charges of alleged misconduct during

Philip's tenure as abbot. But the testimony extracted (through bribery and threats) was "so suspect that Bishop Pafnuty of Suzdal, its most influential member, refused to sign the report. Pafnuty's opposition threatened to abort Philip's trial, leaving the outcome in the hands of the boyar council, many of whose members sympathized with the metropolitan."

In mid-June, the *Oprichnina* launched a punitive campaign against the Kolomna estates of Cheliadnin. The guardsmen set fire to villages and churches and amused themselves by stripping women and girls naked and compelling them to catch chickens in the field. The tsar himself went to one of Cheliadnin's holdings near Tver, "slew his retainers, herded the rest of his servants and domestics into a hut full of gunpowder, and blew them up." Between March and July, some 300 of Cheliadnin's servants were killed. This whole operation was directed by Malyuta ("Stumpy") Skuratov, captain of Ivan's personal bodyguard and soon to preside over the *Oprichnina*'s investigative arm. His chief assistant was Vasily ("Murky") Griaznoy, a former kennelman.

Toward the end of July, Philip and Ivan clashed publicly again. On the 28th, the metropolitan was celebrating a service at the Novodevichy Monastery outside Moscow, and as he led a procession around the walls, the tsar and a band of *Oprichniki* suddenly appeared. Philip noticed that one of them (according to Islamic custom) was standing with his cap on. "Sovereign Tsar," said Philip, "are the Orthodox to uphold Islamic law?" The tsar responded: "How so?" Philip answered: "There he is, one of your own guards, the one who looks like Satan." Ivan looked back, but the man had already removed his cap.

In early September, there were mass executions. Some 450 nobles and their servitors, including several of Philip's relations, were killed. Many had been on Staritsky's conspiracy list. Others had simply been close to Cheliadnin, and they included outstanding members of the military high command, such as the officers in charge of Narva, Svyazhsk, and Kazan. If Kurbsky's charge in 1564 that Ivan was killing off his best generals (as Stalin would do in the 1930s) had at the time been overstated, it was certainly true by 1568.

On the 11th, Cheliadnin himself was summoned to the Kremlin's Golden Chamber where Ivan arrayed him in royal robes and placed him on the throne. Prostrating himself in mock humility, the tsar said: "You have what you wanted. Enjoy it." Then: "What I have given, I can also take away," and (it is claimed) seizing a knife stabbed him in the chest. Afterward, Ivan's myrmidons threw the body into a ditch.

Cheliadnin's fate cowed all vestigial boyar opposition, and despite the

tainted evidence of the investigative commission, the Duma agreed to try
Philip on a range of charges from administrative corruption to sorcery. The
chief witnesses against him were Paisy, Philip's successor as abbot, and
certain elders whom he had repeatedly reprimanded for allowing the monastery's reservoir and dam to fall into disrepair. Their testimony came as no
surprise. In January 1568, in answer to his chiding, they had sent him a
shipment of rotten fish. Surely they would not have dared to do so if Philip's
impending fall had not already been widely assumed. Another cleric with
a grudge was the Archpriest Evstafy, Ivan's current confessor, whom Philip
had reproached for his lack of spiritual counsel to the tsar. And then of
course there was Archbishop Pimen, who hoped at last to be made metropolitan once Philip was out of the way.

As a clergyman, incidentally, Pimen was only interested in strictly liturgical questions; for example, what one was supposed to do if a priest collapsed
in the middle of Communion.

Meanwhile, Ivan did everything he could to intimidate Philip before
his arraignment, and on the eve of his trial decapitated his cousin, Mikhail
Kolychev, and sent him the head sewn up in a leather bag.

Nevertheless, Philip denied all the allegations, and once again reminded
Ivan, in front of the assembled dignitaries: "Your high earthly rank has no
control over death, which sinks its invincible teeth into everything. And
remember that each person must answer for his own life."

Sentence was passed against him in his absence on November 7. The
tsar had wanted him burned at the stake as a heretic, but the clergy successfully united in pleading for his life. However, Ivan was determined to
make his deposition as grotesque as possible—perhaps in revenge for the
public embarrassment he had suffered at the trial. On the following day,
as Philip stood at the altar of the Cathedral of the Annunciation preparing
to celebrate his final liturgy, Aleksey Basmanov burst in with *Oprichniki*
and loudly proclaimed the verdict from a scroll. Seizing him, they stripped
him of his clerical vestments, and roughly buttoning him up in a tattered
sackcloth robe, dragged him out of the cathedral and threw him onto a
sled. Over the next several days he was transferred from monastery to monastery, ever farther from the capital, until he was finally sequestered in a
dungeon at the Otroch Monastery in Tver, where Maksim the Greek had
once languished for twenty years.

Philip's fortitude immediately gave rise to miracle tales. "And some who
went into the dungeon," wrote Kurbsky, "say they found him freed from
his heavy bonds, and standing with his hands raised, singing divine psalms;
and all his fetters lay on one side. Then Ivan ordered a wild, half-starved

bear to be let into his cell and locked in, and on the following morning came himself and had the cell unlocked, hoping to find him eaten by the beast, but again he was found whole, standing in prayer as before."

Such tales became ever more precious to the people as the role of the Church declined. "Where is my faith," Philip had asked, "if I am silent?" But after him the Church was silent for a very long time.

29.

The Great Messenger

In England, Elizabeth had been pondering Ivan's last letter, as "St. Peter's Day next" came and went. Ivan had kept the pressure up. Though he continued to exclude all but the English from his White Sea port, he lent new encouragement to various renegades at Narva, where the two men sent out to manage the Russia Company office—Ralph Rutter and Thomas Glover—had begun, in collaboration with a certain John Chappel, to trade privately and undersell their own collective. To justify themselves, they denounced the company "as a close and oppressive monopoly," and Ivan's advisers, taking up the tune, denounced its merchants as "most greedy cormorants." Alarmed, Elizabeth despatched two emissaries to arrest the mavericks, but the Russians arrested them instead in protest against Elizabeth's neglect of Ivan's request for an alliance.

Ivan's tactics had their effect. Elizabeth relented and sent the "great messenger" Ivan had asked for in 1567. That messenger was Thomas Randolph, a professional diplomat who for several years had coordinated her Machiavellian policy at the Scottish Court.

Randolph's mission was to placate and mislead. He was to assure the tsar of his authority to discuss any subject, and to offer him sanctuary in England, but to refuse the reciprocal offer of refuge in Russia as unnecessary, for "we have no manner of doubt of the continuance of our peaceable government without danger eyther of our subjects or of any forren ennemys." As for "any such legue as is called offensive and defensive," he was told to "pass those matters with silence," pretending that Jenkinson had never conveyed the request to the queen. Finally, he was to negotiate only "for privilegs to the benefit of our merchants. *That is our speciall cause of sendyng you thither.*"

To make out the capable Jenkinson as the bearer of a garbled message on matters of such import was not a sound foundation stone for the embassy. And how was Randolph to pass over in silence what Ivan was bound to bring up?

Nor was he helped much by the personnel he brought along. There were "several gentlemen" who had signed on, "desirous to see the world," and for his personal secretary he had engaged the poet George Turberville, who was utterly bored and resentful, and wrote long verse letters home to friends in rhymed poulter's measure (a kind of doggerel) in which he venomously disparaged every conceivable aspect of Russian life. Thus, for example,

> *Drink is their whole desire, the pot is all their pride,*
> *The sobrest head doeth once a day stand needfull of a guide . . .*
> *Perhaps the muzhik [peasant] hath a gay and gallant wife*
> *To serve his beastly lust, yet he will lead a bugger's life.*
> *The monster more desires a boy within his bed*
> *Than any wench, such filthy sin ensues a drunken head.*
> *The woman to repay her drowsy husband's debts*
> *From stinking stove unto her mate to bawdy banquet gets.*
> *No wonder though they use such vile and beastly trade,*
> *Sith with the hatchet and the hand their chiefest gods be made.*

Fortunately, Randolph also had with him two "trusty wyse" merchants, Thomas Bannister and George Duckett, to advise him on commercial affairs. Those affairs were then in a precarious state, which the Russia Company blamed on Elizabeth's cautious diplomacy. To drive the point home, it furnished Randolph's ship with rancid provisions, "beere starke sower" and "water so ewle as none could be wurse."

But the voyage was savory compared to the world into which Randolph was about to disembark. Arriving at St. Nicholas in late July 1568, he reached Moscow on October 15, shortly after Philip's deposition. En route, he wrote to Lord Burghley:

> Of late [the tsar] hathe beheaded no small number of his nobilitie, cawsinge their heads to be layde in the streats to see who durste beholde them or lamente their deaths. The Chanceler [Cheliadnin] he cawsed to be executed

openlye, leaving nether his wyff, chyldren or brother alive. Divers other have byne cutt in peeces by his comandemente. . . . I intende to be wyth hym so sone as I cane speede as I maye . . . the soner to be owte of hys Countrie whear heads goe so faste to the potte.

That was not to be easy. Ivan was angry, placed Randolph under house arrest for several months, and had his diplomatic correspondence opened, read, and tendentiously translated by the English traitor Ralph Rutter, who also screened Queen Elizabeth's replies. Of Rutter and Glover, Randolph remarked: "In the worlde I am sure ther are no worce excepte that you rake hell to seeke men to serve you"; but they had powerful allies. A strong anti-English faction was ascendant at court, and "maynie practyzes are made agaynst us," he advised Lord Burghley, "with as myche cunninge workinge as yf all the divles in hell were confederate to overthrowe and drive us owte of thys country." About the only sign that the English were not in complete disfavor was a rumor that Ivan was thinking of putting together an English bodyguard—according to "talke in Mosco by men in ther cuppes."

Randolph finally met with the tsar on February 29, 1569, and to his astonishment was received in a friendly manner, as if nothing were amiss. Apologizing for not feting him at a banquet ("I dine not this day openly for great affaires I have"), Ivan referred him to the "Long Duke" (either Viazemsky or Nikita Romanovich), with whom Randolph conferred.

A few days later the Long Duke came to him in the middle of the night, furnished him with some sort of disguise, and led him to "a place farre off" where he spoke with Ivan secretly almost until dawn. The next day the tsar departed for Aleksandrova Sloboda, "the house of his solace."

Randolph conferred again with Ivan in Moscow in mid-April, and then in June followed him to Vologda, where apparently in return for vague (or not so vague) promises of an alliance he obtained a confirmation of all previous commercial privileges the Russia Company had enjoyed, plus the right to mine for iron at Vychegda, to mint coin at Moscow, Novgorod, and Pskov, to expand their facilities at Narva, and to build a new ropewalk at Vologda. The tsar also accepted all company property and personnel into the *Oprichnina*—thus placing them under his protection.

These gains were not as solid as they seemed. Randolph's remonstrances with the tsar about Rutter and Glover had been to no avail, and no sooner was he out of Ivan's sight than he was told by court Anglophobes to be out of his quarters within three days—"much soner then I cowlde, and was threatened to have my baggage throwen out of doores."

Meanwhile, Bannister and Duckett in going over the company accounts had found evidence of "very lewde and untrew praktises," and advised Lord Burghley that had they not come to Russia when they did "the holle trayde had bene utterlye overthrowen." Nevertheless, they believed the trade could be rebuilt and the company itself, gratified too by Randolph's efforts, furnished his return voyage with "good beveraige and bysquyte," as he embarked at the end of July with Andrey Savin, the new Russian ambassador to England.

30.

Muscovy's Neighbors Regroup

Despite his uncompromising objectives in the Livonian War, Ivan, caught up in his eroticized bloodbaths, had been unable to take advantage of the disarray of his Baltic adversaries whose energies had also been drained by their own domestic troubles and the Northern War. And now that window of opportunity was about to snap shut. Sweden was moving obscurely toward a repudiation of its Moscow alliance (before it could be consummated), Poland and Lithuania inexorably toward union. The Northern War itself was drawing to a close. And the Ottoman Empire was turning its fearsome gaze to the north.

Erik's mental disintegration had been apparent for some time. Nor, of course, can it be blamed directly on Ivan. If somebody at court so much as smiled or whispered or cleared his throat, Erik was sure he was being ridiculed; he cast his horoscope repeatedly: it predicted his assassination; he attributed every military setback to the treachery of his commanders, and executed two members of his bodyguard for sorcery: he discovered treason everywhere. As often as Ivan withdrew to his Sloboda, Erik secluded himself in his castle outside Stockholm, and paced back and forth in vengeful agitation through the gloomy halls.

To keep his own rebellious nobility under surveillance Erik also established Sweden's first secret police. Whereas the tsar looked to men like Skuratov and Griaznoy, Erik relied on Joran Persson, a parson's son and clerk, who had been educated by Melanchthon in jurisprudence at Witten-berg. Persson coordinated Erik's network of spies and bent the law of Swe-den to accommodate his sovereign's fears. For example, since only those sentenced to death could be tortured, even misdemeanors were designated capital crimes (subject to commutation) so that any prisoner could be racked for information about conspiracies.

While Erik's brother, Johan, languished in prison, the king fixed his primary suspicions on Nils Sture (grandson of the popular former regent Sten Sture), and astrologically confirmed his threat to the crown. Arrested and led through Stockholm in a mock-triumphal procession—as Cheliadnin had been placed on the Russian throne—Nils in his humiliation aroused such popular indignation that Erik (who had ceased to know his own mind) released him and appointed him to a top post. Then, just as suddenly, he rearrested and imprisoned him in Uppsala Castle with his father, Svante, and other nobles implicated in a plot. On May 24, 1567 (shortly before the arrival of the Russian embassy to extradite Katerina), Erik entered Svante's call, fell on his knees, and implored his pardon. A few hours later, with "his hat pulled down low over his brow," he returned, went directly into Nils' cell, and stabbed him in a frenzy with a dagger. Running out, he began shouting incoherently, changed into a peasant's costume, and at nightfall was discovered wandering, quite alone and distracted, through the woods on the edge of town.

During Erik's convalescence, government ground to a halt, with a disas-trous effect on military operations. The Danes advanced on all fronts, and Rantzau, with a small but picked army, marched from Smaland all the way to Skenninge, burning cities in his wake. Then Varberg fell. The *Riksdag* urged Erik to free Johan, but the king, in his delirium, was convinced his brother had already deposed him. When Johan was ushered into his presence, each insisted on kneeling to the other in a scene of painful and absurd confusion.

Insurrection was inevitable. Johan and a cabal of powerful nobles re-nounced their oath of allegiance, as a rising began in the south and spread through the central provinces to the gates of Stockholm, which were flung open to the rebel army on September 28, 1569. A few days later, Johan was crowned, Erik imprisoned, and the residence of the Muscovite ambassa-dors was sacked.

The coup in Stockholm paved the way for a settlement of the long-drawn-out Northern War. All the participants were financially exhausted, and because Johan and Sigismund had many interests which seemed to coincide, peace between Poland and Sweden was swiftly restored. A year later, by the Treaty of Stettin on November 30, 1570, Sweden's war with Denmark was also brought to a close. Both kingdoms renounced claims to each other's territory and agreed that Livonian territory now in their possession was eventually to be returned to the German emperor once he had paid for the expense of its defense against Moscow. This was a face-saving device. Everyone knew the emperor's coffers were empty. The treaty confirmed the status quo.

In Poland-Lithuania, a new age had also dawned. Just as fear of the Teutonic Knights had once prompted their dynastic union 200 years before, so in the struggle with Muscovy the constituent parts of the loosely knit kingdom coalesced into a more permanent bond. The developing dénouement was unmistakable. By the end of 1568, there was a broad consensus that a constitutional union was imperative, especially (since Sigismund had failed to produce an heir) with the impending demise of the dynasty itself. Yet its consummation was arduous. The Polish Diet insisted on the complete incorporation of Lithuania into Poland; in Lithuania the gentry favored parliamentary union, but the lords an arrangement that would keep the autonomy of the grand duchy intact.

Nevertheless, in late December 1568, a joint diet was convoked at Lublin to decide the issue. The Lithuanians expected concessions; the Poles, gratitude. Above all, the Lithuanians resented the desperate position in which they had been placed—in part by the crafty policies of the king who in his capacity as grand duke of Lithuania had committed that division of his realm to the defense of Livonia, without a similar commitment from the Poles. In the words of one lord: "When we left for the diet, the Muscovites were at our back. Yet we had wanted to join with you in love." By mid-February, negotiations had collapsed; whereupon the king, unwilling to see his great life's work thwarted at the eleventh hour, autocratically decreed on March 5 (in his capacity as grand duke of Lithuania) that the two Lithuanian provinces of Volynia and Podliashie (with strongly pro-union populations) were now "Polish." This changed everything. Rather than see Lithuania absorbed into Poland piecemeal, the dissidents capitulated, and on July 1, 1569, the Act of Union was sealed. Henceforth, Poland and Lithuania were to constitute one commonwealth, state, and people, with one currency and foreign policy, ruled by one sovereign, to be elected by a joint assembly of the united nation. That assembly was to meet in Poland, where the king would also be crowned. Though he would no longer be separately installed as grand duke of Lithuania, he would retain the title, while the Lithuanians were to enjoy some measure of autonomy in the preservation of their own law, administration, and army. Thus was the *Rzeczpospolita* or

Commonwealth born. And at the time it appeared to herald the creation of a vast new eastern empire.

The Ottoman Empire was not pleased by this development, but in its own way, too, felt obliged to respond to the recent growth of Russian might. On the face of it, at least, the Turks had little to fear. Under their most potent sultan, Suleyman the Magnificent, who in 1520 had succeeded Selim the Grim, their domains had spread southward into Egypt, eastward through Baghdad and Tabriz to the Caspian Sea and Persia, and westward into the heart of Europe, along the Balkan Peninsula. In 1521, they had encircled Belgrade, bombarded it with heavy cannon from an island in the Danube, and eventually reduced it by mines. In 1522, they had secured a beachhead on the Mediterranean, at Rhodes, despite the island's heroic defense by the Knights of St. John. Corsairs took Tunis and Algiers and raided as far north as the British Isles. In 1529, the Turks advanced across Hungary to besiege Vienna itself, and though twice repulsed forced the German Empire to accept a partition of Hungary. This led directly to the fall of Moldavia, and in 1538 the transformation of Wallachia into a vassal state.

Thus, by 1569, the sultan's dominions stretched from the Atlantic to the Indian Ocean; and as bombastic as his title read—"Shadow and Spirit of God amongst men, Monarch of the terrestrial orb, lord of two continents and of two seas, and of the east and west"—it was accurate enough as contemporary titles went.

Concurrently, however, Muscovy had become a great northern Russian state, then an empire, and after the conquest of Kazan and Astrakhan, extended its influence along the northern shores of the Caspian Sea to the River Terek and into the north Caucasus. Scattered Tartar tribes such as the Circassians had come under Russian domination, and the Little Nogays, allied to the Ottomans, had been driven to the right bank of the Volga, toward the shores of Azov. In 1559, Ivan had singed the sultan's beard with raids into the Crimean peninsula and at Azov at the mouth of the Don; and in 1561 had confirmed his allegiance with the Circassians by marrying the daughter of their chieftain. In 1567, he made a direct bid for authority in the region by building a fortress, garrisoned and equipped with artillery, on the River Terek, on the borders of Turkestan.

The Turks, hitherto preoccupied with their Persian and Balkan campaigns, were aroused. At the sultan's court, various Tartar exiles, especially the ousted grandees of Kazan and Astrakhan, agitated for recovery of their homelands, while Moslem merchants and pilgrims complained that the Russians interfered with the route through Astrakhan to Mecca. For the sultan as Caliph or Defender of the Faith, this was a significant issue, together with the religious persecution Tartars were said to be suffering in the occupied lands. Finally, the Turks regarded the Crimea, apparently now threatened, as an indispensable source of men for their campaigns, grain, condiments and slaves for their economy, and as a buffer state between themselves and the growing Slavic dominions to the north. Though Suleyman the Magnificent had repeatedly deferred the "Moscow" question, in 1566 it came to the fore when he was succeeded by Selim II the Sot.

Selim, the pitiable remnant of his father's filicide, had none of his predecessors' aptitude for government or war. His one, modest talent, was for poetry, but on the whole it was consumed by his passion for wine. Wine, he confessed, was sweeter to him "than the kiss of a young girl," and he actually once broke peace with a major power to seize an island whose vineyards he prized. As it happened, the power was Venice and the island, Cyprus; and its acquisition was of such strategic importance that perhaps never has a dissolute impulse produced so significant a policy result. Its immediate harvest, however, was to consolidate a "Holy League" between Venice, Spain, and the pope which made possible the historic Turkish naval defeat at Lepanto.

Generally speaking, Selim was "out of it," and relied heavily on advisers, especially on Mehmet Sokollu, his capable grand vizier. During Selim's sober interludes, Sokollu tactfully secured his imprimatur for policies already devised. In 1568, after negotiating a truce with the Hapsburg emperor, Sokollu decided it was time to address the Russian problem to the north.

The plan he came up with included an engineering project of fantastic ambition—a ship canal linking the Don River to the Volga—with a threefold aim: to enable the Turks to check Russian expansion into the north Caucasus by recapturing Astrakhan, and thereby cutting Russian trade with the East; to confirm the sultan's prestige as Grand Caliph by reopening the pilgrim route to Mecca; and by linking the Black Sea, already an "Ottoman Lake," to the Caspian, to enable the Turks to attack Persia from the north.

For some reason (which only lack of experience can explain) the canal itself was not seen as a difficulty, because the two rivers bent relatively close together where Don cossacks were said to portage their boats across.

Kasim Pasha, a Treasury official, was given command of the expedition, and throughout the spring of 1569 at the Black Sea port of Kaffa he assembled ships, troops, munitions, and other supplies, including thousands of shovels, picks, and spades and big stores of hard biscuit for the march through barren terrain. Heavy cannon were shipped from Constantinople; skilled laborers and carpenters were brought in from Moldavia and Wallachia, along with veteran sappers and miners who had shown their mettle during the

Hungarian wars. The Crimeans contributed their cavalry, and joined Kasim at Azov, where his flotilla of galleys arrived in June.

In early July, the galleys began threading their way up the Don, but almost immediately shallows forced delays, and it soon became apparent that heavy cannon and other matériel would have to be unloaded for transport overland. On August 15, the easternmost bend of the Don was reached, but it was found that the rivers were still forty miles apart, and the hilly topography not what Kasim had anticipated. He concluded at once that a canal was out of the question. Instead, for fifteen days his forces labored to level the land so that planks could be laid down to form a road. Some ships were hauled ashore and mounted on wheels, but a whole day's exertions advanced them just a few hundred yards; and then the wheels broke. Extrapolating, Kasim calculated that the portage alone would take a year. Back to Azov went his galleys and heavy cannon, as he marched at the head of a diminished but still mighty host across to the Volga. On September 16, he arrived at the ghost town of old Astrakhan. The new city, built ten miles downstream on a midriver island, was strongly defended with artillery; around it, the wide, deep waters of the Volga formed a natural moat.

Ivan, kept apprised of Turkish plans by his well-connected envoy in Bakchiseray, had offered the shah of Persia muskets for an armed diversion in the Caucasus, but once the expedition got under way, he had to rely on rough dispatches from the field.

Unwilling to strip his regiments on the Western front, where battle lines were being drawn anew, he gathered reserves at Nizhny-Novgorod and despatched a relatively small relief force to Astrakhan, which arrived just ahead of the Turks. This proved enough. Kasim discovered that the island stronghold was out of reach of his field artillery, while the Volga moat rendered his sappers useless. After Tartar reinforcements failed to arrive with provisions, he also despaired of mounting a blockade, especially with winter coming on.

He considered transforming old Astrakhan into a barracks and holding out until spring, when heavy cannon could be brought up the Don and portaged across for a full assault. But opposition to this plan was nearly unanimous, as the winters in Astrakhan were known to be bitter, with an average temperature below freezing, high winds, and heavy snows. The chosen alternative was no less grim, as the army set out for Azov, 500 miles away, across trackless wastes of unmitigated sand. The Tartar contingent, inured to the hardships of seminomadic life, sustained themselves on horseflesh and mare's milk. But at the end of the month-long trek most of the Turkish army lay buried in the sands.

It is said that Devlet Giray was not unhappy about all this, because a canal would have enabled the sultan to expand his power in the Steppe, and in time to annex the Crimea as his own, ending the Giray dynasty. It is even said that he purposely doomed the retreat by leading the Turks astray, so that they invariably failed to encounter the few groves or oxbow lakes that might have relieved their march. However true, the Turkish venture had not been in vain. Ivan elected to abandon his fortress on the Terek (in 1571), and vouchsafed passage for pilgrims to Mecca through Astrakhan.

In the end, of course, it would be the Russians, not the Turks, who would succeed in building a Don-Volga Canal, though not until after the Second World War.

31.

The Sack of Novgorod

Ivan took less comfort from the Turkish fiasco than one might expect, and seemed to attach more significance to the fact that when his cousin Vladimir passed through Kostroma on his way to take command of the reserves at Nizhny-Novgorod, the whole population turned out to cheer him. This combined in his mind with some other recent unpleasant surprises. In January, the Russian defector Timofey Teterin, disguised as an *Oprichnik*, had persuaded the night watch at the fortress of Izborsk to open the gates. A Lithuanian detachment of 800 men rushed in after him, and though Ivan recaptured the fortress two weeks later, he went to extraordinary lengths to get his hands on the fortress commander, Afanasy Nashchekin, who had otherwise enjoyed a distinguished career. He traded a number of Lithuanian prisoners for him in August, and rode all the way from Vologda to Aleksandrova Sloboda to see him tied to a stake and, like Saint Sebastian, riddled with arrows.

Beset by fears that Pskov and Novgorod might emulate the example of Izborsk—that is, capitulate at the first opportunity—he deported 500 "suspect" families from Pskov and 150 more from Novgorod to Tver; at the same time, profoundly shaken by Erik's fate in Sweden, he looked through a glass darkly at Johan and saw Staritsky, the nobility's favorite, who was also popular with the folk. Then, on September 6, 1569, Ivan's second wife, Maria, died of poison. Though their marriage had been "politically" inspired, a chronicler reports that Ivan had also fallen in love with her at first sight. Reputedly wild, cruel, and dissolute, Maria had evidently inspired Kurbsky's rhetorical question in a letter to Muromtsev, "Who is there to accuse the Queen of love of gold?" and it has even been alleged that the *Oprichnina* was her idea. In any case, Ivan reacted to her death by refortifying Aleksandrova Sloboda and by expanding the Vologda Kremlin, which was now to include an adjacent shipyard to facilitate the transport of his treasure to the White Sea.

Staritsky of course was doomed. In October, a conspiracy was concocted around the palace cook, who had gone to Nizhny-Novgorod that summer to procure salmon for the royal table. Apprehended, the cook "confessed" that Staritsky had bribed him with fifty rubles to lace the fish with poison. Vladimir was summoned to the Sloboda to confront his accuser, and in a brief trial at a posting station nearby (Skuratov and Griaznoy presiding) he was condemned to drink a cup of poisoned wine. Afterward, his entire retinue and family were cut down by *Oprichniki*, and an assassin was sent north to strangle his mother, Evfrosinia, in her convent cell. The cook, his two sons, and even the fisherman who had caught the fish and the vendor who had sold it, were likewise executed.

Two months later Ivan embarked on the most infamous atrocity of his reign.

According to the Chronicles, a vagabond malcontent by the name of Peter, from the Lithuanian province of Volynia, had a score to settle with the Novgorod authorities for some discipline he had received at their hands. Resolved to be revenged upon the whole city, he composed a treasonous letter to Sigismund August, as if from the archbishop and other inhabitants, which he concealed in the Cathedral of St. Sophia behind an icon of the Virgin opposite the archbishop's throne. He then hurried to Moscow to disclose the conspiracy to the tsar. Ivan dispatched a secret agent to Novgorod who, of course, discovered the incriminating document in the designated place. And this led to the reprisals.

Recent scholarship suggests that although the facts are askew, the essence of the account is right. Apparently, a prominent *Zemshchina* boyar and artillery commander, Vasily Danilov, who permitted the mutiny and flight of certain Lithuanian prisoners of war, confessed on the rack to intriguing with Sigismund August against the tsar, and wildly implicated whomever it was suggested might also have been involved, including the Novgorod authorities.

This incident dovetails with the recollections of a Venetian abbot, who happened to visit Moscow a few months later, that a traitorous letter had been intercepted, either to or from Poland—evidently alluding to a "Polish note," mentioned in the Kremlin archives, that two state secretaries had turned over to the tsar. Just as Cheliadnin and Philip (a prominent boyar and a hierarch) vaguely linked in a conspiracy had occasioned attacks on both the nobility and Church, so now Danilov and Archbishop Pimen (just as vaguely linked) occasioned the same opportunities for plunder, random violence, and revenge. One of the first boyars to be executed as a result was a certain Grigor Volynsky, hence the "Peter of Volynia" in the Chronicles' account.

Yet perhaps "Peter of Volynia" is a still richer clue than that. As Ivan's tyranny had increased, he feared that Novgorod and Pskov, as former democracies with past political affinities to Lithuania, would be even more strongly drawn by the new and powerful constitutional union which now joined Lithuania with Poland. The political ambivalence of the two former principalities had of course long been a factor in Russian foreign relations, and it cannot be forgotten that in most negotiations between Muscovy and Lithuania for a century or more, Lithuania had claimed both Novgorod and Pskov as her own as firmly as Moscow had claimed Smolensk and Polotsk. The spectacle of the new union, in beckoning contrast to the oppression under the tsar, might well have rekindled whatever democratic sentiment remained. And Volynia had shown the way, for after Sigismund's famously bold act incorporating the province into Poland, its deputies had independently sworn allegiance to the king, compelling the rest of Lithuania to go along. What's in a name? In the compressed and folktalelike Chronicles account, Volynia stood for the attraction of the union—that which Ivan feared most, and which called forth his wrath.

Whether the Lithuanian secret service arranged for some incriminating document to be intercepted, or not, as one Soviet historian suggests, is perhaps not so important as the story itself, which goes to the heart of what was felt to be at stake.

Ivan huddled with his favorites at Aleksandrova Sloboda and decided to sack the two cities and to exterminate everyone in them on his "enemies list." An army of 15,000, including 1500 *streltsy*, was mustered, and the night before setting out, Ivan got up twice before daybreak to go over his plans with Viazemsky, in whom he apparently had absolute trust. It is said, in fact, that he would accept medicine only from Viazemsky's hands.

Located on the Volkhov River about two miles below its outfall from Lake Ilmen, and about 110 miles southeast of where the Neva flows into the Gulf of Finland, Novgorod (much like Budapest) was divided in two. Its kremlin or inner citadel, with great stone walls and nine towers, stood on the left or west bank of the Volkhov and enclosed the archbishop's sumptuous palace and the city's five-domed Cathedral of St. Sophia. On the right or east bank stood the commercial quarter, where organized guilds of merchants had once flourished in conjunction with the Hanseatic factory Ivan III had destroyed.

Novgorod could trace its democratic institutions to 1019 when Yaroslav the Wise had issued the town a charter of self-government. Through its *veche* or town meeting, the people had elected their chief officials by direct democracy, much as in the ancient city-state republics of Athens and Rome. But sovereignty resided in the town itself, which was quaintly styled *Gospodid Veliki Novgorod* ("Lord Novgorod the Great").

A mile and a quarter to the south, on the other hand, where the Volkhov rises in Lake Ilmen, stood the so-called *Rurikovo Gorodishche* or Rurik's hill-fort, traditionally the residence of princes expelled by the *veche* for malfeasance or for attempting to exceed their authority. As such, it came to symbolize hostility to democratic liberties, just as the Cathedral of St. Sophia symbolized the town's freedom, prosperity, and independence. "To stand and die for St. Sophia" meant to fight and die for Novgorod.

St. Sophia was a great Orthodox cathedral, inspired by the original Russian cathedral in Kiev. Its western portal was furnished with a magnificent pair of embossed bronze doors dating from the twelfth century; and its large, beautifully proportioned interior was divided by rows of powerful, cruciform piers into five aisles, with three semicircular apses and a choir gallery. The nave and transept were beautifully lit by windows; the iconography included enthralling figures of eight prophets and the four evangelists; while the huge head and shoulders of Christ Pantocrator looked awesomely down from the central dome.

As Ivan embarked on his infamous revenge, the utmost pains were taken to conceal his intentions. "No one in Moscow," wrote a contemporary, "even knew where he was." Even the commander of the advance guard was kept in the dark, as each morning Ivan gave him a map pinpointing the next night's encampment, with a warning to keep the location secret and under no circumstances to pick another spot. The expedition made a wide detour of the capital, and in accordance with methods he would soon use to enforce quarantines during epidemics, any wayfarer the troops encountered was killed at once so as not to herald their advance.

Wholesale killing and looting started in Klin, a small town en route, and continued in Tver, where the "rebellious" Novgorod families had been resettled. The inhabitants of Tver could only compare what was happening to them to the historic massacres by Khan Uzbek in 1327. On December 23, Skuratov rode to the Otroch Monastery, entered the cell where former Metropolitan Philip remained confined, and sought his blessing for the expedition. Philip refused, and knowing what Skuratov had really come to do, opened his arms to God.

As Skuratov left the monastery, he told the prior that he had found Philip's cell "stifling," and the former metropolitan already dead, "of neglect." The prior found him smothered under his bedclothes.

In Torzhok and Medyno, families recently deported from Pskov were massacred, and many Polish and Lithuanian prisoners of war were shot. Nineteen Tartar nobles faced the same fate, but when they learned what was in store for them they managed to conceal long knives under their robes. As their executioners lined them up in a courtyard, they attacked, killing two. Skuratov was wounded in the stomach, and Ivan himself grazed before the Tartars were cut down.

On January 2, 1570, Ivan came within sight of Novgorod. An advance detachment had completely cordoned off the city with roadblocks and hastily erected watchtowers, while cavalry brigades charged through the suburbs slaughtering local militia and the armed retainers landowners kept on their estates. All the treasuries of neighboring monasteries were impounded, and some 500 clerics—abbots, elders, and deacons—were rounded up and placed under guard. Over the next several days they were regularly subjected to *pravezh* or cudgelings to extort a minimum of twenty rubles from each, and to force the disclosure of any secretly sequestered wealth. Meanwhile, squads of *Oprichniki* fanned out through the city and sealed up the great mansions and parishes, posting sentinels at the doors. Most of the local dignitaries were likewise confined.

The Chronicles assert that Novgorod was taken by surprise. Ivan thought otherwise, but aside from a few high officials (who were helpless to oppose him) the Chronicles are probably right. In any case, Novgorod was so rapidly and efficiently occupied by Ivan's guard that there was little strategic need for the elaborate earthworks and fortifications hastily created to secure the tsar's encampment at Gorodische.

On January 6, he ordered the massacre of all monks who had not paid their twenty rubles or "redemption tax." On Sunday, the 8th, he made his dreaded entry into the city. The clergy, carrying icons and crosses, met him on the Volkhov Bridge. Archbishop Pimen attempted a benediction but the tsar refused it, vehemently cursing the prelate as "a thief, a murderer, a traitor, and a wolf." He proceeded to the Cathedral of St. Sophia, heard Mass (with a trembling Pimen officiating), and reputedly prayed with great fervor. Afterward, he went to the episcopal residence where Pimen had done his best to prepare a banquet.

Ivan began to eat, stood up and shouted "Hoyda!" and at once his myrmidons appeared. They arrested the archbishop and began to ransack the palace. Evstafy, the tsar's confessor (whose piety Philip had presumed to doubt), headed for St. Sophia Cathedral, where he carried off sacred vessels and chasubles and authorized irremediable damage to the ancient Korsun gate of miraculous icons, which was wrenched from the altar. The famed bronze church doors were also ripped from their hinges, and the bronze cathedral bell cut from its tower. Meanwhile, twenty-seven local monasteries were systematically stripped.

Some 400 prominent citizens—boyars, courtiers, abbots, officials, and merchants—were hauled off to Gorodishche for trial. The method of investigation was torture; the invariable verdict, death. Ivan built a kind of hillslide down to the Volkhov River, bound his torn and broken victims to sleds, and sped them precipitously into the icy water, where *Oprichniki* armed with pikes and axes moved about in boats hacking and stabbing at anyone who tried to swim. Others were hanged, beheaded, impaled, or thrown off the Volkhov Bridge.

The Gorodishche massacres continued for five weeks, and ended with a general pillage of Novgorod. Many *Oprichniki* made their fortunes in a night. Von Staden, who had joined the campaign with one horse and two servants, returned to his manor with forty-nine horses—twenty-two of them harnessed to sleds laden with goods. What was not expropriated was vandalized or destroyed.

At length, on February 13, Ivan condescended to pardon all who remained alive. He summoned about sixty elders to Gorodishche, spoke to them "with mildness," we are told, and gazed upon them "with kind and merciful eyes." With the cruelest irony, he asked them to pray that heaven might grant him a long and happy reign.

Pimen was publicly humiliated. Borrowing a page from Gennady's treatment of the Novgorod heretics three-quarters of a century before (which he had obviously studied in Joseph Sanin's account), Ivan sat the archbishop backward on a mare, thrust bagpipes and a zither into his hands, and taunted him with names. This thoroughly believable incident is confirmed by two sources, yet (in what would seem oddly contradictory behavior in any other monarch) he also rebuked Metropolitan Kirill, Philip's successor, for having prematurely declared Pimen stripped of his rank. Ivan wrote to his over-zealous lackey: "Archbishop Pimen may not perform any services, but his style and dignity are not to be removed until he has been judged and sentenced by the Church Council!" When the council met in July, its deliberations were brief. Pimen was defrocked and confined to the Nikolsky Monastery outside Tula south of Moscow, where he died in the following year.

The scale of Ivan's atrocity has been the subject of much debate, and estimates vary widely as to the total number slain. The Chronicles say 60,000: "And every day perhaps a thousand; occasionally fifteen hundred, and if perchance only five or six hundred people . . . the day in question was considered an easy day, one deserving of thanks." But the entire city population cannot have been that large. Another contemporary conjectured 2770 prominent citizens "not counting humbler folk"; a third, 27,000 in all. The second figure more or less agrees with a meticulous sifting of the primary documents by the renowned Soviet historian Ruslan Skrynnikov, who based his calculations on the tsar's subsequently compiled Synodical or memorial list of the dead. Ivan had an extraordinary memory, but the Synodical is known to be incomplete and deliberately omitted those he refused to "forgive." Such anonymous "humbler folk" as *Oprichniki* did away with in back alleys were also obviously not included in the list.

The controversy, however, is frivolous, because it obscures the overall scope of the crime. Aside from those killed on the spot, countless others eventually perished because they had been deprived of their livelihoods, loved ones, winter stores of grain, parts of their bodies, their sanity itself. Moreover, the calamity was followed directly by famine, and famine by epidemics. Death in Novgorod forged a chain, begun by the tsar's atrocities; and link by link it made up an awesome sum.

From Novgorod, Ivan marched on Pskov, where news of what had been happening had long since reached the inhabitants. On February 17, he pitched his camp at the monastery of St. Nicholas on the city's outskirts; and it is said that, as he listened to all the churchbells pealing through the winter night, "his heart was softened and he came to himself," and ordered his soldiers to "blunt their swords with stones." In truth, most of the Pskovians he meant to kill had already been executed on the road to Novgorod.

Ivan entered Pskov from the north, through the Varlaamsky Gate. In a gesture of submission, the people had placed tables spread with bread and salt in front of their dwellings and knelt in the snow before their offerings as Ivan drove through the city in a sleigh. He attended Mass in Holy Trinity Cathedral and prayed at length at the tomb of Saint Vsevolod, a twelfth-century prince and local hero whose mighty sword, inscribed with the words "I surrender my honor to no one," hung nearby. Ivan appeared to stare at it. Emerging from the cathedral he executed forty officials and had several clergymen burned at the stake. Some ransacking of churches and prosperous establishments began. But then, abruptly, it stopped—due, we are told, to the intercession of one Nikolay, a "holy fool."

Nikolay existed. "I saw this imposter or magician," wrote an Englishman, "a fowll creature, went naked both in winter and sommer; he indured both extreme frost and heat; did many streinge things thorow magical illusions of the Divill; much followed, feared and reverenced, bothe of prince and people." If so, then we must give the devil his due.

At the time Ivan came to Pskov, Nikolay enjoyed a considerable reputation as a fortune teller and lived in a soiled and disheveled little house aswarm with pets. Ivan went to see him, ostensibly for his blessing, but probably to learn what his future might hold. As he approached the dwelling, a voice boomed out through the window: "Ivashka! Ivashka![1] How much longer will you continue to shed innocent blood? Enough. Go home! Or a great misfortune will befall you!" Ivan pushed through the door to confront the speaker, who promptly thrust into his hands a slab of raw meat. Flabbergasted, Ivan exclaimed, "I am a Christian. I do not eat meat during Lent." Nikolay inquired politely, "How about Christian blood?" Then he called him "the Emperour bloudsuccer" and warned him he would be struck down by a thunderbolt "if he or any of his army in Pskov did touch a hair in displeasur of the least childs head." Suddenly the sky grew overcast, thunder rumbled from afar, and Ivan's heart changed out of fear.

Though usually dismissed as an apocryphal tale, Nikolay's intercession was remarked upon alike by both the Chronicles and Western contemporaries. Indeed, it was so sensational that it could not long continue to be linked to a secondary saint. Within a few years it belonged to Vasily (Basil) the Blessed, a Holy Fool of more historic standing, and the scene was transferred to Novgorod. As the story goes, Vasily invited Ivan to dinner in a cave beneath the Volkhov Bridge. He set up a little table, and dished up meat and blood. Ivan had a vision of the souls of innocent martyrs rising toward heaven, came to his senses, and commanded the executions to stop. As he did so, the terrible offerings on his plate were transformed into watermelon and wine.

Vasily, in fact, had died several years before, and in 1558 had been canonized. Soon thereafter, the Moscow cathedral commemorating the conquest of Kazan and Astrakhan had been popularly named after him, with an additional chapel added to house his tomb. Thus, the very church Makary had built to exalt the tsardom was dedicated by the people to the conscience which it lacked.

In an act of national contrition, moreover, Metropolitan Philip would be canonized in the following century.

There is a postscript to this story deserving a place beside the miracle tales.

Among the clerics to meet Ivan at the Varlaamsky Gate had been Vassian Muromtsev, Kurbsky's correspondent, and Abbot Kornily of the Pskov-Pechery Monastery. Both were subsequently executed.

Kornily's fate was particularly anomalous.

A protégé of Makary, who had appointed him abbot at the age of twenty-eight, he had (so far as we know) firmly believed in the autocracy, and in the course of his tenure as abbot, had transformed his monastery into a first-class frontier fortress by building two stone churches and a massive, encompassing stone wall with seven towers. Included in the fortifications was the powerful Church of Saint Nicholas the Miracle Worker, which had a subterranean arsenal, gunloops on the walls, and commanded the open triangle of ground between the first and second gates. A wooden statue of Nicholas, nicknamed "the Warrior," depicted the saint with a sword.

A veritable paradigm of the Russian Church Militant, Kornily's monastery had also been associated with the "miraculous" victories at Narva and Fellin early in the Livonian War. Yet, in front of one of the gates, Ivan struck him down. He struck him down and then, the story goes, seized with remorse, took the body into his arms and carried it "with tears of repentance" along an unpaved path known afterward as the "path of Blood" to a church within the grounds.

That path, deliberately left unchanged for generations, was still to be seen as late as 1938.

32.

Faith and Works

Back at Aleksandrova Sloboda, an unrepentant tsar sequestered his plunder in fireproof storehouses, and to commemorate his campaign against the two cities erected two new stone churches. For one of them he cut the bronze doors of St. Sophia down to size.

On May 4, he returned to Moscow to attend to urgent activity on the diplomatic front. As always, Ivan continued to give his attention to a broad range of affairs. He courted an armistice with Poland (to which Sigismund August was amenable to gain time to consolidate the new union of his kingdom) and the normalization of relations with Turkey so as to free his forces for an attack against the Swedes. When Swedish envoys arrived in Russia in January, they were interned in Murom. Two months later, a large and impressive Polish embassy arrived with a suite of 700 for negotiations that culminated on June 22 in a three-year truce.

The linchpin of Moscow's new policy was the idea of establishing a vassal kingdom in Livonia under Denmark's Duke Magnus, who remained barricaded on the island of Oesel. Ivan had had his eye on Magnus for a long time. He knew of his dependent condition and frustrated envy of his brother, King Frederick, who in exchange for Holstein had misled him into hoping for a large Livonian dominion of his own. Even on Oesel he was under the continuous surveillance of one of Frederick's generals. Ivan offered to make his dreams come true. Through Johann Taube and Elert Kruse, two Livonian noblemen captured early in the war who became Ivan's ambassadors without portfolio, he invited Magnus to Moscow to be proclaimed "King of Livonia."

Magnus came, signed a treaty which "guaranteed" the Livonians freedom of religion, with all their hereditary rights and customs, privileges, and laws, and promised them duty-free trade with Muscovy, in return for their submission. He was betrothed to Princess Evfimia, eldest daughter of the late Vladimir Staritsky, and in return for his new title and the privilege of marrying Ivan's niece, was expected to take Reval—the key to securing Estonia. (In all this Ivan was but vaguely following Sigismund's example, who had recently secured Courland through Kettler, his vassal duke.) On June 25—three days after the armistice with Poland was signed—Magnus set out for Reval at the head of a Russian army.

Ivan needed Magnus, however, far more than Sigismund had ever needed Kettler. Fear of living under Russian rule had grown since the beginning of the war, and information about the *Oprichnina* was getting out. In territory under Russian occupation, a brutal policy of reprisal had recently taken hold, while elsewhere anti-Russian propaganda was having its effect. All nations, of course, try to dehumanize the image of their opponents in war, and just as the "wilde" Irish was every Elizabethan's ethnic prototype of the savage ("they never leave a man for dead until they have slit open his belly to remove his heart"), so reports now swept through Europe that the Muscovite-Tartar hordes in Livonia were "eating Livonian children," "not even sparing the child in its mother's womb." "O the lamentable owtcries and cruell slaughters," went another report, "drowninge and burninge, ravizinge of weomen and mayeds, strippinge them naked without mercie or regard of the frossen weather, tyenge and byndinge them by three and by fower at the their horses taiells, dragginge them som alive som dead, all bloudying the wayes and streates . . . into Russia." Ivan's Tartar entourage was invariably singled out as evidence of his savagery, and one delegate to the Polish Diet concluded that "except for his outward form" Ivan had "nothing in common with the human race."

Nevertheless, the new Polish embassy clearly assumed that Ivan might turn out to be a broadminded Christian. And this had produced a curious sideshow.

As it happened, the chief envoy, Jan Krotowski, was an evangelical Hussite[1] who belonged to a Protestant religious community known as the Bohemian Brethren. Along with other Protestant sects, the Brethren enjoyed within Catholic Poland considerable political clout, and in his eagerness to promote friendship between the two powers, Krotowski hoped Ivan might allow the Brethren freedom to evangelize in Moscow. He may even have hoped to convert the tsar himself, and to this end had brought with him Jan Rokyta, one of the leading Hussite preachers of the day.

They had reason to be encouraged. Protestants were tolerated in Russia more than Catholics, and were widely scattered through the realm. In provinces bordering on Sweden and Livonia, a current of Lutheran missionary feeling was indulged for political reasons, while the Anglican English were a substantial presence in the Russian north. At the beginning of the Livonian War, Ivan had also rounded up Protestant Livonian talent (merchants, architects, wheelwrights, gunsmiths, and so forth), deporting many of the artisans into the Russian interior. In 1565, a second wave of deportations from Narva, Dorpat, and other towns gave rise to Protestant communities on the fast-growing Volga trade route, at Vologda, Kostroma, and Nizhny-Novgorod. At this time, too, the nucleus of the so-called "German suburb" southeast of Moscow was formed, where parishioners were allowed two churches, one Lutheran, the other Calvinist.

On the other hand, Ivan was profoundly repelled by the antiauthoritarian strain in Reformation theology and the factionalism it seemed to spawn was absolutely contrary to the dogmatic unity coveted by the Russian Orthodox Church. What he was willing to tolerate in his policy was very different from what he was prepared to proclaim. Therefore, when he accepted Rokyta's invitation to a public debate, he was bound to speak as the "Orthodox Tsar."

The "debate" took place on May 10, 1570, before a large audience in the Kremlin Palace. Ivan sat on an elevated throne and confronted the Hussite preacher, who stood on a carpeted dais. The tsar made a brief, vigorous statement in which he denounced Protestantism in general as "depraved, and clearly contrary to the teaching of Christ and the Church." He then put several questions to the preacher regarding the Brethren's doctrine. Rokyta kept his exposition brisk and, as he no doubt supposed, innocuously simple and direct. Avoiding criticism of Orthodox beliefs, he leveled his indictment at the Roman Catholic Church. Ivan heard him patiently, praised his eloquence, invited him to summarize their exchange in writing, and promised a detailed written reply.

Rokyta, however, had not acquitted himself well. Despite his fifteen years' experience as cosenior spokesman for his church (including a dispute with an anti-Trinitarian in the presence of Sigismund August in 1564), his vague and uncontroversial approach, weakly supported by scriptural quotation, had failed to say anything definite about the Incarnation, the Resurrection, or the Trinity. Ivan's written reply, though occasionally rhetorical and vain, was apostolic in form, designed to admonish and instruct. Rokyta had set little boats upon the water; Ivan, with a tidal wave of Biblical and patristic quotation, swept them all away.

Of the ten questions Ivan had asked, two were paramount: "What is the foundation of your faith—how can man be justified?" and "Why do you not have icons?"—the first going to the heart of Christianity itself; the second, to the heart of the Russian Orthodox Church. To the first Rokyta had replied:

Foremost, everyone has to consider himself a sinner before God, deserving condemnation for the sin of the first parents in Paradise, because of whom everyone is born into this world already in sin and under the wrath of God. And no one can free himself from that sin and satisfy God simply with his deeds and merits. . . . Through them [human deeds] no man has ever been justified before God, but only through faith in Christ Himself, for all holy Scriptures testify that the forgiveness of sins and the gift of eternal life after death are granted only in Christ's name.

And to the second:

Through His Prophets God has strictly forbidden man to make and worship images, and St. John says at the end of his First Epistle: "Little children, keep yourselves from idols." Against this command of the Lord we do not dare to venture to put images of God and the saints in the church, for we know that God has always punished [man] severely for it. . . . The saints, while living in the world, did not allow themselves to be praised, as Peter said to Cornelius: "Get up for I am a man." (Acts 10:26) . . . To every saint a special field is attributed, as if God Almighty neither could nor wanted to do it satisfactorily Himself.

Ivan's complex rejoinder, stamped by his neurotic personality, yet illuminated by an uncorrupted intelligence and literary gift, deserves to be quoted at length:

I did not want to answer you, because you inquire for inquiry's sake and not for the sake of faith. For we are taught by Our Lord Jesus Christ, "Give not that which is holy unto the dogs, neither cast ye your pearls before swine." The saving word is often cause of ruin. For that reason I wanted to keep silent. [But] I will tell you a little, so that you do not think me ignorant. You have written that no one can save himself in any way by good deeds, and you have referred to the epistles to the Romans and the Galatians. . . . Now faith is the substance of things hoped for, the evidence of things not seen. Through faith we understand that the worlds were framed by the Word of God, so that things which are seen were not made of things which appear. Abel offered unto God a more excellent sacrifice than Cain, by which he obtained witness that he was righteous. By faith Abraham, when he was called to go out into a place which he would thereafter receive for inheritance, obeyed; and he went out, not knowing whither he went. Through faith also Sarah herself received strength to conceive seed, and was delivered of a child when she was past age. By faith Moses, when he was come to years, refused to be called the son of Pharaoh's daughter; choosing rather to suffer with the people of God, than to enjoy the pleasures of sin for a season; esteeming the reproach of Christ greater riches than the treasures in Egypt: for he had respect unto the recompense of the reward. By faith he forsook Egypt, not fearing the wrath of the king; for he endured, as seeing him who is invisible. [Yet] it is said in the general epistle of James: "What doth it profit, my brethren, though a man say he hath faith, and have not works? Can faith save him? If a brother or sister be naked, and destitute of daily food, and one of you say unto them, Depart in peace, be ye warmed and filled; notwithstanding ye give them not those things which are needful; what doth it profit? Even so faith, if it hath no works, is dead, being alone. Thou believest that there is one God; thou doest well: the devils also believe, and tremble. Was not Abraham our father justified by his works, when he offered Isaac his son upon the altar? Seest thou how faith wrought with his works, and by works was faith made perfect? . . . By works a man is justified, and not by faith only. Do you think there was a difference of meaning between those Apostles when they wrote, Paul about faith, James about action? No, there was great agreement. One was asserting deeds, the other strengthening faith, and both acted for the same good, for the salvation of men through faith and deeds. . . .

Look at Paul himself writing about deeds: "Where sin abounded, grace did much more abound: That as sin reigneth unto death, even so might grace reign through righteousness unto eternal life by Jesus Christ our Lord. What shall we say then? Shall we continue in sin, that grace may abound? God forbid. . . . But I am afraid of talking too much, for fear of being judged with Judas for having told the secret to the foe.

Ivan then turned to the worship of icons and saints:

There is no salvation in another name, but in the name of the Lord Jesus Christ. We do believe this, but only by His disciples and apostles and divine fathers are we led to it and instructed of the true road. And we pray to the most Holy, Immaculate, Ever Virgin Mary, who was worthy to serve such a mystery and to receive the flame of God in her womb.

We do not worship the apostles. That shall not be. For the Apostle himself says, writing: "I have planted, Apollos watered, but Christ gave the increase." . . . Thus do we honor the divine apostles as students and messengers of the word of God and instructors and leaders of our salvation, and the fathers also in the same way as guides, and we revere the sainted martyrs.

What is difficult in Scripture cannot be thought out on one's own, as did your Luther and yourselves. But Paul preached by means of the Revelation of Jesus Christ and did not lay his own foundation, but that which was laid, which is Jesus Christ. . . .

The apostles, in going forth to preach, left seventy vicars in their place. Following them are the higher priests; from them come also the priests who are the teachers of men even until this day. . . . If Christians did not need that, the apostle would not have written about it. But who appointed you?

You, having bypassed the priests, the teachers, the fathers and the apostles, corrupt the very convenant. . . .
As to the worshipping of idols, you have not distinguished between the holy and the abject. You have judged equal the icon of Christ and the idol of Apollo. . . . Where will you find now . . . the shedding of blood for divine icons as for idols? With idols nothing is accomplished. Concerning the icons of the Church a spiritual prayer is a sacrifice from the heart. Do not think that we idolize them; rather we worship honoring the source of the likeness; we honor neither the paint nor the board, but the image painted of Christ and the Mother of God and of all saints, raising the glory to the source. . . . When the divine Luke had painted the likeness of the Mother of God and brought it to her, she said, "My grace and strength shall be with you." And this icon is, by the order of God, here in the ruling city of Moscow, preserving Christianity.

Ivan concluded:

I cannot look upon you otherwise than as a heretic, for all your teaching is corrupt as compared with the teaching of Christ. . . . You are not only a heretic, but also a servant of the Antichrist. . . . In the future you shall not preach in our country. And we will faithfully pray to our Lord Jesus Christ, the Savior of all, to preserve us, the Russian people, from the darkness of your unbelief.

Ivan's brilliant tract, richly bound and filling eighty-four parchment pages, was solemnly handed to Rokyta in a jewel-studded box on June 18, shortly before the embassy returned to Poland. Whatever Rokyta may have thought of it, it was subsequently recognized by others as authoritative; and a quarter of a century later a Catholic king of Poland would rely more heavily on Ivan's exposition for his Counterreformation propaganda than on all the treatises churned out by the learned Jesuits then crowding his court.

Unfortunately, Ivan's intellectual accomplishments were destined to sing but a lofty descant to the terrible theme. Even as he expounded the theology of redemption with almost apostolic beauty, authority, and power, secret trials were about to create new martyrs of some of the worthiest remaining men in his realm. Having delayed the start of the executions until the Poles departed, with savage promptitude he made up for lost time.

An inquest into Archbishop Pimen's treason named three leading *Oprichniki* as accomplices—Aleksey Basmanov, his son Fyodor, and Prince Afanasy Viazemsky—together with several leading state secretaries including Ivan Viskovaty. If such a broad conspiracy could ever have been forged,

Ivan probably would not have survived it. The Basmanovs were executed (according to Kurbsky, Fyodor was forced to cut off his father's head); and Viazemsky, caught hiding in the house of Ivan's English court physician, Arnold Lindsay, was banished to Kazan.

Viskovaty's condemnation was a national tragedy, to be compared with the assassination of Philip. Though he had "never contradicted the tsar openly," we are told, behind the scenes he had apparently been telling him "to think of God, not to shed so much innocent blood, and not to exterminate his nobility. He begged him," wrote a contemporary, "to reflect on who would choose to live in his realm, to say nothing of fighting on his behalf, if he continued to destroy so many brave men. The Grand Prince replied: 'I have not yet rooted all of you out because I have not really started, but I intend to make every effort to destroy you so completely that no memory of you will survive.' "

Let us remember Ivan Mikhaylovich Viskovaty.

After retiring as head of the Foreign Ministry in August 1562, he had remained as a top aide to the tsar on foreign affairs, while his responsibilities expanded into other areas. On February 9, 1561, he had become *pechatnik* or chancellor, and soon thereafter also keeper of the great seal.

The exceptional favor he was shown at court made such an impression on contemporaries that a half century later it was still remembered that he had "always been served at the tsar's table." One eyewitness, who had ample opportunity to observe the close relationship between the two men, wrote that "Ivan IV loved Viskovaty as he loved himself." Baltazar Russow, the compiler of the Livonian Chronicle and a man "very hostile to the Russians," testified: "Ivan Viskovaty was an excellent man. There was not one like him at that time in Moscow. All the foreign ambassadors were greatly amazed at his mind and diplomatic art."

Though as late as July 12, Viskovaty's loyalty had not been openly questioned, he proved vulnerable to lethal court intrigue, at a time when one's fortunes at law could be called a horoscope of one's impending fate. Shortly before his indictment he lost two *beschestie* suits, one to Prince Vasily Temkin-Rostovsky, a prominent member of the *Oprichnina;* the other to Vasily Shchelkalov, a fellow state secretary and clerk of the Duma.

In the secret indictment Viskovaty was accused of having conspired to surrender Novgorod and Pskov to the Poles, and of clandestine contacts with the Turks to encourage their expedition against Astrakhan.

On July 20, the tsar beheaded Viskovaty's brother, Tretyak, ostensibly because he had impugned the memory of Vladimir Staritsky, now being rehabilitated so as to ennoble Ivan's betrothal of Evfimia to Magnus. Yet it is unlikely his sentence would have been so grim had not his illustrious brother already been condemned.

Ivan put theology behind him. Tretyak's execution got his blood going, and that same evening he jumped up from dinner, shouted "Hoyda!" and ordered his bodyguard to the home of Peter Serebriany, a renowned Muscovite general, who was dragged out of his house and beheaded by Skuratov in the yard. The reasons are obscure, but Serebriany had two broad stripes against him: he had favored Staritsky in 1553 and he belonged to the House of Obolensky.

Five days later, on the Orthodox "Feast of St. James the Apostle" (whose theology of good works Ivan had so recently extolled), a squad of *Oprichniki* cordoned off Red Square and hammered twenty heavy stakes into the ground. Transverse beams were fastened to them, and behind them copper cauldrons of iced and boiling water were hung in pairs.

Ivan rode into the center of the square in full dress armor with breastplate and helmet, surrounded by heavily armed *Oprichniki* and 1500 mounted *streltsy* who silently took up their positions around the gibbets and fires. The people had scattered, but Ivan shouted to them not to be afraid, even as 300 torn and crippled prisoners were brought forth from the dungeons to hear their doom. Gradually, as his subjects reappeared, the tsar addressed them: "I punish only traitors. Is mine a righteous judgment?" The crowd shouted back: "Long live our glorious tsar! May his enemies perish!"

Ivan resumed his place and, as he loved to do, divided the quick from the dead. To the reprieved he announced: "I have no further quarrel with you," and let 184 of the prisoners go.

Vasily Schchelkalov read out the names of the other 116 from a parchment scroll. Viskovaty was made to advance. For each charge pronounced against him Schchelkalov struck him with a whip. But the aged diplomat denied them all, asserting that he had faithfully served Russia and his sovereign throughout his long career. To Ivan's chagrin, he resolutely refused to beg for mercy, and looking around him at the instruments of torture littering the square, exclaimed for all to hear: "A curse on you, you bloodsuckers! God will judge you too, in the next world, for the evil you have done." *Oprichniki* rushed forward to gag him, and trussed him up to a transverse beam as Ivan declared, "Let whomever is most loyal kill him." Skuratov at once cut off his nose, another *Oprichnik* one of his ears, and so on, limb by limb, until he expired.

The next to die was Nikita Funikov, state treasurer since 1561. Though he had wavered during the succession crisis of 1553, since then his service had been exemplary. Schchelkalov read out similarly unsubstantiated charges, which Funikov likewise denied. Two *Oprichniki* took turns savagely dousing him with cold and boiling water "until his skin came off like an eel's."

The third victim was Grigory Shapkin, a *dyak* who had served under Viskovaty. With his wife and two children he was beheaded by Prince Vasily Temkin-Rostovsky, who "laid their decapitated bodies in a row at the tyrant's feet."

And so the slaughter continued, through the long hot summer afternoon, till all had perished; and to their sorry toll many others were destined to be added over the next several weeks.

Nine months later, on April 6, 1571, Vasily Schchelkalov acquired Viskovaty's entire estate, and his older brother, Andrey, became the new head of the Foreign Ministry and the Military Records Bureau. Of Andrey it was said that he was "a very sly man, intelligent and spiteful. He worked night and day like a mule, but always complained that he wanted to do more"—sufficient unto a clerk, perhaps, but hardly the man to fill Viskovaty's shoes.

Ironically, Viskovaty's hideous dismemberment emerged some years later as a gruesome parable of Ivan's just punishment of corrupt officials. In 1588, the new English ambassador to Moscow, Giles Fletcher the Elder, was told of an anonymous *dyak* who had accepted "a goose ready drest full of money" as a bribe. Apprehended, he was brought to "the marketplace in Mosko" where Ivan warned the onlookers that such men "would eate you up like bread"—obviously, an allusion to *kormlenie*. He asked his executioners "who could cut up a goose." One cut off the man's legs at the shins, another his arms at the elbows, as the tsar taunted the dyak with, "That's goose flesh. Is it good meate?" Finally, he ordered him beheaded, "that he might have the right fashion of a goose readie dressed."

Perhaps the tsar himself put this tale into circulation. If so, the ambassador was not deceived, for he remarked: "This might seeme to have been a tollerable piece of justice (as justice goeth in Russia) except his subtill end to cover his owne oppressions."

Much like Henry VIII, in fact, Ivan was a skillful demagogue—affecting to side with the commons against the mighty, and prone to make "a publick example" of officials in order to "transfer the fault" of policy blunders or other unpopular actions. Having told the Turks that Viskovaty had masterminded his aggressive Crimean policy of a decade before, he offered his chancellor's blood to christen the apology.

* * *

Russia staggered under adversity. "God hath plagued it many ways," wrote Jenkinson, "ffirste by ffamyne, that the people have been enforced to eate bread made of barke of trees, besydes many uncleane things," such as pounded wood-pulp, snails, and moss. "One man killed another for a crust of bread," remembered von Staden. "In the storehouses of the court, the Grand Prince had many thousand ricks of unthreshed grain, but would not sell them to his subjects; thus many died [unnecessarily] and were eaten by dogs." It was even reported "for certeyn" that in some places people had "eatten one another," which was true. In Novgorod the bodies of some victims of the *Oprichnina* were salted in barrels like pork.

Famine was followed by plague (apparently cholera),[2] which in 1570 spread throughout the northwest from Novgorod to Moscow to Vologda. Thousands were thrown into common graves. As the government took the most draconian measures to contain it, "military checkpoints were set up on highways and all attempting to leave infected areas were seized and burned in large bonfires, along with their goods, horses and wagons." Infected houses were promptly walled up, entombing the living with the dead. Even so, the pestilence continued so fiercely into 1571 that it is estimated to have killed one out of every fifty people in the land.

Some Russians blamed it on an elephant given to the tsar "along with an Arab who looked after it." The Arab died in Gorodets before he could be executed. His elephant, which stood in a shed with a palisade around it near his grave, was shot by an executioner sent from Moscow.

In the end, "everyone wondered when he met an acquaintance." Ivan holed up at Aleksandrova Sloboda, and when von Staden arrived one day at the *Oprichnina* court in Moscow, "it was all quiet. A guard looked at me peevishly and asked, 'What do you want? Is everything dying at your place, too?'"

33.

The "Evil Empire"

While Ivan's subjects were being variously exterminated, his ambassador in England, Savin, was endeavoring to explain, excuse, and justify the infamous treatment Randolph had received at Moscow. Savin objected (fairly) that Randolph, like every other envoy Elizabeth had sent, "would not give aunswere of the secrite affaires" Ivan had raised but talked only of commerce. Ivan himself wrote to the queen (in an eloquent pronouncement worthy of the most enlightened monarch): "We know that merchant matters are to be heard, for that they are the stay of our princely treasures," yet "princes affaires should be first ended and after that to seeke a gaine." Nevertheless, he implied that Randolph had eventually been forthcoming, and that between them a tentative agreement had been reached, which Savin was now to conclude.

Savin, in fact, had brought with him a unilaterally concocted treaty committing Elizabeth to an offensive and defensive alliance designed to draw her into the Livonian War. To the queen's amazement, Savin demanded she "copy it out in Rousse worde for word," confirm it by kissing the cross, and seal it with the great state seal of England. In addition she was expected to send Ivan "all things necessary for warre"; allow Russians complete freedom to come, go, or settle on English soil, with duty-free access to English merchandise; and pledge refuge for each other in their respective realms. Finally, Savin insisted that Jenkinson be upgraded to ambassador and sent back.

Ivan's insistence on a military alliance put Elizabeth in a difficult position. Protests against the shipment of arms to Russia had begun almost with the inauguration of the English trade. Both Poland and Sweden had issued warnings in 1555, and in 1558, Jenkinson's companion, Thomas Alcock, traveling overland from Moscow, had been detained in Poland and interrogated about the export of technicians and war matériel. Alcock insisted that only one hundred shirts of chain mail had been sent, "such olde thinges newe scowred as no man in Englande woulde weare."

The outbreak of the Livonian War and the Russian capture of Narva had intensified the outcry. It was said in Germany that the arms Elizabeth was buying on the continent were not for her own defense but for reshipment to the tsar. She could scarcely afford to see her continental sources dry up, and (in a letter to the Hamburg Senate, May 6, 1561) denied this "on her royal word." On July 7 she gave identical assurances to the Emperor Ferdinand. Anything to the contrary, she insisted, was "grounded uppon untroth."

But arms (and armament experts) certainly had been shipped, and Elizabeth's official export ban was meant fundamentally to prevent unauthorized merchants from pursuing such commerce on their own and thereby unduly complicating her foreign policy.

On the continent, Elizabeth's roving ambassador, William Herlle, tried to explain what was going on. Some of his explanations were amazingly far-fetched. For example, despite the now-regular commercial traffic between England and Russia by the northern route, he swore that the principal aim of the voyages remained to reach Cathay, with the port of St. Nicholas serving as but "a harbour midway."

The war of words continued. In 1565, Elizabeth promised Frederick of Denmark that English vessels to Muscovy carried only what weaponry and supplies were required for their own defense; but Sigismund August quite saw through her game. And on July 13, 1567, he called her to account. Even if she sent only technicians, he pointed out, "still by their labour . . . everything which can be used in war of which [the Muscovite] has hitherto been ignorant, will be manufactured in that barbarous empire." And he warned that the fate of "the whole Christian commonwealth" was at stake. In mounting frustration he began to outfit warships at Danzig and hired a squadron of privateers to enforce a blockade of Narva. On March 3, 1568, he again urged Elizabeth to understand that Russia was not just "the temporary enemy of our kingdom," but "the hereditary foe of all free nations," and then in an astonishing letter dated December 6, 1569, sternly rebuked her with his most sweeping indictment of her policy yet:

> We know and feele of a surety, the Muscovite, enemy to all liberty under the heavens, dayly to grow mightier by the increase of such things as be brought to the Narve, while not onely wares but also weapons heeretofore unknowen to him, and artificers & arts be brought unto him: by meane whereof he maketh himselfe strong to vanquish all others. Which things, as long as this voyage to Narve is used, can not be stopped. And we perfectly know your Majesty can not be ignorant how great the cruelty is of the said enemy, of what force he is, what tyranny he useth on his subjects, and in what servile

sort they be under him. We seemed hitherto to vanquish him onely in this, that he was rude of arts, and ignorant of policies. If so be that this navigation to the Narve continue, what shall be unknowen to him? Therefore we that know best, and border upon him, do admonish other Christian princes in time, that they do not betray their dignity, liberty and life of them and their subjects to a most barbarous and cruell enemy, as we can no lesse do by the duty of a Christian prince. For now we do forsee, except other princes take this admonition, the Moscovite puffed up in pride with those things that be brought up the Narve, and made more perfect in warlike affaires with engines of warre and shippes, will make assault this way on Christendome, to slay or make bound all that shall withstand him: which God defend.

Thus did Russia's great confrontation with the West begin, and ideas formed then seem almost to have been cast and set in a mold. "Evil Empire" speeches belong to a long tradition, and Sigismund's admonition remains the progenitor of all such diatribes. Roughly speaking, its point of view has animated the case against making Western technology available to Russia up to the present day. Every Baltic nation at the time shared Poland's views. The Russian potential was obvious—as it had been to Chancellor, for example, even before the Livonian War.

Not surprisingly, some of the English experts suffered qualms. One such was Humphrey Locke, an outstanding military engineer, who had come to Russia to make his fortune. But when he saw what a tyrant Ivan was, he wrote frankly to Lord Burghley, "I could do for the Emperour such things, and make him such engynes for his warres, that he might therebye subdue any prynce that wold stand against him, but the goods is evil gotten, and that proffyt precipitates a man down to hell."

Whether or not Elizabeth gave much weight to such opinions, or believed the king's apocalyptic admonitions, it is hard to say. But she felt she could not afford to give up the Russian trade.

The conferences with Savin, in which some of the queen's Privy Council took part, lasted from July 1569 to May 1570. The English insisted on their right to determine the justice of any war before committing their nation to it, and on their obligation to seek an end to hostilities by negotiation before resorting to force. Savin "insisted on the literal transcription of the convention demanded by the tsar, not considering it compatible with the dignity of his sovereign that the justice of his acts should be questioned by Elizabeth."

In the end, she sent Ivan two letters (both dated May 18, 1570)—one a formal reply to Savin's embassy, the other secret, which she sealed with her private seal. In the first, in return for his commercial "favour," she ambiguously agreed to make common cause against "common enemies," and pledged England would "not ayde, comfort, or suffer anie person or potentate to offend you or your countries, that we maie to our power and by justice with reason staie or impeache."

In her secret communiqué, "whereunto none are privie but our most secreite councell," she reiterated her pledge of refuge and promised him decent maintenance in her realm, but said nothing about reciprocal asylum for herself; and instead of Jenkinson, she dispatched Daniel Sylvester as her new ambassador.

Historians have generally exclaimed over the character of Ivan's demands in derisive amazement. Without denying his presumption, several things go a long way to explain their curious place in diplomatic history. To begin with, Ivan's proposal that he and Elizabeth hold friends and enemies in common takes its phrasing from traditional Russian interprincely agreements between equals. Second, there was a notably recent precedent for such an arrangement—in the treaty which the sultan had concluded in 1536 with his "good friend" Francis I, Catholic king of France. That treaty included secret mutual-defense clauses and built on another negotiated in the previous year which bears a remarkable resemblance to the trade agreement England and Russia would later establish between themselves. (The treaty of 1534 had permitted the French to trade on privileged terms throughout the Ottoman Empire, with the Turks enjoying reciprocal privileges in France. It also granted the French merchants religious liberty and "recognized as valid within the Empire the jurisdiction of French consular courts, with a Turkish obligation to carry out consular judgments, if necessary by force.") It is not impossible that Ivan, who monitored Turkish policy closely, modeled his arrangements with the English on Turkish policy toward the French. The French, it is true, never enjoyed a monopoly comparable to what the English received from the tsar, but neither did the sultan expect as much in return. Should not Ivan get more? He knew the Narva trade had been a boost to the English economy; that the northern trade, by fostering seamanship and the English merchant marine, had accelerated the development of the English Navy, which he had also furnished with cable and masts; and that the trade to Persia (on which the English mistakenly continued to pin great hopes) had already resulted in spices superior to those supplied by the Portuguese. One English lord went so far as to predict that Persian silk would revolutionize the clothing industry, and "gretely sett a worke the subjectes of this realm." Given that naval and economic strength were both indispensable to Elizabeth's long-range hopes of withstanding an assault from Spain, all this puts Ivan's requests for armaments in a more equable light. Moreover, his offer of refuge to Elizabeth (generally ridiculed by historians) was not just a face-saving device. Frankly, only a profound disregard of Elizabethan history can so construe it. For though the queen was to prove, in the end, a sturdy, well-beloved, and long-lived monarch (despite Essex's rebellion, which was still ahead of her), Ivan may be pardoned for wondering in 1567 whether her hold on the throne was secure. Chancellor had arrived at the Russian Court in 1553 with a letter from a young Protestant king Edward VI (whom Ivan had been told was in good health), but returned two years later in 1555 with a letter from the Catholic monarchs Philip and Mary. The next envoy arrived with a letter from Elizabeth, who had ascended the throne in 1558. Doubtless Ivan (who quizzed foreign diplomats closely) had also learned of the brief and tragic reign of Lady Jane Grey. Now, whether or not he supposed Edward had been poisoned, he knew for certain that in a mere five years two monarchs had gone to the scaffold, England had officially changed its religion twice, had been horribly torn by civil war, and had crowned four heads of state. Was this a stable realm? Moreover, it was just at this time that Elizabeth's assassination began to be a topic of earnest and sometimes open discussion in the Catholic courts of Europe, even as she was facing domestic rebellion fomented by Catholic extremists in the north: the "Rising of the Earls" of 1569 was just on the horizon, followed by "Dacre's Rebellion"—both instigated by the Catholic nobility. After 1570, only Sir Francis Walsingham's remarkable network of spies would repeatedly save her from assassination. All things considered, Ivan's proposal must have seemed a pretty fair offer to him, timely and just; and this may explain why he reacted with such bitter humiliation when she turned him down.

Ivan was so angry and disappointed that he wrote Elizabeth a letter (dated October 24, 1570) probably unlike anything else she was ever to receive. He reviewed the whole history of Russian-English relations, which he depicted as one-sided—Russian generosity repeatedly met by English ingratitude—and doubted that Jenkinson had ever conveyed his original message to her. He also claimed she had reneged on Randolph's promise of alliance. Then he "got personal":

And how manie lettres have beene brought to us hither, and not one lettre that hath beene sealed with one seale, but everie lettre hath had a contrarie seale, wich is no princelie fashion. . . . And wee had thought that you had beene ruler over your lande, and had sought honor to your self and proffitt to your Countrie,, and therefore wee did pretend those weightie affaires between you and us. But now wee perceive that there be other men that doe rule, and not men, but boors and marchaunts, wich seeke not the wealth and honnor of our maiesties, but there own proffitt of marchandize. And you flowe in your maydenlie estate like a maide.

And seeinge it is so . . . those bowrish Marchaunts that . . . but doe seeke their owne wealthes, they shall see what traffique they shall have here; for our cittie of Musko, before their traffique to it, hath not greatly wanted Englysche commodities. . . . And all those priviledges wich wee have given aforetime be from this daie of none effect.

Such a letter could probably not have gotten past Ivan's Foreign Ministry had he not recently liquidated its most outstanding personnel.

Ivan's sometime contempt for the "bowrishnes" of merchants was disingenuous. He himself was the principal merchant of the realm, and had first choice of all imported goods, though he personally did not engage in trade. Moreover, the power of the merchant class and its influence on government policy was considerable. Its interests had been prominently weighed in all of Ivan's wars; "merchants of credit" had formed part of the welcoming committee at the Kremlin in 1555 for Chancellor, Killingworth, and Henry Lane; reciprocal free-trade agreements had been sought with Sweden in 1557, and with Denmark in 1562; leading wholesale merchants (or *gosti*) enjoyed a greater status under the law than a courtier or junior boyar (as measured by *beschestie* fines); and the *gosti* were the only elite Ivan's abdication rescript of 1564 did not indict. In 1566, they had comprised about 20 percent of the delegates to the *Zemsky Sobor*, and as a class had been relatively spared by the *Oprichnina* terror.

Though it is said that commerce between Russia and England never amounted to much, for reasons Elizabethan historians might wish to explore, the queen went to extraordinary lengths to keep it up. Not only had she begun to risk her own supply of arms on the continent, but little by little she began to yield to Ivan's will. When she learned that Ivan had revoked all of the Russia Company's privileges and confiscated and impounded all its goods, she decided after all to send Jenkinson back. He left in June 1571 with a letter that accredited him as ambassador to "treat very fully all things" including "the greatest and most secret affairs," and in another letter she bent over backward to interpret Anglo-Russian relations in the happiest light. With dignity she defended the use of her private seal "on which are carved the arms and emblems of the Kingdom of England"; affirmed that Jenkinson had been a faithful envoy between them; doubted that Savin had fully conveyed to the tsar what he had been told; and assured Ivan with pride: "No merchants govern our country, but we rule it ourselves, in manner befitting a Virgin Queen, appointed by the great and good God; nor was ever better obedience shown to any Prince than to us by our people." As for the trading privileges Ivan had recently revoked, she hoped they would soon be "royally restored as they were royally given," and as proof of her countrymen's readiness to serve his interests, reminded him that they had "lately seized the King of Polands piratical ships called freebooters, and delivered them into your hands." As for things "necessarie for warre," she said that despite pressure from other powers to desist, the English had "exported merchandize, and every kind of thing to your Empire, to conciliate your goodwill, which we do not allow to be exported to any other Princes in the world."

To put such a revelation in writing suggests how far she was prepared to go.

Overall, she urged Ivan to see the recent strain in their relations as having been due to a misunderstanding, and through Jenkinson to suggest that a *de facto* alliance between the two powers was already in effect. But when Jenkinson disembarked at St. Nicholas on July 26, 1571, he was immediately advised that his life was in danger and that Ivan's "displeasure was such that if ever I came into his countrey againe, I should loose my head." Bravely, he proceeded to Kholmogory, only to be quarantined there for several months by another outbreak of plague.

And there he also learned of an even more frightful calamity.

34.

"A fearfull reveng and spectacle to al generacions"

Since the beginning of the Livonian War the Crimean Tartars had raided Russian territory every year except 1566; and even during a relative lull in the fighting in the West, the empire had remained vulnerable to attack from the south. Perhaps the Chosen Council had been right after all. Russia had been fighting on the wrong front.

Devlet Giray, the Crimean khan, had long contemplated a mighty revenge on Moscow. Though his sphere of influence had been considerably diminished by the loss of Kazan and Astrakhan, he had effectively defended Crimean power in the Steppe, and now the terrible internal decomposition of Muscovy at last gave him a chance to strike back.

The old Oka defense line was obsolete; the new forward line was not only full of gaps, but some of its stronger links had long been neglected during the war. From bitter experience the Muscovites knew what to expect, but most of the veteran civil servants who might have initiated remedial action were dead.

Time was running out. Late in 1570, intelligence reports from the Crimea suggested renewed conscription on a large scale. In September, a scouting party of 6000 Tartars ominously tested Russian frontier defenses and plundered with impunity a town within the outer line. On January 1, 1571, Ivan appointed Mikhail Vorotynsky (perhaps his finest remaining commander) to head a commission on military preparedness in the south. A number of garrison officers and other personnel concerned in regional defense were summoned to Moscow, formulated several decrees, and appealed to the Duma to act on their recommendations without delay.

Vorotynsky proposed a largely revamped front line extending from the Lithuanian border all the way to the Volga south of Kazan. New towns would have to be built to bind the chain of fortifications together, with seventy-three observation posts divided into twelve chains. No post was to be more than two days' ride from the next, and once Tartars were spotted, smoke signals and outriders were to spread the alarm. Special trails were to be cut through wooded areas for Russian patrols.

Though these recommendations were promptly accepted, in April, before they could begin to be implemented, Devlet Giray appeared at the head of 40,000 Tartar cavalry on the Russian frontier.

Much to Ivan's exasperation, Devlet's onslaught coincided with the collapse of Magnus' eight-month siege of Reval. Having pitched his camp before the city on August 21, 1570 (about the time that the plague was beginning to strike the Russian interior), Magnus had promised everything under the sun to get its garrison to surrender. Then he began to batter its walls with artillery. Assault after assault was repulsed, as the Swedes kept the city resupplied by sea. Poland stood with Sweden in this battle, and Magnus got no help from the Danes. On March 16, 1571, he withdrew in humiliation. Taube and Kruse, who had accompanied him as advisers (and may have proposed the "Magnus arrangement") judiciously fled to Dorpat rather than return to Ivan to explain. Subsc͵ently they escaped to Lithuania, where they wrote their memoirs.

Magnus stumbled back to Moscow to find his fiancée, Evfimia, dead from poison, and Ivan frantic to meet the Tartar advance.

As Devlet's army galloped north, a combined Russian force of 50,000 assembled to meet it. The *Zemshchina* regiments, under Ivan Belsky and Ivan Mstislavsky, "moved vigorously to close the fords at Serpukhov," as the tsar with the *Oprichnina* army followed behind. Belsky was stationed at Kolomna, Mstislavsky at Kashira, Vorotynsky at Serpukhov. In overall command, after the tsar, was the Circassian Mikhail Cherkassky.

It is not known precisely with what aims Devlet Giray had set out—whether to re-annex a slice of Russian territory or merely to launch a devastating raid. The khan was now an old man, and apparently ill. Two years before, Ivan had been told that "the insides were falling out of him and sometimes he cannot sit on a horse." But on a horse he certainly was, and riding hard.

Fortified positions gave the Russians the advantage, but it was undercut by two things: first, the hostility between the *Zemshchina* and *Oprichnina* units, who belonged almost to two separate homelands and lacked feeling of common cause; and second, the inside knowledge given the Tartars by Russian defectors acting as their guides. Thus, the khan knew roughly how the Russian forces were disposed, and one turncoat told him of a gap in the line through which he could ride straight to the capital, for "there is nothing standing in your way." When one of the Tartar chieftains looked down at him doubtfully, he added, "If you fail to reach Moscow, you can impale me!"

The Tartars overran Tula, bore down on Serpukhov, then swept west in a wide arc and crossed the Ugra River, just as Ivan, marching from Aleksandrova Sloboda on May 16 with a bodyguard of 1500 *streltsy*, reached the outskirts of Serpukhov. It was now suddenly reported to him that his entire army had been outflanked and that Tartar detachments were just twenty miles to the west. He learned too that Temriuk, Cherkassky's father, had gone over to Devlet's side—perhaps because Ivan, in abandoning the Terek fortress, had proved an unreliable ally. Immediately he supposed that Cherkassky too might be a traitor, and had him shot.

Meanwhile, Vorotynsky's advance guard had been overwhelmed. Convinced of an impending coup, Ivan turned his back on his own country and "marched a wrong way," as one contemporary put it, hastening first to Aleksandrova Sloboda, where he stuffed as much treasure as he could in one night into chests for transport, then hurried on to Vologda, where he made ready for a swift escape up the Dvina to the White Sea where, if necessary, he could board a ship for England.

The tsar's flight utterly demoralized the army, which began to retreat in disorder toward Moscow. With the swift Tartar cavalry on its heels, the commanders were barely able to regroup in a coherent defense. Mstislavsky deployed his troops into the western suburbs inside a loop formed by the Moscow River; Belsky occupied the river's north bank from the Kremlin to the Yauza; across the Yauza, to the east, Vorotynsky was erecting barricades; while the *Oprichniki*, organized by Temkin-Rostovsky, took up positions in their own district. All tactical planning, however, was frustrated by the tens of thousands of refugees streaming into the city, crushing one another against the gates, where in a mingled tumult soldiers and civilians trampled each other down.

Just before sunrise on the 24th of May (Ascension Day in the Orthodox calendar), the Tartars crossed the ford near the Novodevichy Monastery, stormed the *Oprichnina* quarter, and set it ablaze. As in the conflagration of 1547, the day had dawned "clere, fayre & calme," but an unlucky wind arose and blew like a gale. The fire spread through the suburbs, devoured the Kitaygorod, surged over the Kremlin walls, and set off explosions in the powder magazines in the towers. Soon "ther was nothynge but whirlwynds & such noyse as thoughe the hevens shuld have fallen" as the fire "went on with such rage that it consumed the greater part of the citie almost within the space of foure houres." At the beginning of the siege, it is said, all the church bells in Moscow began pealing, then one by one fell silent as they cracked, melted, or fell.

The Tartars had surrounded the city. No one could escape. The metropolitan shut himself up with some of the clergy in the Cathedral of the Assumption. Belsky, to whom the defense of the city had been particularly entrusted, was asphyxiated in a Kremlin vault. The tsar's English physician, Arnold Lindsay, and twenty-five London merchants also perished, along with the English lions Ivan had kept in the Kremlin moat. Those not burned to death were smothered by the "fierie eyre": fully half the population of Moscow and its environs—some 60,000 at least, it is conservatively believed, though contemporary accounts claimed up to a million. "Mosco," wrote one eyewitness, "is burnt every sticke"; another: "The citie is nothynge but walls. . . . I pray God I never see the lyke agayne."

As the Tartars withdrew into the Steppe (with Vorotynsky in brave but hopeless pursuit), they took with them thousands of captives and laid waste far and wide. "What with the Crimme on the one side, and with his crueltie on the other," wrote an Englishman, "[the tsar] hath but few people left." Russians had not seen such destruction at a stroke since the days of Khan Tokhtamysh of the Golden Horde. It would take many months just to cleanse the rivers, ditches, cellars, and streets of the dead, when "noe man could pass for the putrefaction of the air"; and the outer town of Moscow was not to be fully restored for another twenty years.

With appalling unanimity, the English interpreted the calamity as a "fearfull reveng and spectacle to al generacions," and "juste punyshment of God on such a wycked natyon." And more often than not they singled out sodomy as the principal reason for celestial wrath. Few tears were shed for suffering humanity.

Ivan looked for scapegoats to extinguish the memory of his cowardice. The Russian defeat had profoundly discredited the *Oprichnina* troops in his eyes, and to begin with he executed three of its commanders: Lev Saltykov, Temkin-Rostovsky, and Peter Zaitsev. Zaitsev (a charter member of the guard) was hanged from his own court gate. A staged confession of complicity was also exacted from the senior *Zemshchina* commander, Ivan Mstislavsky, after Vasily Schchelkalov arrested one of his servants and "threatened to roast him over an open fire" if he refused to charge his master with collaborating with the khan. By prearrangement, however, Metropolitan Kirill and other Church worthies "interceded" for his life, and three boyars put up 20,000 rubles for his bond. This sum in turn was collected in varying amounts from 285 others, in a flamboyant display of collective responsibility.

Mstislavsky, who remained Ivan's confidant, cooperated in the sham. Briefly "banished" to Novgorod, an inconceivably horrible doom would surely have been his fate if he had really been responsible for the catastrophe.

During Jenkinson's providential delay at Kholmoghory, Ivan's new misfortunes had tempered his wrath toward Elizabeth and her envoy. He needed England now more than ever, even as the personal danger he faced had recently been brought home to him anew by the death of his third wife, Marfa Sobakina, from poison two weeks after their marriage in the fall of 1571. It was therefore a most conciliatory tsar that Jenkinson met with at Aleksandrova Sloboda on March 23, 1572:

> I came before his majestie, who caused mee to kisse his hande, and gave gratious audience unto my oration, gratefully receiving and accepting the Queenes majesties princely letters, and her present, in the presence of all his

nobilitie. . . . Then sitting downe againe, he commaunded all . . . to depart, and avoyde the chamber, saving the chiefe secretarie and one other of the counsell, and willing me to approoch neere unto him with my interpretor, said unto me these words.

Anthony, the last time thou wast with us heere, wee did commit unto thee our trustie and secret message, to be declared unto the queenes majestie her-selfe thy mistresse at thy coming home, and did expect they comming unto us againe at the time wee appointed, with a full answere of the same from her highnesse. And in the meane time, there came unto us at severall times three measengers . . . about . . . merchaunts affaires,

which embassies he reviewed until at last, he explained, a tentative under-standing had been reached with Randolph at Vologda about "princely af-faires," which Savin had endeavored to consummate.

Jenkinson replied that Randolph had denied reaching any new agreement, and that the queen had also conferred with Savin until everything had "seemed to his own contentment." Paraphrasing Elizabeth's letter, he again reminded the tsar of the special shipments Russia had received, and that English ships (under Sir William Garret) two years before had "fought with the King of Poles shippes freebooters, and burnt the same and slew the people, and as many as were taken alive delivered unto thy captaine at the Narve, I trust thy highness doth not forget." Accordingly, he asked for restoration of company privileges, and that Rutter, Glover, and Chap-pell—"such rebels of our nation as . . . lye lurking here seeking to sowe dissentions betwixt our majesties"—be remanded into his custody. After pausing a while, Ivan biblically replied: "It is nowe time which we spend in fasting, and praying, being the weeke before Easter, and for that we will shortly depart from hence . . . you shall goe and tary us upon the way, where wee will shortly come, and then you shall knowe our pleasure and have your dispatch."

Actually, the immediate item on Ivan's agenda was his marriage to Anna Koltovskaya, the daughter of a minor noble from Kostroma. Since a fourth marriage was considered uncanonical, Ivan proclaimed that his third wife Marfa had died a maid. Archbishop Leonid of Novgorod, interim head of the Church after the death of Metropolitan Kirill on February 8, 1572, convoked a council of bishops in March essentially to condone the tsar's wish, but in a face-saving measure the body imposed penance on Ivan for a year.

Jenkinson tarried in Tver until May 13, when Ivan summoned him to Staritsa. Declaring himself satisfied that Jenkinson had been a faithful envoy between himself and the queen, he nevertheless rejected the notion that any satisfactory alliance had ever been forged between the two nations; and though he was prepared for the moment to let it go, "because our minde is now otherwise charged, and we will not ymportunate our Syster any further," at a later date he let it be known, "when occasion shall move us to the like, wee will talke of those matters againe."

Ivan restored the company's privileges, but (as he was wont to do) coupled his generosity with a veiled threat: "If the queene our sister had not sent thee Anthony unto us, God knoweth what we should have done to [certain offending] merchants, or whether we would have called back our indignation."

35.

The Battle of Molodi

Ivan's conduct toward other monarchs soon discarded all pretext of civility. His diplomacy with Sweden, in particular, was based on insult. Aware that Johan was struggling to consolidate his hold on the throne, he hastened to impugn his right to it by casting aspersions on his lineage. "Your father, Gustav," he wrote, "whose son was he? When our merchants used to go to Sweden with wax and tallow in his reign, did they not see him put on gloves and go as far as Vyborg to turn the merchandise over, and haggle about the prices? And you talk of the kings who were your predecessors! What kings? Where did you find them? In your larder?"

But Ivan got as good as he gave. Shortly before the conference with Jenkinson, Devlet Giray's envoy had arrived, accompanied by an imposing mounted escort of Tartar nobles in long black sheepskin kaftans with "curious rich scimitars" buckled to their hips. The tsar at first disparaged their office, shut them away in windowless dark rooms, and fed them on "stinking horseflesh." But "tym was com they must have audience," and, according to one account, the Tartar envoy, ushered in, "thundered owt without reverence in a hellish, hollow voice" that his master wished to know how his vassal (Ivan) "did like the scourge of his displeasur by sword, fier and famen." Then, "pulling owt a fowll rustie kniff," he invited the tsar to cut his own throat to end his misery. Four bodyguards seized him and in a scuffle hustled him out. The khan's official letter to Ivan was comparably brusque: "I came to Russia to avenge Kazan and Astrakhan. I searched for the tsar everywhere but could not find him. Where did the coward go? If you don't relinquish the khanates, beware! I have seen the roads and highways of your kingdom, and I know the way!" In an "agonie of madness" Ivan "tore at his haire and beard," but having recovered himself in a few days' time, composed the following reply: "Tell the miscreant and unbeliever, thy master, yt is not he, but for my sins and the sins of my people against God and Christ, that hath given him, a lym of Satan, the power and oportunitie to be the instrument of my rebuke. [But] by [God's] pleasur and grace I doubt not of revenge."

He had to buy time. Through his ambassador in Bakchiseray, he indicated his willingness to cede Astrakhan in return for an alliance against Lithuania. "The sword remains sharp only for a little while," he pontificated. "Too much use blunts it, and the blade might also break," and he proposed one of Devlet's own sons as the new Astrakhan sovereign, assisted by a boyar, to conduct the khanate's affairs.

The khan, however, had an agenda of his own. Russian prestige had rapidly declined all along the Volga, enabling him at last to unite under one banner most of the disparate tribes, including the Great Nogays, in an almost monolithic anti-Muscovite coalition. He saw no reason to settle for less than Russia itself. So certain was he of prevailing that he actually divided up the towns and provinces of the empire beforehand among his own nobility—who would govern Novgorod or Ryazan, for example, who Vladimir or Zvenigorod—and enlisted members of the Ottoman Secretariat for administrative advice.

Hoping to withstand the inevitable coming attack, Ivan frantically endeavored to implement some of Vorotynsky's recommendations, and according to guidelines laid down by the *Zemshchina* Privy Council, blended battalions of *Zemshchina* and *Oprichnina* troops into unified regiments.

The Russians dug in along a fifty-mile stretch of the Oka River behind double palisades, with a long barricade of wagons and, to deprive the Tartar mounts of feed, burned the grass on the open steppe from the sources of the Vorona to the Dnieper and Desna rivers.

Fearing the worst, however, Ivan decamped to Novgorod at the beginning of June and (it is credibly reported) brought with him 450 cartloads of treasure weighing 164 tons. By mid-July, the attack had not yet come, and Ivan wrote anxiously to an officer at Staritsa, "You must tell me without fail when the Khan approaches the river, and where he will cross, and which direction he will take. Keep a courier ready, equipped with two horses, and see to it that couriers are kept ready at Tver. At all costs keep me informed."

On July 31, a courier at last brought news of the invasion, but could tell Ivan nothing to ease his mind. A day or two later, in a fearful, tense, and penitential mood, the tsar sat down to draft his will, and began with a confession of his sins:

> I, the much sinning and poor slave of God, Ivan, write this confession. . . . My understanding is covered with sores. There is no physician to heal me. I have waited for someone to pity me, but found no comforters. From Adam to this day I have surpassed all sinners. Bestial and corrupt, I have defiled my mind by a liking for unworthy things, my mouth by words of murder, lewdness and other foul acts, my tongue by self-praise, my throat and chest by pride and arrogance, my hands by indecent contacts, by theft and assassination, my loins by monstrous lechery, girding them up for every possible evil deed, and my feet by hastening to commit murder and plunder.

He advised his two sons, Ivan Ivanovich and Fyodor, to master the responsibilities of kingship, but seemed to warn them against following the example he had set:

> Those who serve you in a straightforward manner you should favor and love, protect them from all, so that no one persecutes them. . . . And upon those that are evil you should place your disfavor, not hurriedly but after consideration, not in wrath. And accustom yourselves to all affairs: God's, the priest's, the monk's, the soldier's, the judge's; to the way of life in Moscow, and to all the customs of daily life, and how the various ranks of government are dealt with here and in other states—this you yourselves should know. . . .
>
> And you, son Ivan, should hold, and protect, and love Fyodor, your younger brother, and favor him and wish him well in all things. . . .
>
> And you, son Fyodor, hold Ivan in the place of me, your father, and obey him in all things. . . . Do not negotiate with traitors and evildoers. And you two must not bicker, for even if one acquires much wealth or land he cannot avoid a grave of three cubits, when all that remains is only one thing: that which we have done, be it good or evil.[1]

On his elder son Ivan he bestowed the imperial regalia and the tsardom, but concluded: "Concerning the *Oprichnina* which I have established, it is now within the power of my children, Ivan and Fyodor [to do with it as they wish]; in the manner most advantageous to them, so should they do, but the pattern has been made ready for them."

Though in most respects Ivan's testament conformed to Muscovite princely tradition—with its brief invocation, disposition of territories and possessions, and exhortation to his sons to live together in harmony—its long "confession" was unique, and (we must assume) reflected authentic anguish and contrition at the time.

Meanwhile the Tartar vanguard had raced toward Tula, intending to cross the Oka above Serpukhov. Vorotynsky concentrated his troops south of Kolomna to interdict the routes leading from Ryazan to Moscow, and stationed his vanguard under Prince Dmitry Khvorostinin at Kaluga to prevent the enemy from advancing from the Ugra as before. When the first wave of Tartar cavalry reached the Oka on July 26, Khvorostinin "beat them back from the fords." Devlet's main force now drew up opposite Russian fortified positions, and on the night of the 28th Nogay cavalry seized several key crossing points. At dawn Khvorostinin hastened to cut the Tartars off, but was hopelessly outnumbered and withdrew. Other Russian regiments, trying to block them at the upper reaches of the Nara River, were repulsed. Suddenly Devlet Giray "emerged to the rear of the Russian army and began making his way unopposed along a broad highway toward Moscow."

Khovorostinin, in pursuit, shadowed the Tartar rear guard, commanded by Devlet's sons, and near the small village of Molodi, about thirty miles south of Moscow, took advantage of a break in Tartar ranks and attacked. The khan sent back reinforcements and the fighting spread. Gradually the march on Moscow was arrested as the Tartars redeployed. The main Russian army drew near. A pitched battle promised to develop in the open field.

The Russians had with them a great, prefabricated mobile fortress which they hastily assembled atop a nearby hill. It bristled with cannon, and as Khvorostinin retreated before a counterattack, he lured the enemy well within range of their fire, with devastating effect.

The Tartars regrouped; the Russians entrenched themselves around their fortress and stationed some 3000 musketeers at the foot of the hill. In a massive Tartar assault on the following day the musketeers were annihilated, but around the fortress the fighting raged until evening, and enemy losses were such that although the Russians were outnumbered three to one, the khan spent the next two days trying to reconstitute his army. Meanwhile, the Russians were running out of provisions, and in starvation began to slaughter their horses for meat.

In this grim stand-off, luck tipped the scales. During a rash reconnaissance foray close to the fortress, Divey Mirza, Devlet's eldest son and heir, was captured. At first the Russians were ignorant of their prize, but during the interrogation of some captives, one of them, asked what the plans of the

Tartars were, replied: "All our plans are with you, because you have Divey Mirza." The prince was located and brought to Vorotynsky's tent, where his witless admirer confirmed his identity by throwing himself at his feet. Devlet resolved to liberate his son at all costs. In suicidal abandon on August 2 he threw everything he had against the fortress, and in conjunction with cavalry charges, thousands of Tartars actually rushed to the walls and tried to push them over with their hands. Toward evening, Vorotynsky secretly led a large contingent out of the fortress, "made his way along the bottom of a declivity behind it, and came out to the rear of the enemy." Khvorostinin remained inside with a small body of cavalry and a skeleton crew to man the artillery. At a signal, the cavalry charged, artillery fired, and Vorotynsky attacked the Tartars from behind. The result was a complete rout.

Ivan learned of the victory at Novgorod on August 6, and immediately sloughed off his abject humility like a serpent's winter skin. He wrote another insulting letter to Johan, and promised to invade Swedish Estonia before the end of the year.

The Battle of Molodi was one of the three most important battles of Ivan's reign. It delivered a telling blow to the power of the Crimea coincident with the Turkish defeat at Lepanto, and helped persuade Grand Vizier Sokollu once again to postpone the Russian problem and concentrate on securing Turkish positions in West Africa and the Mediterranean. In domestic affairs, it presaged the abolition of the *Oprichnina*. A reintegration of the nation was begun, as the two separate hierarchies in military and civil administration were gradually fused. Tellingly enough, when the fusion was complete, the numerical domination of the nobility in the Duma was not appreciably different from what it had been before the *Oprichnina* was born.

The restitution of confiscated property was less satisfactorily achieved, for in the burning of Moscow not only some of the property at issue but most of the petitions, records, and receipts needed to adjudicate claims had perished in the flames. What Ivan had appropriated for himself he also kept, and to some degree the *Oprichnina* itself continued, discreetly metamorphosed into his expanded *Dvor*, or Court. To the end of his reign, a large proportion of his staff remained former *Oprichniki*, now called "Court people," while the tsar's abolition decree of 1572 was certainly in keeping with the spirit of the institution itself: "Anyone guilty of chattering about the *Oprichnina* is to be stripped to the waist and publicly beaten with a knout."[2]

36.

A Medley of Monarchs

The death of Sigismund August without heir on July 9, 1572, brought the Jagiellonic dynasty (1386–1572) to a close and threw the crown of the second most powerful state in Eastern Europe open to competition. For years, in anticipation of this day, ministers representing every court on the continent had been intriguing on behalf of various candidates. Their power, influence, and industry flattered the vanity of the Polish nobles, as their wealth aroused their greed. The German emperor Maximilian and his sons, the imperial archdukes Ernest and Ferdinand, Johan III of Sweden, Henry of Valois, duke of Anjou (the son of Catherine de' Medici and brother to the king of France), and, strange to say (but shortly to be explained) Tsar Ivan IV himself, all rushed to the starting gate.

The Polish-Lithuanian constitutional union was still extremely fragile, and Sigismund August's talents as a monarch were only truly appreciated by his subjects once he was gone. Upon ascending the throne in 1548, he had looked insufficient to fill his father's shoes: physically slight and effeminate, and at twenty-eight, less energetic than his father had been as an octogenarian. His speech was soft and deliberate, clever and witty, like that of the ladies and corrupt priests of the Italianate court in which he had been raised, but there was hidden kingship in him, a far-sighted aptitude for policy backed by stamina and patience, and a broadminded cosmopolitan intelligence that made him the right man to manage the state through some of the most turbulent days it would see. The Catholic monarch of a Catholic land, he had taken Jews under his protection and allowed Protestants of all denominations refuge in his realm. Despite the subsequent arrival of capable papal nuncios to regenerate the Catholic Church, followed in 1565 by the first Jesuits—the vanguard of the Counterreformation—Lutheranism remained strong in the cities, Calvinism among the nobility, and the Orthodox faith among the Lithuanian masses. A number of the Orthodox were Uniates, who favored a conditional union with Rome. At the same time, a powerful educational movement, launched in emulation of the new Jesuit seminaries, attempted to check the spread of Catholicism in Lithuania through the founding of Orthodox schools. The chief figure in this endeavor was Prince Konstantin Ostrogski, a fabulously wealthy magnate who set up three printing presses (with the help of Fedorov and Mstislavets, the fugitive Muscovite typographers), as Kurbsky, Artemy, and other exiles threw themselves into the cause.

Despite the ethnic, class, religious, and other divisions within his double kingdom, Sigismund had miraculously forged the new union; and to preserve it from religious strife, his subjects had nobly committed themselves "in matters of faith to keep the peace among ourselves" by the Confederation of Warsaw on January 28, 1573.

In the jostling for electoral advantage, however, that solidarity began to come apart.

The Archduke Ernest was the favorite choice of the Catholic party; Johan, of many Protestants, because he appeared to be one himself and, having married the late king's sister, inspired hopes the dynasty might continue by lateral descent. Henry of Valois, whose cause was richly advanced by Medici gold, was promoted by those afraid that a Hapsburg triumph would lead to confrontation with the Ottoman Empire. Support for Tsar Ivan (or his son Fyodor as a compromise choice) came largely from the Lithuanian gentry, who were ambivalently drawn to Russia by their Orthodox faith, and to Ivan by his reputation for humbling his nobility. They had also suffered the most from the interminable frontier war, and saw this as a stratagem for bringing it to an end. On the other hand, there was Ivan's fearsome reputation, and the danger that if Russian power was brought to the edge of the Balkans, the sultan would launch a preventive war. It was not forgotten that the head of the last Polish king to march against the Turks had ended up in Constantinople preserved in a pot of honey. Yet Ivan's candidacy appeared serious enough to prompt Kurbsky to write, at a furious rate, a whole *History of the Grand Prince of Moscow* which chronicled the development of Ivan's tyranny from his sadistic childhood ("conceived in ferocity, born in transgression and concupiscence") to 1573. His narrative of the tsar's cruelties was conveniently corroborated by a harrowing eyewitness account composed by a Pomeranian, Albert Schlichting, who had served as a translator in the Kremlin from 1565 to 1569.

Ivan made an effort to be tempting. He told the Polish envoy who brought him word of Sigismund's death: "I do not stand for Polotsk, and I am willing to yield it and all its suburbs if only Livonia up to the Dvina is ceded to me. And we shall conclude perpetual peace with Lithuania." Though he declined to make Fyodor available as a candidate ("I have only two sons and they are like the eyes in my head"), he acknowledged his reputation for severity, but declared he had been harsh only to traitors. "Look," he said, "to a good man I would give the jewelled collar from about my neck and the gown from off my back," and as he spoke made as though he would remove them.

The Poles had no desire to explore Ivan's candidacy. But the Lithuanians, acting independently, sent an emissary to Moscow in 1573 to obtain assurances that if elected he would respect their constitutional liberties and return Smolensk. Ivan replied:

> We know that the Emperor and the King of France have been soliciting support, but that is no example for us to follow. They are begging for honours, whereas we are sovereigns descended from Augustus Caesar. And this is known to all men. We wish to hold the Moscow State and the Grand Duchy of Lithuania as one, as Poland and Lithuania have been. Polotsk with all its suburbs and Courland go to Lithuania, and Livonia to Moscow. The Dvina shall be the frontier.

Ivan's offer accorded with a scheme to partition the Commonwealth secretly proposed to him by the Emperor Maximilian, who hoped to unite Catholic Poland with Austria. In his communiqúe, Maximilian had also condemned Henry of Valois for his part in the St. Bartholomew's Day Massacre of Huguenots (August 24, 1572). In reply, Ivan had deplored the carnage as "so much blood shed without sufficient reason."

Nevertheless, in late April 1573, some 40,000 electors pitched their tents on a vast plain outside Warsaw, and in a great "Election Diet" reluctantly chose Henry of Valois to be their king. Before his coronation, however, he had to agree to a number of constraints on his power, including adherence to the Confederation of Warsaw and a pledge not to undertake any military campaign or levy taxes without the electorate's consent. He was also expected to maintain a fleet in the Baltic at his own expense, replenish the royal treasury, and marry the late king's sister, Anna.

Henry, twenty-two years old at the time, absolutely refused to marry Anna, who was forty, but otherwise acquiesced; and on February 21, 1574, he was crowned king in the Cathedral of Cracow.

Meanwhile, Ivan had resumed his aggression in Livonia. Keeping his threat against Johan, he brought a large army through Novgorod to the frontier, and on Christmas Day invaded Swedish Estonia, capturing the fortress of Weissenstein on January 1, 1573. Skuratov was felled by a cannonball in the assault, and in revenge Ivan roasted the fortress commander alive. Subsequently, dividing his army into three columns, he sent one south against Karkus, the second westward as far as Lode, while a third, diversionary force, attacked into Finland as far as Helsingfors.

Ivan was exhilarated. Resurrecting Magnus, whom he now affianced to Staritsky's youngest daughter, Maria, a thirteen-year-old child "still devoted to her playthings," he promised once again to make him "King of Livonia. At their wedding in April, he personally conducted a choir of young monks—whose musical lapses evidently so annoyed him that he beat time on their heads with a stick—and afterward rambunctiously took part in the festivities, dancing and singing songs.

Two of Ivan's most spirited and sarcastic letters also date from this time. One was to Vasily Griaznoy, recently captured in a raid by the Crimean Tartars who hoped to exchange him for Divey Mirza. Griaznoy encouraged the plan, but Ivan rejected it as absurd. He wrote to him:

> Why did you tell them you were a man of prominence? When we were confronted with the treason of the Boyars, we had to surround ourselves with people like you, of lowly birth. But do not forget who your parents were! . . . As for trading Mirza for you, all you want is a soft bed. But Mirza will raise his sword against the Christians.
>
> You should have been more careful, my little Vasily, when you rode after the Tartars. Or did you think that everything would be as easy in Bakhchiseray as cracking jokes at my table?

In a kindred spirit, Ivan wrote to the White Lake Monastery, whose abbot appealed for help in disciplining two tonsured ex-boyars who were living it up there in high style. "Why ask me?" Ivan exclaimed,

> stinking dog that I am, evil and vile? Yet because I am half a monk, I will tell you: It is written, Angels are the light of monks, monks the light of the laity. So it is proper for you to enlighten us. . . . You have the great example of your founder, St. Kirill, and you have his monastic rule. . . . Is it the way of salvation when a boyar becomes a monk and does not shave off his rank? It is not they who have been tonsured by you, but you by them. And now one sits among you in his cell like a tsar and the other calls upon him, together with other monks, and they eat and drink as they did in the world.

As usual enlightened observations combined with mindless violence: the hero of Molodi, Mikhail Vorotynsky, accused by a dismissed servant of witchcraft, was executed along with Mikhail Morozov, Kurbsky's successor as governor of Dorpat. Morozov's crime can only be guessed.

In Poland, meanwhile, young King Henry was proving his unfitness for the throne. Accustomed to the frivolity, obsequious flattery, and profligacy of the Parisian court, he had begun to curse the day of his election. Among other things, he was

> disappointed by the poverty of the Polish countryside: by the wooden houses and gray fields which looked their worst in the damp spring. He disliked the Italian furnishings of the Royal Castle, and ordered a complete refit. He was bored by the constant debates in Polish and Latin which he could not follow, and was affronted by the argumentative demeanor of the senators and envoys. . . . He took to taking pills and potions, to diplomatic absences from court, and to long week-ends at the royal hunting-lodge.

In mid-June, when the death of his brother, Charles IX, made him heir to the throne of France, fraternal grief (if any) was expunged by his sudden reprieve. The Poles, to prevent his departure, virtually confined him to his castle, but on the night of June 18 he donned a disguise, slipped out by a secret exit to a gate which an accomplice had unlocked, and before Polish cavaliers could catch up with him had crossed the Moravian frontier. Poland's loss was not France's gain. Henry had been a non-king. In France he was destined to rule ignominiously as Henry III—"the New Herod"— until his assassination at the age of thirty-eight by a Dominican monk.

In Sweden, Erik in captivity (like Johan before him) had naturally become the hope and instigation of various plots. Johan moved him from dungeon to dungeon; his higher clergy counseled fratricide. "It is to be feared," their spokesman said, "that we have rather offended than pleased God by not killing him thus far." As the king pondered their advice, his German mercenaries in Livonia rebelled at not getting paid. When he gave them three fortresses—Hapsal, Leal, and Lode—as security, they mortgaged them first to Frederick of Denmark, then (when he failed to come up with the capital) to the tsar.

Soaring with confidence, Ivan reopened the whole treaty issue with Queen Elizabeth. Though Jenkinson had smoothed things over, new tensions had since appeared. Elizabeth complained of debts to the company that were piling up, Ivan of English soldiers fighting for the Swedes. Elizabeth replied, "They must be Scots."

Ivan, who had Scots in his army too, nevertheless repeated his charge in August ("many Englishmen stood up against us with the Swede") and in a rambling, repetitive tirade again disparaged her "maidenly" estate of governance, and concluded: "If you wish for more amity and friendship from us, ponder upon that subject and do that business, by which you may increase our amity towards you. Order also your men to bring us ammunition, arms, copper, tin, lead, and sulphur."

In May 1575, Daniel Sylvester tried to persuade Ivan that the queen's two letters of 1570 had amounted to the treaty he sought; and in her own communiqué she explained that in order to keep the league between them secret (as Ivan had required), she had been unable to confirm it, according to his demand, "by oath" because "the leagues which wee confirm by othe doe ordinarily passe our greate seale: which cannot be done but that the same must runne through the hands of so great a numbre of our ministers as in no possibilitie they can be kept secret." As for right of refuge in his realm, she dared not ask for it, because if word got out her subjects might suppose she had some reason to fear them, which "would breed so dangerous a mislikynge in them towards us, as might put us in perill of our estate."

Ivan scoffed at all this in a meeting with Sylvester in November. He noted that he himself had been able to transmit sensitive information to Elizabeth in such a way that only one of his own counselors knew of it; and in a later meeting complained that he detected "a kynde of haughtynes in our systar toward us moved tharto by th'abasynge of our selfe towards her." Sylvester asked him to elaborate. Ivan said: "Our mislyke consisteth in the scruple aunsweres of our systar, that she maketh dayntye to requiar the like of us as our requeste is to have of her according to the symple and playne meaning of our demaunds." Threatening to revoke the company's privileges, transfer its trade to the Venetians and Germans, and negotiate a refuge in Austria, he indicated (as if England were Elizabeth's private property), that had she merely been more forthcoming, "trewly our whole countrye of Russia hadd bene as much at her pleasure as England ys as frelye to have sent or commanded anye thinge thence as out of her own treasurye or wardrope."

As the new crown auction got under way in Poland, the Emperor Maximilian dispatched a high-level delegation to Ivan to ensure his support. The second time around, the candidates were identical, except that Henry had been succeeded by Stefan Batory, prince of Transylvania, as the favorite choice of the Turks. Their recommendation was powerfully and immediately expressed through Devlet Giray, who in early October carried out a huge raid in the Ukraine. In November, the Electoral Diet gathered on the outskirts of Warsaw, and though a Senate proclamation restricted the retinue of each magnate to ten, and the weaponry they carried to the usual halbert and sword, some nobles were accompanied by as many as 1000 retainers, and every voter carried a musket, mace, spiked battle-ax or lance. Fierce political debate was accompanied by the clank and scrape of chain mail. Auxiliary cavalry outnumbered the voters, and a nearby field had to be converted into an artillery park.

The Commonwealth appeared on the verge of civil war.

The Senate was dominated by the papal legate Vincenzio Laureo, a partisan of the Hapsburgs; the Lower House, by Jan Zamoysky, "who fulminated so eloquently against 'the craft and cruelty of the House of Austria' that it determined, on November 30, by an enormous majority, to elect a native Pole." No one, however, stepped forward to accept the honor, whereupon the Senate declared the issue settled and prevailed upon the primate of Poland, Uchanski, head of the interregnum government, to proclaim Maximilian king on December 10.

The Lower House rebelled, nominated Stefan Batory, and on December 14, in the Old Town Square of Warsaw, elected him king of Poland by acclamation. Thus, at the end of 1575, Poland had two kings-elect.

Coincident with these events, Maximilian's delegation to Ivan, led by Hans Kobenzl, a vice chancellor of the Empire, and Daniel Printz, a counselor of the Imperial Appellate Court in Bohemia, had made its way to Muscovy. Detained and interrogated at great length at the border, however, they were not received by Ivan until January 24, 1576, at Mozhaisk, where in part to make up for the discourtesy, he made every effort to enchant them with the extent of his wealth, piety, and charm. Kobenzl in particular was impressed by Ivan's cap "with a ruby as big as an egg on it that shines like a lighted lamp," and his crown "more splendid than the Pope's, so thickly studded with gems as big as walnuts that I marvelled how his head could support the weight." Told of Ivan's zeal for building churches, and of the pious ferocity with which he beat his forehead on the ground, Kobenzl was soon convinced that religious reconciliation with Rome might be achieved without difficulty—"increasing the number [of Catholics] at a stroke by three times the loss incurred recently in Germany and France." This, despite the fact that he himself was clearly viewed as a schismatic, and during an Orthodox Mass had to wait outside in the church *parvis* with a dejected company of men "who had not bathed and washed since lying with women." The credulous Kobenzl also found it hard to believe that the tsar, according to his reputation, was really "addicted by nature to all rigour and cruelty" (as another contemporary put it), especially since "he hath not an illiberall or misshapen countenance as was said of Attila the Hun." On the contrary, he thought Ivan "friendly and sweet," and his stature "so obviously noble that among several hundred peasants dressed exactly the same he would be recognized instantly as a great lord."[1] Printz, more critically observant, has left us this brief but priceless portrait of the tsar at age forty-six:

> He is very tall and physically very powerful, though somewhat tending to fat. He has large eyes which are perpetually darting about, observing everything thoroughly. He has a red beard with a somewhat black coloring and wears it rather long and thick. But like most Russians he wears the hair of his head cut short with a razor. . . . They say that when he is in the grip of anger he foams at the mouth like a stallion, appears close to madness and rages against everyone he meets.

37.

The Enthronement of Simeon Bekbulatovich

Ivan's habitually anxious demeanor had of course been long in the making, but there were, at this time, new and remarkable reasons for it, which allude to the strangest episode of all in Ivan's reign.

While at Mozaisk, Printz heard a rumor that Ivan had secretly abdicated and enthroned another in his place. And this, incredibly enough, was true. The tsar's country estate at Mozhaisk had been hastily embellished to simulate a palace, and the embassy's delay at the border had also been due in part to elaborate efforts to conceal from foreigners what was going on. The tsar confided the facts (if only vaguely) to Daniel Sylvester on November 24, 1575, shortly before Printz and Kobenzl arrived. "We highlye forsawe the varyable and daungerous estate of princes," Ivan told him,

> and that as well as the meanest they are subject unto chaunge, which caused us to suspect oure owne magnificence, and that which nowe inded ys chaunced unto us, for we have resyned the estate of our government which heathertoo hath bene so royally mayntayned into the hands of a straunger whoe is nothinge alyed unto us our lande or crowne. The occasion whereof is the perverse and evill dealinge of our subjects who mourmour and repine at us, forgettinge

loyaull obedience they practice against our person. The which to prevent we
have gyvene them over unto an other prince to governe them but have reserved
in our custodye all the treasure of the lande withe sufficient trayne and place
for their and our relyefe.

According to correlative information Printz obtained, this "straunger" had
been anointed grand prince by the metropolitan in August, but without
the Duma swearing allegiance (an essential part of the coronation procedure);
and though invested with the *barmy* or mantle, was denied Monomakh's
crown. The conditional nature of his enthronement was more obliquely
stressed by Ivan to Sylvester in a second interview on January 29, 1576:

> Although we manifested to thyne aparaunce to have enthronysed an other in
> th'empyryall dignitye and thereunto have enthrowled bothe us and others,
> yet not so muche and the same not so farr resyned, but that at our pleasure
> wee can take the dignitye unto us againe and will yet for that same ys not
> confirmed unto him by order of coronacion nor he by assent elected, but for
> our pleasure. Behoulde allso seaven crownes yet in owr possession with the
> cepter and the rest of the stately ornaments apertaynynge unto th'empyre
> with all the treasures belonginge unto each.

Who was this hand-picked "other . . . nothing alyed unto us our lande
or crowne"—that is, neither a Russian nor a descendant of Rurik—elevated
to take charge of the administration of Muscovy?

He was a Tartar, Sain-Bulat, baptized Simeon Bekbulatovich, of royal
blood and the former tsar of Kasimov, where he had succeeded Shah-Ali
in 1566. A descendant of the eldest son of Genghis Khan, and the great-
grandson of Khan Ahmad of the Golden Horde, he had converted to Christianity in February of 1573 and married the daughter of Prince Ivan Mstislavsky, whose mother was a niece of Vasily III. Though not a blood relation,
he was therefore an in-law of Ivan IV, and his genealogical background
and connections were impeccable. Moreover, as a Muscovite general he
had recently distinguished himself in the attack on Swedish Estonia in the
winter of 1572–1573.

The Chronicles and other sources relate that after Simeon's enthronement
Ivan assumed the role of an appanage prince and called himself simply
"Ivan of Moscow." He lived in a residential suburb, "rode simply, like a
boyar," and passed on to Simeon "all the offices of the tsardom." At the
palace, he "sat with other boyars at a distance from the tsar's place" and
addressed Simeon in self-effacing terms, as in one petition which began:

"To the lord and great prince Simeon Bekbulatovich of all Russia, Ivanets Vasiliev with his children Ivanets and Fedorets incline their heads."

Why this very risky charade, such as "few princes would have done in their greatest extremitie"?

No one really knows. The most obvious explanation is that it was some sort of interregnum experiment, with a caretaker regime, while Ivan was under consideration for the Polish throne. But if so, Ivan was evidently also propelled to it by other factors. To begin with, according to the *Piskarev Chronicle*, soothsayers had warned him that in Anno Mundi 7084 (that is, the year in the Muscovite calendar beginning September 1, 1575), "there would be a change: the Moscow tsar will die." He therefore perhaps untsared himself, and by putting another in his place, sought to give the fates a scapegoat. At the same time, ever the cunning politician, he made use of Simeon to implement one of his most controversial and abiding policy aims:

> All charters graunted to bishoprickes and monasteries, which they had enjoyed manie hundred yeares before, were cancelled. This done (as in dislike of the fact and of misgovernment of the newe king) [Ivan] resumed his scepter, and so was content (as in favor to the Church and religious men) that they should renew their charters and take them of himselfe: reserving and annexing to the crowne so much of their lands as himselfe thought good.
>
> By this practise hee wrung from the bishoprickes and monasteries (besides the landes which he annexed to the crowne) an huge masse of money. From some 40, from some 50, from some an hundred thousande rubbels. And this aswell for the increase of his treasurie, as to abate the ill opinion of his harde government, by a shewe of woorse in an other man.

In other words, Ivan attempted to test through Simeon the possibility of confiscating ecclesiastical property, and used him as a surrogate to show the Church and people how bad things could get, so that after conjuring up the hateful specter of the Tartars, his own re-enthronement would be greeted with relief. Whatever property he deigned to return would therefore be gratefully received.

Yet another explanation can be extrapolated from one of the petitions Ivan submitted to Simeon in the name of himself and his two sons, which allowed him to select a new cadre of servitors, and to expel those he did not trust. "And when we have sorted the people out, then, O Lord, we shall submit their names to you and thereafter we shall take none without your Lordship's express permission." This lent a pretense of legality to an

Oprichnina-like reshuffling of his court—but with Simeon, not Ivan, assuming responsibility for the action, in a procedure far more orderly than the formation of the *Oprichniki* corps.

Peter the Great, incidentally, was to emulate Ivan's morality play of self-demotion at least twice: once when he "enthroned" Menshikov and withdrew to a little wooden house; and secondly, when after the Battle of Poltava he "handed in his 'colonel's report' to Romodanovsky, set upon a throne and dressed up to represent Caesar." In both instances he "desired to give his subjects a striking example of the obedience due to the universal law of service." In the summer of 1576, in what could be construed as a similar example of obedience, Ivan and his elder son were "assigned" by Simeon to Kaluga on the southern frontier "to serve against the coming of the khan."

Yet it is on Ivan's rash remarks to Sylvester that we must finally rely. And they ring with psychological truth. Due to the "perverse and evill dealinge" of his subjects "who mourmour and repine," he had decided (whatever his other reasons) once again to make a spectacle of going away. Just as in his abdication of 1564, he did this finally in order to be recalled— as Simeon's role in expropriating church property makes clear.

To the end, some part of Ivan would remain the hysterical child.

But hysteria on the throne turns gruesome—inevitably, at least, in the case of Ivan IV—and the background to Simeon's elevation is awash with blood. The preceding summer (1575) had indeed been a tumultuous one for the tsar. Among other things, he had sent his fourth wife, Anna Koltovskaya, to a convent; married a fifth, Anna Vasilchikova; defrocked Archbishop Leonid of Novgorod for witchcraft, sodomy ("keeping boyes and beastes"), and the counterfeiting of coin; ransacked the house of his brother-in-law Nikita Zakharin in a punitive measure for some unknown offense; and obliged his new foreign secretary, Andrey Schchelkalov, "to gash the naked back of his young and beautiful wife with a scimitar as a sign of renunciation." In the midst of these events, on August 2, 1575, he had also sent a number of officials to the scaffold; and on October 20 (a month before his revelations to Sylvester) some forty others accused of plotting his assassination were executed in the Kremlin's Cathedral Square.

A central figure in the generation of these purges appears to have been Ivan's sinister court astrologer, apothecary, and necromancer, Dr. Elijah Bomel, a Westphalian by birth who had studied medicine in Cambridge, England. Imprisoned in London for sorcery in the summer of 1570, he managed to make contact with the Russian ambassador, Savin, who invited him to Muscovy. Possibly enlisted as a double agent, he was nevertheless anathema to Burghley, who was glad to be rid of him. After Dr. Lindsay was asphyxiated in the Moscow fire of 1571, Bomel supplanted him as the tsar's physician and "lived in great favour and pompe," casting horoscopes, concocting poisons, and surreptitiously conveying a fortune out of the country. Perhaps he was the mysterious soothsayer who had injudiciously predicted 1575 as a fatal year. In any case, by that summer he had begun to intrigue with Polish and Swedish agents with whom he communicated in cipher and, guessing that some part of his correspondence had been read, shaved off his beard, disguised himself as his own assistant (to whom the tsar had issued a pass to buy herbs at Riga), and with gold sewn into the lining of his coat, fled toward Livonia. But as he passed through the fish market at Pskov, he was recognized and arrested. Charged with treason and placed on the rack, he "confessed much and many things more then was written or willinge the Emperor should knowe. The Emperor sent word they should rost him." Bomel's revelations about plots and other (unrecorded) matters apparently led to the fall executions. Among those to perish was Archbishop Leonid, who was sewn up in a bearskin and mauled to death by dogs. Eleven members of his staff were also hanged, and "his woemen witches shamfully dismembred and burnt."

On September 1, 1576 (Anno Mundi 7085), Ivan reassumed the tsardom and rewarded Simeon for his service with the governorship of Tver.[1]

part four

DEMISE

38.

Stefan Batory

Whatever the explanation for Simeon's enigmatic enthronement, it was symmetrical with Ivan's habits of rule. Having at one time or another divided the territory, people, and government of his realm—choosing an "elect" even among his mendicant population—what was there left for Ivan in the ingenuity of his madness (or political game) but to split his kingship and give duality itself a seat on the throne?

Meanwhile, the potentially bloody but wholly different double kingship of Poland had come to a swift but surprisingly peaceable end. Couriers dispatched to both Transylvania and Vienna had separately congratulated Batory and Maximilian on their election, but while Maximilian temporized (until he believed he had a promise of Russian military support), Batory sped for Cracow, as the sultan warned Vienna that any attempt to interfere with his accession would mean war.

Thus onto the Baltic scene strode an obscure figure of Napoleonic genius—a relatively unknown prince from a tiny principality, whose unhoped-for intercession in the Livonian War was to change the course of Eastern European history.

Born at Somlyo on September 27, 1533, Stefan Batory had studied at the University of Padua (Europe's foremost university), and after 1552 had devoted himself to the Transylvanian independence movement. He soon proved an outstanding general in battles with Austrian troops, and after 1562 took charge of the truce negotiations in Vienna, where his inflexibility so infuriated his Austrian counterparts that they arrested him. Imprisoned for three years, he emerged in 1571 as the Turkish candidate for the Transylvanian throne against Gaspard Bekes, the choice of the Hapsburgs. At this time Transylvania was caught as in a vise between the two great empires, each seeking to dominate the principality as a vassal state. Inevitably, civil war ensued, continuing for four years until Bekes was decisively defeated at the Battle of Maros on July 10, 1575. A few months later, Batory was elected king of Poland—suddenly making him the lord of two realms. Accepting the greater crown without hesitation, he entrusted the government of Transylvania to his brother Christopher, hurried across the Carpathians, and on March 23, 1576, accompanied by 500 Transylvanian knights "with leopard skins slung over their golden breastplates," entered the Polish capital. Astride his huge bay charger, he looked every inch a warrior-king, while a black heron plume, fixed to the front of his tall fur *kolpak* by a ruby, completed the Turkish style of his majesty.

The nobility, Church hierarchs, and great merchants rode in stately procession to meet him. Near the castle gates, a triumphal arch had been erected with a mechanically operated eagle attached to the keystone. The bird flapped its wings thrice in salute and inclined in submission as Batory passed beneath. Cannons thundered their tribute from the castle walls.

Batory agreed at once to the various constraints imposed on his predecessor, and even to marrying Anna; but if the turbulent nobility imagined for a moment that he was to be their marionette they were sadly mistaken. Convoking a Diet directly after his coronation, he warned that all who failed to appear would be condemned as traitors. And to the assembled aristocrats, he declared: "I was born a free man and I will guard my freedom with my life. You called me to this throne and placed the crown upon my brow. I will not be a painted or a ballad king." No magnate, however mighty, could intimidate him. One of the mightiest tried and was executed.

Though autocratic, Batory was not a tyrant. In council he encouraged free and open discussion, and though a fervent Catholic who supported the educational and proselytizing work of the Roman Curia, he preached religious toleration and increased the privileges granted to both Protestants and Jews. "I may reign over persons," he once declared, "but God has reserved unto himself three things: the creation of something out of nothing, knowledge of the future, and the government of conscience." Indeed, despite the limited intelligence some thought to divine from his low brow and "savage Magyar face," Batory was a man of broad Renaissance culture and capacities. Heidenstein, the contemporary Polish historian, wrote of him: "He was the incarnation of majesty, yet possessed of a strange sensitivity and simplicity, together with great humility. A high seriousness marked his contact with everyone, and as a lover of truth he easily recognized it in others and never avoided it on his own behalf. In many people's eyes, he was unduly given to anger and to cruelty, but no person forgave more readily, and he had a long memory for services rendered. . . . It is impossible to say whether he was more feared than loved." So, we may remember, it had been said of the young Ivan, in 1556; yet unlike the tsar, Batory conspicuously sought to the end to be above reproach—from his heroic entry into Cracow (to remind the Poles, after Henry, what a true king was), to the stern self-abnegation and chastity of his private life. Though his marriage to Anna was scarcely a romantic one, he took no mistresses; and in his disdain for luxury and all the ostentatious vanities of court display, hauled out his regalia only when it seemed necessary to demonstrate the authority and dignity of the crown.

Despite numerous physical complaints—chronic rashes, hereditary epilepsy, and (like the legendary Greek archer Philoctetes) a mysterious, unhealing wound in his left leg—he made a constant show of vigor, especially to his troops on campaign. He spent whole days in the saddle, scorned stockings under his boots, ate his meals off a bare wooden trestle, and slept in his tent on straw or a heap of dry leaves.

The works of Caesar were always by his side, but his knowledge beyond military affairs was also enormous, encompassing theology, history, medicine, magic, and alchemy.[1] Though he did not speak Polish, he did speak Latin, which was the language of the Polish court; and his knowledge of Polish history and contemporary issues was exact. Needless to say, he knew the pattern of the Russian invasions, which territories were under dispute and why.

Though perhaps not Ivan's literary equal, Batory had a convincing reputation for eloquence, "his every word," according to Heidenstein, "so weighted that his speech assumed an oracular quality." John Kochanowski (the "Polish Ronsard") had nothing but praise for his Latin style—which meant something in a realm which boasted "more Latinists than ever there were in Latium."

When first notified of Batory's election, Ivan derisively exclaimed: "Who ever heard of this man before?" He was to grieve that he had ever heard his name.

The foremost early challenge to the king came from the "free city" of Danzig at the mouth of the Vistula, which controlled the main artery of Polish commerce with the outside world. Under the pretext of remaining faithful to the Hapsburg cause, it immediately attempted (with Danish connivance) to secede.

Batory mounted a blockade, declared the burghers outlaws, and after failing to subdue the city by land assaults and heavy bombardments, began building a Polish squadron at Elbing to intercept the Danish convoys resupplying the port by sea. When he started to dredge an artificial channel to divert the Vistula from Danzig to Elbing, horrified Danzigers tried to plunder the rival port but were driven off by Hungarian platoons. Danzig's ultimate capitulation ended a challenge which might have destroyed Batory as a king, but instead reinforced his reputation for invincibility. Meanwhile, he had managed to mend his relations with the pope, who had favored the election of Maximilian, and had reaffirmed his amicable relations with the Turks, who pledged to restrain their Crimean vassals from raiding the Ukraine. Thus, by 1577 Batory was freed to concentrate on defending the borders of Western Christendom, as he saw it, from the onslaughts of Moscow and its "Scythian Wolf."

Batory invested himself with all the historic enmity of his adoptive kingdom and confronted Moscow like the most partisan Pole. Convinced that a negotiated settlement to the Livonian War was impossible, he left no doubt in his initial message to Ivan as to where he stood. Calling himself Sovereign of Livonia as well as the King of Poland, he addressed his counterpart as grand prince rather than tsar, and omitted to acknowledge him as lord of Smolensk and Polotsk. But at that passing moment, Ivan had the upper hand. While the king's energies had been diverted by the Danzig rebellion, Ivan in 1575 had captured Pernau, reoccupied part of Estonia in 1576, and in a direct challenge to Batory in the summer of 1577 had overrun two important fortresses, Wenden and Wolmar, in territory supposedly under Polish control. At Wenden the garrison chose death over surrender and blew itself up. At Wolmar, where Kurbsky had written his first, famous letter of defiance more than thirteen years before, Ivan resumed the polemical correspondence, boasting: "In our old age we have gone beyond the far-off towns where you sought refuge. . . . And on the legs of our horses we have ridden all over your roads, from and into Lithuania, and on foot we have gone, and we have drunk water in those places. . . . And who now takes the strong German towns? . . . And to Wolmar, too, your place of rest, has God led us." But there was no rest for Ivan at Wolmar, for none of his old wounds had healed. In the midst of his triumphant taunting, he again reviled Sylvester, who had fallen, he said, only because "I stood up for myself;" and though affirming, as ever, his divine right and qualifications to rule, yet acknowledged "sacrifices to Cronus," and in the guiltiest way anticipated the charge against him of sexual license: "You will say I did not bear [Anastasia's] loss patiently and did not remain true to her—well, we are all human. What about that soldier's wife you took?," adding, "If only you had not stood up against me with the priest! Then none of this would have happened."

*   *   *

As the Russian campaign of 1577 proceeded, Magnus attempted to act independently and to capture towns on his own account. Many capitulated, hoping to avoid Russian reprisals by coming under his protection. So impressed was he with his own success that he warned the tsar not to molest his new "kingdom," listing a number of towns and castles as his own. Ivan rode directly to Kokenhausen, the nearest one on the list, and executed the garrison.

Ivan's fresh conquests were also facilitated by tragic developments in Sweden. On February 24, 1577, Johan had served Erik a bowl of poisoned pea soup, and afterward seized with remorse, tried to bury himself in the study of theology. Long his favorite subject, if never so urgent, he apparently convinced himself that he was destined to be the architect of a universal religious reconciliation, uniting the opposed currents of Protestant and Catholic doctrine into a single stream. He compiled a compromise Manual on Church organization and practice, and a compromise Liturgy, known as the Red Book (after its red parchment cover) massively annotated with his own reflections. He also wrote to the pope, whose agitation for a Catholic restoration in Sweden had already recruited the queen, and had led to at least one covert Vatican operation involving two Jesuits posing as Lutherans sent to Stockholm to infiltrate the faculty of a new Protestant seminary. There, their highly regarded lectures, which deliberately made use of Reformation texts in such a way as to impugn their authority without seeming to do so, had produced classes full of confused and troubled students ripe for conversion.

To convert the king, the pope sent Antonio Possevino, a former general secretary of the Jesuit Order and one-time rector of Avignon, who as a vigorous agent of the Counterreformation in France had hunted Waldensian heretics through the Alps. Learned, politically savvy, if somewhat impetuous and vain, Possevino was prepared to use every means at his disposal to advance the Catholic cause.

On Christmas Day in 1577, he arrived in Stockholm accredited as an imperial envoy and disguised as a cavalier. Johan had approved the masquerade so as not to alarm his subjects, and after several long discussions extending over several months, the king was swayed, made his general confession to the priest, and received communion at his hands. At the conclusion of the Mass, Johan is said to have exclaimed: "I embrace thee and the Catholic Church forever." Six months later, however, he angrily recanted when the pope rejected his compromise reforms and bluntly implied that his Red Book was heretical.

Possevino returned to Sweden, this time openly as a Catholic priest, and supposing pro-Catholic sentiment to be widespread, ordered his confrères to throw aside their disguises. Panic seized the Swedish Church and incited anti-Catholic riots in Stockholm, but in the end it was revealed that there were only a few thousand Catholics in the entire realm.

At long last, Ivan's adversaries began to coalesce. Batory wrote to Johan proposing Reval as a base of operations against Narva. Johan advised Batory to draw his battle lines from Wenden to Pskov—by implication yielding him southern Livonia—while he marched toward Novgorod. If this worked out they could link up for a drive on Moscow. After that they could talk about Russia from Narva to the White Sea and make a race for Kholmogory.

This sort of playful correspondence did not bode well for the tsar. Before the end of the year (1577), the Lithuanians had captured Düneburg, and in January 1578 the Polish Diet voted subsidies for war. Ivan proposed a three-year armistice not applicable to Livonia, but as his two ambassadors made their way across war-torn territory to Batory, they were deliberately delayed by officials appointed to engage them in prolonged discussions as to how the two sovereigns should be designated in the text. By the time they struggled into Warsaw in December, Batory was on the march. Early in 1578, Polish cavalry took Wenden by storm; then Karkus, Helmet, and Ermes fell, securing western Livonia almost in a line from Pernau to the Dvina eighty miles inland from the coast. Magnus barricaded himself up in Oberphalen. When the Swedes captured it, he fled to Courland and renounced his thorny crown.

Ivan resolved to retake Wenden, but the Poles and Swedes combined in defense of the town. As the Russians began their siege, they were attacked from all sides, and only nightfall seems to have spared them extermination. Under cover of darkness, some of their officers fled. Dawn broke and the remaining troops faced massacre. In despair and humiliation, eighteen Russian cannoneers strangled themselves across their own guns.

These Muscovite reversals gave Kurbsky an opportunity to reply to Ivan's taunt of the previous year. He predicted a total Russian defeat, quoted Cicero to prove that enforced flight was not treason, contrasted the virtuous Sylvester with Ivan, who "used the name of virtue" but did "not understand what virtue meant," and accused him of having "shut up . . . free human nature," making Russia "a fortress of hell."

Batory was absolutely determined to break that fortress open, and when the Muscovite envoys were finally ushered into his presence, he neither rose from his seat nor asked after the tsar's health, as protocol required.

They promptly declared themselves unable to discharge their mission—precisely what he had wanted them to do.

At least as early as March 1578, Batory had confided to a handful of advisers that his ultimate aim was to conquer Russia itself. By April, he had begun to hammer out his overall strategy, and every limited campaign he subsequently undertook was so constructed as to fit into this larger design.

He had few firm commitments from allies. The pope promised to promote his cause in Europe; the elector of Brandenburg sent him a few cannon; Denmark agreed to neutrality; Sweden (despite their collaborative action at Wenden) promised nothing in the way of a definite agreement on Livonia, and seemed prepared to rely on the fortunes of war. For the next year or so the Crimean Tartars were out of the picture, since the new sultan (Murad III) needed them for his Persian campaigns. (In 1577 Devlet Giray had died, succeeded by Gazi Giray II. In 1578, Crimean cavalry helped the Turks capture the strategically important "Iron Gate," a mountain pass near Derbend, on the southwestern coast of the Caspian.) Grand Vizier Sokollu was openly skeptical that Batory could prevail: "Great is the power of the Muscovite," he told the Polish ambassador. "With the exception of my master, there is no mightier sovereign on earth." Russia's resilience had certainly been remarkable, yet Ivan realized he could not stand alone. His quest for allies, however, was almost fruitless. When his envoys arrived in Vienna, they found Maximilian dead, and his successor, Rudolph, uninterested in any alliance that did not acknowledge his sovereignty over Livonia. In late August 1578, a Danish embassy under Jacob Ulfeld met with Ivan at Aleksandra Sloboda to conclude a trade agreement, but it was subsequently nullified because Ulfeld had exceeded his instructions. Queen Elizabeth continued to "make dayntie" with his appeals.

At about this time, various Livonian exiles in Germany, clustered about a certain Count Georg Hans, also concocted a scheme for the invasion of Russia from the north. Predicting that a mercenary army of 75,000 men in 200 ships would suffice, the idea was to occupy the Arctic harbors, push south, blockade Moscow, capture Ivan alive, collect his treasure from numerous caches scattered across the land, and deposit it with the Emperor Rudolph—to whom, in fact, this whole scheme was calculated to appeal. Rudolph would get the treasure, Poland and Sweden could carve up Russia as they liked, the Livonian Knights would get back their country, and Ivan would be given an earldom in some foreign land. The bankrupt Rudolph, who would have done almost anything else to replenish his treasury, dismissed the scheme as preposterous, as did every other monarch approached.

Batory, whose plans were real (and more practical than any skeptic could divine), reduced his expenses at court, persuaded a recalcitrant Diet to levy new taxes, stockpiled supplies, and drilled his troops. On the Hungarian model, he diversified his cavalry into light-horse and the heavily mounted and equipped, rearmed his infantry with battleaxes and muskets, tripled its size by new levies among peasants on crown estates, and introduced aristocrats into its ranks to develop its leadership and prestige. Townsmen, too, were called to arms; and to encourage volunteers, he promised liquidation of debts. Foreign auxiliaries were enlisted—Germans, Hungarians, and Scots—along with battle-hardened battalions from the Transylvanian Alps. Dnieper cossacks were integrated into his machine as a cavalry reserve.

Artillery began to roll out of cannon foundries at Danzig, Marborg, Warsaw, and Lvov. From the mouth of the Nieman, it was floated downstream and portaged overland to Svir, where an army of 60,000 had assembled by July 1579.

39.

Polotsk and Veliky Luki

England emerged as the wild card in the war. Hoping to avoid, if possible, a permanent rupture with Muscovy, Daniel Sylvester had hurried back to England in the spring of 1576, where several versions of an Anglo-Russian treaty were apparently prepared. Its wording may never be known. Upon his return, as he was trying on a new satin jacket in an upper room of his lodging at Kholmogory, "the tailor gone scars down the stears," a thunderbolt reputedly "stroeke him dead . . . killed also his boy and dogg, burnt his descke, letters, howse, all at an instant."

Sylvester's curiously absolute incineration, which destroyed every document connected with his embassy, may have been an Act of God, as historians have tended to assume, but in context it is hard not to suspect some other instrument, since so many interests, foreign and domestic, had a stake in keeping England and Russia apart. In any case, the assassination cannot be laid at Ivan's feet. " 'Gods will be donn!' " he said when he heard about it, "but raged and was in desperatt case; his enymies besettinge and besiegginge three partes of his countrye," with Narva "shutt up" (under blockade), in need of powder, saltpeter, lead, and brimstone, but "knew not howe to be furnished thereof but owt of England."

This crisis conducted onto the stage another remarkable Englishman, Jerome Horsey, who had risen from company stipendiary to agent, spoke fluent Russian (as well as Polish and Dutch), and much like Jenkinson won Ivan's affectionate trust. Having originally come to the tsar's attention as an interpreter, he was now summoned to convey a secret message to the queen—though not before Ivan had questioned him closely to assure himself that he was the right man. Horsey remembered:

> He asked me if I had seen his great vessells and barcks built and prepared at Vologda. I told hime I had. "What traitor hath shewed them you?"—"The fame of them was such, and people flockinge to see them upon a festival daye, I ventured with thowsandes more to behold the curious bewty, largnes and streinge fashion of them."—"Whie, what meane you by those words, streinge fashion?"—"For that the portrature of lyons, draggons, eagles, oliphonts and unicorns, wear so lievlie made and so richly sett forth with gold, silver and curious coullers of paintinge, etc."—"A craftie youthe, comendes his own countrimens artificerie," said the Emperor to his favorette standinge by. "Yt is trew: yt seems you have taken good vew of them: how many of them?"—"Yt pleas your Majesty I sawe but 20."—"You shall see fortie, err longe be, noe worss. I comende you. Noe doubt you can relate as much in forren place, but much more to be admired, if you knewe what inestimable treasur they are inwardly to be bewtified with"—

alluding to his contingency plan to abscond to England with the public treasury.

Obviously, Elizabeth's contribution to the Russian war effort was ongoing and considerable. As of 1579, Ivan had twenty great new ships at Vologda alone, and at least twenty more under construction.

The tsar's "favorette standinge by" was probably Bogdan Belsky (unrelated to the great Belsky clan), appointed armorer in 1578, and subsequently chamberlain. Another man on the rise was Boris Godunov, of Tartar princely extraction, who had enrolled in the *Oprichnina* under the sponsorship of Malyuta Skuratov in 1571, and whose sister a few years later married the tsar's son Fyodor. In 1578, Boris himself married Skuratov's daughter,

Maria—which further assisted his advance at court. After his elevation to boyar in 1580, he emerged as the tsar's chief adviser on state affairs.

Ivan liked Horsey's "readie aunswers" and told him: "Be thou trusty and faithfull, and thy reward shal be my goodnes, and grace hereafter." Since it was too late to voyage by the northern route, he was dispatched overland through enemy terrain, with gold ducats sewn into his boots and quilted into his clothes, and the tsar's letters to Elizabeth concealed in the false side of a brandy flask suspended under his horse's mane.

In one night he rode the 90 miles to Tver, and covered 600 miles in the next three days. At Neuhausen, in Livonia, he was arrested, interrogated, and released, but detained again on the island of Oesel and imprisoned as a spy. Admitting nothing, Horsey managed to convince his captors that he was a refugee. All the while he kept the flask "close under my cassocke by daie, and in the night my best pillow under my head." Upon his release, he traveled to Pilton (where he met "King Magnus," who had become an alcoholic), through Courland to Danzig, Lübeck, and Hamburg, where he boarded a ship for England. Home at last, Horsey carefully opened the flask, "toke owt and swetned the Emperors letters and directions, as well as I could; but yet the Queen smelt the savier of the aqua-vitae when I delivered them to her Majesty."

Meanwhile, Batory had perfected his military machine. Before his advent, the Livonian War had been a war of sieges and attrition, of few pitched battles in the open but many incursions, marauding expeditions, and raids. Pillaging had been the principal occupation and preoccupation of the troops, as the possession of districts, citadels, and towns ebbed and flowed. Despite the new weaponry, tactical emphasis on infantry, and so forth, the war had been conducted largely on medieval lines. It was the king who brought to its last phase a method to the long-drawn-out madness of sieges and a strategy of lasting historical note.

At his council of war at Svir in July 1578, he began to unfold his plan: to evict the Muscovites from Livonia, not by a massive counterinvasion, but indirectly by a series of surgical strikes along the Russian frontier that would force Ivan to evacuate most of his army of occupation in order to protect the Russian heartland. At the same time, by opening secondary fronts in Livonia, Batory would oblige him to scatter his remaining troops into isolated strongholds from the Baltic to Moscow. As a result, the Livonian garrisons would fall like dominoes into Polish hands.

Ivan, in fact, had already begun to distribute his Livonian divisions among twenty-four towns, and had split his main army between Novgorod, Pskov, and Smolensk. But the Tartar menace could never be ignored, and though the Crimeans for the moment might be preoccupied with Persia, recent Nogay raids in the Volga Basin had been devastating, obliging Ivan to place detachments at numerous points along the Volga, Oka, Dnieper, and the Don. To make matters worse, the tsar's intelligence network utterly failed him. At Novgorod in July he first learned for certain that Batory had rejected the truce proposed in January, yet was also told the king had been unable to assemble more than "a small army of Lithuanian volunteers." Indeed, the obscurity of the king's encampment at Svir, surrounded by dense forests, as well as "the skillfull division of his forces on the roads leading to this trysting place," had enabled him to conceal his preparations to the eleventh hour.

From his headquarters Batory issued a vigorous manifesto, "crammed with dates, diplomatic texts and epigrams," which reviewed the history of the war, scornfully refuted Ivan's Roman pedigree, and explained that as King of Poland he had drawn his sword not against the people of Russia but their tyrant. He promised to avoid unnecessary devastation and bloodshed, to respect the rights and property of all civilians, and issued specific regulations against wanton killing, rape, and the destruction of crops. To establish a high moral tone, he instituted pious passwords like "Lord, forgive us our sins!" and "God punishes the wicked."

Thus heralded, and accompanied by two official historians, a wind-instrument military band, two printing presses for churning out propaganda, a rabble-rousing theologian to exhort the troops, two Italian doctors and a Polish specialist on syphilis, Batory embarked on the first of his three great Livonian War campaigns.

His target was Polotsk.

Before Ivan even knew where Batory was, his advance guard had stormed Krasny, Susha, and Sitno, three of the city's auxiliary strongholds, while his main army, marching obliquely to the Disna River from Svir, had rapidly crossed over by means of pontoon bridges and was hacking its way through the woods towards its goal.

Meanwhile, Ivan had sent a cavalry regiment over the border into Courland as a diversionary thrust, but hastily withdrew it when he realized Batory was somewhere in the Ukraine. Yet he still couldn't figure out where the king meant to strike; and though he sent one relief force to Polotsk, he sent others equally strong to Nevel and Smolensk. Batory's advance guard intercepted the reinforcements destined for Polotsk and drove them into the fortress of Sokol ten miles to the north.

On August 11, the king emerged from the woods and began bombarding Polotsk with fireballs.

In gruesome defiance the Russians killed the first few prisoners they took, roped them upside down to beams (to brand them as infidels) and floated them down the Dvina River past the king's encampment.

But their own situation was grim. Nor could Ivan promise relief. Johan had 17,000 men in the field, supported by a first-class fleet, and in July (with Batory still at Svir) had bombarded and set fire to the suburbs of Narva. As Swedish infantry also gathered at Reval, Russian forces were tied up by developing battles at Wesenberg and Hapsal, while Batory had opened a third front with raids near Smolensk and across the Dnieper as far as Starodub. Narva was infinitely more important to Ivan than Polotsk, and the cavalry regiment withdrawn from Courland was therefore sent to the Estonian front.

After a three-week siege, Polotsk capitulated. The slaughter was dreadful. One veteran officer said he had "never seen so many corpses together," and despite Batory's Christian regulations, the Polish and Hungarian soldiers "lined up and rushed at each other" in a dispute over the spoils. In ransacking the cathedral for hidden treasure, a priceless library of chronicles and Slav translations of the church fathers was apparently committed to the flames.

When Sokol fell on September 25, the defenders were massacred to a man. Numerous fortresses in the area surrendered throughout the fall.

Kurbsky, who served on Batory's general staff, wrote letters to Ivan from Polotsk and Sokol to celebrate the Russian defeats. In the first, he appealed to the tsar to repent and reminded him that before he had been "corrupted by toadies" and had fallen into "foul despotism, pharaonic disobedience and hardness of heart against God," he had "lived in the commandments of the Lord, surrounded by chosen men of eminence; and not only were you a brave and courageous fighter and a terror to your foes, but also you were filled with Holy Scriptures and sanctified by holiness." In the second, he deplored Ivan's sodomy, his many marriages, and insatiable lust—violating "hordes of pure maidens, dragging them along in wagon-loads"—and cursed the *Oprichniki* as "Satan's band." "You were corrupted," he reminded him, "and then you repented, but afterwards returned to your first state of filth." On that unpleasant note (for Ivan was never to reply), their historic correspondence came to an end.

As Ivan's chief accuser, Kurbsky's own doings merit scrutiny. His life as an expatriate had had its ups and downs. Initially greeted with much fanfare and an extensive grant of estates (including ten villages with 9000 acres of land in Lithuania, plus towns, villages, and Bona Sforza's old castle of Smedyno in Volynia), he had ridden to war against the tsar, and in return for "good, shining, true, and manly service" Sigismund August in 1567 had made his property hereditary. Twice elected to the Diet, he also married into a wealthy branch of the landed aristocracy.

A diligent scholar as well as a venomous pamphleteer, Kurbsky's knowledge of Latin was sufficient to enable him to translate into Church Slavonic the works of several Greek Fathers from Latin redactions, and in the same way to read Aristotle as well as Cicero. In other literary activity, between 1572 and 1576 he compiled an annotated 900-page anthology of Church literature called the *New Margarit*, wrote his polemical history of Ivan's reign, and was active in the Orthodox educational movement sweeping Lithuania. This movement brought him together with many gifted fellow refugees, including Ivan Fedorov and Peter Mstislavets, the pioneer printers of Moscow. Under their auspices, the first full text of the Bible in Church Slavonic was printed at Ostrog in 1580.

But Kurbsky was no saint. He wrangled with his neighbors, who regarded him as an interloper, and when he thought they were poaching on his land, carried out retaliatory raids. He oppressed the peasants on his estates, and his steward was a notorious sadist whose cruelties he failed to curb. His Lithuanian marriage was a disaster. In 1578, he caught his wife *in flagrante delicto* with a valet, but his divorce settlement was unfavorable, and because he failed to secure it on canonical grounds, his subsequent offspring from a later marriage were declared bastards under the law, without right of inheritance. Costly litigation failed to set things right. By the end of his life (in 1583) there was nothing to inherit, since his remaining assets were impounded against his debts.

Ivan's marital problems were of another kind. After his fifth wife, Anna Vasilchikova, died in 1577 (of natural causes), he had married Vasilisa Melentieva, but remanded her to a nunnery before the end of the year. In the summer of 1580 he exceeded the nuptial record of Henry VIII and took his seventh and last wife, Maria Nagaia, the daughter of his long-time foreign-service official Afanasy Nagoi. In Ivan's favor it must be said that (so far as we know) unlike Henry he executed none of his wives.

But his charity had a very narrow range. His immediate reaction to the loss of Polotsk, for example, was to sack the foreign suburb of Moscow. For some time its privileged status had aroused the anger of the Church, especially since its inhabitants had flaunted their modest liberties. Perhaps its seductive role as a prototypical showcase village was now also deemed obsolete. In any case, one night Ivan "sett a thowsand gunors" all in black, like *Oprichniki*, "to robb and take the spoill of the people; stripped them naked, most barbarously ravished and deflowered both yonge and old weomen without respects," and burned the suburb's two Protestant churches to the ground.

In other areas he tried to reconstitute his resources, so thoroughly drained in countless ways. At a Church Council convoked on January 15, 1580, by Metropolitan Anthony (Metropolitan Kirill's indifferent successor), the tsar told the clergy that because of recent military setbacks the Orthodox faith itself was in jeopardy, and that although he, his son Ivan, and the whole civil and military establishment were working night and day to preserve the state, the Church had been standing idly by. The council responded positively by prohibiting Church institutions to acquire any more land or to receive it as a gift by any device under any pretext. Lands currently under mortgage to the Church were to be taken over by the state at once, as were all princely appanage estates the Church had acquired "to the end that there be not loss of service."

But the problem was not so much the land as peasant flight because of the social calamities that had repeatedly struck the population. For at least two decades, war, famine, pestilence, and domestic terror had transformed a once carefully fostered and regulated migration to the borderlands into a frantic flight *en masse*. This had radically thinned out the working population, ruined numerous service estates, thereby reducing the army, whose gentry no longer had the wherewithal to serve—and destroyed the tax base of the economy. Grain prices rose steadily, a problem exacerbated by hoarding, while monasteries competed for the peasantry that remained. Accordingly, the gentry urged the government "to curb the freedom of peasant movement," and in 1581 this led to an edict prohibiting peasants from leaving their plots during certain "forbidden years." By its partial abrogation of the St. George's Day law, it set a precedent for subsequent decrees that would culminate by the end of the century in the outright institution of serfdom. Thus the real momentum toward serfdom derived not so much from measures needed to sustain the *pomestie* system itself, which had become the cornerstone of Russian military power, but from Ivan's overall social and military policies.

The fall of Polotsk had given Batory a communications and supply line all the way to Riga, and from Riga to the sea. Ivan's gateway to Lithuania had become Batory's bridgehead into Muscovy.

The king's next objective was Veliky Luki, long a staging area for Muscovite operations along the frontier. Advancing from Chasniki in July 1580, he skirted Nevel and proceeded east through Vitebsk, as if against Smolensk. Just before crossing the Dvina, however, his army divided into two columns: one, under Jan Zamoysky, the Polish chancellor, cut its way through thick forests to Velizh, a fortress on the lower Dvina; the other, under Batory, crossed the river on pontoon bridges to advance on Usvyat, to the northwest. A third but smaller cavalry contingent (under a daring Lithuanian commander by the name of Filon Kimita) rode from Orsha toward Smolensk.

Scouts kept Ivan posted, but again he found the king's deployments indecipherable. He had to guess—and again guessed incorrectly—and rushed his reserves to Smolensk, Dorogobush, and Toropets.

Velizh capitulated on August 5, Usvyat on the 26th. Kimita, after a sweep around Smolensk to the north, doubled back sharply: all roads to Veliky Luki were cut. In a perfectly timed conjunction, Zamoysky and Batory linked up on August 26 a few miles from their objective, and by September 5 Veliky Luki had been reduced to rubble by fireballs and mines. The garrison tried to surrender, but Hungarian mercenaries, who "counted on sacking the town when it was stormed," killed the delegates sent out to offer terms. Ozerishche fell a few days later; Nevel on September 29; Zavoloche on October 23. Meanwhile, Batory's light-horse cavalry squadrons roamed almost at will as far north as Porkhov and Opochka, burned Kholm on the Lovat River, and dared even to raid the environs of Staraya Rusa, near Novgorod. In Livonia itself his troops took Kreuzberg south of Riga and stormed the castle of Smilton, while the Swedes under Pontus de la Gardie, a French soldier of fortune, swept through Ingria and Karelia. Kexholm fell in November, Padis after a thirteen-week siege, and Wesenberg, Tolsburg, Hapsal, Leal, and Lode by the summer of 1581.

Russia's position appeared hopeless—so hopeless in fact that most Poles and Lithuanians assumed the war had been won. They were tired of fighting, had suffered their own crop failures and epidemics in recent years, and it was therefore with a groundswell of popular support that the Diet which convened at the end of January 1581 not only stated its reluctance to vote funds for a third campaign, but in a move exasperating to the king (who pointed out that the Muscovite ambassadors were listening), declared them the last he would get.

40.

Missio Moscovitica

In a move that took his adversaries completely by surprise, Ivan appealed for the intervention of the pope. Sudden as it seemed, the way had been carefully prepared. To begin with, Ivan's widely publicized talks with Kobenzl had improved his image in Europe, especially at the Vatican, and as a follow-up in March 1580, he had sent an envoy to Vienna to pretend his enthusiasm for an alliance against the Turks. Then in August, in conjunction with the Duma, he decided to invite the pope to mediate the war. As Ivan well understood, the pontiff was almost bound to respond favorably in the hopes of advancing the two projects nearest to his heart: an anti-Turkish Christian league, and the reunification of the Eastern Church with Rome.

A number of things contributed to the Vatican's preoccupation with the Turks. The most obvious, of course, was the relentless growth of Ottoman might, and the alarming fact that the infidel, fought three centuries before in faraway Palestine, was now bivouacked in the heart of Europe. At the same time, the supranational unity which had once made possible the great medieval crusades had long ago vanished, along with the unity of the faith. For more than a century the Holy See had been unable to stay the erosion of its power, and the Catholic sovereigns of France and Spain were just as unwilling as their Protestant counterparts in England or the Burgundian states to tolerate papal interference in their ecclesiastical or secular affairs. After the papacy had been Italianized in 1523, it enjoyed political power only in Italy, while the nepotism of the Curia, the debauchery of some of the pontiffs, and the secular aspirations of intriguing cardinals who hoped to realize their family fortunes in a papal dynasty accelerated the dismal decline in Vatican prestige. To many Christians the call for an anti-Turkish league seemed an obvious bid on the part of the papacy to revive its ecumenical pretensions and recoup the stature it had lost.

All these issues, however, were eclipsed by the spread of Protestantism, and by the Catholic dream of recouping its numerical losses by garnering the Orthodox East, and especially Russia, for Rome.

From the time of Ivan III, in fact, the Vatican had endeavored to lure Russia to its fold[1]—even as Poland and Livonia had tried to foster the idea that wars against the Muscovites were essentially religious crusades. Poland was especially apprehensive that the pope might one day be induced to recognize Muscovite sovereignty over Lithuania, while during the reign of Ivan IV the Vatican had already made at least five unsuccessful attempts to communicate with the tsar—every one thwarted by the Poles. What was altogether new in 1580 was that the initiative had come from the Muscovites.

On September 5, Ivan's courier, Istoma Shevrigin, set out from Moscow to Rome accompanied by two interpreters, Wilhelm Popler, a Livonian convert to the Orthodox faith who knew both Russian and German; and Francesco Pallavicino, a Milanese merchant and sometime Russian agent in Lübeck who knew German and Italian.[2] They traveled by way of Pernau, Denmark, and Saxony to Prague, where Shevrigin delivered a letter from Ivan to the Emperor Rudolph; on to Venice, where he delivered a second letter to the doge, promising Venetians commercial privileges in Muscovy; and then to Rome, where he arrived on February 26, 1581, with Ivan's letter to the pope. "We want to be in alliance and agreement with you," Ivan wrote, "and with the Emperor Rudolph and to struggle together against all of the Moslem rulers in order that from now on . . . no Christian blood will be shed, and Christian people will live in peace, emancipated from the Moslems. And we ask that you . . . command Stefan [Batory] to break with Islam and stop shedding Christian blood."

Though Ivan never mentioned the possibility of religious union, hopes were inevitably raised, and just one week after Shevrigin's arrival, Pope Gregory XIII commissioned the Jesuit Antonio Possevino (whose recent *missio suetica* had been a disaster) to undertake a *missio moscovitica* and mediate a negotiated conclusion to the Livonian War. Though technically no more than a courier, Shevrigin had thus succeeded in bringing about the appearance of a reconciliation between Rome and Moscow, achieving almost automatically what under any other circumstances would have taxed to the utmost the talents of the most gifted and capable ambassador.

The pope was forthright. In his letter to Ivan dated March 15 he made religious union his central theme: "There is one Church, one Christian flock, one only after Christ is his vicar on earth and universal shepherd," and urged Ivan to study carefully the proceedings of the Council of Florence. In the secret instructions conveyed to Possevino on the day of his departure, Church union was set forth as his paramount aim.

Ivan's canny maneuver serves as a useful reminder that while Muscovy's masses may have known little of the outside world, the tsar himself and his advisers were up to date on European affairs. In addition to envoys sent abroad, the Kremlin coordinated a network of spies, culled intelligence from visiting dignitaries, artisans, and merchants, and received regular reports from agents stationed in all the major Baltic ports. Russia's excellent pony express had also long since been extended into Livonia. The Vatican, on the other hand, knew almost nothing about Muscovy. Its staff, for example, had prepared a gift for Possevino to give to Anastasia, who had been dead for twenty years, and described Muscovy as extending northward "from Scythia and Sarmatia, between the Borysthenes [Dnieper] and the Rha [Volga]," thus using geographical (not to mention geopolitical) terms borrowed from Ptolemy and obsolete for a thousand years.

Shevrigin returned through Denmark, Lübeck, and Livonia to Moscow. Possevino stopped at Graz (where he was briefed by Kobenzl), Vienna, and Prague en route to Vilna. At Vienna he was joined by two Jesuit brethren, Paolo Campano and Stefan Drenocki, the latter a Croatian specialist in Slavic languages.

Batory was appalled at how easily the Vatican had fallen for the diplomatic snare. Although documents also reveal that some of the pope's advisers clearly understood the opportunistic motives behind Ivan's appeal, the Vatican in so responding risked alienating a king whose fervent support of the Counterreformation was unrivaled by any other monarch in Europe. Not only had he taken a leading role in fostering Jesuit seminaries throughout Poland, but more recently in Livonia on the heels of his military gains. When Possevino met with him in Vilna in mid-June, and explained his mission—"to negotiate a just peace, and overlook no opportunity of restoring the Prince of Muscovy to the bosom of the Church"—Batory disparaged "the whole idea as useless, because the Muscovites would soon be compelled to give up all of Livonia in any event, and had thought up the entire scheme solely in an effort to improve their chances." Nevertheless, he agreed to cooperate with his embassy.

In the initial diplomatic back-and-forth, Ivan offered to cede the whole of Livonia except for the four towns of Narva, Dorpat, Fellin, and Pernau;[3] Batory insisted on Narva, plus a war indemnity of 400,000 gold crowns. Emboldened by Possevino's mediation, however, Ivan on June 29 retracted his earlier concessions, demanded thirty-six Livonian towns (yielding only Veliky Luki and twenty-four forts), rejected the indemnity as infidel "tribute," compared Batory to Amalek and Sennacherib, and hypocritically appealed to the Council of Florence of 1439 (which the Russians had rejected) as having ruled that the Greek Orthodox and Latin faiths were one: and therefore, "Why do you object to an extension of the Greek faith over Livonia?" Though Ivan told his ambassadors not to insist on his title "being written out in full in the text of any truce," they were nevertheless to declare: "God gave our sovereign his royal title and who can take it from him? Our sovereign is not of yesterday, but the one who is knows that himself." To drive the insult home, he signed his own letter "Tsar and Grand Duke of Russia . . . by the Grace of God, and not by the turbulent will of men." At about the same time, he launched a counteroffensive from Smolensk and sent Russian cavalry across the Dnieper to strike at Orsha and Mogilev. In July, he attempted to retake Kholm and Velizh.

When Possevino asked one of the Russian ambassadors why the tsar had altered his proposals, he declared flatly: "The New Testament wipes out the Old." Possevino's task was a very difficult one. On the one hand, the Poles feared he would sell them out, since Russian enthusiasm for discussing Church union might seem to depend on whether he performed his mission to Moscow's satisfaction; on the other, the Muscovites suspected him as a Catholic of being an instrument of the king. Meanwhile, however, his very presence on the scene helped Ivan by fostering expectations of peace that, coupled with the tsar's threat to break off negotiations, undermined Polish morale: no one wanted to be a casualty in the last days of a needlessly prolonged war.

On July 21, Possevino and his companions crossed the Russian frontier and after a harrowing night camped outside in the rain—during which "Ukrainian cossacks imitated the cries of wild beasts in the woods to frighten us"—they were met at dawn by sixty Muscovite cavalrymen, who escorted them to Smolensk.

Ivan had told the bishop of Smolensk to spruce up his churches, and by a special dispensation had granted permission for Possevino to visit them, even though "it had been a long time since Latins were in communion with the Universal and Apostolic Church." Ivan did not realize that Possevino was under a similar ban, being forbidden to worship with heretics or apostates. Accepting an invitation, as he thought, to dinner (*obied*), he declined at the last moment in embarrassment when he realized he had been invited to attend an *obiedna*, or Orthodox Mass.

His irritation increased as he was conducted (in a deliberately confusing and disconcerting manner) from Smolensk to Staritsa, and he began to chafe at Muscovite protocol. He heard Ivan's interminable titles at every turn, yet noted that everyone else was called by their first name only, "in an undignified manner." At Staritsa, he was greeted by the cavalry commander thus: "Antonio. Ivan Vasilyevich, by the Grace of God Great Hospodor and Tsar and Grand Prince of all Rus, Vladimir, Moscow and Novgorod, Tsar of Kazan, Tsar of Astrakhan, Lord of Pskov, and Grand Prince of Tver, Ingria, Perm, Vyatka, Bulgaria, etc., Lord and Grand Prince of Nizhny-Novgorod, Chernigov, Ryazan, Rostov, Yaroslavl, Beloozero, Livonia, Udorsk, Obdorsk, Kandinskaya Zemlya, and all of Siberia inquires concerning the health of the Most Holy Father, Gregory XIII, the Pope of Rome."

"He is well," replied Possevino simply, "for which God be thanked."

On the following day, he was told to prepare himself "to behold the serene eyes" of imperial majesty, and upon encountering Ivan and his elder son both enthroned with heavy, glittering tiaras "bigger than the Pope's," bridled to hear himself announced: "Antonio and his companions strike their foreheads to the ground before you." When Ivan asked after the pope's health, Possevino seized the opportunity to competitively enumerate his own master's honorifics: "Our Most Holy Lord, Pope Gregory XIII, Shepherd of the Church Universal, Vicar of Christ on Earth, Successor to St. Peter, Lord of Many Realms and Regions, Servant of the Servants of God, greets your Highness and gives you his blessing." Presenting his letters (to Andrey Schchelkalov), he described the gifts he had brought: a sliver of the true cross embedded in a carved rock-crystal crucifix; an image of the Lamb embossed on silver and inscribed with red Cyrillic characters; a beautifully bound copy, in Greek, of the proceedings of the Council of Florence; a rosary of precious stones; ten gold prayer beads; and a crystal goblet with a gold rim. Ivan examined the crucifix "for a long time" and declared it "a gift worthy of the Pope."

(As for the embarrassing letter to Anastasia, Possevino remarked laconically in his memoir: "We learned that she had died a long time ago, and that the Prince's present wife was actually his seventh.")

Meeting with Ivan's inner council of advisers, Possevino set forth the pope's "understanding": namely, that once the war with Poland was over, Ivan would join a league against the Turks, allow papal envoys free transit through his kingdom to Persia, and Catholics freedom of worship in Muscovy. He also expressed the hope that Ivan would acknowledge the primacy of the Holy See.

Ivan led him on. He threw a tremendous banquet in Possevino's honor, proved a pious and most attentive host, "always looking around to see that everyone had everything he wanted, no matter how far away from him they were sitting," and toward the end of the repast "called for silence and made a most impressive speech," which seemed to acknowledge the pope as "the general shepherd of the Christian Republic and the Vicar of

Christ." Nevertheless, no headway was made on the subject of religion in discussions with Ivan's councilors (Ivan even forbade his intepreters to translate whatever pertained to it), but at length the tsar unenthusiastically agreed to take up the whole issue at the conclusion of the war.

Though Possevino had come to Moscow inadequately briefed on Russian affairs, he was a man of unusual discernment, and exceptional in not being bowled over by Ivan's pomp and court display. In his report to Gregory XIII, he unmasked the whole charade:

> The Prince takes great pains to encourage a view of himself as High Priest as well as Emperor, and in the splendor of his attire, his courtiers and his other appurtenances he rivals the Pope and surpasses other kings. He has borrowed these trappings from the Greek Patriarchs and Emperors, and it could be said that he has transferred to his own person the honor that it is proper to pay to God alone. When seated on his throne he wears a tiara stiff with pearls and precious stones, and keeps several others by him, changing them to emphasize his wealth, a practice he claims to have inherited from the Byzantine Emperors. In his left hand he carries a crook or staff with large crystal balls, like knobs, attached to it. He is dressed in long robes, such as the Popes are accustomed to wearing when they solemnly proceed to Mass, and he wears rings set with huge stones on all his fingers. There is an ikon of the Savior to his right, and one of the Virgin above the throne. Both wear white cloaks, and standing as they do on each side of the Prince with wings attached to their shoulders they look like royal bodyguards. . . . When I was engaged in protracted discussions with his Councillors he had various documents and treaties brought out from remote archives in order to buttress his position and oppose the stance taken by the Polish King. He was anxious to have these documents brought to the Pope's attention, as those he had chosen were designed to illustrate the fact that unbroken friendship had existed between his father Vasily and the Popes, Emperors and other rulers since the days of Popes Leo X and Clement VII, as well as between Your Beatitude and himself. They also argued the need for extending the boundaries of his realm. . . . It was the sort of performance the Turks used to give in years past, when they employed the skills of unscrupulous persons to solicit or profess friendship with Christians while they drove on into the heart of Europe.

Not unlike the shah, however, who had obliterated Jenkinson's infidel footprints in the sand, Ivan after his contact with Possevino could not refrain from a ritual insult and "washed his hands in a silver bowl placed openly on a bench in general view, as though he were performing a rite of expiation."

* * *

As both sides jockeyed for advantage, Possevino's arbitration effort stalled. Meanwhile Batory had replied to Ivan's letter of June 29 with an acromonious forty-page rejoinder which heightened tensions considerably. He compared the tsar to Cain, Pharaoh, Nero, and Herod; ridiculed his bogus Roman genealogy; denounced him as a "sneaking wolf" and a "vile venomous cur"; challenged him to single combat; and taunted him as a coward. "Even the humble hen covers her chicks with her wings when a hawk hovers in the air above her," he wrote. "But you, the double-headed eagle, for such your seal proclaims you, do nothing but skulk away and hide." For his coup de grace, he enclosed a couple of Latin pamphlets recently published in Germany that described Ivan as a bloodthirsty despot.

Ivan was probably not unaware of such circulars, since the Livonian War, in fact, had produced a fairly substantial body of literature. The typical pamphlet was four pages long, illustrated by a single woodcut, stitched and bound, with a lengthy heading made up of sensational slogans. The Battle of Nevel had been celebrated as a sort of Trojan War, in which the gods took sides and heroes opposed each other in single combat; hexameter panegyrics had saluted the Lithuanian victory on the banks of the Ula in 1564. Balthasar Russow, a pastor in Reval, had composed an invaluable *Chronicle* published in 1578. After 1578, Batory dominated the "news" with official manifestos and frontline dispatches. His field presses turned out a continuous stream of Latin propaganda that was rushed by couriers to translators all over Europe, and rendered into German, Polish, Hungarian, Italian, and other tongues. Not surprisingly, the fall of Polotsk and Veliky Luki precipitated a flood of minor epics, panegyrics, and odes, while the redefection of the Livonian turncoats, Taube and Kruse, inspired a lampoon. Even Jan Kochanowski (no minor poet) celebrated a daring raid into Staritsa. So many encomia were bestowed on Batory that within a few years they could be gathered into hefty collections published in Rome and Cologne, while Johan III was the subject of at least one history, written by a German Protestant, Laurentius Muller, who also claimed to have discovered the gravestone of Ovid on the lower Dnieper. By contrast, Ivan fared poorly. Almost invariably described as some kind of savage, and typically depicted in woodcuts as "a cruel, cunning Asiatic in a turban or cap," he was variously known in Europe as "Ivan the Hun," the "Scythian Wolf," or the "Basilisk" (from a pun on Basil, the Greek spelling of his patronymic), a fabulous monster with a deadly gaze.

Russia's brief rebound collapsed as Batory drove his challenge home with raids into Starodub and Tver, and a cavalry feint towards Novgorod that threw the city into such panic that it torched its own suburbs to prevent enemy foraging. Along the way outriders approached the tsar's residence at Staritsa, where it is said he could see the glow from the fires. Then, on July 21, Batory set out with 40,000 troops from Polotsk, marched swiftly along forest paths cut in advance by an Hungarian engineer, subdued Ostrov on August 21, and on the 25th appeared before Pskov, "like a wild boar," wrote a Russian chronicler, "emerging from the wilderness."

41.

Pskov

The Battle of Pskov was to prove one of the immortal battles of Russian history. A city comparable in size to contemporary Paris, or so it seemed to a member of Batory's staff, for "whole centuries the chief care of the Pskovians had been to make it impregnable to the attacks of the Livonian knights." It had an oblong triangular Kremlin on a hill above the Velikaya River, wide moats, and colossal stone walls some eight miles in circumference, sixteen feet thick, and thirty feet high. Its considerable garrison—about 16,000, in addition to the local population (which had drastically fallen during Ivan's reign from about 35,000 to 20,000)—bristled with what remained of Muscovy's best arms.

Religious fervor animated the city's defense. Prince Ivan Shuisky, of the still mighty Shuisky clan, was given the command and made to swear before the Icon of Vladimir to defend the city unto death. The whole populace had to repeat the oath when he arrived, as icons were brought in from the Pskov-Pechery Monastery, and the holy relics of St. Vsevolod were carried in procession around the walls. A local gunsmith was visited by the Virgin Mary, "who told him where the cannons should be placed and assured him that the town would not fall." An old man, probably St. Nicholas the Warrior—or was it Kornily?—was seen to ride in a cloud of radiance back and forth between the monastery and Pskov.

Batory's troops dug in, began their artillery barrage on September 7, and on the 8th "made a general assault with such elan that two of the principal bastions were captured." From his distant observation post in a bell tower, the king saw his standards waving over the battlements. His officers exclaimed: "Sire, we shall dine with you tonight in Pskov!" But the Muscovites rallied and hurled the assailants back with heavy casualties.

On the very next day, however, Ivan's worst fears were realized to the north, when Johan at last took Narva. "I set the snare," Batory remarked, "but my brother takes the game," as the Swedes proceeded to subdue Ivangorod, Yama, and Koporie, and before long occupied the whole eastern coast of the Gulf of Finland.

The tsar began to be more attentive to Possevino, promising papal envoys free transit through his realm to Persia and Catholics freedom of worship on his soil. On September 12 he told him: "Go to King Stefan; greet him in my name, and treat for peace with him in accordance with the Pope's instructions. After you have done this, be sure to come back to us, for you will always be welcome, both because of the Pope and because of the loyal and devoted services you are rendering in this cause." He furnished Father Campano with gifts and a letter to Gregory XIII, and turning to Father Drenocki, ominously began to stroke the man's head. "You are to stay here in Muscovy with me," he said, then noting Possevino's alarm, added, "Antonio, be of good cheer; we shall treat your man well. It will be the same as if you were staying yourself."

Winter had come early to Pskov, and when Possevino arrived on October 5, he found snow on the ground, a scarcity of tents, and low morale among Batory's troops. After a month of hard fighting they had failed to crack the Muscovite defenses, and though many had managed to scale the city walls, those who made it over had perished to a man, either between the ramparts or after being driven into wooden houses, which were set ablaze. The Muscovite artillerymen, unassailable in their enclosed tower bastions, kept up a continuous fire, while every tunnel dug by the king's sappers had somehow been discovered, countermined, and destroyed. Meanwhile, Batory's main munitions stockpile, at Susha, had blown up in an accident, and his powder had begun to run out. New shells had to be shipped all the way from Riga. On October 28, one of Batory's specialty teams, equipped with mattocks and crowbars, advanced like a great bronze tortoise under large overlapping shields, and began to dig and wrench about the base of a corner tower. Before they could do much damage, the Russians drove them back with buckets of boiling tar. His convoy of fresh ammunition finally arrived, but another attempt to storm the city failed. The Pskovians were simply heroic. Women and children stood with their husbands, fathers, and brothers on the ramparts, piling up stones and pushing them down from the walls, sifting lime to throw into the eyes of the enemy, carrying food and munitions, or other matériel, back and forth in baskets, aprons, and sacks, and repairing breaches made in the ramparts with amazing speed. They gave "an extraordinarily fine account of themselves," wrote Possevino; and Heidenstein, the Polish historian, could not but salute their "unbelievable fortitude." Batory himself would not disparage them either, and confided to Possevino that he had found Muscovite soldiers in other fortresses who had subsisted on nothing but water and oat dust for a long time, and though "scarcely breathing, still feared their surrender would constitute a betrayal of their oath to serve their Prince to the last."

At the end of October, Batory withdrew to winter quarters and organized a blockade. Thinking to restore confidence to his men, he sent crack divisions with artillery to take the fortified Pskov-Pechery monastery thirty-seven miles away. A Muscovite contingent operating out of the cloister had carried out a number of damaging hit-and-run attacks against his supply lines, but it was really the monastery's mystique Batory sought to smash. To his dismay, if not humiliation, a fierce bombardment and two major infantry assaults on the monastery failed.

As a result of the developing stalemate, in mid-November Kiverova Gora, a tiny hamlet near the ruined village of Yam Zapolsky (equidistant from Veliky Luki and Pskov) was designated the site for negotiations. Across the war-torn zone the drinking water was contaminated, and the plenipotentiaries had to quench their thirst with freshly fallen snow. Meeting in Possevino's wooden hut, "between a temporary altar and a stove," they made determinations that would affect the fate of Eastern Europe for more than a century.

Batory's negotiating team (supervised and directed by Zamoysky), was headed by Michael Haraburda, a Greek Orthodox Lithuanian and a veteran diplomat. The Russian delegation was headed by Roman Alferyev, a veteran of the *Oprichnina* who had once served in the Treasury Department. He was now a privy councilor. A self-confessed illiterate ("I never read reports," he once blurted out, "because I can't read"), he nevertheless had substantial military and negotiating experience and was presumably chosen because of his clear understanding of Russia's strategic needs.

Batory returned to Poland to exact from his Diet one last grant of funds to sustain the siege. Attempting to set an inspiring example for his subjects, he committed his entire personal fortune to the cause. Zamoysky, remaining behind to consolidate the blockade, almost immediately had to hang a number of officers to quell a rebellion, when his troops learned they might have to remain through winter into spring.

The pressure on Moscow was just as intense. After the fall of Narva, Ivan regarded it as pointless to continue fighting with Poland, but considered it an absolute priority to recover Narva from Sweden at any price. For this reason, although the Poles had wanted Sweden included in the negotiations to constrain Johan from further conquests, the Russians—and the Swedes, who now enjoyed a free hand—both refused. However, Moscow's military situation suffered each day a settlement was delayed; and therefore, as the negotiations got under way, although the Russians at first refused to cede a number of major towns, they were gradually whittled down to two fortresses, Nevel and Velizh. The Polish delegates threatened to walk out if no settlement was reached by December 28. On the night of the 27th, the Muscovites, "weeping," went to see Possevino, "asking him what they should do." Possevino told them to yield. They replied that they had already yielded forty fortresses, far exceeding their instructions, and that Ivan would probably kill them as it was. Possevino promised to go surety for them with his own head and to sign a document that he had compelled their capitulation. They responded that even if each of them had ten heads, Ivan would cut off every one. On the following day the two sides compromised. The Russians kept Nevel, but yielded Velizh in exchange for Sebezh, an outpost commanding the outlet from the Velikaya River valley.

The question of the language of the treaty remained. Ivan repeatedly endeavored to insert such formulations as "Hereditary Ruler of Livonia" into the document in order to have a pretext for future claims against the region. For the same reason, he wanted Riga and Courland included among the towns and territories he had relinquished. And of course his envoys also insisted on his title as Tsar. Possevino rebuked them, saying: "If the Grand Prince desires a valid title and a legitimate dignity, he should first negotiate with the Pope, like other Christian rulers," since " 'Tsar' is only an oddity borrowed from the Tartars in an effort to approximate the title held by other Kings." In their spirited but confused rejoinder, they asserted that Ivan's crown had been sent from Rome to Vladimir I by the emperors Honorius and Arcadius. Possevino promptly pointed out that Honorius and Arcadius had lived 500 years before Vladimir. When Alfereyev replied that they had meant another Honorius and Arcadius, Possevino exclaimed, "You have come here not to negotiate but to steal!" and angrily seizing him by the collar pushed him out of the hut.

In the end, the Treaty of Yam Zapolsky, as the document was called, was given a dual text, with the unofficial Russian version more flattering to the tsar. Substantively, the two were the same. Signed on January 15, 1582, the treaty imposed a ten-year truce on the belligerents, obliged Russia to relinquish all of Livonia (aside from territory held by the Swedes) and all recent strategic conquests in Lithuania to Poland. With the loss of Ivangorod, Ivan had even managed to undo the initiative of his grandfather, Ivan III. Thus did his drive to the Baltic, which had begun with a series of quick successes in 1558, end twenty-five years later in catastrophic defeat and humiliation without a square inch of Livonian soil to his name. Estonia was now firmly in the grasp of a resurgent Sweden, and southern Livonia in the power of an expanding Polish Empire directed by a monarch who still hoped, eventually, to bring Moscow to its knees.

It is difficult to tell to what extent Ivan felt the defeat as a personal one. "We know," he apparently told Possevino, "what is due to the majesty of Princes. But the Empire is majesty, and above that majesty stands the Sovereign in his Empire, and the Sovereign is above the Empire."

But the empire was not above tragedy, and the sovereign, apart from his majesty, was not above anything at all, and had begun to taste of hell itself. "Is this then 'contrary to reason,' to live according to the present day? Recall to memory Constantine," he had written to Kurbsky in 1564, "mighty even amongst the tsars; how he killed his own son, begotten by him, for the sake of his kingdom."

42.

"Recall to Memory Constantine"

In 1581, Ivan's namesake and elder son, Ivan Ivanovich, was twenty-seven years old. Thoroughly schooled for the throne, he had from at least the age of eighteen the sound and sensible universal maxims of kingship impressed upon him by his father, who in his Last Will and Testament before the Battle of Molodi had set forth this advice:

> You should become familiar with all kinds of affairs: the divine, the priestly, the monastic, the military, the judicial; with all patterns of life in Moscow

and elsewhere. [You have to know] how the administrative institutions function here and in other states; and what are the relations between this state and other states. All this you have to know. . . . Then you will not depend on the advice of others, but will give directions to them.

The Tsar, of course, had known all these things in his own way, and already at the age of twenty-three himself (according to the Englishman Chancellor) had regarded it as essential to know everyone who served under him directly, and what duties he discharged.

By most accounts the tsarevich emulated his father in this regard, accompanied him on his complex round of government and diplomatic functions, sat with him at court weddings and receptions, and stood with him at the executions in Red Square. They were even rumored to revel together in vice, to share the same women and, in consonant depravity, to take turns torturing the condemned. The evidence on this score, however, is mixed. Taube and Kruse denounced him as "cruel like his father"; but Printz reported that he was endowed with "abundant virtues." The more objective Possevino thought him "capable of ruling" and divined that he was "popularly beloved"—corroborating Horsey's observation that the people's esteem for him made the tsar fear for his own power: "He was the hope of their comfort, a wise, mild, and most worthy prince, of heroicall condicion, of comly presence, beloved . . . of all men." Whatever his qualities, the one thing we know for certain is that Ivan and his son were not of one mind.

Differences between them surfaced early. The tsarevich had his own court circle (Cheliadnin had belonged to it), in which the tsar had uncovered treason; and aside from publicly admonishing his son more than once for insubordination, Ivan had not stopped short of threatening to disinherit him—for example, at a Kremlin reception for Duke Magnus in June 1570, attended by foreign envoys. Nor had the tsar been happy with his son's choice of wives—banishing the first two, Evdokia Saburova and Petrova Solovaya, to nunneries, and persecuting the clan to which his third wife, Elena Sheremetova, belonged. One of her uncles had been executed, another imprisoned, and a third had defected to the Poles. Her father, too, was in disfavor. As for Elena herself, Ivan apparently couldn't stand the sight of her, but in the fall of 1581, as Batory was closing in on Pskov, she was very much in view and conspicuously pregnant with a potential heir.

Coincident with this, the tsarevich had emerged at the head of a kind of "war party." With all of Livonia, including Narva, and part of Russia itself in jeopardy, he became alarmed at the spectacle of his dwindling inheritance, and began to quarrel with his father about the defense of Pskov. Urging him to commit his reserves (held back under Bekbulatovich at Staritsa) to the fray, in a theatrical gesture he also proclaimed himself willing to lead an army to the rescue.

Under the best of circumstances, Ivan could not bear contradiction; but his son's bravado dug at an old wound: the charge that he was a coward. He had heard it before—from Kurbsky, who had documented his timidity at Kazan; from the whole nation in 1571, after his flight before the khan; later from the khan himself; and from Batory, who had called him less valiant than a hen. And now his own son, by implication, had flung the challenge down.

A tsar did what he had to do. "Recall to memory Constantine . . ." The tsarevich thus had three mortal strikes against him: his wife, his personal popularity and conspicuous competence to rule, and his rebellious mind. In his outbursts Ivan presumably told him he didn't have any real grasp of Russia's strategic interests or even know how to choose a suitable consort for the helm; and on November 14, when he came upon Elena "sitting on a bench in a warm room," immodestly attired (unlike a tsarina) in a single chemise, he told her she didn't know how to dress. He struck her fiercely; the tsarevich intervened; Ivan raised his iron-tipped staff and drove the prong of it deep into the side of his head. Some say Boris Godunov was present and in attempting to restrain the tsar was brutally knocked aside.

Elena miscarried. The tsarevich languished, consumed by fever. The wound's infection spread: five days later he died. His remains were brought in procession from Aleksandrova Sloboda to Moscow, to be interred in the Cathedral of the Archangel Michael, and when the cortège reached the outskirts of the city, boyars dressed all in black bore the coffin aloft on the tips of their fingers, as Ivan followed behind on foot.

He was beside himself with grief. He "tore his hair and beard like a madd man, lamentinge and mourninge"; unable to sleep, he cried out at night and "scratched the wall of his chamber with his nails." He grew unkempt, "laid aside his diadem and all other bright adornment," and donated large sums of money to monasteries throughout Muscovy and the Orthodox East, pledging the faithful to pray for his son's soul. On January 6, 1582, after attending Mass with his confessor at Holy Trinity Monastery, he summoned to his bedroom two venerable monks and "began to weep and sob and to implore them" to remember the tsarevich every day in their prayers, "forever, as long as this monastery stands, till the end of time." Yet even in this extremity he could not truly humble himself, but had to couple his pious appeal with an imperial threat: "And whoever will forget and fail to fulfill this will and request . . . will face a trial with me before God at the Second Advent." Whatever was most "terrible" about Ivan is perhaps to be discovered here.

Oral tradition refused to accept the filicide. In the *bylina* or historical songs about it, the plot is reworked: Fyodor falsely accused of treason by his older brother, Ivan Ivanovich, is sentenced to die. Like Shakespeare's Bolingbroke in *Richard II*, who asks: "Have I no friend will rid me . . . ," Ivan asks: "Have I no terrible executioners left?" and a resurrected Malyuta Skuratov at once volunteers. He leads the saintly Fyodor "by his white hands" to the Lobnoe Mesto, but the good Anastasia (still alive!) appeals to her brother Nikita Zakharin to intervene, and like a knight rescuing a maiden, he gallops bareback into the square and whisks Fyodor away in the nick of time. Meanwhile, the tsar has learned the truth and rejoices at Fyodor's reprieve. The tale (as folktales will) thus has it both ways: the father is spared the murder of his son, but the son he actually did kill is stamped with the mark of Cain.

Not long after the tsarevich's interment, Ivan began to compile his *Synodical*, or list of the victims of his terror, to be remembered by the clergy in their prayers. Over 1500 names were inscribed from the sack of Novgorod alone, many followed by the words "with his wife," "with his wife and children," "with his daughters," "with his sons"; while unremembered others were acknowledged by the relentless, sad refrain: "As to their names, O Lord, you know them." Copies of the *Synodical* were circulated to all the principal monasteries in Muscovy for services, supported by special funds.

This "posthumous rehabilitation of the disgraced, whose names it had been forbidden to mention for years," had "political as well as moral overtones." Unless Ivan could appease powerful relatives and survivors, among whom the simple-minded heir-apparent, Fyodor, Ivan's second son, would have to find support in order to rule, the House of Rurik would be doomed. Openly acknowledging before the *Duma* that Fyodor was unfit to succeed him, he invited the nobles to choose one from among their own to take his place. No one was fool enough to propose a name.

Ivan dictated a new will which established a regency council of five to assist his son in affairs of state: Nikita Zakharin, Ivan's brother-in-law; Ivan Mstislavsky, chairman of the Duma; Ivan Shuisky, the hero of Pskov; Bogdan Belsky, the armorer; and Boris Godunov, *de facto* chancellor, whose sister was married to Fyodor.

43.

Tsar and Jesuit Debate the Faith

Under the circumstances it is remarkable that Ivan honored his commitment to Possevino to discuss religious questions at the end of the war. He cannot have been elated with the way the negotiations had gone; while Possevino, setting out for Moscow on January 23, 1582, made no effort to conceal his combative mood. At Novgorod he refused the archbishop's ecumenical invitation to assist at an Orthodox liturgy, but insisted instead on seeing the uncorrupted bodies of two Russian saints. After the tombs were opened and shut very quickly, he exclaimed: "Statues of painted wood!" Twelve days later, on February 13, he was escorted into Moscow on a sleigh carpeted with the pelt of a polar bear.

This was the moment he had been waiting for—to dispute the faith with the tsar. He would have three opportunities to do so; Ivan was ready. Despite his miseries, he had been boning up on his theology, this time in consultation with a visiting Dutch Anabaptist and some Anglican merchants who had given him a book proving that the Pope was Antichrist.

The first encounter took place on February 21. Ivan warned the legate in advance that the whole thing was a bad idea and would only create ill will. "You see that I am now [past] fifty years old[1] and have not much longer to live," he said. "I have been brought up in the true Christian religion, and I cannot change. The Day of Judgment is approaching when God will decide whether our faith or the Latin faith is the repository of truth. I am fully aware that Pope Gregory XIII sent you to champion the cause of the Roman faith, and you may say what you wish."

Possevino began:

> Your Most Serene Highness. . . . I want you to know that under no circumstances is the Pope asking you to make changes in the most ancient Greek religion as taught by the Fathers and in the lawful Synods. He is simply urging you to acknowledge its pristine form, embrace it fully, and preserve it intact in your Kingdom. . . . His Holiness is highly attracted by the suggestions contained in your letter that he arrange for a treaty among the Christian rulers.

He is also impressed with the letter you wrote to King Stefan, in which you said that the Emperor of Constantinople and the whole of the East acknowledged the unity of the faith at the Council of Florence. . . . If you think that the decisions taken at the Council of Florence do not pertain to you, you should summon Greek interpreters . . . and I should be most happy to provide you with the chief citations from the Fathers found in the Greek edition of the proceedings. . . . Heaven will rejoice; you will have every reason to expect that your titles and distinctions will enjoy greater prestige than they have heretofore, and you will soon be called the Emperor of the East, if you advance the cause of the Orthodox Catholic faith there.

Ivan replied: "I do not believe in the Greeks; I believe in Christ. As for any Empire of the East, it is for the Lord of His Own volition to assign realms to whomever he chooses. . . . We do not seek the earthly realm of the whole world, for this would be a sinful tendency."

When Possevino tried to argue that Catholicism was "the most true and Orthodox faith," Ivan remarked: "We received our Christian faith from the early Church at the time when Andrew, the brother of the Apostle Peter, visited these lands on his way to Rome. Vladimir was converted to the faith, and Christianity spread far and wide among us. We received the Christian faith here in Muscovy at the same time you received it in Italy, and we have preserved it intact. . . . When all the Apostles [were sent forth], no man was greater than any other man, and they produced Bishops, Archbishops, Metropolitans and many others. It is from these men that the religious leaders of our country are descended."

To which Possevino said: "Christ sent all the Apostles forth into the world . . . with different degrees of power. But to Peter alone He entrusted the Keys of the Kingdom of Heaven, the strengthening of the brethren, and the care and feeding of the sheep. . . . If we grant that the bishops who are descended from the other Apostles retain their authority, we must also agree that the See of Peter retains much greater authority."

Ivan rejoined: "We acknowledge Peter as a saint, as well as a number of the Popes . . . but the later ones led evil lives." This gave the repartee a new direction. Possevino bridled: "The power of the Sacraments and the administration of the Church conferred upon the Popes do not depend upon the lives they lead, but upon the inflexible precept of Christ." But Ivan went in for the kill:

Our courier, Istoma Shevrigin, told us that Pope Gregory is carried about in a chair. The people kiss the shoes on his feet, and he has a Cross on his shoe.

The Cross carries a representation of the Crucifixion of the Lord our God: now how can such a thing be right? Here is one of the prime differences between our Christian faith and the Roman faith. Our Christian faith considers the Cross of Christ the sign of victory over the Enemy; we revere the wood of the glorious Cross and esteem and honor it as enjoined by Holy Apostolic Tradition and the Holy Fathers in the General Councils. We are forbidden to wear a cross below the girdle; similarly, ikons of the Savior, the Virgin Mary and the Pious Saints must be placed in such a way that when viewed by spiritual eyes they uplift the soul to their source. It is unseemly to place them on the feet. . . . Antonio, you are saying that [Pope Gregory] is the Successor of Christ and the Apostle Peter and that it is incumbent upon all to honor him, and to fall at his feet and kiss them. But the words you utter are said out of cunning. Holy men should not give themselves such airs. . . .

The period from the convocation of the First Council to the Seventh, created, to take the place of the Four Evangelists, the Sees of the Four Patriarchs, the Universal Teachers, [and] witnessed the consecration of innumerable Metropolitans in many places, including our Tsaric realm. . . .

But Pope Gregory XIII does not walk upon the ground; he has himself carried in a chair, calls himself the Successor of Peter, and calls the Apostle Peter the Successor of Christ. But the Pope is not Christ; the chair in which the Pope is carried is not a cloud, and those who carry him are not angels. Pope Gregory has no business pretending to be Christ or His Successor. . . .

The Pope who does not seek to live in accordance with Christ's teaching and Apostolic Tradition is a wolf, and no shepherd.

Possevino exclaimed: "If the Pope is a wolf, I have nothing further to say."

"I warned you," said Ivan, endeavoring to calm both himself and the Jesuit, "that if we discussed the faith it would be impossible for us to avoid harsh words. I am not calling your Pope a wolf; only the Pope who refuses to follow Christ's teaching and Apostolic Tradition do I call a wolf, not a shepherd. But let us terminate our discussion."

This awkward retraction is recorded in the official Kremlin transcript. In his own version, which dramatically diverges at this point, Possevino portrays himself in a heroic light:

Half rising from his seat, the Prince declared: "I would have you know that the Roman Pope is no shepherd." I was highly offended at this insult, [which] effectively slammed the door on any serious discussion. I told my young interpreter, hesitating out of mortal fear, to ask: "Then why did you send to the Pope concerning your problems?"

The Prince flew into a rage and stood right up from his throne. Everyone was sure that he would strike and kill me, as he had others, including even his own son, with the iron-tipped staff he carries the way the Pope does his pastoral rod. "There are peasants outside," he cried, "who would show you what it means to talk to me like a peasant!"

I heard these words impassively [!] and said: "Most Serene Prince, I know that I am speaking with a wise and good ruler. . . . I hope you will not be angry at any statements I make, because they are the words of Christ that I am uttering, and you yourself gave me permission to speak freely of those things." In this way I managed to sooth the Prince, to the amazement of the boyars and the rest of the nobles.

When the Prince had once more resumed his seat, his speech was more moderate, but he kept on asking the same four questions: "Why is the Pope carried in a chair?" "Why does he wear a cross on his feet?" "Why does he shave his beard?" "Why does he pretend to be God?" All [in the audience] were on their feet, for these extraneous issues and false calumnies, combined with their natural fear of the Prince's power, had roused the nobles to such a pitch that a few were openly saying I should be drowned on the spot.

But at length (so Possevino claimed), he was able to explain everything to the tsar in such a satisfactory way that "to the great astonishment of all present, the prince clasped me twice in full embrace . . . and dismissed me in a friendly manner."

Whichever version one cares to credit, Ivan was surely not about to acknowledge the primacy of the pope, either in religion or as the legal source of his imperial power, which would have annulled the theoretical foundations of the Orthodox tsardom and its claim to be the Third Rome. Possevino had called into question Ivan's divine right to rule, and therefore his right to demand obedience from his subjects, whereas his whole reign had been devoted to asserting that authority, and he had stopped at nothing to enforce it. As for the Council of Florence, Possevino seemed not to realize that the Russians had rejected it independently of the Greeks.

The second encounter between the two men took place on February 23. Possevino (taking no chances with Ivan's homicidal wrath) advised everyone in his party first "to make a full confession" and take Communion, but after a brief and cordial exchange in which Ivan either apologized for his earlier remarks about the pope (according to Possevino), or politely reminded the legate of his warning against religious disputations (Kremlin version), Possevino conferred with Ivan's councilors concerning a prisoner exchange and the route papal envoys might take through Russia to Persia.

The third and last encounter took place on March 4. Ivan said: "Antonio, my boyars have told me that you are anxious to visit our churches. I have ordered my nobles to take you to them, where you will see how reverently we adore the Most Holy Trinity, honor the Virgin Mary, and invoke the Saints. You will also perceive the exemplary piety we manifest before the holy icons, and you will behold the icon of the Virgin Mary which was made by St. Luke. But you will not see my Metropolitan or myself carried in a chair."

Possevino disclaimed any desire to witness a Russian Orthodox service as long as the Russians remained schismatics, and instead gave Ivan two treatises: one on "the Chief points in which the Greeks and the Muscovites differ from the Latins in the Faith" and another refuting the charge that the pope was Antichrist. The latter document injudiciously began with a diatribe against the promiscuity of Henry VIII, overlooking the fact that of all contemporary monarchs Ivan alone surpassed Henry in the number of his wives.

Ivan noted politely that Possevino was very fond of giving him things to read.

On the threshold of the Cathedral of the Assumption, which the legate refused to enter, the tsar mocked him: "Antonio, see that you do not take any Lutherans into church with you!" before disappearing into the parvis.

Nevertheless, Possevino managed to secure the release of 210 Lithuanian and Polish prisoners of war, several Livonian noblemen, and fourteen Spaniards and Italians who had recently escaped from a Turkish prison in Azov. However, he reportedly failed to lobby for the release of any Lutherans because "there were already too many Lutherans in Livonia."

Perhaps Ivan had been mocking this discrimination in his charity.

No man had come to Moscow with more enthusiasm; and none was so eager to leave. Setting out on March 14, "without stopping day or night," he traveled the 400 miles to Smolensk in four days, where he waited impatiently for Ivan's embassy to Rome. Continuing on through Courland, he saw many magnificent buildings—now "filled with dirt, their windows broken, their interiors exposed to the elements"—vandalized by the Muscovites in the raid of 1579. As the Russian suite paused to rest in little improvised wooden huts erected beside the still-imposing ruins, Possevino was reminded of the Goths "squatting in the Coliseum, amid the triumphal arches, after their sack of Eternal Rome. And I was no longer surprised at what lurked in the heart of a race that is unable to endure the splendor and majesty of other peoples."

44.

Aftermath

The Treaty of Yam Zapolsky notwithstanding, Ivan still hoped to settle accounts with the Swedes. After taking Narva, de la Gardie had occupied Ingria, and was poised to strike at Novgorod. Meanwhile, he had built up a large army of mercenaries in Finland. Only two Russian strongholds, Oreshek and Ladoga, remained to break the crescent sweep of his drive. The looming catastrophe was accelerated by developments on the eastern frontier, where a general uprising by the Cheremis was followed by Great Nogay raids as far west as Kolomna. The whole region of Kazan was in turmoil. All of Ivan's early accomplishments were disintegrating. He could scarcely hope to recover any losses; he could only hope to hold on to what remained.

The Swedes surrounded Oreshek—an island fortress in the middle of the Neva and (as it would prove) the heroic equivalent of Pskov in the northern zone. To de la Gardie's astonishment, it withstood a fierce, sustained, month-long bombardment begun in early September 1582, and in mid-October, when he twice tried to take the fortress by storm, an inspired garrison crushed the assaults with such heavy casualties that the Swedes abandoned the siege.

Throughout the northwest, both armies dug in as negotiations were conducted on the River Pliusa near Gdov. But Sweden could bargain from strength, and by a three-year armistice, signed on August 5, 1583, secured every one of its conquests—and was destined to stand between Russia and the Baltic until the reign of Peter the Great.

To the new empire of Poland, victory was also sweet. Commemorative medals were struck, and there was public rejoicing, with parades and marching bands, throughout the land. In 1583, the marriage of Zamoysky to Batory's niece furnished an occasion to celebrate the triumph in the capital in grand neoclassical style. Both Batory and Zamoysky were, after all, humanists, each in his own way a scholar and Latin stylist of renown; and though the wedding was Catholic, the revelry of the nuptial festivities certainly recalled their student days in Padua more than the stern Counterreformation to which the king was otherwise attached. In a cavalcade of floats, there were rockets and fireworks, a carriage pulled by children representing the hours "with clocks on their heads, and stars on their backs," and a gray-bearded Saturn grasping a scythe. Another figure personified Time, and after him a couple representing the Sun and Moon. There was a contraption which emitted an horrific rumble, surmounted by Jove clutching his thunderbolt; Cupid sitting among choristers; Venus "drawn by a pair of whales, whose jaws, nostrils, and eyes emitted clouds of aromatic oil"; and "a bevy of goddesses dressed in gold" dragging Trojan Paris by a rope. A hunting party led by Diana signified "relaxation after the toils of war." But the centerpiece was a "Victory Car"

> displaying the effigies of hostile countries, and carrying prisoners of war and captured booty. A woman walked alongside representing the province of Livonia over which the war had been fought. At her feet lay the conquered foe. After that, four white horses pulled a chariot to which the Enemy was shackled, together with his defeated generals, officers and people at large. A placard made fun of the boastful epithets which he had used before the war had started. The whole float was surrounded by white-haired old men, carrying sweet-smelling censers. They represented the decline and lethargy of the Enemy's power.

The cosmopolitan variety and Renaissance wit of this extravaganza contrasted strangely with the neo-medieval world of gloom and extreme privation into which Muscovy was now absolutely plunged. The "decline and lethargy of the Enemy" was as awesome as his once-vaunted might.

Incessant calamity, upheaval, and peasant flight had turned whole provinces into wastelands. The cumulative desolation was almost beyond belief. In the northwest, out of a total of 34,000 settlements listed in land registers of the 1580s, 83 percent were described as empty. The three main reasons given in the census records were: military service, impoverishment, and death. In the central regions the average number of suburban houses had declined by almost half, and most of the remaining population consisted of untaxed clergy, dependents, and military personnel. In Kashira, for example, only 18 houses out of 315 remained inhabited; in Kolomna, only 34 out of 696; in Mozhaisk, roughly 400 out of 1778; in Murom, 111 out of 738.[1] The teeming villages which Chancellor had seen in 1553, "so well filled with people that it is a wonder to see them," had become ghost towns. "No one lives in them," wrote Possevino, "the fields are deserted, and the forest growth over them is fresh." Moscow, despite a decade of rebuilding, was still no more than half its former size, and only 17 percent of the surrounding arable land remained under cultivation. Smolensk, Novgorod, and Pskov had been reduced by about a third. Nor were the monasteries exempt from this toll. Roughly 45 percent of the settlements owned by Trinity Monastery, for example, had been abandoned.

New farmsteads were seldom recorded in surveys except on the borderlands, ironically enough, especially in the twenty-six districts between the first and second fortified lines on the southern frontier. A kind of inversion had taken place, where the population preferred to live in the wilds or in areas vulnerable to Tartar attack rather than be exposed to the continuing horrors of the interior.

Against such a background Ivan's substantive accomplishments appear futile. As enumerated by a contemporary, he had "mightely inlarged his country and kingdoms everie waye," reformed the law, defined the faith, doctrine, and discipline of the Russian Orthodox Church, built 40 "faire stone churches," more than 60 monasteries, 155 fortresses, 300 towns in the wilderness, a new stone bell tower in the Kremlin with 30 great "swaet soundinge bells," and a stone wall around Moscow. But the law had been forgotten, the doctrine of the Church betrayed, the fortresses stocked with mercenaries and stained with civilian blood, the towns deserted, and the stone wall built too late. As for the 60 monasteries, the example he had set for his nation at the Bacchanalian cloister of Aleksandrova Sloboda may be suggested by the continuing breakdown of discipline at the White Lake Monastery, once so renowned for its ascetic life. Ten years after humbling the unruly brethren with his ironic letter of rebuke, elders were "drinking wildly in the wine cellar," and one had created a sort of Bower of Bliss for himself in the wilderness, financed with embezzled funds and fortified with muskets, like any secular stockade.

45.

Sir Jerome Bowes

Jerome Horsey's urgent mission to Elizabeth had resulted in new military shipments from England in 1581, though obviously not enough to affect the outcome of the war. In May 1582, while still fighting the Swedes, Ivan had also despatched Fyodor Pissemsky to England to reopen discussions for a comprehensive military alliance, and this time sought to bind and consummate the pact by marrying a relative of the queen's. The ill-fated Elijah Bomel had apparently once suggested to Ivan that "yt was very feacable for him" to marry Elizabeth herself; more recently, his new English physician, Robert Jacob, had commended Lady Mary Hastings, daughter of the earl of Huntington, a descendant of George, duke of Clarence, and Elizabeth's niece. Though Ivan's seventh wife, Maria Nagaia, was then pregnant, Pissemsky was authorized to declare that in order to marry English "bloud royall," the tsar was prepared to put her aside. Perhaps Ivan was cynical enough to assume that a daughter of Henry VIII would have no problem with the idea of marriage as a consecutive career.

But he wanted the lady's particulars first: some confirmation of her pedigree, and details as to her figure, age, and complexion, as confirmed by her portrait painted on paper or wood.

Pissemsky arrived in England on September 16 (just prior to the Swedish assault on Oreshek), but failed to obtain an audience with Elizabeth's advisers until December 18 or with the queen herself until January 18, 1583. She was very gracious, but hedged on the alliance and was quick to disparage her niece as a suitable bride: her face, she explained, was pitted by smallpox; she had not yet recovered from the disease. Then embarrassing news arrived that the tsarina had given birth to a son. (This was the tsarevich Dmitry, destined for tragedy in a later reign.) It was therefore not until April that Pissemsky was allowed to behold Lady Mary (briefly) in the lord chancellor's garden. According to one account, he "cast down his countenance; fell prostrate to her feett, rose, ranne back from her, his face still towards her, she and the rest admiringe at his manner. Said by an interpreter yt did suffice him to behold the angell he hoped should be his masters espouse."

But according to another, he merely stared at her, exclaimed "Enough!" and walked away. No rapture, in any case, is evident in his report, which evasively describes her as "tall and slender, with a pale face, grey eyes, a straight nose, and long tapering fingers." Perhaps the portrait was supposed to fill in the blanks.

Lady Mary's friends playfully began to call her the Empress of Muscovy. She didn't want to be anything of the sort. For humane and other reasons Elizabeth also discouraged the match: familiar with Ivan's infamous attempt to procure Katerina from Erik, she doubtless assumed he would automatically incorporate Lady Mary into his English policy as a hostage.

In her discussions with Pissemsky, she inevitably concentrated on issues of trade. In particular she was upset that in contravention of the White Sea monopoly a Dutch merchant, John de Wale (known as White Beard) had been doing business that way since 1576, and that after the fall of Narva the French had moved their trade in wines and manufactured goods to Kola, another Arctic port. Pissemsky insisted that England alone could not possibly meet all of Russia's import needs.

Elizabeth, in fact, was just as unwilling as Ivan to put all of her eggs in one basket, and had recently signed broad trade agreements with the sultan that launched the Levant Company, or the "Company of Turkey Merchants." In November 1582 (with Pissemsky still patiently waiting to see her), she had appointed her first ambassador to the Sublime Porte.

Her new ambassador to Russia was Sir Jerome Bowes. Though adept at court intrigue and a well-educated diplomat of the rhetorical school, in other respects he was an irritable, conceited, petty, insolent fop. He arrived at Rose Island on July 23, 1583, and almost immediately began to draw up a laundry list of complaints. No Muscovite official, from Kholmogory to Moscow, seemed able to treat him right. Two miles from Moscow he was met by a large cavalry escort, but refused to dismount to receive a message from the tsar. On his way to the palace, crowds filled the streets, and a thousand *streltsy* in red, yellow, and blue uniforms lined the route—surely no insult here; but when three hundred noblemen, led by Prince Ivan Shuisky (the hero of Pskov), were sent to accompany him, he thought Shuisky's horse better than his own and demanded its equal. This kept the tsar waiting. In the Kremlin the reception prepared for him was lavish, but he complained at having to address Ivan from a formal distance, "as yf I had been to have made a proclamation," and at having to deliver the queen's gift and letter to the foreign secretary, Andrey Schchelkalov, "esteminge me unworthy to delyver them my selfe," though this was standard.

All such slights, real or imagined, he blamed principally on two of the tsar's chief councilors, Schchelkalov and Nikita Zakharin, whom he claimed were Anglophobes in the pay of the Dutch.

His initial discussions with Ivan were stormy. Reiterating Elizabeth's position that an alliance was possible only if Ivan agreed to attempt third-party mediation of disputes before hostilities were declared—"thinking it requisite," she wrote in her letter, "both in Christianity, and by the law of nations, and common reason not to profess enmity, or enter into effects of hostility against any prince or potentat, without warning first given" — he had come prepared, for example, to mediate between Russia and Sweden in their ongoing war. But Ivan scoffed at the offer (which had come too late) and rejected the conditional alliance as practically useless.

On the marriage question, he would not be calmed. The queen's letter indicated that there had been resistance on the part of Lady Mary's family and that "as over the rest of our subjects, so especially over the noble houses, and families, we have no further authority than by waye of persuasions to induce them to like of such matches as are tendered them." Ivan found this incredible, yet remained "so inflamed with his desier" for an English bride that he was secretly prepared to make any concession for it—even to promise that "her yshue should inherit the crown." He swore "he would send againe into England to have one to wife," according to Horsey, "and if her Majestie would not send him such a one as he required, himselfe would then goe into England, and cary his treasure with him, and marry one of them there."

This passion threatened to interfere with the plans of Boris Godunov, whose dynastic hopes were linked to Fyodor, and he reportedly began plotting "to cross and overthrow all such designes."

Ivan was of two minds as to how Bowes should be handled. Though the envoy had made enemies right and left by his petty complaints and "unreasonable and needless findinge fault from tyme to tyme, so much to disquiett the Kinge and state, as never any ambassador did," at one point, to try to elicit concessions from him, Ivan apparently had the Schchelkalov brothers and Nikita Zakharin beaten, and thereafter they smoldered with desire for revenge. On another occasion, however, Ivan pelted Bowes with insults, even disparaging Elizabeth as a petty monarch. When the ambassador allegedly leaped to her defense, declaring her "as great a prince as any was in Christendome, equall to him that thought himselfe the greatest," Ivan fumed, but (according to Bowes) was secretly overcome with admiration for his performance and told his ministers he "wished himself to have such a servant." Thus, "I became a great man with the Emperor," Bowes wrote, and secured new privileges for the company.

His tale may be doubted: other evidence indicates that the negotiations ended in a deadlock, while not far from St. Nicholas the Dutch had already begun to dig their great new port of Archangel, destined to become "the center of the maritime trade of the Empire."

46.

The Conquest of Siberia

As momentous as the founding of Archangel was, a development of far greater magnitude was also at hand. Scarcely had the signatures dried on the Treaty of Yam Zapolsky signifying Ivan's ignominious defeat when "at the other end of his huge dominions an unforeseen and mighty compensation for the loss of Polotsk and Livonia was beginning to appear. Siberia, distant, mysterious, far extending, was opening her arms."

How far-extending Siberia really was no one could have guessed. First mentioned in the Chronicles in the eleventh century, a fragment of the region had long been familiar to Novgorod merchants trading in furs with tribes of the lower Ob, and in 1376 St. Stephen of Perm had bravely established a church in the Upper Kama, where a former missionary had been skinned alive. Before his death he managed to discredit local idolatry and stop the sacrifice of reindeer. Subsequently the Tartar Khanate of Western Sibir, extending east of the Urals to the Irtysh River, had fallen well within the orbit of Muscovite political and military relations. Ivan III and Vasily III had meddled in Siberian politics, and in 1555, the khan, by paying a token tribute, had acknowledged the suzerainty of Ivan IV. Somewhat prematurely Ivan had thereupon incorporated "Tsar of Sibir" into his title. But no one knew that, beyond the Ob, Greater Siberia comprised the whole of northern Asia between the Urals and the Pacific Ocean. This was as unimaginable to the most daring Russian explorer as the Pacific Ocean itself had been to Balboa and his men.

Until 1552, the only route into Siberia lay to the north. After the capture of Kazan, the Kama River and its tributaries had opened a route to the south. Past the Urals and into Siberia the Russians plunged, in a clash of forces not inaptly symbolized by the culinary opposites of "beef Stroganov" and "steak Tartare."

The Stroganovs were financiers and industrial magnates, the Rockefellers and Rothschilds of Muscovy. Their wealth was founded on salt, ore, grain, and furs (the mainstays of the economy), and their assets and properties, accumulated through shrewd dealing over the course of two centuries, extended by the mid-1550s from Ustyug and Vologda to Kaluga and Ryazan.

Though Novgorodians, their political loyalties had always been Muscovite. In 1445–1446, they had helped ransom Vasily II from Tartar captivity, and after Ivan III subdued Novgorod, a Stroganov was commissioned to arbitrate disputed real-estate claims along the Northern Dvina. Needless to say, his official report gratified the Kremlin. The Stroganovs had always had an influential friend at court. In 1517, Vasily III granted them forest land in Ustyug to support their newly established salt works on the Vychegda River at Solvychegodsk, with tax-exempt status for colonists and legal and administrative jurisdiction over the local population that gave them remarkable autonomy. At a time when appanage principalities were becoming a thing of the past, the government allowed a new and semi-independent principality to develop in the north, which became the vital center of the Stroganovs' huge commercial empire.

In the sixteenth century, the paterfamilias of the clan was Anika Stroganov (1497–1570), a fabulously wealthy patron of the arts who wore hand-me-down kaftans, built churches "with the same zeal as he showed in the construction of his salt works," and, notably before his deathbed, took monastic vows. As commercial agent in the 1550s for both Ivan and Metropolitan Makary, he had enjoyed an inside advantage over such industrial rivals as the Solovetsky Monastery, and at an opportune time had enrolled his family in the *Oprichnina*. After his death, Stroganov interests were promoted at court by Boris Godunov.

A rapid series of land grants secured the family's absolute commercial domination of the Russian northeast: in 1558, along the Kama River and its tributaries south of Perm; in 1564, upstream on the Orel "where there is brine"; in 1568, in the Chusovaya River valley; and in 1570, on the Sylva and Yaiva rivers. The charter of 1558 (drafted by Adashev) served as a model for the rest. In each case, in return for long-term tax-exempt status for themselves and their colonists, the Stroganovs pledged to fund and develop industries, break the soil for agriculture, train and equip a frontier guard, prospect for ore and mineral deposits, and mine whatever was found.

They enjoyed jurisdiction over the local population and had the right to protect their holdings with garrisoned stockades and forts equipped with artillery. Thus, a lengthening chain of military outposts and watchtowers soon dotted the river route into Siberia. The stone fort of the Stroganovs on the Orel was to Siberia what Veliky Luki might have been to Lithuania, or what Vasilsursk and Svyazhsk had been to Kazan.

As the colonization advanced to the foot of the Urals, the Stroganovs endeavored to subject a number of native tribes, such as the Voguls and the Ostyaks, to their authority. This brought them into conflict with the new khan, Kuchum, a fiercely ambitious and anti-Muscovite prince who had recently come to power by a coup.

A lineal descendant of Genghis Khan, Kuchum had proclaimed himself "Tsar" of Western Sibir, and after purging the Ostyak and Vogul leadership of opponents, felt strong enough by 1571 to renounce the tribute to Moscow. Moscow, indeed, was in flames, and Ivan quite unable to reassert his claim.

The advancing Stroganov settlements also provoked increasing native unrest. Russian suzerainty was one thing; Russian occupation of the land another. In 1572, there were massacres near Kankor and Keredan, and in 1573 a general uprising of the Cheremis, who struck at settlements along the Kama and Chusovaya all the way to Kazan. To quell the revolt, Ivan sent a large expedition into the region.

Daring prospectors had meanwhile located deposits of silver and iron ore east of the Urals on the Tura River, and it was not erroneously supposed that the same district contained sulfur, lead, and tin. And scouts had seen the rich pastures by the Tobol River where the Tartar cattle grazed. In 1574, the Stroganovs petitioned for a new charter "to drive a wedge between the Siberian Tartars and the Nogays" by means of fortified settlements along the Tobol, Tura, Irtysh, and Ob, in return for license to exploit the resources of the land. The new land allotted to them amounted quite literally to the northern half of the Khanate of Sibir. In a singular measure (impelled by the manpower drain of the Livonian War), the Stroganovs were also permitted to enlist runaways or outlaws in their militia and were urged to organize and finance a campaign, spearheaded by "hired Cossacks and artillery," against Kuchum "to make him pay the tribute."

Enter Yermak Timofey, enemy of the state, future hero of the empire. Yermak was a cossack; that is, he belonged to that turbulent border population of frontiersmen whose ranks were a moil of disaffected elements—tramps, runaways, religious dissenters, itinerant workers, fugitive slaves, bandits, and adventurers driven into the no-man's-land of forest or steppe by taxation, famine, debt, serfdom, repression, and hope of refuge from the long, strong arm of Muscovite law. In the wild country, where they "mingled and clashed" with the Tartars, adopted Tartar terminology and ways (including the horse-tail standard as their common emblem of authority), and gradually displaced certain tribes, they carved out for themselves a new and independent life.

That life was seminomadic, sweet with freedom, bitter with strife. The cossack might be a hunter, fisherman, or farmer; a solitary wanderer or rough mystic; a freebooting cutthroat or buccaneer. Though some, like Yeats' Irish recluse, chose to "live alone in the bee-loud glade," most gathered into homesteading communities and lived in fortified villages strategically placed on river islands or high riverbanks.

Armed societies arose to protect them, and the most famous were those banded together under *atamans* or chieftains into semimilitary confraternities along the Volga, the Dnieper, and the Don. They raided Tartar settlements or poached on Tartar land, preyed on Muscovite river convoys and ambushed government army patrols sent out to catch them and "hang 'em high." The whole cossack story, in fact, with its rugged individualism and worship of democracy, its "badmen," posses, ranchers, cattle rustlers, sheriffs, and so forth bears close comparison with the folkloric picture of the American "wild west." In the simplest and most obvious configuration, the cossack represents the American pioneer, the Tartar the Red Indian, and the Russian Army the U.S. cavalry.

Some cossacks were half-breeds. The word itself derives from the Turkish *kazak*, meaning "rebel" or "freeman," and the original cossacks were not Russian but Tartar renegades. As late as 1483, the Tartar element predominated, when Moscow complained that "Cossack bandits from the Crimea, Azov and Kazan" were attracting malcontents from its border towns. By 1549, the situation was reversed. Don cossacks had built several river forts from which to launch attacks on the Nogays, and by 1551 it was not the tsar but Suleyman the Magnificent who was complaining (with prescient exaggeration), that "the hand of the Russian Tsar Ivan is high. . . . He took the land and rivers away from me. His cossacks from the Don collect tribute from Azov." By 1556, a mighty Cossack stronghold—the Zaporozhian Sech or "clearing beyond the rapids"—had been established on the island of Khortitsa in the Dnieper as a hideout, south of the river's thirteen cataracts; and by the late 1570s, the Tartar component had so far dissolved into the Slavic mass that Ivan could refer to the Cossacks generally as "runaways from our state and the Lithuanian lands."

Yet he could not disown them. He had long since recognized their usefulness in extending his southern frontiers, and at various times had used them as auxiliary troops. But they were unreliable allies. Manipulated as an instrument of policy, they often willfully went against its grain and clashed with the Crimeans and Nogays at diplomatically inconvenient times. Government policy acknowledged a clear distinction in their ranks. Those lured to frontier service (as scouts, trackers, and so forth), were known as "town" cossacks, and came under the jurisdiction of the Streltsy Bureau; relations with the free cossacks were supervised by the Foreign Ministry.

After 1556, regular army patrols sought to enforce the tsar's authority along the Volga trade route, and a series of expeditions designed to crush or subdue outlaw bands culminated in 1577 in a great sweep along both sides of the Volga. With the tsar's cavalry in hot pursuit, some fled down the river to the Caspian Sea, others to the Terek. A third group, under Yermak, the most notorious river pirate of his day, raced up the Kama River into the wilds of Perm—where they were enthusiastically welcomed into the Stroganovs' frontier service.

Exceeding the tsar's commission, the Stroganovs organized a military expedition with a threefold aim: to secure the Kama frontier; bring part of Siberia within their mining monopoly; and gain access to Siberian furs. Their principal objective may have been the third.

Fur was Russia's most valuable export commodity. Especially prized were sables "unripped, with bellies and feet," but quality pelts of all kinds had been exported in such abundance by 1558 to Western Europe, as well as to Bokhara and Samarkand, that a domestic shortage resulted, with hats and coats having to be pieced together out of mangy remnants of rabbit and squirrel. The price of furs rose sharply; by the 1570s, foreign consumption (which helped finance the war effort) had led to the near extermination of fur-bearing animals in the north. Already a large proportion of the best pelts displayed on the Volga markets or at Solvychegodsk were obtained by barter with Siberian natives, who (as no American will be surprised to hear) proved pathetically willing to part with their precious merchandise in return for a couple of trinkets or cheap manufactured goods. Indeed, like the United States and Canada, Siberia owed its opening and first exploitation primarily to the fur trade.

On September 1, 1581, a Cossack army of 840 men, including 300 Livonian prisoners of war, two priests, and a runaway monk impressed into service as a cook, assembled under Yermak on the banks of the Kama River near Kankor. The official chronicles tell us that the men set off "singing hymns to the Trinity, to God in his Glory, and to the most immaculate Mother of God," but this is unlikely. Who knows what they sang; but their secular fellowship was given muscle by a rough code of martial law.

Anyone guilty of insubordination was bundled headfirst into a sack, with a bag of sand tied to his chest, and "tipped into the river." Some twenty grumblers were "tipped in" at the start.

Such a force hardly seemed adequate to conquer a khanate, but the odds against surviving were not as bad as many thought. Though vastly outnumbered, they were well-led, well-provisioned (with rye flour, biscuit, buckwheat, roasted oats, butter, and salt pig), and armed to the teeth. The Tartars of Sibir were "Tartare"—comparatively primitive; Yermak's army had the new technology, and it was their military superiority through firearms that would prove decisive, as it had for Cortés in Mexico and Pizarro in Peru.

Yermak proceeded along a network of rivers to the foothills of the Urals, where he pitched his winter camp. In the spring, he embarked downstream, swung into the Tura River, and for some distance penetrated unmolested into the heart of Kuchum's domain. A skirmish at the mouth of the Tobol proved costly, but it was downstream where the river surged through a ravine that the Tartars laid their trap. Hundreds of warriors hid in the trees on either side of a barrier created with ropes and logs. The first boat struck the barrier at night. The Tartars attacked, but in the enveloping darkness most of Yermak's flotilla managed to escape upstream. At a bend in the river, the cossacks disembarked, made manikins out of twigs and fallen branches, and propped them up in the boats, with skeleton crews at the oars. The others, half-naked, crept around to surprise the Tartars from behind. At dawn, just as the flotilla floated into view, they opened fire.

The result was a complete rout.

Infuriated, Kuchum resolved to annihilate the intruders before they could reach his capital, even as Yermak knew he had to take the town before winter or his men would perish in the cold. Though so far victorious, their provisions were dwindling, while ambush and disease had already reduced the expeditionary force by half. Still they pressed on, past the meadowlands whitening with hoarfrost and the hardening salt-marshes glazed with ice, toward the tall wooden ramparts of Sibir.

The decisive confrontation came in late October, at the confluence of the Tobol and Irtysh rivers, where the Tartars had erected a palisade at the base of a hill. Kuchum himself, blind and carried in a litter, listened at some distance for Tartar shouts of victory.

Instead he heard tumult and confusion, followed by cries of despair. As the cossacks charged, they fired their muskets into the densely massed defenders with devastating effect. Many of the Tartars, conscripted by force, at once deserted; more fled as the palisade was stormed. This gave the cossacks a chance. In hand-to-hand combat, the battle raged till evening, 107 cossacks falling before they prevailed.

A few days later, when they came to Sibir itself, they found it deserted, with few of its fabled riches left behind. Instead (for which they were probably more grateful) the men discovered stocks of barley, flour, and dried fish.

Immediately there were scattered defections to the Russian side as Yermak began accepting tribute from former subjects of the khan. But to consolidate his position he needed reinforcements and artillery, and to obtain them he dispatched Ivan Koltso (also a renowned bandit, and his second in command) with fifty others to Moscow. Traveling on skis and on sleds drawn by reindeer, they took the fabled "wolf-path" shortcut over the Urals disclosed to them by a Tartar chieftain who acted as their guide.

Back in Moscow, however, the expedition was in disgrace. No one yet knew of Yermak's achievement, but they knew that in retaliation for his invasion the Voguls had been rampaging through the upper Kama Valley, burning Russian settlements to the ground. This had prompted the military governor of Perm to accuse the Stroganovs of leaving the frontier undefended, and in a letter dated November 16, 1582, the tsar had bitterly reproved the industrialists for "disobedience amounting to treason." Narva had just fallen to the Swedes; the Poles had just blockaded Pskov, when Koltso arrived to cheer the gloomy capital with his sensational news. Prostrating himself before the tsar, who had planned to hang him, he announced Yermak's conquest of Sibir and proclaimed Ivan Lord of the Khanate. To a stunned court he displayed his convincing spoils, including three captive Tartar nobles and a sledload of pelts equal to five times the annual tribute demanded from the khan. Ivan pardoned Koltso on the spot and Yermak in absentia, promised reinforcements, and sent Yermak a magnificent suit of armor embossed with the imperial coat of arms.

At the Kremlin, Koltso kissed the cross in obedience; back in Siberia, as Yermak struggled to extend his authority up the Irtysh, natives were made to swear allegiance by kissing a bloody sword. Those who resisted were hanged upside down by one foot (which meant an agonizing death), yet in his own way Yermak tried to Christianize the tribes. In one contest of power, a local wizard ripped open his own stomach with a knife, then miraculously healed the wound by smearing it with grass; Yermak simply tossed the local wooden totems on the fire.

By the end of the summer of 1584, his jurisdiction extended almost to the river Ob. In November, long-awaited reinforcements tramped into Sibir on snowshoes, but having brought no provisions of their own, Yermak's reserves were rapidly consumed. During the long winter, part of the garrison starved. In the spring, Kuchum's adherents stepped up attacks on foraging sorties; and in two grievous blows to the garrison's hopes for survival, twenty cossacks were killed as they dozed by a lake, while Koltso and forty others were lured to a banquet and massacred.

In early August 1585, a trap was baited for Yermak himself. Informed that an unescorted caravan from Bokhara was nearing the Irtysh, he hastened with a company of cossacks to meet it, and that night bivouacked on an island in midstream. A wild storm arose and drove the watchmen into their tents. A party of natives disembarked unobserved, attacked, and killed the cossacks almost to a man. Yermak managed to struggle into his armor and fight his way to the river bank. But, as he plunged into the water, the tsar's fatal gift bore him down beneath the waves.

The cossack remnant retreated to the Urals, where as they made their way through a mountain pass, they met a hundred *streltsy* equipped with cannon moving east—too little, too late. Yet the way had been shown; and over the next few years the reconquest of Western Siberia was to be accomplished with remarkable speed.[1] River highways facilitated the advance, with outposts established at strategic locations and blockhouses scattered through the forests and tundras of the north. After the founding of the city of Tobolsk in 1587, no tribe could doubt that the Russians were there to stay.

The soldiers came in waves, followed by the hunters and trappers in a "Fur Rush" as frantic as the Gold Rush of Alaska. With any luck a man could strike it rich in a season. A few good fox pelts alone, for example, could buy fifty acres of land, a decent cabin, five horses, ten head of cattle, and twenty sheep. Yet a progressive exhaustion of the hunting grounds drove the hunters ever farther east. In their wake came farmers, and after the farmers, artisans and state employees. For three-quarters of a century, in fact, despite all the perilous hardships of pioneering equal to the experience of "winning" the American West, nothing would arrest the Russians' advance, until they entered the Amur Valley and were stopped by the Chinese.

Yermak was to be posthumously canonized in both Russian and Tartar folklore, and the names of the cossacks who had fallen in the battle for Sibir were engraved on a memorial tablet in the Cathedral of Tobolsk. Legend has it that some months after Yermak's death his body was dredged up from the Irtysh by a Tartar fisherman who recognized it at once by the double-headed eagle emblazoned on the chain-mail hauberk. Beneath the armor, Yermak's flesh was "found to be uncorrupted, and blood gushed from his mouth and nose." In awe, the natives buried him at the foot of a pine tree by the river, and for many nights thereafter the spot was marked by a column of fire.

47.

Endgame

Siberia belonged to Russia's future. Ivan had nothing to do with its conquest, and though it fell like a ripened apple into his lap, before he could possibly taste what it meant he belonged to Russia's past. Not even the addition of another khanate to his imperial dominions could undo the tragedy of his life and reign. And notwithstanding his continuing pursuit of complicated policy, his third (if least crafty) abdication, and his masterful debate in the midst of his grief with a leading Jesuit apologist of the age, the contemporary judgment was, and may be right, that "his mourning and passion after his sonnes death never left him till it brought him to his grave." Possevino was told that he often "called out to the tsarevich in a lamenting voice, and acted as if he talked with him," as if he were still alive. And whereas in his youth he had composed hymns of praise to the Vladimir Icon and to Metropolitan Peter, a fourteenth-century saint of the Russian Church, his despair now moved him to compose a canon to the Angel of Death.

Tyrants tend toward pitiable declines, and in his last days Ivan was as bloated and riddled with disease as Henry VIII; as fatuously ascetic as Suleyman the Magnificent, who stopped listening to the singing of choir boys and began to eat off earthenware plate; and as hopelessly superstitious as the Byzantine emperor Andronikos II, who kept asking the stars if they could do any better for him than his doctors.

For some time Ivan had suffered from a painfully severe form of ankylosing spondylitis (a crippling malady akin to rheumatoid arthritis), which resulted in the degeneration of his joints and eventually fused the vertebrae of his spine into a single rod. Long, hot baths and mercurials in the form of ointments and salves were used to relieve the pain and inflammation, but the mercurials may also have affected his mind. His robust and athletic habits (as vouched for by Kurbsky) and straight-backed regal posture were coincidentally therapeutic, but the former were steadily undermined by dissipation, and in the end his back was bent like a bow. "Age doth not rectify but incurvate our natures" is a wise and witty adage, and seldom more apt than in Ivan's case.

It has sometimes been suggested (to explain his aberrant behavior) that Ivan was made "criminally insane" by some form of syphilis. Though he probably had a number of venereal diseases, his pathological behavior was not obviously progressive (which also complicates a diagnosis of extreme paranoia), and he remained brilliant and lucid to the end. Only slightly more interesting is the notion that there was something wrong with his "stock": namely, the "vitiated blood of the Paleologi, with all that predisposition to nervous complaints which was so strongly marked among them." This theory associates Ivan's high-strung temperament with the fact that his brother was a deaf-mute; his son Fyodor an imbecile; and his last-born, Dmitry, suffered from epileptic fits. Perhaps a geneticist can connect such afflictions; but whatever his stock bequeathed, there is no doubt that his vicious life also caught up with him in the end.

By January 1584, he had begun to show signs of internal putrefaction, to "griviously swell in his coddes," wrote Horsey, "with which he had most horriblie offended, boasting of a thowsand virgins deflowered." Carried each day from room to room in a chair, he doted often on his fabulous treasury, tormented at all he would have to leave behind.

Sixty Lapland witches, "sent forth owt of the North," were brought in haste to Moscow where they were daily consulted by Bogdan Belsky, who conveyed their predictions to the tsar. Belsky dared not tell Ivan all, for the witches unanimously agreed that "the signes constellaccions and strongest planetts of heaven were against the Emperower," and flatly predicted his death for March 18. Belsky warned them they had better be right.

One day, from the palace balustrade, Ivan saw a comet flash through the sky, its tail forming a nebulous cross which lingered between the domes of two cathedrals. He stared at it gloomily and proclaimed to his attendants: "This portends my death."

Circulars were sent to all the monasteries of the realm soliciting prayers.

March came. On the 10th, he was too ill even to discuss state affairs and directed that a Lithuanian embassy, on its way to Moscow, be delayed at Mozhaisk. But on the 15th, he rallied, gave it clearance to proceed, and later that day invited Horsey and others to accompany him into his treasury, where he discoursed on the occult properties of sundry items in the vaults. "The load-stone you all know hath great and hidden vertue," he began, "without which the seas that compas the world ar not navigable, nor can the bounds or circle of the earth be knowen." He explained that magnetism enabled the steel tomb of the Prophet Mohammed at Derbent to hover in midair, and marveled at some magnetized needles hanging in a chain. Proceeding next to his gem collection, he commanded one of his attendants to place brightly colored turquoise and coral on his hand and arm. The colors paled. "Declares my death," he exclaimed, "I am poisoned with disease. Reach owt my staff roiall!" A unicorn's horn garnished with gems was fetched and used to scrape a circle on a board. "Seeke owt som spiders!" Three were obtained: one ran off; two placed within the circle died. "It is too late," cried Ivan, "it will not preserve me." He was carried over to his precious stones. Pointing first to the diamond, he said: "I never affected it; yt restreyns furie and luxurie and abstinacie and chasticie; the least parcell of it in powder will poysen a horss geaven to drinck, much more a man." Next, the ruby: "O! this is most comfortable to the hart, braine, vigar and memorie, and clarifies congelled and corrupt bloud." Then the emerald: "An enemye to uncleannes. Try it: though man and wiff cohabitt in lust together, havinge this stone aboute them, yt will burst at the spendinge of natur." Fourth, the sapphire: "Preserves and increaseth courage, joies the hart, pleasuring to all the vital sensis, precious and verie soveraigne for the eys, clears the sight, takes away bloud shott, and streingthens the mussels and strings thereof." Finally, he took the onyx in his hand: "All these are Gods wonderfull guifts, secreats in natur, and yet reveals them to mans use and contemplacion, as frendes to grace and vertue and enymies to vice. I fainte, carie me awaye till an other tyme."

March 18 arrived. Ivan awoke with gusto. In the afternoon he read over his will, yet supposing himself now "unbewitched," looked to confirm his optimism by some astrological sign. He summoned his chief apothecary and physicians to apply their ointments and rubs, others to draw his bath, and dispatched Belsky again to the witches "to know their calculacions." Belsky, furious and tired of the whole routine, confronted them: "The daye is come; he is hartt and holl as ever he was," and swore to see them all burnt for their "fals illucions and lies." They answered: "Sir, be not so wrathfull. You know the daie is com and ends with the setting of the sun." Belsky hurried back, found Godunov and others standing about, dutifully assisted the tsar with his ablutions, and soon they all heard him "as he useth to do," splashing about and singing in his bath. Four hours later Ivan emerged refreshed, sat down on the edge of his bed in a loose gown, and called for his chessboard. He began to assemble the pieces but could not make the king stand up. Suddenly he fainted and fell backward. There was a "great owt-crie and sturr," aqua vitae, marigold and rose water were fetched to revive him; physicians, apothecary, and confessor all came running, but found him "starke dead."

Hastily Ivan was tonsured (according to his wish) and posthumously rechristened Jonah. Dressed in a monk's robe and cowl, with Calvary depicted on the shawl, a few days later he was laid to rest among his ancestors in the Cathedral of St. Michael the Archangel, in the place of honor near the altar, beside his eldest son. At the head of his white-stone sarcophagus was set a blue and yellow goblet of enameled Venetian glass containing the sacramental ointment which had purged him of sin in an instant and transformed him into a monk. The sarcophagus, in turn, was placed in a brass-covered casket embossed with the eight-pointed cross.

"Though garded daye and night," wrote Horsey, "he remained a fearfull spectacle to the memorie of such as pass by or heer his name who ar contented to cross and bless themselves from his resurrection againe."

No sooner had Ivan expired than Godunov, as lord protector, acted to prevent a coup. He went onto the Kremlin terrace, "cried owt to the captaines and gunners to kepe their gard stronge and the gaetts shure, with their peces and matches lighted," and when Horsey offered to place his own men, powder, and pistols at his disposal, cheerfully replied, "Be faithfull and fear not." Within six or seven hours the treasuries had been sealed, new officers of the guard appointed, military governors with fresh garrisons dispatched to the chief border strongholds of Kazan, Novgorod, Pskov, and Smolensk, and 12,000 gunners assigned to strategic locations along the walls of the capital. "To see what speede and policie here was used," wrote Horsey, "was a thing worth beholding." Meanwhile, the high clergy and nobility flocked to the Kremlin to swear allegiance to Fyodor.

Ivan's demise put Jerome Bowes, still in Moscow, in mortal danger. The powerful officials who had suffered so much for his arrogance were the very men at whose mercy he now stood. "Thy English Tsar is dead," he was informed by Andrey Schchelkalov, his deadliest enemy; and for nine weeks he remained under house arrest as the nobles debated whether or not to kill him.

Horsey was summoned for his opinion. He personally disliked Bowes, but as a servant of the queen eloquently pleaded for his life. That night Godunov took him aside, warned him not to say too much on Bowes' behalf—"the lords take it ill"—but promised to do what he could to save him.

At length, Bowes was brought to the palace and told that as an example to others who might "so much forgett themselves" he deserved to be dismembered. Mercifully, however, they merely stripped him of his cloak, dagger, and sword and "in verie short garments," to his great humiliation, hustled him into the presence of Fyodor. Denied an interpreter and (perhaps for his own good) refused an opportunity to speak, Bowes was given curt letters for the queen rejecting his embassy. "Lett him thank God: God was his gud God," Schchelkalov told Dr. Robert Jacob the next day, for he had otherwise "bene torne in peeces and throwne over the walls."

Horsey helped Bowes pack up his belongings, and on May 29 accompanied him to the outskirts of Moscow where Bowes swore his everlasting gratitude. Despite fears of an ambush, he made it unmolested to St. Nicholas, but once safely on board an English ship, began to shout obscenities at the Russians on shore and in full view actually tore up Fyodor's letters to the queen. The chief agent of the Russia Company wrote home: "Wolde he had never come here!"

Back in England, Bowes put the best face on things at court, but one year later when Horsey returned and was debriefed, his damaging testimony combined with other evidence to confirm that the embassy had been a disaster. Called to account, Bowes tried to discredit Horsey by inducing one Finch, who had been in Russia with them, to charge that he had almost been roasted by Ivan as a spy because Horsey had betrayed him. Horsey's star plunged; but when Finch was examined by the Privy Council, he proved "so faint, faultering and fearfull, ever loking upon Bowes what he should saye," that after a few stern glances from the mighty ministers he broke down and confessed to the frameup. Horsey was rehabilitated; Bowes was permanently banished from court; and Finch was clapped into irons and told by Lord Burghley: "Though you wear not rosted, sirra, yt was pittie you had not ben a littell scorched."

Fyodor was crowned tsar on June 10, 1584. Cannon thundered in salute on the outskirts of Moscow, and thousands of musketeers in silk and velvet, standing eight ranks deep for a length of two miles, discharged their weapons twice in orderly succession. At the head of a huge body of cavalry, he rode through the city to the Kremlin.

Despite his warrior pose, the new tsar had almost nothing in common with his father except for a Mediterranean nose and weirdly late dentition. Variously described as a simpleton, an idiot, or a "fool in Christ," he doted on the antics of dwarfs and jesters, and above all loved to run to church, "hang firmly from the bells, and ring them himself." Even as heir apparent after 1582, he had been an embarrassment to his father who, except on rare occasions, had kept him out of sight. Giles Fletcher the Elder, Elizabeth's brilliant choice to repair Russian-English relations, fills his portrait out:

> For his person of a meane stature, somewhat lowe and grosse, of a sallowe complexion, and inclining to the dropsie, hawke nosed, unsteady in his pase by reason of some weakenes of his lims, heavie and unactive, yet commonly smiling almost to a laughter. For qualitie otherwise, simple and slowe witted, but verie gentle, and of an easie nature, quiet, mercifull, of no martial disposition, nor greatly apt for matter of pollicie, very superstitious, and infinite that way. Besides his private devotions at home, he goeth every weeke commonly on pilgrimage to some monasterie or other that is nearest hand.

Possevino thought Fyodor "quite unguilty" and hoped he might even prove tolerant toward Catholics; a knowledgeable Polish diplomat suggested that he was, perhaps, "not unlike the Emperor Claudius, pretending to be an idiot to escape a worse fate."

Be that as it may, the people adored him, preferring to be ruled by a gentle bellringer manipulated by able advisers than chastised by an arbitrary tyrant who would save their souls through fear. Everyone, says Horsey, held Fyodor's accession "for their redemption—as a day of jubilee." Corrupt officials were dismissed, many taxes canceled or reduced, due process restored to the law, the prisons opened—"all peaceably as bred great assurance and honor to the kingdom."

That promise, however, was not to be fulfilled. Ivan's tormented regime had "so troubled the country, and filled it full of grudge and mortall hatred" that no wise policy in the short term could mend it, nor even a long season of goodwill. "God hath a plage in store for this people," wrote Horsey. "What shall we say?" Fletcher had the answer: civil war. In the Time of Troubles, which loomed just over the horizon, Russia would again be ripped asunder, the Swedes would occupy Novgorod, and the Poles the capital itself, where they would install a Polish tsar.

Though Ivan was "utterly tragic in his inward struggle with self waged concurrently with his struggle against the enemies of his country," he was most deeply tragic as a monarch who came to see his own people as the foe. Whatever the early accomplishments of his reign, or the historical trends to which he may have been attuned, calamities substantially of his own creation overwhelmed them, and the scourge of his epithet remains.

What shall we say? Though *grozny*, rendered "terrible," originally meant "dread" or "awesome," denoting majesty, the same mistranslation occurs in every language—*Ivan der Schrecklich* in German, for example, and *Jean le Terrible* in French. On the one hand, Ivan was "dread" as all contemporary monarchs were automatically dread by virtue of their office—even the young and gentle King Edward VI, "our most dread and soveraigne Lord"—and "terrible" as Pope Julius II was *il Papa Terribile*, the fearsome pope. But in Russia the idea of majesty in the word was uniquely reinforced by both pagan and Christian tradition. As a cognate of *groza* (storm), it recalled Perun, the Thunder Lord, the supreme pagan deity of pre-Christian Slavs. Perun's Christian counterpart was Christ Pantocrator, the Lord Omnipotent enthroned, who in the typical Byzantine-Russian icon of Christ looked severely down upon the congregation from the cathedral dome. This was the Christ who judged, who saved through fear. The Last Judgment was called the "Terrible Judgment" by the Greek and Russian Orthodox, and Christ the "just and terrible heavenly tsar," as one court pamphlet, for example, had put it in 1551. Ivan rather self-consciously assumed the role. "It was no wise prince who trusted his people," he once remarked, "who had betrayed the Redeemer of the world." For Ivan, Judas was the prototypical traitor, and the Biblical story of the Crucifixion seems to have stood in his mind as the eternal example of what a divinely ordained monarch could expect from his subjects. It is not impossible (speaking psychiatrically) that Ivan's extreme identification with divinity worked obscurely within him toward the sacrifice of his own son, even as he dedicated his reign, in imitation of Christ, to separating out the damned from the redeemed.

Though folklore stubbornly sustained his early reputation as a hero against the infidels and his self-projected image as an ally of the poor against the oppressions of the rich, even sympathetic anecdotes of his life tend to be ambiguous, while "terrible" in its colloquial sense became indelibly attached to his name.

What began as a mistranslation can be called a verdict of history. Ivan's case recalls that of Selim I, the Ottoman sultan and bigoted Sunni who (among his other atrocities) killed or imprisoned 40,000 Shiites in Anatolia in 1513. Among his own "orthodox" subjects this massacre won him the name of "the Just." History justly remembers him as "the Grim."

As Ivan was entombed, so was he found and resurrected 369 years later on earth, when a "blue ribbon commission of Soviet archaeologists, historians, and specialists in forensic medicine" opened his sarcophagus on April 23, 1953. His remains were analyzed, his skull reconstructed. A residue of the sacramental chrism unaccountably remained in the goblet of enameled glass.

Notes

1.

1. The name then given indiscriminately by the Russians to any Mongol, Turkic, or Islamic people.
2. Elena was a great-great-great-granddaughter of Mansur Kiyat, Mamay's son.
3. Louis XIV, also considered a miracle at his birth and likewise the occasion of a thanksgiving church, was supposedly born with two fully developed teeth, and "one wet nurse after another proved unable to sustain the punishment of feeding him." Hugo Grotius, the Swedish minister to France in 1638, wrote: "It is for the neighbors of France to fear this precocious voracity." The story about Ivan carried a similar but more ominous message.
4. Catherine (the "spouse of Christ" in a dream) converted outstanding pagan philosophers at an audience with the Roman emperor in Alexandria in 305, and subsequently converted the empress herself. For this, she was tortured on a spiked wheel and beheaded. Angels transferred her relics to Mt. Sinai. How they happened to be in the Kremlin is a mystery.
5. Referring to an ancient Bulgar state in the region of the middle Volga, near Kazan.

2.

1. Strictly speaking, the genealogical and service records, carefully maintained by eminent individual families, were not formally compiled into unified central directories until the 1550s.
2. In the Eastern Orthodox Church, a metropolitan ranks above an archbishop but below a patriarch. In 1533, there were four patriarchs: at Constantinople, Alexandria, Antioch and Jerusalem. The Russian primate was granted patriarchal status in 1589.
3. This Catholic innovation in the Creed (established at Constantinople in 381) apparently first appeared around 589 in Spain. In 809 Charlemagne approved it

at Aachen; and in 1014, Pope Benedict VIII sanctified it at his anointing of King Henry II.

4. Botanists have since identified it as the cotton plant.

3.

1. After the Muscovite defeat at the battle of Orsha two decades before, he had hanged all of the city's pro-Lithuanian nobles from the walls.

4.

1. Not to be confused with Elena's uncle.
2. Nevertheless, it is a pity. The Kremlin library was said to contain a priceless collection of some 800 rare Greek, Hebrew, and Latin manuscripts (including a copy of the Homeric hymns) preserved in part from the famous library of Yaroslav the Wise and supplemented by volumes brought to Russia by Sophia Palaeologa and Maksim the Greek. Maksim indeed lamented that many had been abandoned in a basement of the Kremlin as "food for worms." As late as 1960, Soviet scholars were still hoping to locate them in a Kremlin crypt.
3. Thus, for example, Helmut Schmidt, former chancellor of West Germany, quoted in *The New York Times*, September 16, 1984: "The political behavior of Russia hasn't really changed much since Ivan III or Ivan IV. . . . I think it's a mix of a never really satisfied drive for expansion and a strong and subconscious belief that Mother Russia will bring salvation to the world. This idea of salvation by Russia was in the minds of Russian intellectuals . . . long before Communism— Moscow as the Third Rome, after Byzantium."
4. This tale was first promulgated in the *Legend of the Princes of Vladimir*, composed at the end of the fifteenth or beginning of the sixteenth century.
5. The *Shapka Monomakh*, probably of Central Asian origin, would be featured in every coronation ceremony, if not worn by every Russian tsar, until the revolution of 1917. The earliest mention of the *barmy* and crown is to be found in the Testament of Ivan I Kalita, ca. 1339; of the sardonyx box in the Testament of Ivan II (ca. 1358); of the cross, in the Testament of Vasily II (1423). In one version of the legend, the sardonyx box becomes a cup from which Augustus "once made merry."

5.

1. The passage is actually from a sixth-century treatise on ideal kingship presented by the deacon Agapetus of the Church of St. Sophia in Constantinople to the Emperor Justinian.

8.

1. A monastery located on an island in Lake Lagoda northeast of the Gulf of Finland.
2. Originally composed in Arabic around 950 A.D., the *Secreta Secretorum* had been translated into Latin in the thirteenth century and subsequently into a number of the vernacular languages of Europe. The copy in the Kremlin Library was exceptional in having been translated from the Hebrew.
3. Historians remain divided as to whether sufficient crown land about Moscow was found to support a resettlement on this scale.

9.

1. This and many other inflated statistics were repeated by numerous contemporaries even among Moscow's neighbors, especially when it came time for them to put together "defense budgets."

10.

1. Two daughters, Anne and Marie, had been born to Ivan and Anastasia in 1549 and 1551, respectively. Anne had died in 1550. Marie would die in 1554.

11.

1. Prince Ivan Mstislavsky, Prince Vladimir Vorotynsky, Ivan Scheremetev, Mikhail Morozov, Prince Dmitry Paletsky, and Daniel and Vasily Zakharin.
2. Prince Dmitry Kurlyatev (who was close to Sylvester) and the treasurer Nikita Funikov.
3. The interpolations occur in the *Tsarstvennaya Kniga*, or *Book of the Tsar*, and include the celebrated description of Sylvester as all-powerful (quoted earlier). Though generally attributed to Viskovaty, one outstanding Soviet scholar, Ruslan Skrynnikov, believes the author to be Ivan himself. A certain caustic restraint in their style makes this unlikely, as does their relatively omniscient point of view. Moreover, The *Tsarstvennaya Kniga* was largely compiled under Viskovaty's direction during his tenure as keeper of the state archives, and according to the distinguished scholar Nikolay Andreyev, "the technical directions for the binders are written in the same hand."
4. Including Prince Semeon Lobanov-Rostovsky, Prince Peter Shchenyatev, Prince Ivan Turontay-Pronsky, Prince Peter Serebriany, and Prince Semeon Mikulinsky.
5. Twice in the following year, in April and May of 1554, Vladimir had to sign supplementary bonds, each with a special clause directed against intrigue by his mother.

12.

1. There is no question of his guilt. His son, Nikita, had been caught at the border near Toropets on an errand to the king of Poland to obtain a writ of safe conduct to assist his father's flight.
2. The ambassador had reportedly told Maksim: "Let my beard be tied to a dog's tail if I do not lead the Sultan onto the prince's land."
3. Maksim wrote voluminously. Some 350 works have been attributed to him, including dictionaries, grammars, philological and polemical treatises which introduced unfamiliar literary genres, such as the Dialogue, as well as new methods of textual criticism into Russian culture.

14.

1. Yadigar, baptized Simeon, fought loyally for Ivan as a general in the Moscovite Army until his death in 1565. Utemysh, often seated next to Ivan at court banquets, died prematurely in 1566 at the age of nineteen, and was buried in the Cathedral of the Archangel Michael, near the tsars.
2. Located on the Kerch Strait, not at the mouth of the Volga.
3. In the second edition of *The Great Menology* it was claimed that the patriarch had addressed Ivan as "pious sovereign, Tsar and Grand Prince . . . Autocrat of all Russia . . . crowned by God . . . our new ruler and good and chosen master."
4. Insecurity about their title would trouble the tsars of Russia even to the time of Peter the Great. When a letter addressed by the German emperor Maximilian to Vasily III as emperor was unearthed in the Kremlin archives in 1717, Peter was so pleased that he promptly had it translated into several foreign languages and distributed to all the foreign ambassadors.
5. The famous apocryphal story about the blinding of the "foreign" architect, however, probably comments as much on Moscow's tradition of brutal ingratitude toward foreign artisans as it does on either the uniqueness of the church's beauty or Ivan's sadistic whims.
6. In the time of Ivan IV, the entire cathedral complex, including the sheet iron over the cupolas, was white.

16.

1. I.e., from the northern shore of the Gulf of Guinea, then Europe's principal source of supply.
2. Dee, a Renaissance magus, was to become Queen Elizabeth's court astrologer. He determined the date most propitious for her coronation, and she remained his steadfast patron despite his lurid renown. John Aubrey in his *Brief Lives*

wrote: "The vulgar did verily believe him to be a conjurer. He had a great many mathematical instruments and glasses in his chamber, which did confirm the ignorant in their opinion, and his servitor would tell them that sometimes he would meet the spirits coming up his stairs like bees." Elizabeth, not one of the vulgar, allowed him to do what he wished in alchemy "and none should check, control, or molest" him.

3. Not out of tolerance, but as an encroachment on canon law.

17.

1. In 1466, by the Peace of Thorn, West Prussia was incorporated into the Polish Kingdom as an autonomous province, and East Prussia, still under the rule of the Teutonic Knights, was enfeoffed to Poland as a vassal state. Subsequently, as the spread of Lutheranism depleted the grand master's ranks, he struck a bargain whereby in exchange for submission the king would enfeoff him as hereditary duke of a secularized domain. This arrangement was consummated in 1525.

20.

1. Sigismund, fearing some additional arrangement between Moscow and the German Empire (Poland's long-time political antagonist in Eastern Europe), also procured the support of the elector of Brandenburg by agreeing to delay the day when the rule of East Prussia would revert to the Polish crown. This costly gambit was to haunt the history of Poland well into the twentieth century.

21.

1. Some of the medallions representing Livonian localities had been hastily incorporated: the coat of arms of Reval, for example, was confused with that of Wenden, and Riga was represented by the escutcheon of the von Fürstenbergs. Oddly enough, Smolensk was also confused with Tver.

22.

1. These details are translated from Kurbsky's subsequent *History* of Ivan's reign.
2. Makary had written to Ivan at Kazan: "*If the Tsar's heart is in the hand of God*, then is it fit for all to act and obey, with fear and trembling according to God's will and the imperial command; for thus said the Apostle Peter: 'Fear God and

honor the Tsar'; and also because the Apostle said: 'the Tsar bears the sword not in vain, but for vengeance unto evil-doers, and for the praise of the good!' " In closely repeating Makary, however, Ivan neglected the essential idea. (Italics mine.)

24.

1. The extensive and very revealing correspondence between Ivan and Elizabeth has been unaccountably neglected by Elizabeth's biographers. Her letters reveal her at her shrewdest, wisest, and literary best, and Ivan's responses are cumulatively as rich in revelations about his character and style as his celebrated correspondence with Kurbsky.

25.

1. From 1505 on, no law could be passed unless it was ostensibly the unanimous wish of the Diet. The simple utterance of the phrase "I protest" not only put an end to further discussion of an issue; it ended the session of the Diet.
2. Among other things Zosima had been charged with alcoholism and sodomy.

31.

1. A familiar form of Ivan.

32.

1. The Hussites were followers of Jan Hus, a Czech admirer of Wycliffe.
2. The Black Death did not spare Russia entirely, however, as some have supposed. Thus, for example, this unmistakable description from the Novgorod Chronicle in 1417: "First of all it would hit one as with a lance, choking, then a swelling would appear, or spitting of blood with shivering, and then fire would burn in all the joints; and then the illness would overwhelm."

35.

1. Ivan's colorful counsel against reckless territorial ambition was evidently derived from the Byzantine emperor Basil's advice to his son Leo: "If thou hast strived

to subject by arms the whole world, thou shalt have nonetheless after death but a space of three cubits."

2. Stalin in 1947 told the great film director Sergey Eisenstein (whose *Ivan the Terrible*, Part I, had been awarded the Stalin Prize, first class, in the previous year) that "the only mistake Ivan had made was his failure entirely to liquidate those who opposed him, and that the *Oprichnina* had been a positive force in Russian society." Though implicitly warned, Eisenstein had his own interpretation, and in the following year Part II was condemned by the Central Committee of the Communist Party for showing Ivan's "progressive army of *Oprichniki* as a band of degenerates in the style of the American Ku-Klux-Klan."

36.

1. Compare an admirer on Louis XIV in his prime: "Even should he disguise himself, one would recognize immediately that he is the master, for he has the air by which we recognize those whom we speak of as having the blood of the gods."

37.

1. Simeon was eventually to pay a heavy price for his prominence. Removed from office after Ivan's death, he was subsequently blinded and died at the Solovetsky Monastery in 1616 as the monk Stephen.

38.

1. John Dee, incidentally, met three times with Batory in the course of a transcontinental tour devoted to crystal gazing in 1585.

40.

1. Vatican promotion of his marriage to Sophia Paleologa was fundamentally a scheme to win Russia for Catholicism and, collaterally, the first attempt to enlist Russia in a pan-European, anti-Turkish crusade.

2. The two men did not like each other, and on their way back from Italy Popler assassinated his colleague.

3. Ivan's ambassadors, Evstafy Pushkin and Fyodor Pissemsky, incidentally, were also instructed to rebuke Kurbsky for his "rude letter" to the tsar.

43.

1. He was fifty-two.

44.

1. All these statistics refer not to a single cadastral survey in a single year, but to a cluster of surveys in the late 1570s and early 1530s.

46.

1. The complete conquest of Greater Siberia (1,555,448 square miles of land) was another matter.

Bibliography

ABBREVIATIONS

AB-S	*Acta Baltico-Slavica*
AHR	*American Historical Review*
ASEER	*American Slavic and East European Review*
C-ASS	*Canadian-American Slavic Studies*
CH	*Church History*
CHR	*Catholic Historical Review*
CSP	*Canadian Slavonic Papers*
CSPF	*Calendar of State Papers, Foreign, 1547–1589*
DOP	*Dumbarton Oaks Papers*
HRM	*Historica Russiae Monumenta*
HSS	*Harvard Slavic Studies*
IZ	*Istoricheskie Zapiski*
JGOE	*Jahrbücher für Geschichte Osteuropas*
JHI	*Journal of the History of Ideas*
OCP	*Orientalia Christiana Periodica*
OSP	*Oxford Slavonic Papers*
RH	*Russian History*
SEER	*Slavonic and East European Review*
SR	*Slavic Review*

ALEF, G. "Muscovy and the Council of Florence," *SR*, 20 (1961), 389–401.
ALPATOV, M. V. *Art Treasures of Russia*. London: Thames and Hudson, 1969.
ANDERSON, M. S. *Britain's Discovery of Russia*. London: Macmillan, 1958.
ANDREYEV, N. "Filofey and his Epistle to Ivan Vasilievich," *SEER*, 38 (1959–60), 1–31.
_____. "Interpolations in the Sixteenth Century Muscovite Chronicles," *SEER*, 35 (1956–57), 95–115.
_____. "Kurbsky's Letters to Vas'yan Muromtsev," *SEER*, 33 (1954–55), 414–36.

_____. "The Pskov-Pechery Monastery in the Sixteenth Century," *SEER*, 32 (1953–54), 318–43.

_____. *Studies in Muscovy. Western Influences and Byzantine Inheritance.* London: Variorum Reprints, 1970.

BACKER, G. *The Deadly Parallel: Stalin and Ivan the Terrible.* New York: Random House, 1950.

BACKUS, O. P. "A. M. Kurbsky in the Polish-Lithuanian State (1564–1583)," *AB-S*, 6 (1969), 29–50.

_____. "Muscovite History in Recent Soviet Publications," *SR*, 20 (1961), 517–22.

_____. "The Problem of Feudalism in Lithuania, 1506–1548," *SR*, 21 (1962), 639–59.

BADDELEY, J. F. *Russia, Mongolia, China*, Vol. 1. London: Macmillan, 1919.

BAIN, R. N. *Slavonic Europe: A Political History of Poland and Russia from 1447 to 1796.* Cambridge: Cambridge University Press, 1908.

BAKER, J. N. L. *A History of Geographical Discovery and Exploration.* London: Harrap, 1937.

BAKHRUSHIN, S. V. " 'Izbrannaia rada' Ivan Groznogo," *IZ*, 15 (1945), 29–56.

BARBARO, JOSAFA, and CONTARINI, AMBROGIO. *Travels to Tana and Persia.* Trans. W. Thomas. New York: Burt Franklin, reprint of Hakluyt Society, 1873.

BARING, M. *The Russian People.* London: Metheuen, 1911.

BARON, S. H. "A Guide to Published and Unpublished Documents on Anglo-Russian Relations in the Sixteenth Century in British Archives," *C-ASS*, 11 (1977), 354–87.

_____. "Ivan the Terrible, Giles Fletcher and the Muscovite Merchantry: A Reconsideration," *SEER*, 56 (1978), 563–85.

_____. (Ed. and trans.) *The Travels of Olearius in Seventeenth Century Russia.* Stanford: Stanford University Press, 1967.

_____, and SHEER, N. W. (Eds.) *Windows on the Russian Past.* Columbus, OH: American Association for the Advancement of Slavic Studies, 1977.

BARON, S. W. *The Russian Jew under Tsars and Soviets.* New York: Macmillan, 1976.

BAYNES, N., and MOSS, H. ST. L. B. (Eds.) *Byzantium.* Oxford: Clarendon Press, 1948.

BERRY, L. E. (Ed.) *The English Works of Giles Fletcher the Elder.* Madison: University of Wisconsin Press, 1964.

_____, and CRUMMEY, R. O. (Eds.) *Rude & Barbarous Kingdom. Russia in the Accounts of Sixteenth Century English Voyagers.* Madison: University of Wisconsin Press, 1968.

BEUCLER, A. *La Vie de Ivan le Terrible.* Paris: Gallimard, 1931.

BILLINGTON, J. H. *The Icon and the Axe.* New York: Alfred A. Knopf, 1966.

BLUM, J. *Lord and Peasant in Russia from the 9th to the 19th Century.* Princeton: Princeton University Press, 1961.

BOND, E. A. (Ed.) *Russia at the Close of the Sixteenth Century.* London: Hakluyt Society, 1856.

BUSHKOVITCH, P. "Taxation, Tax Farming, and Merchants in Sixteenth Century Russia," *SR*, 37 (1978), 381–98.

Calendar of State Papers, Foreign, 1547–1589. London: His Majesty's Stationery Office, 1861–1950.

Cambridge History of Poland, Vol. 1. Cambridge: Cambridge University Press, 1950.

CHADWICK, N. K. *Russian Heroic Poetry.* Cambridge: Cambridge University Press, 1932.

CHERNIAVSKY, M. "Holy Russia: A Study in the History of an Idea," *AHR,* 63 (1958), 617–37.

———. "Ivan the Terrible and the Iconography of the Kremlin Cathedral of Archangel Michael," *RH,* 2 (1974), 3–28.

———. "Ivan the Terrible as Renaissance Prince," *SR,* 27 (1968), 195–211.

———. "Khan or Basileus: An Aspect of Russian Medieval Political Theory," *JHI,* 20 (1959), 459–76.

———. "The Reception of the Council of Florence in Moscow," *CH,* 24 (1956), 347–60.

———. *Tsar and People.* New Haven: Yale University Press, 1961.

CHEW, A. F. *An Atlas of Russian History: Eleven Centuries of Changing Borders.* New Haven: Yale University Press, 1967.

CHRISTIANSEN, E. *The Northern Crusades.* London: Macmillan, 1980.

CHYZHEVSKYI, D. *History of Russian Literature from the Eleventh Century to the End of the Baroque.* 's-Gravenhage: Mouton, 1960.

CONTAMINE, P. *War in the Middle Ages.* (Trans. M. Jones.) New York: Basil Blackwell, 1984.

CROSS, A. (Ed.) *Russia Under Western Eyes, 1517–1825.* New York: St. Martin's Press, 1971.

CROSS, S. H. (Ed. and trans.) *The Russian Primary Chronicle.* Cambridge: Harvard University Press, 1930.

CROSKEY, R. M. "Hakluyt's Accounts of Sir Jerome Bowes' Embassy to Ivan IV," *SEER,* 61 (1983), 546–64.

CULPEPPER, J. M. "The Kremlin Executions of 1575 and the Enthronement of Simeon Bekbulatovich," *SR,* 24 (1965), 503–06.

DAVIES, N. *God's Playground. A History of Poland,* Vol. 1. New York: Columbia University Press, 1982.

DEWEY, H. W. "Charters of Local Government Under Tsar Ivan IV," *JGOE,* 14 (1966), 10–20.

———. "The Decline of the Muscovite *Namestnik,*" *OSP,* 12 (1965), 21–39.

———. "The 1497 *Sudebnik:* Muscovite Russia's First National Law Code," *ASEER,* 15 (1956), 325–28.

———. "The 1550 *Sudebnik* as an Instrument of Reform," *JGOE,* 10 (1962), 161–80.

———. "Historical Drama in Muscovite Justice: The Case of the Extorted Deed," *CSP,* 2 (1957), 38–46.

———. (Ed. and trans.) *Muscovite Judicial Texts, 1488–1556.* Ann Arbor: *Michigan Slavic Materials,* No. 7, 1966.

———. "Muscovite Princes and Monasterial Privileges," *SEER,* 49 (1971), 453–57.

———. "Old Muscovite Concepts of Injured Honor (*Beschestie*), *SR,* 27 (1968), 594–603.

———. "Tales of Moscow's Founding," *C-ASS,* 6 (1972), 595–605.

————, and KLEIMOLA, A. M. "Coercion by Righter (*Pravezh*) in Old Russian Administration," *C-ASS*, 9 (1975), 156–67.

————, and STEVENS, K. B. "Muscovites at Play: Recreation in Pre-Petrine Russia," *C-ASS*, 13 (1979), 189–203.

Dictionary of National Biography. London: Oxford University Press, 1967.

DMYTRYSHYN, B. (Ed.) *Medieval Russia: A Source Book, 900–1700*. New York: Holt, Rinehart and Winston, 1967.

DONNELLY, A. S. *The Russian Conquest of Bashkiria, 1552–1740*. New Haven: Yale University Press, 1968.

DONNERT, E. *Der livländische Ordensritterstaat und Russland*. Berlin: Rütten & Loening, 1963.

————. *Russland an der Schwelle der Neuzeit*. Berlin: Akademie-Verlag, 1972.

DUBNOW, S. M. *History of the Jews in Russia and Poland*, Vol. 1. Philadelphia: The Jewish Publication Society, 1916.

DVORNIK, F. *Byzantine Missions Among the Slavs*. New Brunswick, NJ: Rutgers University Press, 1970.

————. "Byzantine Political Ideas in Kievan Russia," *DOP*, 9–10 (1956), 73–121.

EATON, H. L. "Cadasters and Censuses in Muscovy," *SR*, 26 (1967), 54–69.

————. "Decline and Recovery of the Russian Cities from 1500 to 1700," *C-ASS*, 11 (1977), 220–52.

ECK, A. *Le Moyen âge russe*. Paris: Maison du livre étranger, 1933.

ECKARDT, H. v. *Ivan the Terrible*. (Trans. C. A. Phillips.) New York: Alfred A. Knopf, 1949.

EISENSTEIN, S. *Ivan the Terrible. A Film Script*. New York: Simon and Schuster, 1970.

————. *Notes of a Film Director*. New York: Dover, 1970.

FEDOTOV, G. P. *The Russian Religious Mind*. 2 vols. Cambridge: Harvard University Press, 1966.

————. *St. Filipp, Metropolitan of Moscow*. Belmont, MA: Nordland Publishing Co., 1978.

————. *A Treasury of Russian Spirituality*. New York: Sheed & Ward, 1948.

FENNELL, J. L. I. (Ed. and trans.) *The Correspondence between Prince A. M. Kurbsky and Tsar Ivan IV of Russia 1564–1579*. Cambridge: Cambridge University Press, 1955.

————. *The Emergence of Moscow 1304–1359*. London: Secker & Warburg, 1968.

————. *Ivan the Great of Moscow*. London: Macmillan, 1961.

————. *Prince A. M. Kurbsky's History of Ivan IV*. Cambridge: Cambridge University Press, 1965.

————, and STOKES, A. *Early Russian Literature*. Berkeley: University of California Press, 1974.

FILIPOWSKI, J. (Ed.) *Etienne Batory*. Cracow: Académie Polonaise des Sciences et des Lettres, 1935.

FISHER, A. *The Crimean Tartars*. Stanford, CA: Hoover Institution Press, 1978.

FISHER, A. W. "Muscovy and the Black Sea Trade," *C-ASS*, 6 (1972), 575–94.

FISHER, R. H. *The Russian Fur Trade 1550–1700*. Berkeley: University of California Press, 1943.

FLETCHER, GILES. *Israel Redux*. London, 1667.

———. *Of the Russe Common Wealth.* In *Russia at the Close of the Sixteenth Century.* (Ed. E. A. Bond.) London: Hakluyt Society, 1856.

FLORINSKY, M. T. *Russia: A History and Interpretation,* Vol. 1. New York: Macmillan, 1955.

FLOROVSKY, G. *Ways of Russian Theology.* Belmont, MA: Nordland Publishing Co., 1979.

FRENCH, P. J. *John Dee: The World of an Elizabethan Magus.* London: Routledge & Kegan Paul, 1972.

GERASIMOV, M. M. *The Face Finder.* (Trans. A. Broderick.) London: Hutchinson, 1971.

GRABAR, A. "God and the 'Family of Princes' Presided Over by the Byzantine Emperor," *HSS,* 2 (1954), 117–23.

GRAHAM, H. F. (Ed. and trans.) *"A Brief Account of the Character and Brutal Rule of Vasil'evich, Tyrant of Muscovy* (Albert Schlichting on Ivan Groznyi)," *C-ASS,* 9 (1975), 204–72.

———. (Ed. and trans.) "The *Missio Moscovitica,*" *C-ASS,* 6 (1972), 437–77.

———. (Ed. and trans.) *The Moscovia of Antonio Possevino, S.J.* Pittsburgh: Pittsburgh University Center for International Studies, 1977.

GRAHAM, S. *Ivan the Terrible.* London: Ernest Benn, 1933.

GREY, I. *Boris Godunov.* New York: Charles Scribner's Sons, 1973.

———. *Ivan the Terrible.* London: Hodder and Stoughton, 1964.

———. *Ivan III and the Unification of Russia.* London: English Universities Press, 1964.

GROBOVSKY, A. N. *The "Chosen Council" of Ivan IV: A Reinterpretation.* New York: Theo. Gaus's Sons, 1969.

GUDZY, N. K. *History of Early Russian Literature.* New York: Macmillan, 1949.

GUTERMAN, N. (Trans.) *Russian Fairy Tales.* New York: Pantheon, 1945.

HAKLUYT, R. *The Principal Navigations Voyages Traffiques & Discoveries of the English Nation,* 1589. 12 vols. New York: Augustus M. Kelley reprint, 1969.

HALE, J. R. *Renaissance Exploration.* New York: W. W. Norton, 1968.

HALECKI, O. *A History of Poland.* New York: David McKay, 1981.

———. "Possevino's Last Statement on Polish-Russian Relations," *OCP,* 19 (1953), 261–302.

HALPERIN, C. J. "The Epistle of Patriarch Antonius I to Grand Prince Vasilii I: A New Reading," *C-ASS,* 11 (1977), 539–50.

———. "Judaizers and the Image of the Jew in Medieval Russia: A Polemic Revisited and a Question Posed," *C-ASS,* 9 (1975), 141–55.

HAMEL, J. V. *England and Russia.* (Trans. J. S. Leigh.) New York: Da Capo Press, 1968.

HANEY, J. V. *From Italy to Muscovy. The Life and Works of Maxim the Greek.* Munich: Wilhelm Fink, 1973.

HELLIE, R. *Enserfment and Military Change in Muscovy.* Chicago: University of Chicago Press, 1972.

HERBERSTEIN, SIGISMUND VON. *Notes upon Russia.* 2 vols. (Ed. and trans. R. H. Major.) London: Hakluyt Society, 1851–52.

HINGLEY, R. *The Tsars.* London: Weidenfeld and Nicolson, 1968.

Historica Russiae Monumenta, Vol. 1. (Ed. A. I. Turgenev.) St. Petersburg, 1841. *Supplementum,* 1848.

HORSEY, JEROME. *The Travels of Jerome Horsey*. In *Russia at the Close of the Sixteenth Century*. (Ed. E. A. Bond.) London: Hakluyt Society, 1856.

HOWES, R. C. (Ed. and trans.) *The Testaments of the Grand Princes of Moscow*. Ithaca: Cornell University Press, 1967.

HOWORTH, H. H. *History of the Mongols from the Ninth to the Nineteenth Century*, Part 2. London: Longmans and Green, 1880.

HULBERT, E. "The Zemsky Sobor of 1575: A Mistake in Translation," *SR*, 25 (1966), 320–22.

HUTTENBACH, H. R. "Anthony Jenkinson's 1566 and 1577 Missions to Muscovy Reconstructed from Unpublished Sources," *C-ASS*, 9 (1975), 179–203.

_____. "New Archival Material on the Anglo-Russian Treaty of Queen Elizabeth and Tsar Ivan IV," *SEER*, 49 (1971), 535–49.

_____. "The Search for and Discovery of New Archival Materials for Ambassador Jenkinson's Mission to Muscovy in 1571–72. Four Letters by Queen Elizabeth to Tsar Ivan IV." *C-ASS*, 6 (1972), 416–36.

IVAN IV, TSAR. *Poslaniya Ivana Groznogo* (*Epistles of Ivan the Terrible*). (Eds. D. S. Likhachev, Ia. S. Lur'e, and V. P. Adrianova-Peretts.) Moscow-Leningrad: Akademii nauk SSSR, 1951.

JENKINSON, ANTHONY, and others. *Early Voyages and Travels to Russia and Persia*. 2 vols. London: Hakluyt Society, 1886.

KALMYKOW, A. "A Sixteenth Century Russian Envoy to France," *SR*, 23 (1964), 701–05.

KANTOROWICZ, E. H. *The King's Two Bodies. A Study in Medieval Political Theology*. Princeton: Princeton University Press, 1957.

KAPPELER, A. *Ivan Groznyi im Spiegel der ausländischen Druckschriften seiner Zeit*. Frankfurt: Peter Lang, 1972.

KARAMZIN, N. M. *A Memoir on Ancient & Modern Russia*. (Trans. R. Pipes.) Cambridge: Cambridge University Press, 1959.

_____. *Histoire de l'Empire de Russie*. 11 vols. (Trans. St. Thomas & Jauffret.) Paris, 1820–26.

KARGER, M. *Novgorod the Great*. Moscow: Progress Publishers, 1973.

KARLINSKY, S. "Domostroi as Literature," *SR*, 24 (1965), 497–502.

KASHTANOV, S. M. "The Centralised State and Feudal Immunities in Russia," *SEER*, 49 (1971), 235–54.

KEEN, M. *Chivalry*. New Haven: Yale University Press, 1984.

KEENAN, E. L. *The Kurbskii-Groznyi Apocrypha*. Cambridge: Harvard University Press, 1971.

_____. "Muscovy and Kazan: Some Introductory Remarks on the Patterns of Steppe Diplomacy," *SR*, 26 (1967), 548–58.

_____. "Vita: Ivan Vasil'evich, Terrible Tsar, 1530–1584," *Harvard Magazine*, Jan.-Feb. 1978, 4.

KEEP, J. "Bandits and the Law in Muscovy," *SEER*, 35 (1956–57), 201–22.

KELLY, L. (Ed.) *Moscow*. New York: Atheneum, 1984.

KERNER, R. J. *The Urge to the Sea: The Course of Russian History*. Berkeley: University of California Press, 1942.

KINROSS, LORD. *The Ottoman Centuries*. New York: Morrow Quill, 1979.

KIRCHNER, W. *The Commercial Relations Between Russia and Europe, 1400–1800*. Bloomington: Indiana University Press, 1966.

_____. *The Rise of the Baltic Question.* Westport, CT: Greenwood Press, 1970.

_____. "The Russo-Livonian Crisis, 1555: Extracts from Joachim Burwitz' Report of February 19," *JMH,* 19 (1947), 142–51.

KLEIMOLA, A. M. "The Duty to Denounce in Muscovite Russia," *SR,* 31 (1972), 759–79.

KLYUCHEVSKY, V. O. *A History of Russia.* 5 vols. (Trans. C. J. Hogarth.) New York: E. P. Dutton, 1911–31.

KONDAKOV, N. P. *The Russian Icon.* (Trans. E. H. Minns.) Oxford: Clarendon Press, 1927.

KONOVALOV, S. "Two Documents Concerning Anglo-Russian Relations in the Early Seventeenth Century," *OSP,* 2 (1951), 128–41.

KONRAD, A. N. *Old Russia and Byzantium.* Wien: Wilhelm Bräumüller, 1972.

KOSLOW, J. *Ivan the Terrible.* New York: Hill and Wang, 1961.

KRAUSSE, A. S. *Russia in Asia, 1558–1899.* New York: Holt, Rinehart and Winston, 1899.

KRISTOF, L. K. D. "The Rumanian Ivan the Terrible and Some Problems of Communist Historiography," *SR,* 20 (1961), 685–94.

KURAT, A. N. "The Turkish Expedition to Astrakhan in 1569 and the Problem of the Don-Volga Canal," *SEER,* 40 (1961–62), 7–23.

KURBSKY, A. M. *Skazaniia Kniazia Kurbskogo (Stories of Prince Kurbsky).* (Ed. N. G. Ustryalov.) St. Petersburg: Imperatorskaia akademiia nauk, 1868.

LANTZEFF, G. V. and PIERCE, R. A. *Eastward to Empire.* Montreal: McGill-Queens University Press, 1973.

LERMONTOV, M. Y. "A Song About Tsar Ivan Vasil'yevitch." In *A Lermontov Reader.* (Trans. G. Daniels.) New York: Macmillan, 1956.

LEROY-BEAULIEU, A. *Empire of the Tsars and the Russians.* 3 vols. New York: G. P. Putnam, 1902–3.

LIUBIMENKO, I. *Istoriia torgovykh snoshenii Rossii s Angliei (History of the Commercial Relations Between the Russians and the English).* Iur'ev: K. Mattisen, 1912.

_____. *Les Relations Commerciales et Politiques de L'Angleterre avec la Russie avant Pierre le Grand.* Paris: Honoré Champion, 1933.

LOEWE, K. v. "Juridical Manifestations of Serfdom in West Russia," *C-ASS,* 6 (1972), 390–99.

LONGWORTH, P. *The Cossacks.* New York: Holt, Rinehart and Winston, 1970.

LUR'E, IA. S. "Problems of Source Criticism with Reference to Medieval Russian Documents," *SR,* 27 (1968), 1–22.

LYASHCHENKO, P. I. *A History of the National Economy of Russia to the 1917 Revolution.* New York: Macmillan, 1949.

MANGO, C. *Byzantium.* New York: Charles Scribner's Sons, 1980.

MASSIE, R. K. *Peter the Great.* New York: Alfred A. Knopf, 1980.

MARGERET, JACQUES. *Estat de L'Empire de Russie et Grand Duché de Moscovie,* 1606. Paris: Editions du Genet, 1946.

MAVOR, J. *An Economic History of Russia,* Vol. 1. New York: E. P. Dutton, 1914.

MEDLIN, W. K. *Moscow and East Rome: A Political Study of Relations of Church and State in Muscovite Russia.* Geneva: Librairie E. Droz, 1952.

_____, and PATRINELIS, C. G. *Renaissance Influences and Religious Reforms in Russia: Western and Post-Byzantine Impacts on Culture and Education (16th–17th Centuries).* Geneva: Librairie E. Droz, 1971.

MEYENDORFF, J. *Byzantium and the Rise of Russia.* Cambridge: Cambridge University Press, 1981.

MICHELL, R., and FORBES, N. (Trans.) *The Chronicle of Novgorod, 1016–1471.* Hattiesburg, MS: Academic International Press, 1970.

MILIUKOV, P. *Outlines of Russian Culture.* 3 vols. Philadelphia: University of Pennsylvania Press, 1948.

MILLER, D. B. "The Coronation of Ivan IV of Moscow," *JGOE*, 15 (1967), 559–74.

――――. "Legends of the Icon of Our Lady of Vladimir: A Study of the Development of Muscovite National Consciousness," *Speculum*, 43 (1968), 657–70.

――――. "The Literary Activities of Metropolitan Macarius: A Study of Muscovite Political Ideology in the Time of Ivan IV," unpublished doctoral dissertation, Columbia University, 1967.

――――. "The Viskovatyi Affair of 1553–54: Official Art, the Emergence of Autocracy, and the Disintegration of Medieval Russian Culture," *RH*, 8 (1981), 293–382.

MILTON, JOHN. *A Brief History of Moscovia,* 1682. In *The Works of John Milton.* (Ed. F. A. Patterson, others.) New York: Columbia University Press, 1937.

MITCHELL, B., and ZGUTA, R. (Eds. and trans.) "The Sixteenth Century 'Account of Muscovy' Attributed to Don Felippo Prenestain," *RH*, 8 (1981), 390–412.

MORFILL, W. R. *Russia.* London: T. Fisher Unwin, 1890.

MORGAN, E. D., and COOTE, C. H. (Eds.) *Early Voyages and Travels in Russia and Persia.* London: Hakluyt Society, 1886.

MORLEY, C. *Guide to Research in Russian History.* Syracuse: Syracuse University Press, 1951.

MOUSSINAE, L. *Sergey Eisenstein: An Investigation Into His Films and Philosophy.* (Trans. D. S. Petrey.) New York: Crown, 1970.

NICOL, D. M. *Church and Society in the Last Centuries of Byzantium.* Cambridge: Cambridge University Press, 1979.

NICOLINI, G. B. *The History of the Jesuits.* London: Henry G. Bohn, 1854.

NORRETRANDERS, BJARNE. *The Shaping of Czardom under Ivan Groznyj.* Copenhagen: Munksgaard, 1964.

OBOLENSKY, D. *The Byzantine Commonwealth.* New York: Praeger, 1971.

――――. *Byzantium and the Slavs.* London: Variorum Reprints, 1971.

ODERBORN, PAUL. *Ioannis Basilidis Magni Moscoviae Ducis vita.* Wittenberg, 1585.

ORCHARD, G. E. "Counterblast to Keenan?," *CSP*, 16 (1974), 448–59.

OSTROGORSKY, G. *History of the Byzantine State.* (Trans. J. Hussey.) Oxford: Blackwell, 1956.

――――. "The Byzantine Emperor and the Hierarchical World Order," *SEER*, 35 (1956–57), 1–14.

PARES, B. *A History of Russia.* New York: Vintage, 1965.

PARKER, W. H. *An Historical Geography of Russia.* London: University of London Press, 1968.

PARRY, J. H. *The Age of Reconnaissance.* London: Weidenfeld and Nicolson, 1963.

PARSONS, S. L. "The Enserfment of the Russian Peasantry: A Reexamination," *C-ASS*, 6 (1972), 478–89.

Payne, R., and ROMANOFF, N. *Ivan the Terrible.* New York: Thomas Y. Crowell, 1975.

PELENSKI, J. "Muscovite Imperial Claims to the Kazan Khanate," *SR*, 26 (1967), 559–76.

———. *Russia and Kazan*. The Hague: Mouton & Co., 1974.

PENROSE, B. *Travel and Discovery in the Renaissance*. Cambridge: Harvard University Press, 1952.

PERRIE, M. "The Popular Image of Ivan the Terrible," *SEER*, 56 (1978), 275–86.

PHIPPS, G. M. "Manuscript Collections in British Archives Relating to Pre-Petrine Russia," *C-ASS*, 6 (1972), 400–15.

PIERLING, PAUL (Ed.) *Antonii Possevini missio moscovitica*. Paris: Ernest Leroux, 1882.

———. (Ed.) *Bathory et Possevino*. Paris: Ernest Leroux, 1887.

———. *Rome et Moscou, 1547–1579*. Paris: Ernest Leroux, 1883.

———. *La Russie et le Saint-Siège*. Paris: Librairie Plon, 1897.

PIPES, R. (Ed.) *Of the Russ Commonwealth. Giles Fletcher*. Cambridge, MA: Harvard University Press, 1966.

PLATONOV, S. F. *Boris Godunov*. (Trans. L. R. Pyles.) Gulf Breeze, FL: Academic International Press, 1973.

———. *Ivan the Terrible*. Gulf Breeze, FL: Academic International Press, 1974.

———. "Ivan the Terrible in Russian Historiography," in *Readings in Russian History*, Vol. 1. (ed. S. Harcave.) New York: Thomas Y. Crowell, 1962.

———. *Moscow and the West*. Gulf Breeze, FL: Academic International Press, 1972.

POKROVSKY, M. N. *History of Russia from the Earliest Times to the Rise of Commercial Capitalism*. New York: International Publishers, 1931.

POLČIN, S. "Une tentative d'Union au XVIᵉ siècle: La Mission Religieuse du Père Antoine Possevin S.J. en Moscovie (1581–1582)," *Orientalia Christiana Analecta*, 150 (1957).

Polnoe sobranie russkikh letopisei (The Full Collection of Russian Chronicles). 26 vols. St. Petersburg: Akademii nauk, 1841–1959.

PRAWDIN, M. *The Mongol Empire: Its Rise and Legacy*. London: Allen and Unwin, 1940.

PRITSAK, O. "Moscow, the Golden Horde, and the Kazan Khanate from a Polycultural Point of View," *SR*, 26 (1967), 577–83.

PUSHKAREV, S. G. *A Source Book for Russian History from Early Times to 1917*, Vol. 1. New Haven: Yale University Press, 1972.

RAEFF, M. "An Early Theorist of Absolutism: Joseph of Volokolamsk," *ASEER*, 8 (1949), 79–89.

RALSTON, W. R. S. *The Songs of the Russian People*. London: Ellis, 1872.

READ, C. *Mr. Secretary Walsingham and the Policy of Queen Elizabeth*. 3 vols. Oxford: Clarendon Press, 1925.

RIAZANOVSKY, N. V. *A History of Russia*. New York: Oxford University Press, 1963.

RICE, D. T. *Russian Icons*. London: Penguin, 1947.

RICE, T. T. *A Concise History of Russian Art*. New York: Praeger, 1963.

RIHA, T. (Ed.) *Readings in Russian Civilization*, Vol. 1. Chicago: University of Chicago Press, 1969.

ROBERTS, M. *The Early Vasas. A History of Sweden, 1523–1611*. Cambridge: Cambridge University Press, 1968.

RUNCIMAN, S. "Byzantium, Russia and Caesaropapism," *CSP*, 2 (1957), 1–10.

Russian Primary Chronicle (Ed. and trans. S. H. Cross). Cambridge: Harvard University Press, 1930.

RYAN, W. F. "The Old Russian Version of the Pseudo-Aristotelian *Secreta Secretorum*," *SEER*, 56 (1978), 242–60.

RYWKIN, M. "The Prikaz of the Kazan Court: First Russian Colonial Office," *CSP*, 18 (1976), 293–300.

SAKHAROV, A. M., others. *Ocherki russkoi kul'tury XVI veka* (*Essays on Russian Culture in the 16th Century*). Moscow: Izdatelistvo universiteta, 1977.

Sbornik Imperatorskogo russkogo istoricheskogo obshchestva (*Collection of the Imperial Russian Historical Society*). St. Petersburg, 1882–1892.

SCHMEMANN, A. *The Historical Road of Eastern Orthodoxy*. New York: Holt, Rinehart and Winston, 1963.

SEREGNY, S. J. "The *Nedel'shchik:* Law and Order in Muscovite Russia," *C-ASS*, 9 (1975), 168–78.

ŠEVČENKO, I. "Byzantine Cultural Influences," in *Rewriting Russian History*. (Ed. C. Black.) New York: Praeger, 1956, 143–223.

――――. "Muscovy's Conquest of Kazan: Two Views Reconciled," *SR*, 26 (1967), 541–47.

――――. "A Neglected Byzantine Source of Muscovite Political Ideology," *HSS*, 2 (1954), 141–79.

SIMMONS, E. J. *English Literature and Culture in Russia, 1553–1840*. Cambridge: Harvard University Press, 1935.

SKRYNNIKOV, R. G. *Ivan the Terrible*. (Ed. and trans. H. F. Graham.) Gulf Breeze, FL: Academic International Press, 1981.

――――. "On the Authenticity of the Kurbskii-Groznyi Correspondence: A Summary of the Discussion," *SR*, 37 (1978), 107–15.

――――. "Who Was the Editor of the Sixteenth-Century Illuminated Codex?," *C-ASS*, 13 (1979), 163–65.

SLOCOMBE, G. *A History of Poland*. New York: Thomas Nelson & Sons, 1939.

SMIRNOV, I. I. "The Revolt of Andrei Staritsky, 1537," *IZ*, 50 (1955), 269–96.

SOKOLOV, Y. *Russian Folklore*. (Trans. C. R. Smith.) Hatboro, PA: Folklore Associates, 1966.

SOLOVIEV, A. V. *Holy Russia: The History of a Religious-Social Idea*. The Hague: Mouton, 1959.

SOLOVIEV, S. M. *Istoriia Rossii s drevneishikh vremen* (*The History of Russia from the Earliest Times*). 29 vols. Moscow: Izdatel'stvo sotsial'no-ekonomicheskoi literatury, 1960. See also the in-progress translation under the auspices of Academic International Press, Gulf Breeze, FL, of which the following are now available: Vol. 7, *The Reign of Ivan III* (Ed. and trans. J. D. Windhausen), 1978; Vol. 8, *Russian Society in the Age of Ivan III* (Ed. and trans. J. D. Windhausen), 1979; Vol. 9, *The Age of Vasily III* (Ed. and trans. H. F. Graham), 1976; and Vol. 24, *The Character of Old Russia* (Ed. and trans. A. V. Muller), 1980.

STADEN, HEINRICH VON. *The Land and Government of Muscovy. A 16th Century Account*. (Ed. and trans. T. Esper.) Stanford: Stanford University Press, 1967.

STÄLIN, K. *La Russie. Des Origines à la Naissance de Pierre le Grand*. Paris: Payot, 1946.

STÖKL, G. *Testament und Siegel. Ivans IV*. Opladen: Westdeutscher Verlag, 1972.

STEMOOUKHOFF, D. "Moscow the Third Rome: Sources of the Doctrine," *Speculum*, 28 (1953), 84–101.

SZEFTEL, M. "Joseph Volotsky's Political Ideas in a New Historical Perspective," *JGOE*, 13 (1965), 19–29.

———. "The Title of the Muscovite Monarch up to the End of the Seventeenth Century," *C-ASS*, 13 (1979), 59–81.

TCHARYKOW, N. "Le chevalier Raphael Barberini chez le tsar Jean le Terrible," *Revue d'histoire diplomatique*, 18 (1904), 252–74.

TIKHOMIROV, M. N. *Rossiia v XVI stoletii (Russia in the 16th Century)*. Moscow: Izdatelistvo akademii nauk SSSR, 1962.

TOLSTOI, G. *The First Forty Years of Intercourse Between England and Russia 1553–1593*. St. Petersburg, 1875.

TOUMANOFF, C. "Moscow the Third Rome: Genesis and Significance of a Politico-Religious Idea," *CHR*, 40 (1954–55), 411–47.

TREUER, GOTTLIEB SAMUEL. *Apologia Pro Joanne Basilide II Magno Duce Moscoviae*. Vienna, 1711.

Tsarstviennaia Kniga (Chronicle of the Reign of Ivan IV). St. Petersburg, 1769.

TUMINS, V. A. *Tsar Ivan IV's Reply to Jan Rokyta*. The Hague: Mouton, 1971.

TURGENEV, A. I. (Ed.) *Historica Russiae Monumenta*, Vol. 1. St. Petersburg, 1841. *Supplementum*, 1848.

ULFELDT, JACOB. *Legatio Moscovitica*. Frankfurt, 1608.

VALLOTTON, H. *Ivan le Terrible*. Paris: Artheme Fayard, 1959.

VASILIEV, A. A. *History of the Byzantine Empire*. Madison: University of Wisconsin Press, 1952.

———. "Medieval Ideas of the End of the World: West and East," *Byzantion*, 16 (1942–43), 462–502.

VERNADSKY, G. "The Heresy of the Judaizers and the Policies of Ivan III of Moscow," *Speculum*, 8 (1933), 436–54.

———. *The Mongols and Russia*. New Haven: Yale University Press, 1953.

———. *The Origins of Russia*. Oxford: Clarendon Press, 1959.

———. *Russia at the Dawn of the Modern Age*. New Haven: Yale University Press, 1959.

———. *Russian Historiography. A History*. Belmont, MA: Nordland Publishing Co., 1978.

———. *The Tsardom of Moscow, 1547–1682*. New Haven: Yale University Press, 1969.

VESELOVSKY, S. B. *Issledovaniia po istorii oprichniny (Essays on the History of the Oprichnina)*. Moscow: Izdatelistvo Akademiia nauk SSSR, 1963.

VILJANTI, A. *Gustav Vasas Ryska Krig, 1554–57*. (English summary, 765–78) Stockholm: Almqvist & Wiksell, 1957.

VOYCE, A. *Moscow and the Roots of Russian Culture*. Norman: University of Oklahoma Press, 1964.

———. *The Moscow Kremlin*. Berkeley: University of California Press, 1954.

WALISZEWSKI, K. *Ivan the Terrible*. (Trans. Lady M. Lloyd.) Philadelphia: Lippincott, 1904.

WIECZYNSKI, J. L. "Archbishop Gennadius and the West: The Impact of Catholic Ideas Upon the Church of Novgorod," *C-ASS*, 6 (1972), 374–89.

————. "The Donation of Constantine in Medieval Russia," *CHR*, 55 (1969), 159–172.

————. "Hermetism and Cabalism in the Heresy of the Judaizers," *Renaissance Quarterly*, 28 (1975), 17–28.

WILLAN, T. S. *The Early History of the Russia Company, 1553–1603.* Manchester: Manchester University Press, 1956.

WIPPER, R. *Ivan Grozny.* (Trans. J. Fineberg.) Moscow: Foreign Languages Publishing House, 1947.

WOLFF, R. L. "The Three Romes: The Migration of an Ideology and the Making of an Autocrat," *Daedalus*, 88 (1959), 291–311.

WRETTS-SMITH, M. "The English in Russia during the Second Half of the Sixteenth Century," *Transactions of the Royal Historical Society*, 4th series, 3 (1920), 72–102.

YACOBSON, S. "Early Anglo-Russian Relations (1553–1613)," *SEER*, 13 (1934–35), 597–610.

YANOV, A. *The Origins of Autocracy. Ivan the Terrible in Russian History.* (Trans. S. Dunn.) Berkeley: University of California Press, 1981.

YARESH, L. "Ivan the Terrible and the *Oprichnina*," in *Rewriting Russian History.* (Ed. C. Black.) New York: Praeger, 1956, 224–41.

YARMOLINSKY, A. "Ivan the Terrible contra Martin Luther. A 16th Century Russian Manuscript," *NYPLB*, 44 (1940), 455–60.

ZENKOVSKY, S. A. (Ed. and trans.) *Medieval Russian Epics, Chronicles and Tales.* New York: E. P. Dutton, 1963.

ZERNOV, N. *Moscow the Third Rome.* London: Macmillan, 1938.

————. *The Russians and their Church.* London: Macmillan, 1945.

————. "Vladimir and the Origin of the Russian Church," *SEER*, 28 (1949–50), 123–38 and 425–38.

ZIEGLER, C. *Ivan IV, dit le Terrible. Son Peuple et son temps.* Paris: L'Institut des Sciences Historique, 1957.

ZIMIN, A. A. *Oprichnina Ivan Groznogo (The Oprichnina of Ivan the Terrible).* Moscow: Izdatelistvo sotsial'no-ekonomicheskoi literatury, 1964.

————. *Reformy Ivan Groznogo (The Reforms of Ivan the Terrible).* Moscow: Izdatelistvo sotsial'no-ekonomicheskoi literatury, 1960.

————. "Towards the History of the Military Reforms of the 50s of the 16th Century," *IZ*, 55 (1956), 344–59.

————. "Zemsky Sobor 1566 goda," *IZ*, 71 (1962), 196–235.

Source Notes

For abbreviations used in the notes, and for full titles and other bibliographical information on books, articles, manuscripts, and documents cited, the reader is referred to the Bibliography.

Preface

PAGE 15
"the new Emperor," "the New City": Vasiliev, "Medieval Ideas of the End of the World," p. 501.

PAGE 16
"an enemy to all liberty": Hakluyt, *Principal Navigations*, v. 2, pp. 485–487.

1. The Death of Vasily III

PAGE 26
"We found lying": John of Plano Carpini, in *Mongol Mission*, ed. C. Dawson, p. 29.

"though an empire," "saddle": Quoted in Riasanovsky, *History of Russia*, p. 82.

"our forefather Mosokh": Dewey, "Tales of Moscow's Founding," p. 600.

"he did everything": Ibid., p. 595.

PAGE 27
"in a clean field": Michell and Forbes (tr.), *Chronicle of Novgorod*, p. xxi.

PAGE 29
"In the power": Herberstein, *Notes Upon Russia*, v. 1, pp. 30, 32.

PAGE 30
"the living law": Obolensky, *Byzantium and the Slavs*, p. 100.

"to make the Grand Prince love": Soloviev, *History of Russia*, v. 9, p. 247.

"Who will rule": Ibid., p. 101.

"Sovereign, when a fig tree": Ibid., p. 248.

"Knowing that she was barren": Ibid.

PAGE 31
"How dare you oppose": Ibid., p. 249.

PAGE 32
"the whole country": Waliszewski, *Ivan the Terrible*, p. 116.

"A Tsar is born among you": Quoted in Pelenski, *Russia and Kazan*, p. 219.

PAGE 33
"If you do this evil thing": Quoted in Karamzin, *Histoire de l'Empire de Russie*, v. 7, p. 381n.

"the child had two fathers": Platonov, *Ivan the Terrible*, p. 24.

"Is it serious?": Soloviev, op. cit., v. 9, p. 105.

"a great deal of pus," etc.: Ibid., pp. 105–110.

PAGE 34
"a ceaseless round": Skrynnikov, *Ivan the Terrible*, p. 3.

PAGE 35
"I would cut myself to pieces": Soloviev, op. cit., v. 9, p. 107.

"dozed and dreamed," etc.: Ibid., pp. 108–110.

PAGE 36
"And instead of a stench": Cherniavsky, *Tsar and People*, p. 49.

2. The Realm of Muscovy

PAGE 37
"that emptying themselves": Bond (ed.), *Russia at the Close*, p. 6.

"The sharpenesse of the aire": Ibid., p. 5.

PAGE 38
"so fresh and so sweete": Ibid., p. 6.

"fully as powerful": Voyce, *Moscow Kremlin*, p. 25.

"when dried": Soloviev, *History of Russia*, v. 7, p. 103.

PAGE 39
"a sepulchral chronicle": Voyce, op. cit., p. 39.

PAGE 40
"he knew no rest": Soloviev, op. cit., v. 8, p. 60.

"frozen whole": Barbaro and Contarini, *Travels to Tana and Persia*, p. 162.

PAGE 41
"walled about with bricke": Hakluyt, *Principal Navigations*, v. 2, p. 440.

"cast up": Bond, op. cit., p. 13.

"sulphur in abundance": Ibid.

PAGE 42
"Naught thereof": Klyuchevsky, *History of Russia*, v. 2, p. 199.

PAGE 43
"by right of origin": Ibid., p. 42.

"thousands of baptized": Florinsky, *Russia*, v. 1, p. 312.

PAGE 44
"he set a precedent": Blum, *Lord and Peasant in Russia*, p. 138.

PAGE 47
"buried alive": Voyce, *Moscow and the Roots of Russian Culture*, p. 72.

"First test your heart": Dvornik, "Byzantine Political Ideas in Kievan Russia," p. 113.

PAGE 48
"allure men to their fold": Herberstein, op. cit., v. 1, p. 61.

"and thinke that they are purged": Bond, op. cit., p. 127.

"like a prince of this world": Ibid.

"an annual purification": Fedotov, *Russian Religious Mind*, v. 2, p. 250.

"so strictly, and with such blinde devotion": Bond, op. cit., p. 129.

PAGE 49
"Of friers they have an infinit rabble": Ibid., p. 114.

"When one visits another": Herberstein, op. cit., v. 1, p. 107.

"they would not pray": Graham, H. F. (ed. and tr.), *"Missio Moscovitica,"* p. 475.

"horrible excess," "prostrating and knocking": Bond, op. cit., pp. 127–128.

"When you hear Scripture": Gudzy, *History of Early Russian Literature*, p. 330.

"Yakim stood here": Karger, *Novgorod the Great*, p. 93.

PAGE 50
"starke naked," etc.: Bond, op. cit., p. 177.

"I talked with one": Ibid., p. 116.

PAGE 51
"made disauthentique": Ibid., p. 126.

"dreaded no people more": Halperin, "Judaizers," p. 153.

"killed with a knife": Soloviev, op. cit., v. 7, p. 103.

PAGE 52
"Lord Jesus Christ," "May a dog": Herberstein, op. cit., v. 1, p. 80.

"somewhat grosse": Bond, op. cit., p. 146.

"mightily brawned": From appendix to Herberstein, op. cit., v. 2, p. 251.

"bellies bygge": Hakluyt, op. cit., v. 3, p. 131.

"hose without feet": Ibid., p. 424.

"picked like unto a rike": Hakluyt, op. cit., v. 2, p. 270.

"black as jeat": Ibid., p. 447.

"bad hue of their skinne": Bond, op. cit., p. 147.

"I cannot so well": Hakluyt, op. cit., v. 2, p. 447.

"easily and for a small price": From appendix to Herberstein, op. cit., v. 2, p. 253.

"seldom bydden forth," "abrode some great": Ibid., p. 252.

PAGE 53
when there is love: Hakluyt, op. cit., v. 2, p. 445.

"knocking her head," etc.: Bond, op. cit., p. 132.

"to make himself soft": Chyzhevskyi, *History of Russian Literature*, p. 289.

"neighing like a horse": Soloviev, op. cit., v. 9, p. 176. See also Cherniavsky, "Ivan the Terrible as Renaissance Prince," p. 197.

PAGE 53
"not only with boys": Kelly (ed.), *Moscow*, p. 257.

PAGE 54
"this people live": Bond, op. cit., p. 164.

"the whole countrie": Ibid., p. 151.

"Drinke is the joy": Cross (ed.), *Russian Primary Chronicle*, p. 184.

"dranke away their children": Hakluyt, op. cit., v. 2, p. 423.

"to drinke drunke": Bond, op. cit., p. 146.

"Blessed are those": Quoted in Fedotov, op. cit., v. 2, p. 250.

"to which their diet": W. H. Graham (ed. and tr.), *"Missio Moscovitica,"* p. 470.

"grosse meates": Hakluyt, op. cit., v. 2, p. 423.

PAGE 55
"you shal see them": Bond, op. cit., p. 147.

"Formal written authorizations": Dewey, "Muscovites at Play," p. 197.

"that the people": Bond, op. cit., p. 56.

"establish his identity": Ibid., p. 197.

PAGE 56
"a personal stake": Kleimola, "Duty to Denounce," p. 769.

"boyars kept busy": Ibid., p. 770.

"What I heard, Sire": Quoted in Kleimola, op. cit., p. 759. See also Soloviev, op. cit., v. 9, p. 100.

PAGE 57
"that all the light": Hakluyt, op. cit., v. 2, 434.

"take them up": Ibid., p. 435.

"for love, and in token": Ibid., p. 436.

"A dancing woman": Quoted in Fedotov, op. cit., v. 1, p. 105.

PAGE 58
"games and masquerades," "when the

moon": Haney, "On the 'Tale of Peter and Fevroniia,' " p. 159.

"by tying and untying": From appendix to Herberstein, op. cit., v. 2, p. 225.

"eate one another": Anderson, *Britain's Discovery of Russia*, p. 16.

"if any merchants" Morgan and Coote (eds.), *Early Voyage and Travels*, v. 1, p. 106.

"With you I wish": Chadwick, *Russian Heroic Poetry*, p. 10.

3. Interregnum

PAGE 59
"in an attempt to remove": Payne and Romanoff, *Ivan the Terrible*, p. 32.

"like Olga": Soloviev, *History of Russia*, v. 9, p. 177.

PAGE 62
"Our ruler will never accept": Ibid., p. 193.

"no one came out": Fedotov, *St. Filipp*, p. 39.

PAGE 63
"in memory of the deceased": Soloviev, op. cit., v. 9, p. 183.

"a mere spot": Ibid., p. 184.

"The grand prince is a boy": Fedotov, op. cit., p. 38.

PAGE 64
"it was impossible": Ibid., p. 185.

"behind the palace": Platonov, *Ivan the Terrible*, p. 27.

PAGE 65
"The hostility was based": Ibid., p. 28.

"arbitrarily attached themselves": Skrynnikov, *Ivan the Terrible*, p. 9.

PAGE 66
"The present ruler": Soloviev, op. cit., v. 9, p. 241.

"refrain from acts": Ibid., p. 239.

You are to establish: Ibid., p. 240.

PAGE 67
"acting in the name of": Vernadsky, *Tsardom of Moscow*, p. 22.

"blood flowed," "The infidels": Quoted in Grey, *Ivan the Terrible*, p. 46.

"You told me the Russians": Soloviev, op. cit., v. 9, p. 232.

PAGE 68
"We shall take it": Ibid., p. 233.

PAGE 69
"Christ-like tranquillity": Miller, "Literary Activities of Macarius," p. 41.

"retrieve the reigns," "shape the official": Ibid.

PAGE 70
"monks lived a communal life": Soloviev, op. cit., v. 9., p. 156.

"Sire, thou art appointed": Quoted in Miller, op. cit., p. 103.

thrown to the dogs: Dewey, "Decline of Muscovite *Namestnik*," p. 39.

4. The Education of a Tsar

PAGE 71
"leaning with his elbows": Fennell (ed. and tr.), *Correspondence Between Kurbsky and Ivan*, p. 75.

PAGE 72
"all my subjects": Ibid., p. 77.

"he played the leading role": Vernadsky, *Tsardom of Moscow*, p. 23.

"like a beggar": Soloviev, *History of Russia*, v. 9, p. 213.

"was my will": Fennell, op. cit., p. 75.

PAGE 73
"to observe their pain": Vernadsky, op. cit., p. 24.

"from this moment on": Skrynnikov, *Ivan the Terrible*, p. 13.

PAGE 74
"taller than any man": Eisenstein, *Notes of a Film Director*, p. 86.

"with the halo": Platonov, *Ivan the Terrible*, p. 33.

"all the books": Ibid.

PAGE 75
"to catalogue, exhibit and define": Miller, "Literary Activities of Macarius," p. 173.

"to impart an authentic aura": Graham, H. F. (ed. and tr.), *"Missio Moscovitica,"* p. 445.

"The favor of God": Cross (ed.), *The Russian Primary Chronicle*, p. 54.

PAGE 76
Our ruler of the present: Baynes and Moss (eds.), *Byzantium*, p. 385.

"once prized": See Howes, *Testaments of the Grand Princes*, pp. 101–102.

PAGE 77
"There are two great blessings": Schmemann, *Historical Road of Eastern Orthodoxy*, p. 151. See also Vernadsky, op. cit., p. 18.

"an exceptional shrewdness": Klyuchevsky, *History of Russia*, v. 2, p. 97.

"rhetorician of lettered cunning": Ibid.

"one of the finest orators": Ibid., p. 93.

5. Tsar Ivan IV

PAGE 79
"a king that giveth not": Hakluyt, *Principal Navigations*, v. 2, p. 438.

"the sovereign offended us": Vernadsky, *Tsardom of Moscow*, p. 31.

"with our ancient titles": Miller, "Coronation of Ivan IV," p. 561.

"chosen by God": Ibid., p. 563.

"It befits thee": Ibid., p. 568.

PAGE 80
"Though an Emperor in body": Ševčenko, "Neglected Byzantine Source," p. 147.

"general for both": Szeftel, "Title of Muscovite Monarch," p. 71.

6. The Glinskys

PAGE 81
"In their double dealing": Pokrovsky, *History of Russia*, p. 121.

"without any lime": Bond (ed.) *Russia at the Close*, p. 19.

"resist and expell": Hakluyt, *Principal Navigations*, v. 2, p. 269.

"once fired burneth": Bond, op. cit., p. 19.

PAGE 82
"And every flower garden": Platonov, *Ivan the Terrible*, p. 38.

PAGE 83
"the old witch Anna," "like magpies": Skrynnikov, *Ivan the Terrible*, p. 20.

7. The Chosen Council

PAGE 84
"company of honestly-disposed": Andreyev,

"Kurbsky's Letters to Vas'yan Muromtsev," p. 422.

"what was best": Kurbsky quoted, ibid., p. 421.

"felt such affection": Kurbsky quoted, ibid., p. 422.

"to follow wise councilors": Miller, "Coronation of Ivan IV," p. 568.

PAGE 85
"there came to him a man": Fennell (ed. and tr.), *Kurbsky's History of Ivan IV*, p. 17.

"all-powerful. Everybody obeyed": Quoted in Andreyev, "Interpolations," p. 108.

"scaring me with bogies": Fennell (ed. and tr.), *Correspondence Between Kurbsky and Ivan*, p. 141.

PAGE 86
"I was not so afraid": Fennell and Stokes, *Early Russian Literature*, p. 165.

"Punish your son": Karlinsky, "Domostroi as Literature," p. 502. See also Medlin and Patrinelis, *Renaissance Influences*, p. 28.

Beatings should not: Chyzhevskyi, *History of Russian Literature*, p. 386.

PAGE 87
"like unto the angels": See Fennell, *Kurbsky's History of Ivan IV*, p. 179.

"many a time": Ibid.

"a gathering of Ivan's friends": Platonov, *Ivan the Terrible*, p. 42.

"accustomed to guardianship": Ibid.

8. The First Wave of Reforms

PAGE 89
"Maintain a warrior": Pokrovsky, *History of Russia*, p. 125.

"When an emperor is mild": Gudzy, *History of Early Russian Literature*, p. 333.

PAGE 90
"Do not fear things": Ryan, "Old Russian Version," p. 251.

"Let the litigants": Dewey, "1550 *Sudebnik*," p. 175.

"not to set his heart": Platonov, *Ivan the Terrible*, p. 47.

"I cannot now redress": Soloviev, *History of Russia*, v. 9, p. 223.

PAGE 91
"Aleksey, I have raised you": Ibid., p. 224.

"In every chancellory": Staden, *Land and Government of Muscovy*, p. 14.

"not according to geneological rank": Soloviev, op. cit., v. 8, note on p. 153.

PAGE 92
"the sum at issue": Dewey, op. cit., p. 162.

"being pushed off a bridge": Ibid., p. 167.

PAGE 93
"whatever compensation": Ibid.

PAGE 94
"if a man," "a fixed scale": Blum, *Lord and Peasant in Russia*, p. 190.

"Many an impoverished landowner": Fennell and Stokes, *Early Russian Literature*, p. 143.

PAGE 95
"a suitable donation," "impecunious aspirants": Florinsky, *Russia*, p. 133.

"To speak of the life of": Bond (ed.), *Russia at the Close*, p. 117.

"so pinched with famine": Bond, op. cit., p. 151.

"There is no people": Hakluyt, *Principal Navigations*, v. 2, p. 448.

"the wealth of the Church": Blum, op. cit., p. 135.

PAGE 96
"obedience without reasoning": Soloviev, op. cit., v. 8, p. 114.

"If the monasteries": Florinsky, op. cit., p. 172.

PAGE 97
"Now in homes": Soloviev, op. cit., v. 8, p. 116.

"the shadowy Croation": Wieczynski, "Archbishop Gennadius," p. 380.

PAGE 98
"See how the king of Spain": Soloviev, op. cit., v. 8, p. 115.

"Our people are simple": Quoted in Billington, *The Icon and the Axe*, p. 384.

"Behold the army of Satan!": Soloviev, op. cit., v. 8, p. 116.

"Unrepentant heretics": Chyzhevskyi, *History of Russian Literature*, p. 264.

"struck Simon Magus blind": Ibid.

"Do understand that there is a difference": Ibid., p. 265.

PAGE 99
"of dazzling white": Wieczynski, "Donation of Constantine," p. 167.

"Do not transgress": See Miller, "Literary Activities of Macarius," pp. 75–77.

PAGE 101
"grew up neglected": Soloviev, op. cit., v. 9, p. 221.

"In your deliberations": See Vernadsky, op. cit., p. 45, and Fedotov, St. Filipp, p. 72.

PAGE 102
"worn by the prophets": Quoted in Massie, Peter the Great, p. 235.

"Is it pleasing unto God": Klyuchevsky, History of Russia, v. 2, p. 182.

"thus hath the tsar commanded": Ibid., p. 270.

9. Military Affairs

PAGE 108
"bore cold and hunger" Waliszewski, Ivan the Terrible, p. 162.

nothing els but: Bond (tr. and ed.), Russia at the Close, pp. 78–79.

"horrible noyse": Bond, op. cit., p. 78.

"When the ground": Milton, A Brief History, p. 354, based chiefly on Hakluyt, Principal Navigations, v. 2, pp. 258–259.

"How justly may": Hakluyt, op. cit., v. 2, p. 259.

PAGE 110
The Ishmaelites are capable: Quoted in Pelenski, Russia and Kazan, p. 124.

PAGE 111
"fierce, cruel looks": Bond, op. cit., p. 94.

"very suddaine," "you would think": Ibid.

"preposterously depraved," "gorged themselves": Herberstein, Notes Upon Russia, v. 2, p. 53.

"mare's milk soured": Hakluyt, op. cit., v. 2, p. 464.

"mylke mingled with bloude": Bond, op. cit., p. 92.

"iron nail": Herberstein, op. cit., v. 2, p. 54.

"May you abide": Ibid., p. 56.

"crouched like monkeys": Longworth, The Cossacks, p. 12.

"but once into the target zone": Ibid.

"harvesting the steppes": Ibid., p. 14.

PAGE 112
"If we consider": Klyuchevsky, History of Russia, v. 2, pp. 119, 321.

10. Kazan

PAGE 113
converted this defensive war: Platonov, Ivan the Terrible, p. 64.

PAGE 114
"You know that Kazan": Pelenski, Russia and Kazan, p. 70.

"Kazan is my yurt": Ibid., p. 41.

PAGE 115
"at the same hour": Soloviev, History of Russia, v. 9, p. 234.

PAGE 116
"the fishermen to fish": Pelenski, op. cit., p. 44.

"must not do this": Platonov, op. cit., p. 67.

PAGE 117
"just as in antiquity": Pelenski, op. cit., p. 238.

PAGE 118
"won by the people": Ševčenko, "Muscovy's Conquest of Kazan," p. 546.

PAGE 119
"And Thou shalt be": Quoted in Pelenski, op. cit., p. 256.

"like a swallow": Quoted in Gudzy, History of Early Russian Literature, p. 349.

PAGE 120
"We saw the citadel": Fennell (ed. and tr.), Kurbsky's History of Ivan IV, p. 36.

PAGE 121
"lived on gruel": Chadwick, Russian Heroic Poetry, p. 188.

"operating from both concealed": Platonov, op. cit., p. 70.

PAGE 122
"Better to die," "Then straight away," "And from that hour": Fennell, op. cit., p. 53.

"Your enemies": See Waliszewski, Ivan the Terrible, p. 164.

PAGE 123
"his face changed": Fennell, op. cit., p. 57.

"whether he liked it or not": Ibid., p. 62.

"And the rest of us": Ibid., p. 61.

"swooped swift as famished eagles": Gudzy, op. cit., p. 345.

"No quarter": Vernadsky, *Tsardom of Moscow*, p. 56.

PAGE 124

"clothed as for bright Easter Sunday": Gudzy, op. cit., pp. 350–351.

"the dragon in its lair": Pelenski, op. cit., p. 123.

PAGE 125

"The tsardom has been impoverished": Vernadsky, op. cit., p. 60.

11. The Crisis of 1553

PAGE 126

"the varyable and daingerous": Tolstoi, *First Forty Years*, p. 179.

"he hardly recognized": Andreyev, "Interpolations," p. 107.

PAGE 127

"as with one": Platonov, *Ivan the Terrible*, p. 75.

"Why do you not let": Ibid., p. 108.

"We are ready": Ibid., p. 110. Also, Vernadsky, op. cit., p. 62.

"there was great trouble": Platonov, op. cit., p. 110.

"If you do not swear": Ibid.

PAGE 128

"And you, why are you": Ibid.

"I don't know what will": Ibid., p. 111.

"What kind of bond": Ibid., p. 112.

12. Vassian Toporkov Versus Maksim the Greek

PAGE 129

"I was born to rule": Fennell (ed. and tr.), *Correspondence Between Kurbsky and Ivan*, p. 193.

"took control of the splendid": Soloviev, *History of Russia*, v. 9, p. 151.

PAGE 130

"like some sort of": Quoted in Haney, *From Italy to Muscovy*, p. 176.

"our saints prayed," "our sainted martyrs": Backer, *Deadly Parallel*, p. 50.

PAGE 131

"God is everywhere," "If you neglect": Fennell, *Kurbsky's History of Ivan IV*, p. 87.

"cunning and cruelty": Fennell, *Correspondence*, p. 187 n.

"If you wish to be": Fennell, *Kurbsky's History*, p. 90.

"a big ax": Ibid., p. 91.

PAGE 132

"Attend to all matters": Dvornik, "Byzantine Political Ideas," p. 113.

13. Art and Heresey

PAGE 133

"confined in a shed": Skrynnikov, *Ivan the Terrible*, p. 40.

"heresy is abroad": Ibid., p. 39.

"the tsar loved him": Miller, "Literary Activities of Macarius," p. 91.

"he ought to have known": Andreyev, "Pskov-Pechery Monastery," p. 329.

"Bashkin consulted": Miller, "Viskovatyi Affair," p. 301.

PAGE 134

"I am horror-struck": Andreyev, "Interpolations," p. 103.

"for we have only the description": Voyce, *Moscow and the Roots of Russian Culture*, p. 39.

"allowed the illiterate faithful": Miller, op. cit., p. 295.

Upon the gates of Heaven: Kondakov, *Russian Icon*, p. 147.

"Let the glory": Florovsky, *Ways of Russian Theology*, p. 30.

"And when I behold": Ibid.

PAGE 135

"changed his mind": Miller, op. cit., p. 302.

PAGE 136

"You started with a crusade": Vernadsky, *Tsardom of Moscow*," p. 76.

PAGE 137

"the [two] close and trusted": Andreyev, op. cit., p. 102.

14. On to Astrakhan

"if I did not acquiesce": Fennell (ed. and tr.), *Correspondence Between Kurbsky and Ivan*, p. 93.

"deeming me incapable": Ibid., p. 87.

PAGE 139
"a disaster": Ibid., p. 117.

"Your men go to trade": Pritsak, "Moscow, the Golden Horde, . . . ," p. 581.

"tsar and Orthodox sovereign": See Miller, "Literary Activities of Macarius, p. 416.

PAGE 140
"It is written": Medlin and Patrinelis, *Renaissance Influences*, p. 32.

"a really royal lineage": Ibid.

"supreme Lord and Emperor" (*potentissimo Domino, Imperatori*): Szeftel, "Title of the Muscovite Monarch," p. 75.

PAGE 141
"wilfull humiliations": Miller, op. cit., p. 587.

This is the Book of Degrees: See Miller, p. 332, and Gudzy, *History of Early Russian Literature*, p. 345.

"Of a noble root," "This noble, God-appointed heir": Gudzy, op. cit., p. 346.

PAGE 142
"so embellished its material": Ibid., p. 345.

"banded together": Voyce, *Moscow Kremlin*, p. 100.

15. A Hammer for Lapland

PAGE 144
"on a par": Davies, *God's Playground*, p. 387.

16. "A Thousand Kingdoms We Will Seek From Far"

PAGE 146
"There is left but one way": Hakluyt, *Principal Navigations*, v. 2. p. 161.

"short and easy": Hale, *Renaissance Exploration*, p. 77.

PAGE 147
"which involved a degree": Penrose, *Travel and Discovery*, p. 197.

"might have seemed": Milton, *Brief History*, p. 366.

"Commoditye farre passing": French, *John Dee*, p. 180.

PAGE 148
"filthy tales," etc: See Hakluyt, op. cit., v. 2, pp. 195–208.

"the best quadrant": See Hamel, *England and Russia*, p. 23.

"in all places": Hakluyt, op. cit., v. 2, p. 209.

"courtiers came running": Ibid., p. 244.

"such flawes of winde": Ibid., p. 212.

PAGE 149
"platter in hand": Willan, *Early History of Russia Company*, p. 15.

"If the rage": Hakluyt, op. cit., v. 2, p. 247.

"sailed so farre": Ibid., p. 248.

"prostrated themselves": Ibid., p. 249.

"our men beganne": Ibid., p. 255.

"rich and very massie": Ibid., p. 228.

"with napkins on their shoulders": Ibid.

"drank them off": Ibid.

"in such sort": Ibid., p. 258.

PAGE 150
"I could scarce beleeve": Ibid., p. 229.

"Now what might be made": Ibid., p. 231.

"as for whoredom": Ibid., p. 238.

"fetcheth the defendant": Ibid., p. 263.

PAGE 151
"ffree markett," etc.: Ibid., p. 272.

"the broad seale": Ibid.

PAGE 152
"were filled": Hamel, op. cit., p. 93.

"without any customs, duties," etc.: See Hakluyt, pp. 297–303.

"tooke it into his hand": Ibid., v. 3, p. 333.

17. Hanseatic Merchants and Red Cross Knights

PAGE 154
"We need Tokhtamysh": Vernadsky, *Tsardom of Moscow*, p. 93.

"dreamed of expanding," "of consolidating," "both Sweden and Poland": Graham, H. F. (tr. and ed.), *"Missio Moscovitica,"* p. 440.

PAGE 155
"to the mass": Pokrovsky, *History of Russia*, p. 138.

PAGE 157
"might have insured Muscovy": Graham, op. cit., p. 440.

PAGE 158

"counts himself happy," "much eating": Kirchner, "Russo-Livonian Crisis, 1555," p. 145.

"no mustering": Ibid., p. 146.

PAGE 160

"Your ancestors came": Quoted in Grey, *Ivan the Terrible*, p. 132.

18. The Second Wave of Reforms

PAGE 162

"for centuries": Dewey, "1550 *Sudebnik*," p. 175.

"coveting wealth": Vernadsky, *Tsardom of Moscow*, p. 60.

PAGE 163

"redemption tax": Dewey, "Decline of the Muscovite *Namestnik*," p. 37.

"was the free services": Dewey, "Charters of Local Government," p. 16.

"out of pity": Dewey, "Decline of *Namestnik*," p. 36.

"to measure and record": Platonov, *Ivan the Terrible*, p. 59.

"Thus, nobles and warriors": Skrynnikov, *Ivan the Terrible*, p. 45.

"for campaigns recently undertaken": Dewey, "Decline," p. 39.

19. "To Subdue and Conquere His Enemies"

PAGE 164

"dashed to pieces": Tolstoi, *First Forty Years*, p. 10.

"fourscore merchants," etc.: Hakluyt, *Principal Navigations*, v. 2, p. 352.

"the most rytch prynce": Anderson, *Britain's Discovery of Russia*, p. 21.

"Hee is very mistrustful": Hamel, *England and Russia*, p. 157.

PAGE 165

"sailed through," etc.: Morgan and Coote (eds.), *Early Voyages and Travels*, v. 2, p. 342.

"the manner of entering": Ibid., v. 1, p. 4.

"a pitifull crie": Hakluyt, op. cit., v. 2, p. 415.

"like a semicircle": Ibid.

PAGE 166

"Pyneaple trees": Morgan and Coote, op. cit., v. 1, p. 24.

"men of warre": Hakluyt, op. cit., v. 2, p. 430.

"faire ordinance," etc.: Ibid.

"Now what might": Ibid., p. 231.

"to be of higher": Ibid., p. 439.

"was set a Monke": Ibid., p. 427.

[The tsar] is no more afraid: Ibid., p. 438.

20. The Collapse of Livonia

PAGE 167

"And we went through": Fennell (ed. and tr.), *Kurbsky's History of Ivan IV*, p. 107.

PAGE 168

"And all that fire": Ibid., p. 112.

"The idea of submission": Kirchner, *Rise of Baltic Question*, p. 119.

"If any power": Quoted in Wipper, *Ivan Grozny*, p. 83.

PAGE 169

"he believed in God": Kirchner, op. cit., p. 135.

PAGE 170

"You call Livonia yours": Quoted in Karamzin, *Histoire de l'Empire de Russie*, v. 8, p. 370.

PAGE 171

"Do you not see": Staden, *Land and Government of Muscovy*, p. 23.

"who had already begun": Fennell, op. cit., p. 49.

21. Turning Point

PAGE 173

"Being young and riotous": Bond (ed. and tr.), *Russia at the Close*, p. 157.

"honored, beloved": Ibid.

"one single little word": Fennell, *Correspondence Between Kurbsky and Ivan*, p. 99.

"If God send": Chyzhevskyi, *History of Russian Literature*, p. 386.

PAGE 174

"They ought to be brought": Fennell, *Kurbsky's History of Ivan IV*, p. 157.

PAGE 175
"no person": Hakluyt, *Principal Navigations*, v. 3, p. 16.

"If only you": Fennell, *Correspondence*, p. 191.

PAGE 176
"lived in great danger": Bond, op. cit., p. 172.

PAGE 177
"not warmly attached": Roberts, *Early Vasas*, p. 195.

PAGE 178
"at the apex": Wipper, *Ivan Grozny*, p. 90.

PAGE 179
"The banner of Christ": Stökl, *Testament und Siegel*, p. 50.

PAGE 180
"with the cherubim": Fedotov, *St. Filipp*, p. 80.

22. Sacrifices to Cronus

PAGE 181
"wax mightie and enlarge": Bond (ed.), *Russia at the Close*, p. 32.

"by degrees to clip": Ibid.

"who would provide": Blum, *Lord and Peasant in Russia*, p. 144.

"made advantage": Bond, op. cit., p. 33.

"kissing his fingers": Andreyev, "Kurbsky's Letters to Vas'yan Muromtsev," p. 431.

"at the very altar": Fennell (ed. and tr.), *Kurbsky's History of Ivan IV*, p. 181.

"on his way": Ibid.

PAGE 182
"went in tears": Graham, H. F. (ed. and tr.), "Albert Schlichting," p. 217.

"to show how": Ibid., p. 214.

"the modest men marvelled": Skrynnikov, *Ivan the Terrible*, p. 148.

"who wanted to be considered": Graham, op. cit., p. 252.

PAGE 183
"artillerie house at Musko": Bond, op. cit., p. 79.

"immediately ordered new ones": Wipper, *Ivan the Terrible*, p. 208.

PAGE 184
"retaineth and well rewardeth": Hakluyt, *Principal Navigations*, v. 2, p. 439.

"to put fresh heart": See Fennell, op. cit., p. 137.

PAGE 185
"Your governorship": Andreyev, op. cit., p. 427.

"threatened thunderings": Ibid., p. 416.

"the commanders given to you," etc.: Fennell (ed. and tr.), *Correspondence Between Kurbsky and Ivan*, pp. 3–9.

"red-hot pincers": Fennell, *Kurbsky's History*, p. 145.

PAGE 186
"prove through Scripture": Tumins, *Ivan IV's Reply to Jan Rokyta*, p. 41.

"the lofty language": Fennell and Stokes, *Early Russian Literature*, p. 186.

"Your epistle has been received": Fennell, *Correspondence*, p. 33.

"Ethiopian face," "pale blue eyes": Ibid., p. 143 n.

"stinking hound": Ibid., p. 149.

"one little word": Ibid., p. 99.

"I am only human": Ibid., p. 39.

PAGE 187
Is this then: Ibid.

Who placed you: Ibid., p. 42.

It is one thing: Ibid., p. 59.

PAGE 188
"The beginning of our Autocracy": Ibid., p. 13.

"was that sweet": Pares, *History of Russia*, p. 114.

"that cur," "raised from the gutter": Fennell, *Correspondence*, p. 85.

"trampled his own vows": Ibid., p. 87.

"the cunning [truce]": Ibid., p. 119.

PAGE 189
Man made gods: Ibid., p. 107.

I have received: Ibid., p. 181, and Gudzy, op. cit., p. 336.

PAGE 190
"I do not understand": Fennell, *Correspondence*, p. 183.

"No Christian Tsar": Graham, op. cit., p. 217.

23. Satan's Band

PAGE 195
"In doubt and despair": Skrynnikov, *Ivan the Terrible*, p. 84.

PAGE 196
"to govern as he pleased": Vernadsky, *Tsardom of Moscow*, p. 108.

"smash everything": Pokrovsky, *History of Russia*, p. 144.

PAGE 197
"in his hatred and wrath": Quoted in Vernadsky, op. cit., p. 137.

"These two men": Graham, H. F. (ed. and tr.), "Albert Schlichting," p. 72 n.

PAGE 199
"the slightest suspicion": Florinsky, *Russia: History and Interpretation*, p. 199.

"ennobled and countenanced": Bond (ed.), *Russia at the Close*, p. 163.

"for having considered": Fedotov, *St. Filipp*, p. 76.

"sang from memory": Ibid.

PAGE 200
"to begin to pull": Pokrovsky, *History of Russia*, p. 151.

"He did not accuse": Ibid.

PAGE 201
"Many beautiful estates": Quoted in Fedotov, op. cit., p. 102.

24. English Interlude

"both merchants and peasants": Andreyev, "Kurbsky's Letters to Vas'yan Muromtsev," p. 432.

PAGE 202
"laid the matter": Hamel, *Russia and England*, p. 221.

PAGE 203
"went in over": Hakluyt, *Principal Navigations*, v. 2, pp. 334, 337.

"bloodie idols": Ibid., p. 338.

"I could have bought": Morgan and Coote (eds.), *Early Voyages and Travels*, v. 1, p. 58.

"sette up the redde crosse": Ibid., v. 1, p. 97.

"in a little rounde house": Ibid., v. 1, p. 67.

PAGE 204
"certaine Characters": Ibid., v. 1, p. 77.

PAGE 205
"we have none," etc.: Ibid., v. 1, p. 147.

"all sortes and colours": Willan, *Early History of Russia Company*, p. 56.

"though an Italian": Morgan and Coote, op. cit., v. 2, p. 184.

PAGE 206
"We understand": Hamel, op. cit., p. 175.

25. The Zemsky Sobor of 1566

PAGE 207
This Emperor of Moscovia: Morgan and Coote (eds.), *Early Voyages and Travels*, v. 2, pp. 187–188.

"a gunshot away": Staden, *Land and Government of Muscovy*, p. 48.

"catch the sun and breeze": Ibid., p. 49.

PAGE 208
"constitutional seduction": Billington, *Icon and Axe*, p. 99.

PAGE 209
"they petitioned him": Graham, H. F. (ed. and tr.), "Albert Schlichting," p. 248 n.

"You have not yet": Fedotov, *St. Filipp*, p. 83.

PAGE 210
"he realized he could not serve": Ibid., p. 39.

PAGE 211
"concentrate on bringing": Ibid., p. 86.

"custom of intercession": Ibid., p. 30.

"constant intervention": Vernadsky, *Russia at the Dawn of the Modern Age*, p. 156.

PAGE 212
"a man of about thirty": Herberstein, *Notes Upon Russia*, v. 1, p. 54.

"He does not instruct": Schmemann, *Historical Road of Eastern Orthodoxy*, pp. 313–314. See also Fedotov, op. cit., p. 30.

"an abasement which even": Fedotov, op. cit., p. 78.

PAGE 213
"not to be silent": Quoted in Fedotov, op. cit., p. 153.

"You should not obey": Wieczynski, "Archbishop Gennadius and the West," p. 386.

26. The Tsar at Chess with Elizabeth and Erik

PAGE 214
"ride and goe," "superfluous burdens": Morgan and Coote (ed. and tr.), *Early Voyages and Travels*, v. 1, p. 215.

"If they do not amende": Ibid.

"should henceforth be permitted": Willan, *Early History of Russia Company*, p. 72.

"feeling the mounting costs": Huttenbach, "Anthony Jenkinson's 1566 and 1577 Missions," p. 189.

PAGE 215
"technical experts": Ibid., p. 188.

"such as are cunning" etc.: Quoted in Huttenbach, op. cit., p. 197.

"the Baltic had become": Ibid., pp. 184–185.

"obscure destitute men": Ibid., pp. 199–200.

"We prayse God alone": Ibid., p. 201.

PAGE 216
The Emperour requireth: Tolstoi, *First Forty Years*, p. 38.

PAGE 217
"not to sacrifice": Kirchner, *Rise of Baltic Question*, p. 186.

"What God hath joined": Ibid.

27. Conspiracies

PAGE 219
"the only honest judge": See Staden, *Land and Government of Muscovy*, p. 9.

PAGE 221
It was a pitiful sight: Taube and Kruse quoted in Fedotov, *St. Filipp*, p. 116.

"which came out": Bond (ed.), *Russia at the Close*, p. 172.

"they prepared the whip": Quoted in Payne and Romanoff, *Ivan the Terrible*, p. 226.

PAGE 222
"This caused the spirits": Quoted in Dewey, "1550 *Sudebnik*," p. 178.

"torn to pieces": Staden, op. cit., p. 101.

"We came to a place": Ibid., p. 120.

PAGE 223
"The later laws": Quoted in Massie, *Peter the Great*, p. 748.

28. The Martyr's Crown

PAGE 224
"Blood often splashes": Graham, H. F. (ed. and tr.), "Albert Schlichting," p. 229.

"liked to execute": Fedotov, *St. Filipp*, p. 111.

PAGE 225
"beggars and cripples": Bond (ed.), *Russia at the Close*, p. 208.

PAGE 226
"If you are high": Fedotov, op. cit., p. 117.

"kept away from the hierarch": Ibid., p. 119.

"like Chaldean boors": Ibid., p. 121.

"We are offering": Ibid.

"It would be better": Ibid., p. 122.

"We shall see": Ibid.

"In the past": Ibid., p. 123.

PAGE 227
"so suspect": Skrynnikov, *Ivan the Terrible*, p. 114.

"slew his retainers": Ibid., p. 113.

"Sovereign Tsar": Fedotov, op. cit., p. 126.

"You have what": Graham, op. cit., p. 224.

PAGE 228
"Your high earthly rank": Fedotov, op. cit., p. 129.

"And some who went": Fennell (ed. and tr.), *Kurbsky's History of Ivan IV*, p. 239.

29. The Great Messenger

PAGE 229
"as a close": Willan, *Early History of Russia Company*, p. 97.

"most greedy cormorants": Ibid.

"we have no manner," etc.: Tolstoi, *First Forty Years*, p. 44.

"pass those matters" etc.: Ibid.

PAGE 230
"several gentlemen," "desirous": Berry and Crummey (eds.), *Rude & Barbarous Kingdom*, p. 46.

"Drink is their whole desire": Ibid., pp. 75–76.

"trusty wyse": Ibid., p. 46.

"beere starke sower": Willan, op. cit., p. 101.

Of late [the tsar]: Morgan and Coote (eds. and tr.), *Early Voyages and Travels,* v. 2, p. 257.

PAGE 231
"In the worlde": Ibid.

"maynie practyzes": Willan, op. cit., p. 105.

"talke in Musco": Morgan and Coote, op. cit., v. 2, p. 263.

"I dine not": Hakluyt, *Principal Navigations,* v. 3, p. 106.

"a place farre off": Ibid., p. 107.

"the house of his solace": Ibid.

"much soner than I cowlde": Morgan and Coote, op. cit., v. 2, p. 278.

PAGE 232
"very lewde and untrew": Willan, op. cit., p. 101.

"the holle trayde": Ibid.

"good beveraige and bysquyte": Morgan and Coote, op. cit., v. 2, p. 279.

30. Muscovy's Neighbors Regroup

PAGE 234
"When we left": Quoted in Vernadsky, *Russia at Dawn of Modern Age,* p. 244.

31. The Sack of Novgorod

PAGE 239
"Who is there": Andreyev, "Kurbsky's Letters to Vas'yan Muromtsev," p. 431.

PAGE 241
"No one in Moscow": Graham, H. F. (ed. and tr.), "Albert Schlichting," p. 233.

PAGE 242
"stifling," "neglect": Fedotov, *St. Filipp,* p. 136.

"a thief": Dmytryshyn, *Medieval Russia: A Source Book,* p. 205.

PAGE 243
"with mildness": Ibid.

PAGE 244
"And every day": Dmytryshyn, op. cit., p. 206.

"his heart was softened": Andreyev, op. cit., p. 436.

"blunt their swords": Ibid.

PAGE 245
"I saw this imposter": Bond (ed. and tr.), *Russia at the Close,* p. 161.

"if he or any": Ibid.

PAGE 246
"tears of repentance," "path of Blood": Andreyev, "The Pskov-Pechery Monastery," p. 338.

32. Faith and Works

PAGE 248
"they never leave a man": Froissart, anticipating the sentiment. Quoted in Contamine, *War in the Middle Ages,* p. 291.

"eating Livonian children": Kirchner, *Rise of Baltic Question,* p. 44.

"O the lamentable owtcries": Bond (ed.), *Russia at the Close,* p. 160.

PAGE 250
Foremost, everyone: Tumins, *Ivan IV's Reply to Jan Rokyta,* p. 479.

Through His Prophets: Ibid., p. 484.

I did not want: Ibid., pp. 295–305.

PAGE 251
There is no salvation: Ibid., pp. 307–326.

PAGE 252
"I cannot look": Ibid., p. 334.

PAGE 253
"to think of God": Graham, H. F. (ed. and tr.), "Albert Schlichting," p. 272.

"always been served": Andreyev, "Interpolations," p. 101 n.

"very hostile to the Russians": Quoted, ibid., p. 102 n.

"Ivan Viskovaty was an excellent man": Quoted, ibid., p. 102.

PAGE 254
"I have no further": Graham, op. cit., p. 261.

"A curse on you": Ibid.

"Let whomever": Ibid., p. 170.

PAGE 255
"until his skin": Waliszewski, *Ivan the Terrible,* p. 256.

"laid their decapitated bodies": Graham, op. cit., p. 263.

"a very sly man": Vernadsky, *Tsardom of Moscow,* p. 156.

"a goose ready drest": Bond, op. cit., p. 55.

"This might seeme": Ibid.

PAGE 256
"God hath plagued it": Morgan and Coote (eds.), *Early Voyages and Travels*, v. 2, p. 336.

"One man killed another": Staden, *Land and Government of Muscovy*, p. 29.

"for certeyn": Morgan and Coote, op. cit., v. 2, p. 336.

"military checkpoints": Skrynnikov, *Ivan the Terrible*, p. 118. See also Staden, op. cit., p. 29.

"everyone wondered": Morgan and Coote, op. cit., v. 2, pp. 336–337.

"it was all quiet": Staden, op. cit., p. 122.

33. The "Evil Empire"

PAGE 257
"would not give aunswere": Morgan and Coote (eds.), *Early Voyages and Travels*, v. 2, p. 278.

"We know that merchant matters": Tolstoi, *First Forty Years*, p. 129.

"copy it out": Ibid., p. xxv.

"all things necessary": Ibid., p. 77.

"such olde thinges": Hakluyt, *Principal Navigations*, v. 2, p. 399.

PAGE 258
"on her royal word": Willan, *Early History of Russia Company*, p. 64.

"grounded uppon untroth": Ibid.

"a harbour midway": Ibid., p. 65.

"still by their labour," etc.: Hamel, *England and Russia*, pp. 184–185.

"the temporary enemy": Ibid., p. 185.

We know and feele: Hakluyt, op. cit., v. 2, pp. 455–457.

PAGE 259
"I could do for the Emperour": Hamel, op. cit., p. 177.

"insisted on the literal": Tolstoi, op. cit., p. xxv.

PAGE 260
"not ayde, comfort, or suffer": Morgan and Coote, op. cit., v. 2, p. 288.

"whereunto none are privie": Ibid., pp. 290–291.

"gretely sett a work": Willan, op. cit., p. 74.

PAGE 261
And how manie letters: Morgan and Coote, op. cit., v. 2, pp. 294–297.

PAGE 262
"treat very fully": Ibid., p. 297.

"on which are carved," etc.: Huttenbach, "Search for and Discovery of Archival Materials," p. 433.

PAGE 263
"displeasure was such": Morgan and Coote, op. cit., v. 2, p. 306.

34. "A fearfull reveng and spectacle to al generacions"

PAGE 265
"moved vigorously": Skrynnikov, *Ivan the Terrible*, p. 132.

"the insides were falling": Payne and Romanoff, *Ivan the Terrible*, p. 308.

"there is nothing," "If you fail": Quoted, ibid., p. 309.

"marched a wrong way": Bond (ed.), *Russia at the Close*, p. 185.

PAGE 266
"clere, fayre & calme": Morgan and Coote (eds.), *Early Voyages and Travels*, v. 2, p. 338.

"ther was nothynge": Ibid.

"fierie eyre": Bond, op. cit., p. 165.

"Mosco," etc.: Hakluyt, *Principal Navigations*, v. 3, p. 168.

"What with the Crimme": Ibid., p. 170.

PAGE 267
"noe man could pass": Bond, op. cit., p. 165.

"fearfull reveng": Ibid., p. 164.

"juste punyshment": Morgan and Coote, op. cit., v. 2, p. 308.

"threatened to roast": Graham, H. F. (ed. and tr.), "Albert Schlichting," p. 226 n.

"I came before his majestie": Tolstoi, *First Forty Years*, p. 128.

PAGE 268
"seemed to his own contentment": Ibid., p. 131.

"fought with the King": Ibid., p. 132.

"such rebels": Ibid.

"It is nowe time": Ibid., p. 133.

PAGE 269
"because our minde": Morgan and Coote, op. cit., v. 2, p. 326.

"If the queene": Tolstoi, op. cit., p. 141.

35. The Battle of Molodi

"Your father, Gustav": Waliszewski, *Ivan the Terrible*, p. 202.

"curious rich scimitars," etc.: Bond (ed.), *Russia at the Close*, pp. 166–167.

PAGE 270
"agonie of madness": Ibid., p. 167.

"Tell the miscreant": Ibid.

PAGE 271
"I, the much sinning," "Those who serve," "Concerning the *Oprichnina*": See Howes, *Testaments of Grand Princes of Moscow*, pp. 307–359; Vernadsky, *Tsardom of Moscow*, p. 136; and Gerasimov, *The Face Finder*, p. 187.

PAGE 272
"beat them back": Skrynnikov, *Ivan the Terrible*, p. 152.

"emerged to the rear": Ibid., p. 153.

PAGE 273
"All our plans": Payne and Romanoff, *Ivan the Terrible*, p. 327.

"made his way": Skrynnikov, op. cit., p. 154.

"anyone guilty": Ibid., p. 157.

36. A Medley of Monarchs

PAGE 275
"conceived in ferocity": Fennell (ed. and tr.), *Kurbsky's History of Ivan IV*, p. 9.

"I do not stand": Wipper, *Ivan Grozny*, p. 179.

"I have only two," "Look, to a good man": See Turgenev, *Historica Russiae Monumenta*, v. 1, pp. 229–232.

PAGE 276
"We know that the Emperor": Wipper, op. cit., p. 181.

"so much blood shed": Quoted in Vernadsky, *Tsardom of Moscow*, p. 148.

PAGE 277
"still devoted": Kirchner, *Rise of Baltic Question*, p. 118.

"stinking dog": See Gudzy, *History of Early Russian Literature*, p. 340.

PAGE 278
"disappointed by the poverty": Davies, *God's Playground*, p. 416.

"many Englishmen": Tolstoi, *First Forty Years*, p. 153.

"If you wish for": Ibid., p. 158.

PAGE 279
"the leagues which wee": Ibid., p. 164.

"would breed so dangerous": Ibid., p. 165.

"a kynde of haughtynes": Ibid., p. 183.

"Our mislyke": Ibid., p. 184.

"trewly our whole countrye": Ibid., p. 185.

PAGE 280
"who fulminated so eloquently": Bain, *Slavonic Europe*, p. 95.

"with a ruby": Mitchell and Zguta (ed. and tr.), "The Sixteenth Century 'Account of Muscovy,' " p. 409.

"increasing the number": Ibid.

"who had not bathed": Ibid., p. 402.

"addicted by nature": Hakluyt, *Principal Navigations*, v. 2, p. 191.

"friendly and sweet": Quoted in Kappeler, *Ivan Groznyi*, p. 161.

"so obviously noble": Quoted, ibid., p. 163.

PAGE 281
He is very tall: Quoted in Payne and Romanoff, *Ivan the Terrible*, p. 355.

37. The Enthronement of Simeon Bekbulatovich

"We highlye forsawe": Tolstoi, *First Forty Years*, p. 179.

PAGE 282
Although we manifested: Ibid., pp. 184–185.

"rode simply": Pritsak, "Moscow, the Golden Horde, . . . ," p. 577.

"sat with other boyars": Ibid.

PAGE 283
"To the lord": Quoted in Payne and Romanoff, *Ivan the Terrible*, p. 351.

"few princes": Bond (ed.), *Russia at the Close*, p. 56.

"there would be a change": Vernadsky, *Tsardom of Moscow*, p. 146.

all charters graunted: Bond, op. cit., pp. 56–57.

"And when we have sorted": Quoted in Payne and Romanoff, op. cit., p. 351.

PAGE 284
"handed in," "desired to give": Waliszewski, *Ivan the Terrible*, p. 262.

"the perverse and evill dealinge": Tolstoi, op. cit., p. 179.

"keeping boyes": Bond, op. cit., p. 188.

"to gash": Berry and Crummey (eds.), *Rude & Barbarous Kingdom*, p. 299.

PAGE 285
"lived in great favour": Bond, op. cit., p. 187.

"confessed much": Ibid.

"his woemen witches": Ibid., p. 188.

38. Stefan Batory

PAGE 290
"with leopard skins": Davies, *God's Playground*, p. 423.

"I was born a free man": Ibid., p. 424.

"he was the incarnation": Ibid.

PAGE 291
"his every word": Ibid.

"Who ever heard": See Waliszewski, *Ivan the Terrible*, p. 303.

PAGE 292
"In our old age," "more vicious," "You will say": Fennell (ed. and tr.), *Correspondence Between Kurbsky and Ivan*, pp. 189–197.

PAGE 294
"used the name of virtue": Ibid., p. 219.

PAGE 295
"Great is the power": Wipper, *Ivan Grozny*, p. 208.

39. Polotsk and Veliky Luki

PAGE 296
"The tailor gone scars down": Bond (ed.), *Russia at the Close*, p. 184.

PAGE 297
"Gods will": Ibid., p. 185.

He asked me: Ibid., p. 186.

PAGE 298
"Be thou trusty": Ibid., p. 189.

"close under my cassock," etc.: Ibid., p. 192.

PAGE 299
" a small army": Skrynnikov, *Ivan the Terrible*, p. 184.

"the skillfull division": Waliszewski, *Ivan the Terrible*, p. 306.

"crammed with dates": Ibid., p. 307.

"Lord, forgive us": Ibid., p. 309.

PAGE 300
"lined up and rushed at each other": Wipper, *Ivan Grozny*, p. 404.

"corrupted by toadies," etc.: Fennell (ed. and tr.), *Correspondence Between Kurbsky and Ivan*, p. 231.

"hordes of pure maidens," etc.: Ibid., p. 245.

PAGE 301
"good, shining, true": Backus, "A. M. Kurbsky," p. 42.

PAGE 302
"sett a thowsand gunors": Bond, op. cit., pp. 194–195.

"to the end": Klyuchevsky, *History of Russia*, v. 2, p. 195.

PAGE 303
"counted on sacking": Wipper, op. cit., p. 204.

40. Missio Moscovitica

PAGE 305
"We want to be in alliance": Quoted in Vernadsky, *Tsardom of Moscow*, p. 160.

PAGE 306
"From Scythia": Graham, H. V. (ed. and tr.), *"Missio Moscovitica,"* p. 469.

"the whole idea": Ibid., p. 450.

PAGE 307
"Why do you object": Quoted in Vernadsky, op. cit., p. 162.

"God gave our sovereign": See Waliszewski, op. cit., p. 319.

"The New Testament": Ibid., p. 320.

"in an undignified manner": Graham, op. cit., p. 453.

PAGE 308
"Antonio. Ivan Vasilyevich": Ibid.

"to behold the serene eyes": Ibid., p. 455.

"bigger than the Pope's": Ibid., p. 456.

"Antonio and his companions": Ibid.

"for a long time," "a gift worthy": Ibid., p. 457.

"We learned that she had died": Ibid.

"always looking around": Ibid., p. 459.

"called for silence": Ibid., p. 460.

"the general shepherd": Ibid., p. 460.

PAGE 309
The Prince takes great pains: Graham, H. F. (ed. and tr.), *Moscovia of Antonio Possevino*, pp. 47, 57.

"washed his hands": Ibid., p. 47.

PAGE 310
"sneaking wolf" etc.: Bain, *Slavonic Europe*, p. 126.

"a cruel, cunning Asiatic": Skrynnikov, *Ivan the Terrible*, p. 150.

"Scythian Wolf": Kappeler, *Ivan Groznyi*, p. 151.

"Basilisk": Massa, *A Short History*, p. 15.

PAGE 311
"like a wild boar": Quoted in Davies, *God's Playground*, p. 430.

41. Pskov

"who told him": Davies. *God's Playground*, p. 430.

"made a general assault": Bain, *Slavonic Europe*, p. 127.

PAGE 312
"I set the snare": Quoted in Roberts, *The Early Vasas*, p. 269.

"Go to King Stefan": Graham, H. F. (ed. and tr.), *"Missio Moscovitica,"* p. 462.

"Antonio, be of good cheer": Ibid., p. 463.

PAGE 313
"an extraordinarily fine account": Graham, H. F. (ed. and tr.), *Moscovia of Antonio Possevino*, p. 7.

"unbelievable fortitude": Quoted in Skrynnikov, *Ivan the Terrible*, p. 190.

"scarcely breathing": Graham, *Moscovia*, p. 124.

"between a temporary altar": Waliszewski, *Ivan the Terrible*, p. 337.

"I never read reports": Graham, *"Missio,"* p. 464 n.

PAGE 314
" 'Tsar' is only": Ibid., p. 129.

"You have come here": Graham, *Moscovia*, p. 171 n.

PAGE 315
"We know": Waliszewski, op. cit., p. 390.

42. "Recall to Memory Constantine"

You should become: Quoted in Vernadsky, *Tsardom of Moscow*, p. 170.

PAGE 316
"cruel like his father": Quoted in Kappeler, *Ivan Groznyi*, p. 173.

"abundant virtues": Quoted, ibid.

"capable of ruling": Quoted, ibid.

"He was the hope": Bond (ed. and tr.), *Russia at the Close*, p. 195.

PAGE 317
"sitting on a bench": Skrynnikov, *Ivan the Terrible*, p. 195.

"tore his hair": Bond, op. cit., p. 195.

"scratched the wall": Graham, H. F. (ed. and tr.), *Moscovia of Antonio Possevino*, p. 13.

"laid aside his diadem": Ibid., p. 14.

"began to weep": Vernadsky, op. cit., p. 169.

PAGE 318
"And whoever will forget": Ibid.

"Have I no friend": Shakespeare, *Richard II*, Act V, Scene iv, 2.

"Have I no terrible": Chadwick, *Russian Heroic Poetry*, p. 195.

"As to their names": Vernadsky, op. cit., p. 169.

"posthumous rehabilitation": Skrynnikov, op. cit., p. 196.

43. Tsar and Jesuit Debate the Faith

PAGE 319
"Statues of painted wood": See Graham, H. F. (ed. and tr.), *"Missio Moscovitica,"* p. 474.

"You see that I am": Graham, *Moscovia of Antonio Possevino*, p. 67.

Your Most Serene Highness: Ibid.

PAGE 320
"I do not believe": Ibid., p. 69.

"the most true": Ibid.

"We received": Ibid.

"Christ sent": Ibid., p. 71.

"We acknowledge Peter": Ibid.

Our courier, Istoma Shevrigin: Ibid., p. 174.

PAGE 321
"If the Pope": Ibid., p. 176.

"I warned you": Ibid., p. 177.

Half rising: Ibid., p. 72.

PAGE 322
"to the great astonishment": Ibid., p. 75.

"to make a full confession": Ibid.

"Antonio, my boyars": Ibid., p. 77.

PAGE 323
"the Chief points": Ibid., p. 80.

"there were already": Kirchner, *Rise of the Baltic Question*, p. 122.

"without stopping": Graham, *"Missio,"* p. 467.

"filled with dirt": Graham, *Moscovia*, p. 22.

"squatting in the Coliseum": Ibid.

44. Aftermath

PAGE 325
"with clocks," etc.: Davies, *God's Playground*, pp. 252–253.

"so well filled": Hakluyt, *Principal Navigations*, v. 2, p. 225.

PAGE 326
"mightely inlarged," etc.: Bond (ed. and tr.), *Russia at the Close*, pp. 206–207.

"drinking wildly": *Russian Private Law*, pp. 9–10.

45. Sir Jerome Bowes

PAGE 327
"yt was very feacable": Bond (ed. and tr.), *Russia at the Close*, p. 187.

"cast down his countenance": Ibid., p. 196.

PAGE 328
"tall and slender": Quoted in Pelenski, *Russia and Kazan*, p. 127.

"as yf I had been": Tolstoi, *The First Forty Years*, p. 231.

"esteminge me unworthy": Ibid.

PAGE 329
"thinking it requisite": Ibid., p. 203.

"as over the rest": Ibid., p. 204.

"so inflamed": Bond, op. cit., p. 199.

"and if her Majestie": Hakluyt, *Principal Navigations*, v. 3, p. 323.

"to cross and overthrow": Bond, op. cit., p. 199.

"unreasonable and needless": Ibid., p. 204.

"as great a prince": Hakluyt, op. cit., v. 3, p. 320.

PAGE 330
"wished himself to have": Ibid., p. 321.

"I became a great man": Ibid., p. 324.

"the center of the maritime": Waliszewski, *Ivan the Terrible*, p. 297.

46. The Conquest of Siberia

"at the other end": Waliszewski, *Ivan the Terrible*, p. 349.

PAGE 331
"with the same zeal": Lantzeff and Pierce, *Eastward to Empire*, p. 87.

PAGE 332
"to drive a wedge": Ibid., p. 89.

"hired Cossacks": Ibid.

PAGE 333
"the hand of the Russian Tsar": Ibid., p. 76.

"runaways from our state": Longworth, *The Cossacks*, p. 19.

PAGE 334
"unripped, with bellies": Fisher, *Russian Fur Trade*, p. 21.

"singing hymns": Longworth, op. cit., p. 53.

PAGE 335
"tipped into the river": Ibid.

PAGE 337
"found to be uncorrupted": Baddeley, *Russia, Mongolia, China*, p. lxxiii.

47. Endgame

PAGE 338
"his mourning": Bond (ed. and tr.), *Russia at the Close*, p. 121.

"called out": Oderborn, quoted in Kappeler, *Ivan Groznyi*, p. 162.

PAGE 339
"vitiated blood": Waliszewski, *Ivan the Terrible*, p. 379.

"griviously swell": Bond, op. cit., p. 199.

"sent forth": Ibid., p. 199.

"the signes constellaccions": Ibid.

"The load-stone": Ibid., p. 200.

PAGE 340
"Declares my death," etc.: Ibid., pp. 200–201.

"to know their calculacions": Ibid., p. 201.

"The daye is come" etc.: Ibid.

PAGE 341
"Though garded daye and night": Ibid., p. 209.

"cried owt to the captaines": Ibid., p. 202.

"To see what speede": Hakluyt, *Principal Navigations*, v. 3, p. 337.

"Thy English Tsar": Tolstoi, *First Forty Years*, p. xxxix.

"the lords take it ill": Bond, op. cit., p. 203.

PAGE 342
"so much forgett themselves": Ibid., p. 204.

"in verie short garments": Tolstoi, op. cit., p. 234.

"Lett him thank God": Ibid., p. 235.

"Wolde he had never": Hakluyt, op. cit., v. 3, p. 325.

"so faint, faultering": Bond, op. cit., p. 216.

"Though you wear not": Ibid., p. 217.

"hang firmly from the bells": Kappeler, op. cit., p. 174.

PAGE 343
"quite unguilty": Quoted, ibid.

"for their redemption": Bond, op. cit., p. 202.

"all peaceably": Ibid., p. 277.

"God hath a plage": Ibid., p. 206.

"utterly tragic": Quoted in L. Moussinae, *Sergey Eisenstein*, p. 71.

PAGE 344
"il Papa Terrible": See Cherniavsky, "Ivan the Terrible as Renaissance Prince," p. 205.

"It was no wise prince": Oderborn, quoted in Kappeler, op. cit., p. 157.

"blue ribbon commission": Keenan, "Vita," p. 4.

Index